Preparing Every Teacher to Reach English Learners

Preparing Every Teacher to Reach English Learners

A Practical Guide for Teacher Educators

Edited by

Joyce W. Nutta

Kouider Mokhtari

Carine Strebel

Harvard Education Press

Cambridge, Massachusetts

Library of Congress Control Number 2011941944

Paperback ISBN 978-1-61250-127-7
Library Edition ISBN 978-1-61250-128-4

Published by Harvard Education Press,
an imprint of the Harvard Education Publishing Group

Harvard Education Press
8 Story Street
Cambridge, MA 02138

Cover Design: Sarah Henderson
The typefaces used in this book are Aldine 401 and Univers Light.

Joyce:
For Francesca, who has always told me, "Go, Mamma, go!"

Kouider:
For my wife, children, brothers and sisters, parents,
students, and friends who have given me far more
than I have given them.

Carine:
For Ray, my biggest and most caring supporter, and for
all educators who are part of the solution by attending to the
personal and academic well-being of English learners
in their daily practice.

Contents

Preparing All Teachers to Address the Language and Content Needs of English Learners in Mainstream Classrooms

In this book, we argue that all teachers can and should be prepared to effectively teach English learners (ELs) in the mainstream classroom. While we do not suggest that all teachers should view themselves English as a second language (ESL) teachers, we propose that they augment their preparation by (a) gaining a basic understanding of the nature of language and the processes involved in second language acquisition, (b) learning and using accommodations in instruction and assessment for English learners at different levels of English language proficiency; and (c) familiarizing themselves with the characteristics of discourse and text in their own disciplines to better support ELs' language, literacy, and content learning in English. This chapter lays out a rationale based on our premise that every English learner deserves and can benefit from mainstream teachers who know how to support second language development and academic achievement.

Changing Demographics

During the past two decades, a number of global challenges have transformed core practices of teacher educators. One of the most salient changes is the dramatic shift in school demographics. Recent demographic data show that linguistically and culturally diverse students constitute an increasingly strong presence in schools and communities in practically every state in the United States. There are approximately 5 million ELs in the United States, and this number is on the rise.[1] It is estimated that two-thirds of these students are in at least one course taught by mainstream teachers. Growth in K–12 EL enrollment has skyrocketed in the past twenty years. One in twenty public K–12 students was an EL in 1990; in 2008, it was one in nine. Projections suggest that in twenty years it will be one in four.[2]

National demographic data during the past decade indicate that ELs represent the fastest-growing student population in U.S. schools, with significant growth in grades six through twelve. During the 2007–08 school year, ELs represented 10.6 percent of the K–12 public school enrollment, or more than 5.3 million students. Table I.1 displays the remarkable increases of ELs in most states, particularly in states that are not accustomed to serving their academic needs.[3]

An examination of the growth in EL enrollment during the past decade indicates that while the number of all preK–12 students increased by 8.5 percent (from 46 million in 1997–98 to 49.9 million in 2007–08), the number of ELs increased by 53.2 percent (from 3.5 million to 5.3 million) in the same ten-year period.[4] As these demographics continue to shift, educator preparation professionals, school leaders, education researchers, and policy makers are understandably paying increasing attention to the learning and teaching needs of students for whom English is not their native language.

Notwithstanding these statistics, the argument for preparing all educators to teach and assess ELs should be more than an appeal to respond to demographic trends. Student headcount matters little to the individual English learner struggling to understand instruction in an English-speaking classroom. For that individual student, what matters most is a teacher who is sensitive to ELs' needs and can apply knowledge and skills specific to meeting those needs. Whether a teacher works in San Antonio, Texas, or Minot, North Dakota, she should be well prepared to teach and assess ELs placed in her class from the first day of enrollment. We contend that on this principle alone, teacher preparation must expand its focus to address the needs of ELs. Yet unequivocally, our principled call to action is intensified by the escalating EL enrollment nationwide.

English Learner and Teacher Preparation Performance Data

It is hard to ignore the fact that many ELs tend to perform less well on standardized tests and drop out of school at higher rates than their English-speaking peers. This gap is due in part to difficulties associated with reading, writing, and learning in a new language. For several decades, national literacy achievement tests such as the National Assessment of Educational Progress (NAEP) show significant achievement gaps for historically underperforming subgroups of students in fourth and eighth grades. For instance, the 2007 NAEP report indicates that ELs in fourth and eighth grade scored 36 and 42 standard-scale points, respectively, below the performance of their native English–speaker peers.[5] Academic achievement gaps indicate that many ELs may not have attained the English language proficiency or subject matter content needed to participate fully in grade-level classes and programs. Taking into account the linguistic, cultural, and literacy challenges these students face in the classroom, it is easy to understand the performance discrepancies.

The discussion of the achievement gap between ELs and native speaker peers warrants a deeper investigation of what the gap actually represents, however. The fact that there is a collective gap does not necessarily indicate a crisis in the education of ELs. As will be noted in the following section, language learning is a process that takes time.[6] Classification as an English learner means that this student has not reached a selected metric of English proficiency approved by local or state educational agencies. Therefore, by definition an EL would most likely not have reached native-speaker proficiency in, for example, English literacy skills. If we examine reading scores of ELs in contrast to those of native speakers, we would expect native speakers to score significantly higher.

Table I.1

Top 12 States with the Largest EL Student Enrollment (2007–2008)[1]

State	Total preK–12 Enrollment 2007–2008	EL Enrollment 2007–2008	% EL among all preK–12 Students	% Change in EL Enrollment from 1997–1998
United States	49,914,453	5,318,164	10.7	53.2
California	6,275,445	1,526,036	24.3	8.5
Texas	4,674,832	701,799	15.0	38.4
Florida	2,666,811	234,934	8.8	–3.6
New York	2,765,435	213,000	7.7	–3.1
Illinois	2,112,805	175,454	8.3	28.8
Arizona	1,087,447	166,572	15.3	48.0
Nevada	429,362	134,377	31.3	341.7
North Carolina	1,458,035	106,180	7.3	269.8
Washington	1,030,247	94,011	9.1	65.2
Virginia	1,230,857	89,968	7.3	261.7
Colorado	801,867	82,347	10.3	NA
Georgia	1,649,589	72,613	4.4	246.7

1. State Title III Directors and 2007/08 State CSPR; National Clearinghouse for English Language Acquisition and Language Instruction Educational Programs (NCELA), "The Growing Numbers of Limited English Proficient Students, 1997/98–2007/08," (Washington, DC: NCELA, The George Washington University, 2010).

We see a somewhat different picture when we examine reported gaps in mathematics skills. Clearly, it is impossible to teach and assess mathematics without the use of language—English, in U.S. schools. However, to the degree that a mathematics exam can isolate knowledge and skills in mathematics without dependence on language, all other factors being equal, the EL who has had appropriate instruction in math should be able to demonstrate math competence at a level closer to native speakers than he or she could demonstrate on a test of reading in English. In other words, the reading test measures English language skills directly and the mathematics test measures math skills, mediated to a degree by English language skills.

Educators analyzing state and national test data must take care to develop realistic educational goals for ELs, keeping these sorts of nuances and mediating factors in mind. Focusing on the individual student can help clarify the target. For any given English learner, there is a need to close the achievement gap over time. If a student is categorized as a beginning EL student upon enrollment, the expectation is that at some point he or she will reach grade-level competency in language arts and other subjects in English. Collectively, however, as long as new ELs continue to enroll in schools, the general achievement gap will remain. This does not mean that these measures are meaningless. They can provide important data to assess performance goals.

When examining national test data for ELs, rather than simply making outright comparisons of their performance with native speakers, researchers are beginning to collect other more informative data; for example, English language development as measured by tests such as the Comprehensive English Language Learning Assessment (CELLA). We believe that two overarching goals can be furthered by examination of ELs' second language development as well as general literacy and academic achievement data and should direct educators' efforts to improve instruction for ELs. Instructional and assessment practices that are directed to EL needs should aim to (a) accelerate learners' rate of acquisition of English language proficiency and of subject matter knowledge and skills; and (b) elevate learners' ultimate attainment in both areas to the highest levels of achievement.

Numerous individual factors affect these goals, not least of which may be intrinsic to the learner, but teacher preparation should focus primarily on what the teacher can do to further the goals through EL-specific instructional and assessment practices. Any review of collective figures must maintain this critical perspective through (a) examination of the length of time ELs remain classified as needing services and monitoring test scores of former, or exited, ELs over time and (b) careful investigation of the relationship between these data and the types of instructional and assessment support the students received as well as the preparation of their teachers to provide this support.

At the national level, federal legislation, such as the No Child Left Behind Act of 2001 (NCLB) and the 2008 reauthorization of Higher Education Opportunity Act, presently contain provisions holding public schools, state departments, and higher education institutions accountable for the education of ELs. Under NCLB, schools, districts, and state education agencies are held accountable for the progress of ELs in two ways: (a) making Adequate Yearly Progress (AYP) for reading and mathematics under Title I, and (b) achieving Annual Measurable Achievement Objectives (AMAOs) under Title III, demonstrating satisfactory progress in learning English and attaining English proficiency. The reauthorization of the Higher Education Opportunity Act in 2008 includes new provisions for goals and assurances that "general education teachers receive training in providing instruction to limited English proficient [LEP] students," and that states report on the "extent to which teacher preparation programs prepare teachers, including general education and special education teachers, to effectively teach students who are limited English proficient."[7] These accountability measures have the potential to change the ways in which teacher preparation programs are evaluated. Some policy makers suggest that teacher preparation programs should be evaluated on the basis of the demonstrated ability of their graduates to improve the educational outcomes of *all* the students they teach, including ELs.

In light of these developments, educator preparation professionals, many of whom admittedly lack knowledge and skills regarding teaching and assessing ELs, face the dilemma of rethinking their curriculum and instruction practices, allowing them to more effectively prepare their pre-service teacher candidates to address the needs of all students, including ELs, in mainstream classrooms. At the same time, more and more committed classroom teachers, who normally do not have special training in ESL or bilingual education, are faced with the challenge of educating these students in their classrooms.

Due to the increased inclusion of ELs in general education classrooms, we believe it is essential for all teachers, including those who teach content classes, to have the knowledge, skills, and dispositions to effectively teach these students, even though some teachers may not yet view this as their responsibility. No matter the instructional delivery model ELs are enrolled in, they may be assigned to mainstream classrooms for all or part of the day. When bilingual and/or ESL specialists partner with generalist teachers who are knowledgeable and skilled in teaching and assessing ELs, the potential for accelerating ELs' progress and elevating their ultimate level of achievement increases.

Shortage of Teachers Prepared to Instruct English Learners

Addressing the needs of ELs will require deliberate and sustained efforts on the part of public schools and higher education institutions to put in place changes in curriculum, instruction, and assessment practices. Providing high-quality instruction for ELs requires a variety of curricular, instructional, and assessment skills. Members of the National Literacy Panel on Language Minority Children and Youth reported that ELs face distinct challenges in transferring conceptual knowledge and intellectual skills from their native language and in making progress in English, which depend on the level of language proficiency when they begin learning English and the strength of the literacy skills they have developed in the first language.[8]

The recent nationwide call for high accountability standards for all students and the renewed emphasis on high-quality teaching imply that all U.S. public school teachers, whether they have had ESL preparation or not, are expected to be adequately prepared to educate the growing EL population. Unfortunately, it is evident that much remains to be done to ensure that mainstream teachers are prepared to provide the instruction that will enable ELs to successfully learn academic content while developing language proficiency. According to the National Comprehensive Center for Teacher Quality, only Alaska, Arizona, California, Florida, New York, and Pennsylvania require all teachers to have some preparation to teach ELs.[9]

However, research shows that the majority of mainstream classroom teachers feel unprepared to teach ELs. In one survey conducted by the National Center for Education Statistics, researchers found that 54 percent of K–12 public school teachers had ELs in their classrooms but only 20 percent felt that they were well prepared to address such students' needs.[10] A related survey conducted by the National Education Association found that only 2.5 percent of teachers with ELs in their classrooms hold a degree in either ESL or bilingual education. Although the number of teachers of ELs increased to 44 percent in the 2003–04 school year, only about 14 percent of the teachers surveyed reported that they had received some training or professional development (eight hours or more) to teach these students.[11]

The shortage of adequately prepared teachers is consistent with findings of other researchers. For instance, Antunez reported that fewer than 13 percent of all teachers in the 2001–02 school year had received training or professional development focused on teaching ELs.[12] In a national study, Menken, Antunez, Dilworth, and Yasin found that: (a) only a small minority of institutions of higher education surveyed offer a teacher preparation program in bilingual education or Teaching English to Speakers of Other Languages (TESOL), and (b) fewer than 17 percent of educator preparation programs require that mainstream elementary and secondary teachers are prepared to teach ELs.[13] Additionally, Menken et al. found that many states require little of teachers seeking an endorsement or certification to teach ELs. For instance, in Texas, they reported that endorsements were awarded to teachers for merely passing a paper-and-pencil examination coupled with one-year teaching experience involving one or more ELs.[14]

Research by Ballantyne, Sanderman, and Levy found that while most mainstream teachers have at least one EL in their classrooms, fewer than 30 percent of those teachers have opportunities for professional development focused on the education of these students.[15] The shortage of teachers who are prepared to provide high-quality instruction to the growing population of ELs led the U.S. Department of Education's Office of English Language Acquisition (OELA) and the National Clearinghouse for English Language Acquisition (NCELA) to convene a roundtable on Teacher Education and Professional Development of EL Content Teachers in 2008. The purpose was to elicit suggestions for improving the initial and continuing education of pre-service and practicing teachers as they pertain to teaching ELs in mainstream classrooms. Members of the roundtable drafted a report that outlines a vision of teacher preparation and professional development that has the following attributes:

1. Is ongoing and integrated throughout the working life of educational personnel;
2. Is effective and relevant along a continuum of teacher education for pre-service and in-service teachers within a university setting, as well as staff development tailored to novice teachers, experienced teachers and experts;
3. Is effective and relevant for all educational personnel, including paraeducators, teachers, principals, district staff, and SEA staff;
4. Is tightly intertwined with disciplinary standards and pedagogical content knowledge;
5. Involves collaborative active learning within professional learning communities;
6. Is driven by research and data and is continually evaluated and refined;
7. Attends to multiple dimensions of diversity and fosters cross-cultural learning; and
8. Results in improved student outcomes and a narrowing of the achievement gap for English language learners.[16]

How Well-Prepared Teachers Can Make a Difference for English Learners

While it seems logical to assume that preparing all teachers to instruct and assess ELs will lead to enhanced teacher practices and student learning outcomes, significant research findings and theory that explains them are needed to confirm this assumption. Only recently has preliminary research emerged that hints at the positive impact that such preparation can lead to. In the absence of conclusive research on the effectiveness of pre- and in-service teacher preparation in raising ELs' achievement, the following section offers a pragmatic, reasoned argument, based on interactionist second language acquisition (SLA) theory, to explain how mainstream teacher preparation can support students' English language development and subject matter achievement.[17]

Before examining the main factors comprising the interactionist approach, a broader look at SLA is warranted. Ellis notes that SLA research seeks to answer three overarching theoretical questions: (a) how learners acquire the language, (b) why there are differences in individuals' rates of acquisition, and (c) why certain learners do not attain full proficiency. Ellis points to the three factors that provide answers to these questions: the environment, linguistic features internal to all learners (i.e., our ability to see patterns in visual and oral input, or what Ellis calls the "black box"), and individual learner factors, such as aptitude. Because classroom teachers influence primarily the environment, we focus on this aspect of SLA in our argument for preparing mainstream teachers to teach ELs.

Our rationale for preparing teachers to provide an optimal language development environment draws on the interactionist model of SLA, which focuses on the role of the environment in language development. The interactionist approach identifies three necessary communicative elements for ELs' second language (English) development that pertain to all language acquisition contexts, either through formal instruction or informal communication in or out of the classroom: second language learners need to receive *input* that is comprehensible, they must have opportunities to produce meaningful *output*, and they benefit from *interaction*, which encompasses input and output and provides opportunities for negotiation of meaning.[18] ESL classes can manipulate communication situations to elicit each of these three elements in an efficient way. Mainstream classes naturally include these three elements as part of classroom communication, but they may not be accessible to ELs if the language used and the context clues are not adjusted for their levels of English proficiency.

To understand how these practices can support ELs' language development and academic achievement, it is important to note how the education of ELs in ESL models has changed in the past twenty years.[19] Not long ago, ESL specialists taught language in ESL classes, and mainstream teachers knew little about ELs. Instructional practice for ELs in the mainstream drew from general pedagogical research and theory, and instructional practice in the ESL classroom was based on research and theory in the field of methods of teaching English to speakers of other languages. A closer look at this separation of instructional priorities reveals a parallel division in second language acquisition research and scholarship during this time period. Many of the published studies in SLA looked at the acquisition of English language proficiency in two broad contexts: (a) in ESL classes that focused on teaching language, or *instructed SLA* or formal study; (b) outside of the ESL classroom, through immersion in a community of English speakers, or *naturalistic SLA* or "picking up" a language.[20] These perspectives on second language development environments can shed light on the role of the ESL specialist and the mainstream teacher (what we term *teacher of ELs*) in the education of preK–12 ELs.

The older paradigm was, in a sense, dichotomous. English learners acquired English formally in ESL classes, yet they picked it up informally in the mainstream classroom, since instruction there was not focused on their specific language learning needs. The naturalistic English acquisition environment of the mainstream classroom was in effect a sink-or-swim approach, while the instructed English acquisition of the ESL class resembled a foreign language class. There was little connection between the two. The mainstream classroom did not take second language issues into account. It focused on teaching academic content to all students, and partitioned language arts into mainstream instruction for native speakers and a separate ESL class for ELs,. The unspoken assumption was that language proficiency preceded academic content learning, so substantial focus was directed on developing what Cummins terms *social language* rather than the academic language required for achievement in various subjects.[21] A sample indicator from the 1997 TESOL standards, "Persuade peers to join in favorite game, activity, hobby," illustrates this type of social language focus, whereas the majority of 2006 TESOL standards are organized around language for academic success, for example, "Describe steps in solving mathematics problems using tools or technology (e.g., protractors, calculators)."[22] While there is no denying that social language takes less time to master than academic language, there is no reason to delay a focus on academic vocabulary and other language necessary for comprehending subject matters in English.[23]

Given the exponential growth in EL enrollment preK–12, particularly in regions that had not previously served this population, coupled with increased accountability demands for all students' achievement, educators who previously considered improving educational outcomes for ELs as the domain of ESL and bilingual specialists now seek to be part of the solution. Now that schools are evaluated on their ELs' progress and ELs are required to meet common core standards, school leaders and teachers of all grade levels and subject matters are striving to make instructional time, whether in the mainstream or ESL classroom, as profitable as possible. The goal is for ELs to master academic content and develop English proficiency simultaneously, efficiently, and in a reasonable time frame. All teachers are expected to contribute to ELs' academic achievement and language development, and the ESL specialists are now expected to support ELs' mastery of subject matter content.

The new paradigm moves the two EL instructional contexts to a more integrated position on the naturalistic/instructed continuum. A mainstream classroom, if led by a teacher well versed in making adaptations and accommodations for ELs, begins to approximate a more optimal language development environment. When mainstream teachers differentiate instruction to accommodate ELs at multiple levels of English proficiency, they provide linguistic input that the ELs can acquire more readily. When mainstream teachers and native-speaking classmates interact verbally with ELs, attending to successful expression, comprehension, and negotiation of meaning, they support language acquisition through interaction. When mainstream teachers support ELs in expressing meaning in English, they push ELs' output to incorporate increasingly complex language. There is substantial research that shows that all three forms of supported communication lead to second language growth.[24] And, of course, increased English proficiency improves ELs' comprehension of academic subject matter and ability to express knowledge of and demonstrate skills in academic content in English. Similarly, improved comprehension and expression of content learned in English leads to further language growth, which continues to build through this cycle of success in language development and subject matter achievement.

As the shift in instruction for ELs has occurred in the mainstream classroom, following a trend called *content-based instruction*, the ESL classroom has moved away from teaching language for language's sake.[25] Instead of teaching dialogues such as, "Excuse me, where is the public library?" the current ESL classroom might develop English reading skills through examining the expository style of scientific texts. This approach develops language skills for mastering academic content as well as meeting language arts standards at grade-level proficiency. In addition, grammar and vocabulary are studied. There is substantial evidence that this study, particularly what Ellis terms a *focus on form*, positively impacts the rate and ultimate level of attainment of English proficiency.[26] This is especially true for older learners, mainly adolescents and beyond. Focusing on form can be effectively linked to the study of academic subjects as well in as in language arts instruction.

Collaborative Instructional Model for ELs

Our approach to preparing mainstream teachers presumes that a well-prepared mainstream teacher of ELs collaborates effectively with ESL teachers. In what we term a *collaborative instructional model* for ELs, the ESL teacher and mainstream teacher partner to reinforce each other's efforts. This model moves both ends of the naturalistic-instructed continuum toward the center. The mainstream class, with its focus on literacy development and academic content instruction through supporting ELs' comprehension and expression of the subject matter in English, now offers an environment that is conducive to developing English proficiency. Conversely, the ESL class, with its emphasis on language development expanded to application of language skills in content areas, now resembles a more individualized and supportive mainstream class that is targeted to the specific needs of ELs.

So what would this collaborative instructional model for ELs look like? It involves mainstream instruction and assessment that: (a) is attentive to the English language demands of instruction and assessment and the gap between those demands and ELs' level of English proficiency; (b) provides adjustments to the language demands appropriate for English proficiency levels through modified input, supported interaction, and accommodated output as well as increased contextual support; and (c) provides individualized language skill development within the context of the subject matter; for example, focusing on comparatives (e.g., *bigger than* and *more buoyant*) and superlatives (e.g., *heaviest* and *most absorbent*) for a discovery learning activity in science. Its primary purpose, however, remains mastery of subject matter. Complementary to the EL-supported mainstream instruction and assessment is language arts instruction provided by ESL and bilingual specialists and, where possible, native language support for subject matter instruction and assessment. As oral proficiency in a second language has a major effect on literacy skills in that language, the expertise of ESL teachers is needed to target integration of listening, speaking, reading, and writing to the precise level of English proficiency that the EL possesses in each of those skill areas.

In a collaborative instructional model, self-contained ESL classes for ELs would include: (a) language skill development focusing on listening, speaking, reading, writing, grammar, and vocabulary at each EL student's level of English proficiency; and (b) academic content learning through content-based language instruction. This involves the same modified input, supported interaction, accommodated output, and increased contextual support employed in the mainstream classroom, but they can be more finely tuned to the individual needs of ELs in the sheltered environment. Although ESL classes now encompass academic content instruction, their primary purpose remains English language development. In a collaborative model of EL instruction, both instructional contexts support each other in fostering EL academic achievement and English language development.

Our book's approach to preparing mainstream teachers is based on this collaborative model of EL instruction. We focus specifically on preparing mainstream teachers, not ESL or bilingual specialists. There are many excellent books on that subject. We want to make it very clear that we are advocates for the crucial role that ESL and bilingual specialists provide, and we base our model on the assumption that mainstream teachers who are well prepared to teach ELs are most successful when collaborating with these specialists. When all teachers are well versed in best practices in teaching and assessing ELs, whatever the context, those students' chances for success increase. Our goal is to prepare teacher candidates to support ELs' learning in the mainstream classroom through feasible instructional and assessment accommodations, balancing the needs of ELs and native speakers. We seek to better demarcate the knowledge and skills required for mainstream teachers to support ELs' success, aiming to avoid asking too much as well as not expecting enough.

Over the past fifteen years, we have continued to refine a model that has tested aspects of this goal. Our approach is pragmatic, based on piloting elements of the model and preliminary research on implementation of piloted components. We hope this book succeeds in posing new and different questions and sparks discussion about the obligation of all educators to contribute to ELs' success. In our research, we have seen several teacher preparation programs give attention to the instruction of students from diverse cultural and linguistic backgrounds. While this is certainly consistent with recent calls to improve the initial and continuing education of pre-service and practicing teachers as they pertain to teaching ELs in mainstream classrooms, we believe that most educator preparation programs are just beginning to embrace the responsibility of preparing all teachers to teach ELs in mainstream classrooms.

The challenges we outlined call for innovative ways of addressing the needs of ELs in all classrooms, beginning with the preparation of teacher candidates. We concur with Lucas that "Teachers cannot simply teach ELLs the way they teach other students; to teach [ELs] well, they need special expertise—and this requires special preparation."[27] Educating ELs requires specialized knowledge and skills that can and should be meaningfully incorporated or infused across teacher preparation programs. Competent teachers of ELs, including teachers of students in primary and early grades and content area teachers in middle and high schools, understand how these students acquire language, how they become literate, and how to create the conditions under which these students can learn. Teacher preparation programs are uniquely positioned to enhance EL learning and achievement through innovative pre-service teacher preparation initiatives.

The notion that teacher candidates should be well prepared to address the needs of ELs in all classrooms clearly requires some rethinking of how education preparation programs are designed and implemented. Adjustments may be needed in how teacher educators approach their work and how programs are structured. For instance, to provide consistency in curriculum and instruction across all educator preparation, initiatives can be put in place to engage diverse faculty in collaboration and teamwork when addressing EL curriculum and instruction. With respect to program design, some content, assignments, or activities may be revised or added in certain courses within the program. As well, it should not take a major program change to establish school-university partnerships to provide opportunities for teacher candidates to work directly with ELs in real classrooms under the mentorship of field-based educators and practicing teachers with expertise in EL education. Any of these options can be a good first step toward enhancing the curriculum to include a focus on ELs.

In this book, we seek to accomplish two primary objectives. First, we present a realistic EL infusion model, the *One Plus* model, that teacher educators can use as a guide for preparing all teachers to address the needs of ELs in the mainstream classrooms. Designed to be flexible yet comprehensive, the model incorporates all aspects of teacher candidate preparation, including courses, field/clinical experiences, candidate assessment, faculty development and scholarship, and program administration, evaluation, and accreditation. We use the phrase *One Plus* to indicate the stackable nature of the model, which enables programs to build up from simply developing candidates' rudimentary knowledge and skills regarding educating ELs to attaining qualification in teaching various subjects to them. Either of these options may be pursued through application of this model, which we will describe more fully in chapter 3.

Second, throughout the book, we provide a set of insights and examples of how EL competencies can be infused across the teacher preparation curricula. The first three chapters of the book lay the foundation for the One Plus model. In chapter 1, we review some of the prevailing approaches of delivering content through infusion and offer an operational definition of EL infusion inspired by principles of interdisciplinarity, instructional design, and effective instruction and assessment of ELs, which guided the development and implementation of the One Plus model. In chapter 2, we trace the evolution of EL infusion, beginning with a response to a Florida Consent Decree that highlighted the need for the preparation of teachers to teach ELs. We then describe the development of the early iterations of the Florida English for speakers of other languages (ESOL) infusion model, which was originally designed for language arts teachers only and leads to the attainment of the full ESOL endorsement. Finally, we explain how we adapted the Florida ESOL infusion model and built in resources, procedures, and policies to develop the One Plus model. In chapter 3, we provide a detailed description of the One Plus model, which addresses a diverse array of teaching specializations and credentials. We focus on the two institution-granted credentials at the center of the One Plus model, namely, EL-qualified for teaching academic subject areas in mainstream classrooms and EL-qualified for teaching language arts in mainstream classrooms. Finally, for institutions considering adoption of the One Plus model, we offer a framework for designing, implementing, and evaluating such programs.

Chapters 4 and 5 address issues pertaining to the process of embedding EL content across the curriculum, faculty development, and resources. Chapter 4 presents a step-by-step process for infusing EL content across courses and programs, and provides tools and strategies for engaging faculty in the infusion process. In chapter 5, we provide guidance in planning and delivering faculty development in EL content and share a set of resources that teacher educators can use to support the development and implementation of the model in their own contexts.

Chapters 6 through 9 provide practical examples of EL-embedded courses and activities from several disciplines, including general education; specific content area such as science and social studies, and language arts; and other professional education specialties. Chapter 6 includes four sample EL-embedded course summaries at the basic, or 1+, level of infusion representing the areas of human development, early childhood education, learning disabilities, and social foundations. Chapter 7 features six sample course summaries at the intermediate, or 2+, level of infusion representing the areas of classroom management and instructional strategies, physical education, mathematics education, middle school science, adolescent mathematics, and social studies education. Chapter 8 offers four sample course summaries at the more complex 3+ level of infusion in language arts education, including children's and young adult literature, foundations of language and literacy, and developmental reading. Chapter 9, opening with a reflection by Edwidge Crevecoeur-Bryant, features three sample course summaries of professional preparation courses that are more closely aligned with the 1+ level, representing the areas of counseling, school psychology, and educational administration.

Chapter 10, authored by Florin Mihai and Eleni Pappamihiel, provides examples of content in EL-specific courses and/or field experiences. The chapter describes the addition of two EL-specific courses, and offers suggestions for incorporating content from these courses, along with related field experiences, across the teacher preparation curricula.

In chapter 11, authors Jeannie Ducher, Martha Castañeda, and Amy Fisher Young address candidate assessment and evaluation of EL-infused programs and present a culturally responsive framework for evaluating EL-infused programs and assessing teacher candidates' preparation to teach ELs in mainstream classrooms.

Although this book focuses on pre-service education, much of the contents pertain to practicing teachers as well. Novice and veteran teachers, as much as teacher candidates, benefit from considering EL issues when planning, implementing, or assessing instruction. Similar to the infusion of the teacher preparation curriculum in pre-service programs, professional learning can be enhanced by integrating EL competencies. Florida school district supervisors, for example, have noted the improved attitudes of participants in professional learning programs when EL issues were integrated into general topics rather than offered separately as compliance measures. Participation and engagement increased in professional learning on ELs with exceptionalities when it was incorporated into expanded professional learning in response to intervention rather than offered as an independent seminar.[28]

We hope the conceptual foundation for the One Plus model, along with the guidelines, examples of EL-embedded course summaries, and faculty resources, will offer support and helpful guidance for teacher educators who are responsible for preparing teachers to teach all students, including ELs.

PART I

EL Infusion from Theory to Practice: The One Plus Model

CHAPTER 1

The Characteristics of EL Infusion

In this chapter, we position English learner (EL) infusion within an array of possibilities for preparing teacher candidates to instruct and assess ELs, consider the definition of infusion and the infusion of various types of information and skills in other postsecondary disciplines and teacher preparation programs, provide our definition of EL infusion, and examine EL infusion experiences in teacher preparation programs around the nation. We conclude the chapter with a brief overview of the One Plus model, whose development and details are expounded in chapters 2 and 3.

What Is Infusion?

The subject of this book, infusion of EL issues into teacher preparation curricula, is only one of a number of responses to the need for better-prepared teachers of ELs. In a review of the literature on this broad subject, Lucas and Grinberg identified four structural strategies for preparing all teachers to teach ELs: "adding a course to the program, modifying existing courses and field experiences to give attention to ELLs, adding or modifying program prerequisites, and adding a minor or supplemental certificate program."[1] Of these four categories, the first two are common elements of EL-infused programs, and the latter two are complements or alternatives to infusion. Depending on program goals and resources, institutions may choose to address the need for enhanced teacher preparation in a piecemeal or add-on approach, or they may adopt a more comprehensive structure that EL infusion models can facilitate. Before discussing the specifics of EL infusion, we explore the definition of infusion and its track record in other disciplines in higher education.

Infusion is generally defined as the introduction of a new element or quality into something. Additionally, the term can refer to a drink, remedy, or extract prepared by soaking the leaves of a plant or herb in liquid; in this sense, it involves combining two or more properties into a new form that contains elements of both, such as the combination of mint leaves and hot water to make herbal tea. This aspect of infusion is a fitting metaphor for the subject of this book—infusing EL issues into general teacher preparation curricula. Just as the contents of both elements are perceptible yet transformed in making tea, so can the subjects of teaching and assessing English learners combine with the general theory and practice of learning, teaching, and assessing to form an EL-infused teacher preparation program.

However, the tea metaphor applies as well to the major potential flaw of infusion. If there aren't enough mint leaves or the water is too cold, the tea may seem more like water than mint. In other words, the infused element may be so diluted or compromised that it is undetectable. Similarly, programs that fail to plan systemically for infusion risk effacement of the infused content, making the focus on teaching and assessing ELs diffused, marginalized, or even imperceptible. This inherent potential weakness in infusion has been noted in the literature on infusing various content in postsecondary curricula, and we have experienced this issue in multiple programs and states.

Infusion in Other Post-Secondary Contexts

Curricular infusion in fields other than teacher preparation has been studied in the literature on higher education. Topics such as information technology, critical thinking, and communication have been infused across postsecondary curricula to embed the acquisition or application of skills considered necessary for students' success. Institutions in the United Kingdom, such as University of Luton and Napier University, have infused subjects—information fluency, presentation skills, and problem solving, among others—into courses in disciplines as diverse as travel and tourism, health-related fields, and software engineering. Infusion innovators from these institutions researched students' impressions of what they term *embedded* content. They found that the majority of students and faculty at Napier University favored embedded over stand-alone instruction of the skills. Relevance to the subject matter was cited as the reason for this preference. Presumably, applying problem solving, for example, to an issue in a student's field is a more direct way of promoting transfer of skills than teaching a problem-solving protocol in isolation or applied to a general issue, as might be done in a seminar on critical thinking skills. However, for the minority who preferred stand-alone skill instruction, the concern of "sidelining" the targeted skills, as well as the greater likelihood that students might not be as aware of the embedded skills, was an issue.[2]

Similar to the infusion of these skill-building activities, academic content has been distributed throughout postsecondary curricula in the form of common themes. For example, undergraduate students at the University of Central Florida selected *sustainability* as the theme that permeates general education, common core, and various specialization courses within majors.[3] With the support of the administration, faculty who design and update undergraduate courses are invited to participate in paid seminars on infusing sustainability issues into their classes and receive other incentives upon the completion of one or more sustainability instructional modules. The types of modules can vary from a research paper assignment on sustainability in a composition course to a project measuring the financial implications of corporate policies that further sustainability in an economics course. Regular colloquia on sustainability are scheduled, as well as seminars with noted lecturers, community engagement projects, and other forms of reinforcement and incentives for the common theme.

Infusion in Teacher Preparation

For several decades, the integration or infusion of curricula within teacher preparation has been a common practice in mathematics, science, and social studies education, among others. A standard practice among teacher preparation professionals who have integrated their curricula consists of using project- or problem-based learning or employing themes that cross two or more disciplines. While approaches to curriculum integration differ from institution to institution, faculty who have integrated their curriculum in these disciplines often have clearly identified or intentional curriculum overlaps, align their assessment systems with their infused curricula, and participate in ongoing collaboration when planning, implementing, and evaluating the impact of infused curricula on teacher candidate preparation.

The notion of infusion has also been practiced in various other curriculum areas in U.S. teacher preparation programs, most notably in the areas of instructional technology and exceptional education. Through curriculum infusion, teacher educators in these areas aspire to improve teacher candidates' instructional practices, which in turn promote students' engagement and enhance learning and achievement. Because space does not permit a broad review of the literature focused on curriculum integration in these two areas, we highlight two recent examples of infused curriculum projects (one in instructional technology, the other in special education) that have resulted in improved teacher candidate preparation.

Bowling Green State University: Vannatta and O'Bannon used the International Society for Technology in Education (ISTE)'s essential conditions for technology integration as a framework for developing Project PICT (Preservice Infusion of Computer Technology), an initiative designed to prepare pre-service elementary education teacher candidates to effectively use technology as a tool for enhancing teaching and learning.[4] The authors reported that Project PICT had significant effects on technology proficiency, the process of curriculum infusion within the program, and the strengthening of the vision to infuse technology across the curriculum among participating higher education faculty and K–6 teachers. In addition, the project activities had a significant positive effect on technology proficiency among elementary education methods students. The authors noted that while they espouse all ten of ISTE's essential conditions for technology integration (shared vision, access, skilled educators, professional development, technical assistance, content standards and curriculum resources, student-centered teaching, assessment, community support, and support policies), they found the conditions of shared vision, access, incentives, professional development, and community support to be particularly helpful in developing a successful technology infusion program at their institution.

Northern Illinois University: A team of teacher educators developed Project ACCEPT (Achieving Creative and Collaborative Educational Preservice Teams), an initiative aimed at infusing special education competencies across the curriculum for pre-service teacher candidates. In this model, a restructuring of teacher preparation classes and field experiences enhanced existing programs with critical competencies for working with individuals with disabilities. In partial fulfillment of the project requirements, the fifty-three teacher candidates who voluntarily participated enrolled in a designated section of an inclusion course, attended a ten-hour institute prior to the start of the semester, and completed a field experience in a real-world inclusive classroom. The findings indicate that participation in Project ACCEPT resulted in more substantial gains among these teacher candidates, particularly with respect to increasing their content knowledge of the field, in comparison with a control group of teacher candidates who did not partici-pate in the project.[5]

Definition of EL Infusion

It is important to establish what we consider EL infusion and where the model we developed for planning, implementing, and evaluating its location in the spectrum of options. EL infusion, also known as *ESOL infusion* or *ESL infusion*, is one approach to ensuring that teacher candidates are prepared to teach and assess ELs in mainstream classrooms.[6] An infusion approach involves integrating, rather than simply appending, curricular content and assessment that promotes development of the desired knowl-edge, skills, and dispositions. The term *EL* or *ESOL infusion* has been used to describe both the process and outcome of embedding EL issues into existing coursework, as well as the overall process and product of incorporating an EL focus into the teacher preparation curriculum through various measures, including embedded courses. To clarify the scope of our references to EL infusion, this book uses the term *infused* to denote incorporation of EL content throughout the curriculum and the term *embed-ded* to describe the addition of EL content into teacher preparation courses, which also encompass field/clinical experiences. In other words, when we refer to infusion, we are not only referencing the addition of an EL focus to teacher preparation courses but also to all the other curricular components that contribute to teacher candidates' preparation to teach and assess ELs.

We further define *EL infusion* as the addition of EL content into a general teacher preparation program in *an interconnected, cohesive, and interdisciplinary manner*. What we term *EL content* includes *EL-focused* topics, objectives, instructional materials and media (for example, articles, books, multimedia, websites), in-class activities, course assign-ments, field/clinical experiences, and assessments.[7] This EL-focused content can be built into EL-specific courses (also known as *ESL education* or *ESL stand-alone* courses) as well as distributed across other teacher preparation courses. The purpose of EL infu-sion is to prepare teachers of all subjects and grade levels to support the achievement of ELs rather than to prepare specialists who focus on teaching ESL or bilingual educa-tion. EL infusion aims to prepare teachers for the many possible instructional contexts and models implemented in preK–12. It does not supplant the preparation of ESL and bilingual specialists but rather complements it by educating generalists to partner more effectively with them. We affirm that the ESL and bilingual specialists remain central figures in ensuring appropriate instruction and assessment for ELs. Whether mainstream teachers are part of a bilingual, pull-out ESL, or inclusion instructional model, it is essential that they be knowledgeable about and skilled in meeting their ELs' educational needs.

EL infusion is a means of preparing generalist teachers to support the academic success and language development of ELs. Institutions' responses to addressing this goal may meet the criteria for infusion in different ways. However, the extent to which these three qualities of EL infusion—interconnectedness, cohesion, and interdisciplinarity—are met depends on the intent and implementation at each institution. While there are published descriptions of EL-infused programs that have added EL content without consideration of what we consider the essential qualities of infusion, we propose that curricular interconnectedness, cohesion, and interdisciplinarity should be the aspiration of programs seeking to prepare teachers of ELs through infusion.

Curricular infusion connotes more than simple adhesion. Rather, infusion entails both surface and deep connections at multiple points of thematic concurrence. *Interconnectedness* between existing general assignments and EL-focused assignments requires compatibility of format and content. In discipline-based field/clinical experiences, for example, an interconnected EL-embedded assignment might involve working with an individual English learner. Instead of appending a self-contained set of procedures for working with the English learner in isolation, an interconnected assignment might expand an informal reading inventory assignment for a native speaker to explore specific reading issues that the second language reader faces, such as lack of oral proficiency in English. Having the opportunity to compare and contrast the two inventory experiences can bring about useful insights. Interconnectedness in an EL-embedded course such as Social Foundations of Education might involve adding a focus on immigrant experiences of Latinos/as adjusting to U.S. schools, finding points of commonality across particular existing course topics. Interconnectedness implies an exploration of the common and contrasting features of the added EL content and the themes and topics to which it is related. As with any aspect of EL infusion, a constant challenge is to keep the EL content connected to thematic commonalities within the broader curriculum, yet discrete in reflecting the distinct body of knowledge about ELs.

Because of their distributed nature, EL-infused programs risk becoming less than the sum of their infused parts. Even if excellent interconnected EL content is infused, the entirety of the infused elements may represent nothing more than scattered facts in candidates' developing knowledge about teaching. If the same distributed EL content were delivered solely through EL-specific courses, the focus on the English learner would be comprehensive and would convey a sense of completeness. A coming together of the various infused elements can be accomplished through infusion, however. *Cohesion* can be achieved through measures such as reflective portfolios, benchmark reviews of candidates' developing knowledge and skills at key points in the program of studies, cumulative summative assessments, and capstone experiences with ELs, among others. Moving away from traditional course structures toward infusion presents unique opportunities to cultivate cohesion in candidates' perceptions of ELs and how to teach and assess them in comprehensible and equitable ways.

We maintain that the primary factor that distinguishes EL infusion from other approaches to EL teacher preparation is *interdisciplinary* collaboration with the common goal of improving ELs' academic achievement in K–12 settings. As noted in the introduction, all teachers, not only ESL specialists, are being held accountable for ELs' success. By necessity, teacher educators of all subjects and grade levels are called on to prepare teachers capable of sharing responsibility for meeting this goal. ESL and bilingual faculty cannot accomplish this alone. Preparation must be situated within the knowledge base of each discipline, the knowledge base on instruction and assessment of ELs, and the intersection of these disciplinary areas. Upholding an interdisciplinary ethos in the process and product of infusion fosters a more comprehensive and collaborative response to the call for well-prepared teachers of ELs.

EL Infusion in North America

During the first decade of the twenty-first century, various approaches to preparing teachers of English language learners have been implemented, supported largely by federal grants. The U.S. Department of Education's Office of Bilingual Education and Multilingual Affairs—which later became the Office of English Language Acquisition (OELA)—supported institutions of higher education in addressing the growing need for generalist teachers who are knowledgeable and skilled in teaching ELs. The literature indicates that while educator preparation professionals are often guided by similar standards with respect to expected teacher knowledge, skills, and dispositions for teaching ELs, they have also used an array of instructional approaches and strategies that vary widely in terms of target audiences, theoretical and research grounding, content focus, and instructional delivery venues.[8] These approaches tend to fall into four broad categories:

- Use of particular instructional procedures or strategies, such as instructional scaffolding, that help make instruction and assessment comprehensible to ELs in the classroom[9]
- Use of specific lesson frameworks during specific blocks of instruction such as sheltered instruction[10]
- Use of linguistically and culturally relevant conceptual frameworks to inform and guide EL instruction[11]
- Use of comprehensive and systemic models designed to prepare teachers and other school personnel to effectively address the language, literacy, and content needs of ELs in all classrooms[12]

While these approaches all attempt to enhance teacher practices with the goals of enhancing student achievement, they differ in important ways. For purposes of this book, we focus on EL infusion as an approach for enhancing teacher educators' instructional practices when preparing teacher candidates to teach ELs.

While EL infusion is a relatively new approach for preparing teachers to address the needs of ELs in all classrooms, it is being used in a small but growing number of institutions in the United States and Canada. In response to the challenges faced by teachers who work with ELs in mainstream classrooms and the need to prepare all educators to teach these students, the OELA recently provided financial support to teacher preparation institutions that incorporate EL competencies into general teacher preparation programs through its National Professional Development Grants initiative. Several states with high numbers of ELs have begun incorporating EL competencies into their teacher preparation programs; however, most have focused on the preparation of teachers working in sheltered or EL-only environments. The following are a few examples of published EL infusion initiatives:

Ontario Institute For Studies in Education: During the past ten to fifteen years, the Ontario Institute for Studies in Education (OISE), under the leadership of Antoinette Gagne, spearheaded a program to infuse EL issues and teaching strategies into teacher preparation and professional development programs in Ontario.[13] In response to financial cutbacks in ESL specialists' budgets in Ontario's schools, OISE has been providing resources and support for mainstream teachers with ELs in their classrooms. Program leaders report that the program has been beneficial for mainstream teachers who have ELs in their classrooms.

Boston College: At Boston College, Costa, McPhail, Smith, and Brisk developed a project that engages teacher preparation faculty in ESL professional development training to "change the teacher education curriculum to better prepare teachers to work with linguistically and culturally different students."[14] Voluntary faculty members attend a series of Faculty Institute sessions on ELs, receive mentoring by institute facilitators, and have access to various resources supporting their efforts to infuse EL teaching strategies and issues into their curriculum. It is not clear, however, whether such EL infusion efforts were institutionalized or extended to other teacher preparation curricula.

University at Albany: At this state university in Albany, New York, Carla Meskill developed and implemented a program aimed at infusing EL competencies throughout teacher preparation core curricula, as well as extending knowledge to practicing teachers and other school personnel.[15] The project worked toward its goals of curricular revision and enhancement through various means, including working directly with teacher candidates and providing curriculum infusion assistance activities such as: (a) "push-in" work, where an EL expert goes into a faculty member's classroom and works directly with students on an ongoing basis to address EL issues and (b) peer presentations, in which graduate students trained in EL competencies provide presentations for students and faculty on demand. Program developers report that though both of these infusion activities directly affected the curricula and instruction, project leaders initially maintained responsibility for educating students about EL competencies and gradually shifted the responsibility to the actual faculty with ongoing support throughout the year. Preliminary evaluation data indicate that the project was beneficial to both faculty and teacher candidates.

Miami University: In 2007, Miami University of Ohio received federal funding to develop EL-infused programs through project ESOL MIAMI, aimed at preparing all educators to address the needs of ELs. The ESOL MIAMI project was inspired and guided by an EL-infusion model originally developed and field-tested by Joyce Nutta at the University of South Florida, with funding support from an OELA grant, entitled ESOL TAPESTRY.[16] Kouider Mokhtari and Bruce Perry served as principal investigators for this grant. A major focus of the ESOL MIAMI project was enhancing higher education faculty capacity to prepare teacher candidates to teach ELs in mainstream classrooms. The ESOL MIAMI framework used a multifaceted approach incorporating EL-embedded courses, extended field experiences, and optional completion of specialized EL-specific coursework, which led to an EL certificate. Preliminary evaluation data indicated that the ESOL MIAMI project positively impacted participating faculty instructional practices, as well as teacher candidates' self-confidence in their ability to effectively teach ELs.

ESOL Infusion in Florida

As will be discussed at length in chapter 2, Florida initial certification degree programs are required to graduate candidates with preparation in teaching and assessing ELs. Nearly all state-approved programs have adopted an infusion approach for candidates whose certification areas require the ESOL endorsement, called *ESOL infusion* in Florida. We highlight two Florida programs that received funding to develop EL-infused programs and with which the coauthors have been involved.

University of South Florida: Funded by an OELA Training for All Teachers grant, the ESOL TAPESTRY (Training for All Pre-service Educators, Stressing Technology-Based Resources) project's goal was to revise the pre-service teacher preparation curriculum to prepare candidates to work with ELs. Joyce Nutta was the principal investigator of this project. Programs in early childhood, elementary, exceptional, English, and foreign language education were infused to include EL-embedded and EL-specific courses, and the ESOL TAPESTRY website, which provides faculty development resources for ESOL infusion, was established.[17] Over a five-year period, fifty-seven teacher preparation courses added EL content, and 208 full-time and adjunct faculty and graduate teaching assistants attended a series of seminars and workshops focusing on ELs and second language acquisition.

University of Central Florida: In 2000, under the leadership of Gail West, the College of Education at UCF received funding from a U.S. Department of Education grant to develop Project Jericho, a faculty development program. Project Jericho provided College of Education faculty with professional development events and resources and established online tutorial modules on various topics pertaining to teaching and assessing ELs, all of which supported the college's EL infusion initiative. Joyce Nutta and

Carine Strebel have been updating the EL-infused curriculum and faculty development at UCF since 2007; chapters 2 and 4 contain a description of this process.

Preview of the One Plus Model of EL Infusion

From our experiences at the University of South Florida, Miami University, and the University of Central Florida we developed the EL infusion model, which is briefly described in the introduction. Applying core principles and practices from the Florida ESOL infusion model, the One Plus model stratifies three major programmatic outcomes and provides additional procedures and resources to achieve them. At the program level, the infusion outcome can range from what we term *basic coverage*, which denotes rudimentary knowledge and skills about educating ELs attained through EL-embedded courses and field experiences alone, to a university-granted credential we term *EL-qualified*, which is differentiated for content or language arts teachers in mainstream classes with ELs. Figure 1.1 illustrates program outcomes.

Similarly, the depth of EL content in EL-embedded and EL-specific program courses is categorized into three levels, each one adding more applications of EL content to the course subject. Figure 1.2 depicts the course outcomes of the One Plus EL infusion model

Because the One Plus model does not focus solely on the preparation of ESL specialists, as the Florida model does, the term *EL infusion* better describes the primary emphasis—the preparation of mainstream teachers of all subjects and grade levels

Figure 1.1

One Plus model program outcomes: Increasing depth of preparation for teaching English learners

Figure 1.2

One Plus model course outcomes: Increasing proportion of English learner content in program courses

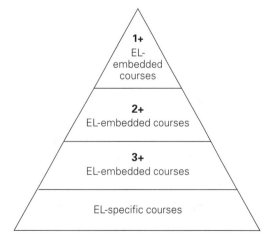

to teach and assess ELs. The model is designed to promote the three central qualities of interconnectedness, cohesion, and interdisciplinarity. In addition, the model promotes comprehensive, curriculum-wide infusion as well as a process for achieving this outcome with maximum participation of faculty, administrators, and other key stakeholders. Fully aware of the potential shortcomings of infused curricula, we offer a model for systemic infusion that takes the risk of EL-infused content dilution into account throughout each phase of program development and across involved faculty and administrators. A number of issues can diminish the development of teacher candidates' competence in teaching and assessing ELs, including: (a) teacher preparation faculty's varying commitment to embedding their courses as well as varying consistency among different sections of the same embedded courses; (b) partner school districts whose teachers are not good models for teaching ELs in their classes or that have few ELs enrolled; and (c) a lack of resources for supporting the curricular change infusion requires. Though these and other factors that threaten the quality, authenticity, and salience of the infused content are affected by local context and interpersonal dynamics, following organizational and procedural guidelines grounded in a shared commitment to the value of EL infusion can mitigate these threats. The following chapters offer specifics regarding the organizational and procedural model we propose and its implementation in various teacher preparation institutions.

TERMS USED

EL infusion: The preparation of generalist teachers to instruct and assess ELs in the mainstream environment through the addition of EL content into a general teacher preparation program in an interconnected, cohesive, and interdisciplinary manner. *Infusion* has become an established term in the higher education literature. Although it can imply a transparency that conceals the nature of the infused content, we believe the word is a fitting reminder of the need for ever-present pressure to uphold its quality and salience. The terms *ESOL infusion* or *ESL infusion* are also used in the literature, but to clarify that infusion is primarily intended to prepare mainstream teachers with ELs in their classes rather than ESL specialists who teach English as a second language, we use *EL infusion*.

EL-infused curriculum or EL-infused program: Integrating EL content into the various components of teacher preparation curricula, including program courses, field/clinical experiences, and candidate assessment as well as through EL specific courses and field/clinical experiences.

EL-embedded course: Teacher preparation course or field/clinical experience that incorporates EL content; also referred to as an *ESOL-infused* or *ESL-infused* course.

EL-specific course: An EL-focused course that connects to other elements of the EL-integrated curriculum; also referred to as a *stand-alone* ESOL or ESL course. We prefer the term *EL-specific*, which conveys the course's connection to EL-embedded courses rather than isolation (i.e., stand-alone) in the curriculum.

EL content: EL-focused topics, objectives, instructional information, materials, and media (e.g., articles, books, multimedia, websites, and guest lectures), class activities (e.g., group discussions, demonstrations, simulations), course assignments, field/clinical experiences, and assessments added to existing curricular elements.

Teacher preparation faculty: Instructional and clinical faculty who are not ESL education specialists.

ESL education faculty: Instructional and clinical faculty who are experts in second language acquisition and TESOL (Teaching English to Speakers of Other Languages).

ESL: English as a second language, a subject of study. An ESL specialist teaches the English language using instructional practices grounded in second language acquisition and ESL teaching methodology.

ESOL: English for speakers of other languages; this term is often used interchangeably with ESL, but in general ESOL is used more in preK–12 and adult education and ESL is used more in post-secondary settings. There are differences from state to state, but the international professional organization TESOL (Teachers of English to Speakers of Other Languages) uses the term ESL for preK–12, so we also use the term ESL. When we refer to ESL certification in states that use the term ESOL, we use each state's term (for example, the ESOL endorsement in Florida).

ELL: English language learner; this term refers to the student rather than the subject (English as a second language). Although some refer to English learners as ESOL or ESL students, this indicates their enrollment in ESOL/ESL classes, not their status as students who are not fully proficient in English and receive support services such as home language instruction or accommodations in mainstream classes. The word *language* in English language learner is intended to clarify that these are students learning the English language, not students from the United Kingdom. However, as of 2011, the Office of English Language Acquisition began using the term *English learner* (EL), which is briefer and whose meaning should be clear to any educator. We use the terms *English learner*, *EL student(s)*, and *EL(s)* in this book unless we are quoting those who refer to ELLs.

ESL teacher: One whose responsibility is to teach English as a second language to English learners in pull-out, push-in, or self-contained classes exclusively for English learners or who serves as an ESL specialist or resource teacher at a school with ELs. We contrast this term with *teacher of ELs*, which implies a teacher who has ELs in a mainstream classroom that includes native English speakers. In other words, the teacher of ELs is not an ESL specialist.

CHAPTER 2

The Origins and Evolution
of the One Plus Model
# of EL Infusion

In this chapter, we provide an overview of the evolution of the One Plus model from a Florida initiative to a comprehensive framework for preparing teachers to reach ELs. We begin with a history and description of the Florida Consent Decree, the response to which served as the starting point of our experiences with EL infusion.

Professional Development Requirements of the Florida Consent Decree

In 1990, the Florida Department of Education entered into a Consent Decree agreement with a consortium of EL advocacy groups, including the League of United Latin American Citizens (LULAC) and Haitian Refugee Center, both of which were legally represented by Multicultural Education Training Advocates (META).[1] This agreement set in place a combination of measures to improve education for ELs in Florida schools, the most sweeping of which required professional development for practicing teachers. Categorized by certification areas, the professional development requirements ranged from eighteen to three hundred clock hours. The majority of academic subject matter teachers were required to complete sixty clock hours, and teachers whose certification areas include responsibility for teaching language arts (early childhood, elementary, English, and exceptional education) were required to obtain the full English as a second language (ESL) endorsement.[2] The endorsement had been approved as a state credential in the 1980s and consisted of fifteen graduate credits, including the following five 3-credit courses: (a) Methods of Teaching English to Speakers of Other Languages (TESOL), (b) ESOL Curriculum and Materials Development, (c) ESOL Testing and Evaluation, (d) Cross Cultural Communication and Understanding, and (e) Applied Linguistics. These courses formed the core of many MA programs in TESOL, and since most Florida colleges of education at the time did not offer bachelor's degrees in ESL education, they were the most readily available courses once the Consent Decree was implemented.

As part of MA programs in TESOL, whose primary purpose in most cases was to prepare ESL teachers for jobs in intensive English programs at universities or for teaching English as a foreign language abroad, the ESL endorsement programs directed coursework toward teaching ESL and typically did not include general learning theory, methods, or assessment courses as a foundation for later discipline-specific coursework, as colleges of education commonly do. Therefore, the five courses included an introduction to general pedagogical issues and principles and then applied them to teaching ESL. Certified teachers taking the five courses became frustrated by the duplication of content from the teacher preparation coursework they had completed for initial certification in their fields and the ESL coursework required for the ESL endorsement.[3] Clearly, teachers did not need to learn the definitions of validity and reliability or the characteristics of cooperative learning more than once. What they needed to know, for example, was how to determine if assessment was valid and reliable in measuring ELs' academic achievement and how to structure cooperative learning activities to provide optimal interaction conditions for comprehensibility. In other words, certified language arts teachers needed to learn about the specific needs of ELs and relevant targeted instructional and assessment strategies, not the general background information on teaching and learning that comprised a portion of the ESL courses. Nonetheless, the courses continued to be offered unchanged.

Beginning in 1992, the Florida Department of Education tried to address this curricular overlap by creating alternatives to the five-course ESL endorsement model. In-service components entitled Empowering ESOL Teachers: Volumes I & II and then Teaching Excellence and Cultural Harmony (TEACH) were designed to build on teachers' existing knowledge and skills by applying them directly to ELs. While these alternatives were being implemented, recent graduates of initial teacher certification degrees expressed frustration with school district policies that made completion of the three hundred hours a condition of hire.

State of Infusion: The Beginnings of the Florida Model of Infusion for the ESOL Endorsement

As the new teachers struggled with the challenges of their first year in the profession, they bore the additional responsibility of completing these three hundred hours of professional development in the evenings. The in-service requirement impacted new teachers in particular, since the Consent Decree grandfathered in Florida teachers who could document two years of successful teaching of one or more ELs prior to the 1990–91 school year, reducing the three hundred-hour requirement to sixty hours. Many decried the extensive professional development required upon graduating with a teaching certificate and questioned why new teachers didn't complete those requirements as part of their degree programs. Doing so would eliminate the demands of in-service professional development during graduates' critical first years of teaching. There was an even greater benefit to moving the ESL professional development to pre-service teacher preparation: new teachers with ELs in their classrooms would not need to learn how to instruct and assess them over a period of years, but would possess the knowledge and skills that would enable them to meet ELs' needs from day one.

In 1995, the Florida Board of Education adopted rules requiring colleges of education in the Florida University System to provide teacher candidates with "the instruction necessary to enable them to teach students having limited proficiency in English. The instruction must be a required part of the teacher-preparation program in each college."[4] Southeastern Florida boasts the highest EL enrollment in the state, so the universities that serve the region, Florida International University (FIU) and The University of Miami (UM) in Miami and Florida Atlantic University (FAU) in Boca Raton, were compelled to address the pre-service issue before other universities followed suit. A conflicting policy complicated their efforts, however. During the same period of the mid-1990s, the Florida legislature was enforcing a 120-hour limit on bachelor's degrees. As a result, teacher education programs had to trim, in many cases, seven to ten credits from their programs of study; and thus could not add fifteen hours of coursework for the ESOL endorsement at the same time.

The confluence of three factors—the need to graduate teachers with the ESOL endorsement, the 120-hour rule, and the overlap in content of the five endorsement courses with the general teacher education curriculum—prompted educators to consider an alternative approach that came to be known as *ESOL infusion* in Florida.[5] As noted in chapter 1, the concept of infusion has been implemented at universities in the United States and United Kingdom, but no precedent for infusion of EL content had been established outside of Florida. Educators at FAU, UM, and FIU began planning a route to ESOL endorsement that eventually included infusing approximately three-fifths of the fifteen-credit ESOL endorsement coursework into the elementary education bachelor's degree curriculum. It was recognized that ESL faculty should teach crucial knowledge and skills regarding ELs, so the policy of adding what have come to be known as *EL-specific* courses—from the original five ESOL endorsement courses—was proposed. Following discussions with the Florida Department of Education, a five-hour waiver of the 120-hour rule was instituted to support the addition of the EL-specific courses.

The southeastern Florida institutions submitted proposals to the Florida Department of Education requesting approval of their infused approaches to the ESOL endorsement. Because it was charged with upholding the Consent Decree, and since the five-course sequence was its only noted option for the endorsement, the department moved cautiously forward with the reviews. Attorneys from the original plaintiffs and the department began negotiating about an infusion approach, while a professional panel assembled by the department reviewed the proposals. A similar give-and-take process occurred between the department and the universities, with requests for more information and more rigor and specificity in the infused curricular elements. Eventually, what became the Florida ESOL infusion model evolved, comprising a set of twenty-five ESOL endorsement standards based on the five ESL courses as well as a recurrence of some requirements for in-service teachers in teacher preparation programs. For example, the professional development the Consent Decree had required of in-service teachers became a mandate for teacher preparation faculty teaching courses with embedded ESL competencies and EL content (which we refer to as *EL-embedded* courses). Any faculty who taught a course addressing an ESOL endorsement standard had to complete the equivalent of a three-credit ESL course for eligibility to be instructor of record.

The EL infusion process, its content, and the quantity of EL-embedded course elements were not clearly established as the Florida model emerged from prolonged negotiations. Questions remained about how much EL content should be embedded in teacher preparation courses and what existing content from these courses addressed the broad ESOL endorsement standards. Redundancy of some of the embedded content with the existing content meant the added elements were less extensive than would have been the case if the disciplines that were fused shared no foundational topics. While the amount cannot be quantified, this overlap could reduce perhaps up to the equivalent of one of the five ESOL endorsement courses. But even the apportionment of one-fifth of the ESOL endorsement content to overlap and the reduced requirement of two EL-specific courses left a substantial amount of ESOL endorsement course content that needed to be embedded. As a key component of the Florida ESOL infusion model, the EL-specific courses were in complementarity with the teacher preparation courses that embedded EL content. If a program was unable to embed the teacher preparation courses broadly and deeply, then more EL-specific courses were required to compensate for the lack of EL content. Figure 2.1 shows this complementary relationship.

In addition to EL-specific and EL-embedded courses, candidates were required to document meeting the ESOL endorsement standards through a portfolio or some other assessment system that tracked mastery of the standards in these courses and field/clinical experiences. Documentation was also required for an early field experience with ELs and a full-time internship in the certification area that included one or more ELs and that was supervised by an ESOL-endorsed teacher. The following list summarizes what became the Florida model of infusion for the ESOL endorsement:

- Minimum of two of the five ESOL endorsement courses (EL-specific courses) taught by qualified faculty
- Faculty development for teacher educators—three-credit course or equivalent

Figure 2.1

Complementary relationship between EL-embedded and EL-specific courses

EL-embedded courses and clinical experiences

EL-specific courses and clinical experiences

- Adequate depth and breadth of embedded EL content in teacher preparation courses—core foundations, content area methods, etc.
- Early field experience and full-time internship with ELs
- Portfolio or assessment system documenting each candidate's attainment of the ESOL Endorsement Performance Standards

From Infusion to Confusion: Moving Beyond Southeastern Florida

After extended negotiations, the Department of Education granted conditional approval for the southeastern Florida institutions to pursue the infusion route to ESOL endorsement, and other institutions began investigating the feasibility of developing similar options. At this point, Joyce Nutta was a foreign language and ESL education faculty member in the College of Education at the University of South Florida (USF; which, despite its name is located in west central Florida). Because of her qualifications in ESL, she was asked to serve as subject matter expert to the college administration as it pursued state approval for the ESOL endorsement through infusion. Although USF had an established MA in TESOL program in the College of Arts and Sciences, the College of Education had no ESL education programs. Unlike UM, FIU, and FAU, USF served an area that had varying access to ELs in local schools. Whereas southeastern Florida had a heavy concentration of ELs in most zones and schools, only certain parts of west central Florida enrolled ELs in public schools, so meeting the field/clinical experience requirements was challenging. Another obstacle was the continuing lack of specifications for approval of ESOL endorsement programs through infusion. Despite these difficulties, the administration committed to seeking the endorsement through infusion and secured substantial funding from the provost to develop EL-specific courses and search for faculty to teach them. It was decided that five undergraduate initial teacher certification programs (Early Childhood, Elementary, English, Exceptional, and Foreign Language Education) would pursue approval for granting the ESOL endorsement through infusion. Doing so, it was argued, would lead to greater enrollment in the EL-specific courses for which the majority of the project funding was secured.

While the administration and ESL faculty began developing the program approval proposal, a plan was conceived to prepare the teacher preparation faculty for the task of embedding their courses with EL content. Major changes in Florida Department of Education rules had moved institutions away from documenting courses and credits to documenting standards, and a prior experience with general teacher education standards affected the initial infusion process. The college faculty had only recently been required to indicate which parts of the teacher preparation curriculum addressed new Florida teacher education standards—the Florida Educator Accomplished Practices (FEAPs). The twelve FEAPs spanned all knowledge and skills that accomplished preservice teacher candidates should have developed by graduation. Since these were broad competencies that all teacher education programs already addressed, faculty were asked to list the standards they believed their courses touched on. Following the approach that had been taken with the FEAPs, the college administration scheduled a faculty seminar that presented the ESOL endorsement standards required for state approval of an infused program. Once the ESOL standards were explained, faculty were asked to complete a form indicating which ones they were addressing, or could reasonably address, in their courses. Faculty from a wide range of content areas marked a substantial number of ESOL standards—up to twenty-five in one course alone. The forms became the basis for the EL-embedded content. Having aligned FEAPs with the existing general teacher preparation curriculum, many of the faculty and administration treated embedding the content of the ESOL standards as an identical process. But for most places and circumstances, EL infusion is an additive process, not one that simply tags elements of the existing general curriculum as ESL-related. Although some teacher preparation faculty actually had already been addressing EL content in their courses and could rightly claim the ESOL standards they indicated, a sizeable number of standards noted did not reflect explicit treatment of EL competencies. In a number of cases, ELs were not mentioned in course syllabi even though the courses listed multiple ESOL standards. The overlap of foundational education topics between the ESOL standards and the teacher preparation curriculum further confused the point of embedding EL content. As with in-service teacher training, confusion over what, in fact, addressed EL issues and competencies clouded the process. This initial identification of ESOL standards would be revisited as the programs approached completion of their academic degree approval dossiers.

Mandatory Pre-Service ESOL Endorsement

As the ESOL infusion movement headed north, Florida state board rules were amended to address ESOL endorsement and minimal requirements for pre-service teachers, mandating that as of 2004, all graduates of state-approved initial teacher certification programs would meet the following regulations:[6]

- ESOL Endorsement required for candidates in Early Childhood, Elementary, English Language Arts, and Exceptional Education
- All other candidates complete a three-credit ESL Education course
- Foreign language education candidates are required to complete the three-credit course, but this is the only degree program/certification area that may opt to include the ESOL endorsement through infusion[7]

With the mandate also came the need for a set of policies and criteria to guide universities in submitting proposals for approval of infused ESOL endorsement programs. In 2001, the Florida Department of Education contracted with Joyce Nutta to coauthor a guidebook and provide on-site technical assistance for institutions who planned to submit a proposal.[8] As institutions attempted to adhere to the Florida mandate, a lack of resources impeded the process of infusion, however. In particular, the department's requiring faculty development without providing funds to develop and offer it presented new challenges. In some universities, teacher preparation faculty charged with embedding EL content were required to attend undergraduate EL-specific courses along with the same students they taught in their own classes, then expected to incorporate what they learned in the course into their class, regardless of subject matter. But although operating under a mandate to meet the many requirements of the infusion model prompted confusion and occasionally discord, it forced institutions to find a way to put the essential elements in place.

ESOL TAPESTRY

To address the growing need for professional development in teaching ELs in mainstream classes across the United States, the OELA funded Training for All Teachers and National Professional Development Grants, which supported teacher preparation institutions that incorporated competencies for teaching ELs into their curricula. Seeking resources for teacher-educator faculty development, USF submitted a proposal entitled ESOL TAPESTRY (ESOL Training for All Pre-service Educators Stressing Technology-based Resources), which aimed to create a variety of materials and resources for faculty development as well as provide other support for embedding EL content into teacher preparation courses. Requiring teacher preparation faculty to complete undergraduate EL-specific courses had proved to be an inadequate measure to equip them to embed EL content, so feasible alternatives were needed.

The proposal was funded for a five-year period at the beginning of which the project staff conducted a thorough review of the literature on the preparation of mainstream teachers of ELs to ground the initiative in scholarship and best practices in the field. Although the TAPESTRY project's primary purpose was faculty development and support for embedding teacher preparation courses, the actual scope of the effort extended to all aspects of developing and implementing the infused ESOL endorsement programs at USF. Project leaders explored curriculum theory and other models to guide the work, but what the initiative needed was an actionable set of procedures and parameters that could propel the infusion process to successful completion.

Because project team members had expertise in instructional design, this systematic process was applied to establishing interdisciplinary teams to guide the faculty development and EL embedding process, which enabled revision of the original outcomes resulting from the initial endeavors to assign ESOL standards to courses. Implementing this formalized process led to the appointment of ESL subject matter experts from the MA in TESOL program to collaborate with teacher preparation faculty in particular areas. For example, one ESL subject matter expert was assigned to work with Early Childhood faculty, another with English Language Arts, and so forth. The ESL experts began by attending the first regular program meeting of the academic year to introduce themselves and the support they offered. Over the course of the year, they interacted with individual faculty, who exhibited different degrees of enthusiasm and interest. Some faculty formed communities of practice, acting as early adopters that their peers could join and emulate; others pursued only the most expeditious route to compliance. Faculty units met with their assigned ESL experts each semester to coordinate the embedding of EL content across courses, and the ESL faculty met monthly to discuss the process and progress toward project goals. The structured interaction of experts in each field, ESL faculty, and teacher preparation faculty from various subjects led to insights that transcended participants' disciplinary boundaries. The faculty's developing understanding that these were indeed interdisciplinary encounters pointed to the power of framing the effort as interdisciplinary scholarship. Through these exchanges project team members eventually designed embedded EL content for fifty-seven courses and constructed a flexible faculty development plan tailored to individual needs. In addition, an array of resources was developed, from online video lectures of leading national experts to annotated bibliographies on teaching different subjects to ELs at various grade levels.

With resources from ESOL TAPESTRY, a multiyear action research agenda was established and approved by USF's Institutional Review Board. A variety of data were collected, including faculty surveys, individual and focus group interviews, and student assignments and portfolios. In addition, ESL faculty kept monthly reflections on the course embedding process, and detailed minutes were recorded for the monthly meetings of the ESL subject matter experts team, which were compiled and reviewed on an annual basis as part of formative assessment. Affiliated research, such as surveys of candidates' perceptions of self-efficacy in teaching ELs, was also conducted.[9] Analysis of these data revealed a number of widespread issues for the major components of infusion, which are summarized below, along with the actions taken to address them.

Embedding Teacher Education Courses with EL Content

Of all elements of infusion, embedding teacher preparation courses and field/clinical experiences with EL content proved to be the most problematic. Although all faculty agreed in principle with the need to prepare candidates for teaching and assessing ELs, there was pronounced variation in individual responses to the call to develop a basic level of knowledge about ELs and to embed EL content into individuals' courses. Some faculty developed an interest in ELs and SLA or had ESL experience; others were willing to go along with infusion if the amount of work was streamlined and the tasks were straightforward, since ELs were not their area of focus; and yet others developed an interest in engaging with the process if there were incentives. Working with the college administration, the project team explored and implemented measures to engage faculty in faculty development and the development of EL-embedded content, in a trial and error fashion. Strategies included: (a) supporting and coordinating interdisciplinary research on ELs; (b) supporting scholarship of teaching and learning by participating in and funding research on their process of embedding EL content into courses and field/clinical experiences; (c) providing mini-grants for special project development; (d) offering stipends for completing modules that participating faculty and instructors of other sections could use; and (e) formalizing recognition of embedded EL content as a form of "the scholarship of integration" in the annual review and tenure and promotion processes.[10] Despite some faculty's lack of interest, the ESL subject matter experts found that a uniform level of commitment was not necessary, and that various faculty responded to different approaches and incentives.

After building faculty members' commitment to embedding, the team needed to develop a process. Although some faculty were willing to dedicate substantial time to participating in time-consuming, generative routes to embedding (as can be the case with, for example, communities of practice), the majority of faculty wanted clear parameters from start to finish. Besides wanting to see what embedded syllabi might look like, faculty requested help in knowing where to begin. As scholars in a given field, faculty are accustomed to deep interaction with subjects in their disciplines, but for the EL embedding process, this approach left many faculty feeling overwhelmed. It would be impractical, if not impossible, to treat the embedded EL content with the same level of depth that faculty pursued in their areas of specialization. Likewise, it would be impractical and ill-advised to ask faculty to give the focus and time to EL content that they did to their subject areas. At the same time the faculty was removing disciplinary boundaries by codeveloping new ways of approaching the instruction of ELs in various subject areas, this innovative embedding process needed bounding. From this need for structuring was developed a categorization of courses, the 1+2+3+ framework, which served as an organizing principle in addition to a minimal standard from which to depart. By indicating what minimal outcomes were expected for each type of course in the teacher preparation curriculum, the infusion team enabled faculty to apprehend the extent of their task before beginning it.

Faculty Development

Although the Florida model required that all faculty complete the same amount of faculty development and that the focus was to survey the five original ESOL endorsement courses' content, the TAPESTRY grant provided funds for creating faculty development suitable for faculty in various contexts. Infusion leaders found in their interdisciplinary interactions that faculty had diverse needs. Some faculty already had backgrounds in teaching ELs or studying Second Language Acquisition and therefore did not need to relearn the information. In addition, faculty members' course subjects required different background knowledge and skills pertaining to ELs. For example, in a course on teaching writing, faculty need to know about common grammatical errors that are developmental for ELs and when and how to correct them. However, that information would not be pertinent to a faculty member teaching mathematics education courses. The team began identifying knowledge, skills, and dispositions that they believed all faculty should possess and then went on to identify them for each discipline. This led to a categorization of faculty development according to the nature of the embedded courses. Parallel with the 1+2+3+ course categorization, specifications for faculty development for each of the three categories were developed.

Candidate Assessment

Early in the implementation of the infused programs, team members noted that if course assignments were expanded to include EL content and competencies, there was no guarantee that candidates would demonstrate mastery. Conceivably, a candidate could pass a course and fail the EL-embedded assignment. Moreover, by distributing various competencies across embedded courses, the focus on the EL became fragmented. A portfolio was proposed to alleviate these issues.

Candidates collected assignments from each EL-embedded and EL-specific course and field/clinical experience and reflected on their increasing competence as teachers of ELs. This measure helped to bring together the scattered curricular elements, but it also served a different programmatic purpose. Since the ESL faculty teaching the EL-specific courses reviewed the reflections and course artifacts, they could identify where there was slippage in the embedded content. If a new adjunct teaching an embedded course hadn't been informed of its importance, or if an embedded course was offered in a new format (for example, online or in a condensed schedule), the embedded assignments might be changed or even overlooked. The ESL faculty took note of these instances and discussed them with the infusion team members. In some cases these issues were resolved, but not all. This caused a certain degree of tension, since some teacher preparation faculty were not comfortable with ESL faculty viewing their students' graded assignments, and some ESL faculty were not comfortable pointing out discrepancies in their colleagues' courses. However, over time the portfolio proved to be the clearest evidence of both the candidates' overall competency in teaching and assessing ELs as well as the durability of the EL-embedded content in the teacher preparation curriculum.

Clinical and Field Experiences with English Learners

Because west central Florida schools had varying EL enrollment, placing candidates in early field experiences and later internships involved the development of a multidistrict plan. School district representatives expressed concern about "wearing out" schools with high EL populations, so a staggered model of placement and supervision was developed. The early experiences included family and adult ESL, with service learning options. Internship experiences occasionally required candidates to travel to schools with high concentrations of ELs or, in some cases, arrange for special placements in other communities or even study-abroad internships.

Program-Specific Challenges

In addition to general infusion issues, challenges specific to particular program areas were identified:

Early Childhood: In developing assignments for embedded courses, it was difficult to isolate a substantial knowledge base regarding what is different about teaching and assessing preschool ELs, since all students at that age are immersed in contextualized activities that integrate language skill development. For example, in a course assignment to develop a lesson plan appropriate for three-year-olds, the candidate might include concrete objects, printed labels, and hands-on experiences linked to oral vocabulary that is being introduced, so what accommodations would be necessary in that case for ELs? Faculty in both disciplines began studying the research on ELs at this age and identified common characteristics and successful instructional practices that eventually became part of the embedded course content. For instance, a number of courses emphasized assessing and building on emergent literacy in the native language to support literacy development in English.

Elementary: Many faculty assumed that instructional and assessment strategies intended for native speakers worked identically for ELs, especially since the literature in both fields used the same terminology, such as process writing and shared reading. Lost in translation was the actual implementation of the strategies with the different learners. For example, an experienced faculty member in literacy education identified numerous activities and assignments in her course that addressed ELs. When infusion team members reviewed the assignment directions, there was no mention of ELs. The faculty member was asked how the assignments focused on teaching and assessing literacy skills of ELs. She replied that she had read articles about teaching these learners and concluded that just as with native speakers, teaching reading and writing to ELs is "all scaffolding." A number of ESL faculty at different Florida universities experienced these sorts of interchanges with elementary education faculty and began calling this mindset the "just good teaching" misperception. To address this issue, ESL faculty collected and presented speech and writing samples of ELs at different levels of English proficiency, examining the effect of proficiency level on performance in various reading and writing tasks. In addition, ESL faculty developed a sequence of immersion experiences in languages other than English for teacher preparation faculty, giving them the perspective of ELs.

English Language Arts: Many courses are taken in the English department, so there were fewer teacher education courses that can embed EL content. In addition, there is a substantial gap between the language demands of English language arts instruction and assessment at the secondary level and ELs at lower levels of English proficiency, so that narrowing the gap requires a high degree of skill. Regardless of their level of English proficiency, ELs in Florida must meet the same language arts standards required of native speakers. At the secondary level, this would include very challenging outcomes such as the English Language Arts Grade 11-12 standards that require writing explanatory texts for complex concepts, using varied syntax, domain-specific vocabulary, and maintaining an objective tone and formal style.[11] Supporting ELs to achieve at this level requires substantial specialized knowledge and skills.

Exceptional Education: Certain strategies used in exceptional education are also used with ELs, but for different purposes. For instance, using multiple modalities to introduce new information may assist students with learning disabilities, as with using movement coupled with storytelling for students with ADHD. The same strategy might be appropriate for beginning ELs because the movement illustrates the meaning of vocabulary and sentence structures that are new to them in English. Connecting the action with the language used to describe it improves comprehension and facilitates language growth. Some exceptional education faculty maintained that by using exceptional education strategies, teachers met ELs needs, but there was no discussion in their courses about the differing reasons why some strategies worked for ELs as well as students with exceptionalities. Omitting the reasons and conditions for using the same or similar strategies with ELs could leave candidates with the false assumption that the category of *English learner* is equivalent to that of *exceptional studen*t, which could in turn promote overidentification of ELs as needing special education services.

From ESOL TAPESTRY to the One Plus Model

With project ESOL TAPESTRY, the infusion team developed resources, established procedures, and adopted a theoretical framework, but over time realized that an ESOL infusion model with two EL-specific courses, field/clinical experiences with ELs, and embedded EL content did not form an ESL specialist, which is what the ESOL endorsement represents. Everything added up to well-prepared mainstream teachers of ELs, so the TAPESTRY team began building a model based on the effective elements of the Florida approach. To support the least stable element, EL-embedded teacher preparation courses, the model offered guidance for embedding and developed criteria and essential components for complementing the embedded content. As shown in figure 2.2, the Florida ESOL infusion model includes a number of provisions necessitated by contextual factors as well as the intended outcome of preparing ESL specialists, but it also includes essential elements of a quality EL-infused program, no matter the context. The TAPESTRY team found that many of these educators generally did not perceive these elements (the inner circle in figure 2.2) as a subset; instead, they felt everything inside the Florida model was essential. Similarly, many educators outside of Florida did not perceive the inner circle as a subset representing the core of any quality EL-infused program. In their view, every component of the Florida model was replaceable. A clear

Figure 2.2

Relationship of Florida ESOL infusion to EL infusion

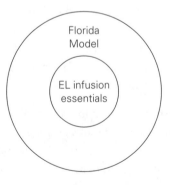

Figure 2.3

Approaches for preparing all teacher candidates to teach ELs

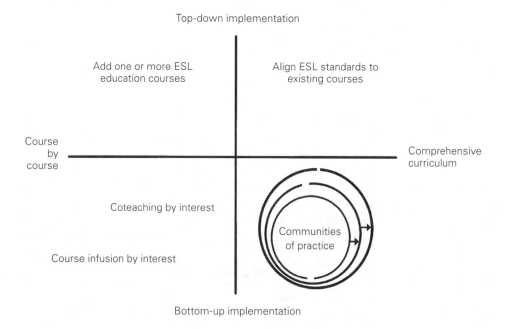

model, including the tested, adaptable elements of the Florida approach and general elements that applied to different contexts, was needed.

Project leaders surveyed the literature, consulted with programs in other states, and reviewed a range of strategies for preparing teachers of ELs. From experiences with programs in Florida and a number of other states, as well as a review of published scholarship on preparing mainstream teachers of ELs, the team identified essential criteria for the developing model. Strategies adopted by programs outside Florida's ranged from adding an EL-specific course to the teacher preparation curriculum to developing faculty-led communities of practice to embed courses. These strategies had varying degrees of impact on the teacher preparation curriculum and involved different degrees of collaboration between faculty, administrators, and other agents of infusion. Figure 2.3 summarizes some of the common strategies discussed in chapter 1. The team determined that the model had to be comprehensive and that faculty and administrators had to be invested and involved. The result was the One Plus model, described in detail in chapter 3. Table 2.1 contrasts the One Plus model with the Florida model.

Beyond the Mandate State: ESOL MIAMI

Once the basic elements of a more flexible and defined infusion model were in place, the ESOL TAPESTRY team had an opportunity to apply the One Plus model in a completely different context. In 2007, a competition for National Professional Development Grants took place, and the dean of the School of Education, Health, and Society

Table 2.1

Comparing the Florida Model of Infusion to the One Plus Model of Infusion

		EL Infusion Models	
		Florida ESOL Infusion	*One Plus*
Components	*Outcome(s)*	ESOL endorsement	• 2 "EL-qualified" options: Language arts & academic subjects • "Basic coverage" option
	Measures of Competency	Florida ESOL Standards	EL Curricular Competencies based on NCELA Roundtable Recommendations
	Candidates	Language arts teacher candidates	• Language arts teacher candidates • Academic subjects teacher candidates
	Faculty Development	60 hours and same content for all: • Overview of ESL Methods, Curriculum, Assessment, Culture, & Applied Linguistics	• Number of hours and content varies by course category (1+2+3+ Framework) • Individual plans based on menu of options
	Field & Clinical Experiences	Some form of early field experience: • Teach 1 or more ELs under supervision of ESL-endorsed teacher during student teaching in certification area	• Early field experiences in EL-embedded & EL-specific courses • Clinical experience with ELs varies by program area
	EL-Specific Courses	2 required	• 1 for all programs leading to EL-qualified credential • 2 for language arts programs leading to EL-qualified credential
	EL-Embedded Courses	Uniform criteria for all courses	Criteria by course category (1+2+3+)
	Assessment	Documentation of attaining each ESOL Standard	Documentation of attaining EL curricular competencies in a reflective portfolio

at Miami University (Oxford, Ohio) invited Kouider Mokhtari and Joyce Nutta to write a proposal to prepare candidates to serve ELs. Ohio had experienced exponential growth in EL enrollment; the overall K–12 population decreased 6.4 percent between 1995 and 2005, but during that same time period the EL population increased 108.4 percent.[12] Miami University had begun conversations with local districts to address the need for pre- and in-service professional development for teachers and other professionals. The project, ESOL MIAMI (Mentoring Initiative for Academics and Methods Infusion), aimed to apply the One Plus infusion model the ESOL TAPESTRY team had designed and further elaborated from the Florida infusion approach.

A needs assessment administered to twenty-two randomly selected Miami University teacher preparation faculty, revealed that 76 percent felt that Miami University graduates were not adequately prepared to teach ELs. Fewer than 5 percent indicated including instruction in teaching ELs while a majority (69 percent) devoted either minimal focus (69 percent) or did not address instruction (27 percent) in teaching ELs. However, 90 percent were willing to participate in faculty development in teaching ELs, and the majority of these respondents indicated their willingness to dedicate up to sixty hours per year to do so. The needs assessment also showed that the preferred method of professional development delivery was a combination of workshops and seminars (64 percent), field-based observations (46 percent), and consultation with ESL experts through distance technologies (90 percent). A great majority of faculty members indicated a strong commitment to working with an expert mentor in the ESL field to incorporate EL content into their teacher preparation courses. The results of the needs assessment showed a widespread acknowledgement of the existing gaps in preparing Miami University teacher candidates to instruct ELs and the commitment to close the gaps through the objectives and activities in Project ESOL MIAMI.

The infusion initiative supported by ESOL MIAMI reached beyond teacher preparation to all professions that impact the education of ELs, including social work, health, and administration.[13] Miami University developed an infusion plan that identified courses common to numerous programs and degree-specific courses. Curricular requirements varied according to licensure area, but all courses in every program were tasked with fostering at least a basic understanding of ELs' learning needs by highlighting cultural and linguistic issues as they relate to the course content. In addition, at different points in the curriculum, teacher candidates spent time observing, teaching, and assessing ELs. This included a special short-term experience that required travel to a school with a substantial EL population, or other alternative placements, such as service learning. Lastly, teacher candidates collected documentation of their achievement in teaching ELs in paper or electronic portfolios. This option enabled faculty to review not only candidates' preparation but also the depth and effect of the infused content.

Because Miami University operated without a mandate to graduate candidates with a credential for teaching ELs, programs made the EL-qualified credential of the One Plus model an elective, add-on option. To address this variation, the One Plus model expanded to include the outcome of *basic coverage* for programs whose candidates do not complete the additional requirements (for example, EL-specific courses and clinical experiences with ELs) of EL-infused programs leading to a credential. Although these candidates may not develop the competencies required to teach and assess ELs in mainstream classrooms, they obtain at least rudimentary knowledge and skills for educating ELs. The ESOL MIAMI team made the EL-qualified designation an elective credential, building on embedded courses with EL-specific courses and additional clinical experiences leading to a special Miami University-granted certificate, the TELLs Certificate. The basic coverage designation also applied to the noninstructional professional preparation programs that were involved in the EL infusion efforts supported by ESOL MIAMI. Their focus on ELs was limited to the embedded EL content in various courses, since it was not feasible to develop EL-specific courses for these noninstructional specializations.

Preliminary Research on Infusion in Florida

Research on the implementation of infusion has been ongoing with ESOL TAPESTRY and ESOL MIAMI, as well as other projects. The majority of this research has focused on teacher preparation faculty's and teacher candidates' impressions of the infusion process and components. As mentioned previously, measures of candidate change in attitude toward and perceived efficacy in teaching ELs have also been examined. Only recently has research on the effect of infusion on candidates' impact with ELs begun to be published. Project DELTA (Developing English Language and Literacy through Teacher Achievement) assessed the impact of an ESOL-infused elementary education program at a Florida university on EL achievement. Coady, DeJong, and Harper conducted surveys, interviews, and case studies of graduates and analyzed data from Florida's Education Data Warehouse (EDW).[14] Graduates identified field and clinical experiences with ELs as the most helpful aspects of their program of studies. In a comparison of graduates from different preparation paths, the researchers found statistically significant differences in ELs' math and reading achievement scores between teachers who graduated from ESOL-infused endorsement programs (significantly higher means in math and reading) and those who did not earn the ESOL endorsement.

Since 2005, Florida's ELs' average scale reading scores at the fourth and eighth grades have continued rising and are above the national scores, which either remained flat or decreased.[15] These NAEP results hint at positive effects of the pre-service and in-service requirements for teaching ELs, although a number of factors may affect the results. As reported by a deputy director of OELA, the nation is looking at Florida's apparent success in increasing EL achievement.[16] Clearly, more research must be conducted to determine the effect of EL-infused teacher preparation on EL achievement.

Summary

Teacher preparation institutions beginning the planning process of infusing EL issues into programs of study may operate under a state mandate for all licensure degrees, as in Florida. Others have no mandate but infuse in response to immediate local and state needs. Similarly, some institutions infuse to stay ahead of foreseen local and state needs. Some institutions, seeing their role as preparing candidates to teach anywhere in the nation, commit to infusing in response to the projected national growth in the preK–12 EL population.

Options for the preparation of teacher candidates from different disciplines will vary, depending on the circumstances that push institutions toward infusing, If a mandate specifies the details of infusion, then the institution's options are restricted. In nonmandate states, institutions may face limitations in the types of field experiences they can provide if local schools have low ELs enrollment.

Although an institution may be committed to preparing all candidates for teaching ELs, resources, both human and financial, affect the outcome. As we note throughout this book, we advocate for requiring all teacher candidates to complete at least one EL-specific course taught by an ESL education expert, but not all institutions have personnel with that expertise or the funds to hire them. In these cases, the goal might be simply promoting candidates' acquisition of rudimentary knowledge and skills regarding teaching ELs through embedding EL-focused content into selected teacher education courses. Other teacher education institutions may invest substantial funds in preparing all candidates to be qualified to teach ELs in mainstream classes through EL infusion and may in addition offer add-on ESL specialist options for teacher candidates who want to work exclusively with ELs, as with Miami University.

An extension and refinement of the Florida infusion approach, the One Plus model offers flexibility in developing and implementing infused programs with differing contexts. The chronology of the model's development in this chapter highlighted a number of considerations that the model needed to account for. The following chapter presents the details of the model and how it addresses the considerations.

CHAPTER 3

A Description of the One Plus Model

The One Plus model of EL infusion includes various measures to incorporate a focus on teaching and assessing English learners throughout teacher preparation curricula. Because teacher preparation programs' resources and goals vary, the model accounts for differing circumstances and contexts while upholding quality assurances for whatever level of commitment an institution can support. Designed to be flexible yet comprehensive, the model encompasses all aspects of teacher preparation, including courses, field/clinical experiences, candidate assessment, faculty development, and scholarship, as well as program administration, evaluation, and accreditation. The term *One Plus* indicates the stackable nature of the model, which enables programs to build up from developing candidates' rudimentary knowledge and skills about educating English learners to developing qualifications in teaching various subjects to ELs, as well as to the possibility of extending the model to specialization in teaching ESL. Any or all of these options may be pursued through application of the model.

As noted in chapter 2, the One Plus model is an adaptation and extension of Florida's ESOL infusion model. Although the Florida model is intended for language arts teachers only and leads to the attainment of the full ESL endorsement, the One Plus model addresses various teaching specializations and credentials. In this book we focus on the two institution-granted credentials at the center of the One Plus model: (a) EL-qualified for teaching academic subject areas in mainstream classrooms; and (b) EL-qualified for teaching language arts and literacy in mainstream classrooms. The One Plus model also allows for the limited outcome of fostering rudimentary knowledge and skills about educating English learners—what we term *basic coverage* of EL topics—through embedded EL content only, which does not lead to a credential. Our partners from the Miami University School of Education, Health, and Society have implemented this option with noninstructional professional preparation programs such as educational leadership and are duly credited for its inclusion in this model. In addition to these field-tested options of the One Plus model, we propose the additional potential outcome of attainment of endorsement or certification in ESL (in other words, the preparation of ESL teachers and specialists), which requires substantial additional ESL education coursework. In summary, although the model includes three outcomes that have been implemented and field-tested as well one proposed outcome that is yet to be implemented, the focus of this book is to provide guidance and resources in establishing the two EL-qualified credentials in various degree programs.

Figure 3.1 outlines the major components of the model. All outcomes other than basic coverage combine EL-embedded coursework and field and clinical experiences from the teacher preparation curriculum with one or more EL education, or *EL-specific*, courses with field/clinical experiences with English learners. In addition, all outcomes include a compilation of candidate artifacts, with EL-qualified or ESL endorsement programs requiring demonstration of mastery of the established competencies or standards. The EL-qualified for academic subject areas credential may be the established outcome for any number of degree programs, such as math, science, or social studies education. Likewise, the EL-qualified for language arts credential could apply to secondary English, early childhood, elementary, or even exceptional education degrees if their preparation includes certification in language arts.

One Plus Model: Program Outcomes

Institutions pursuing EL infusion may establish different goals based on financial resources, academic degree areas, and local context. Some may aspire to preparing teachers capable of differentiating instruction and assessment for ELs, while other may elect to begin with a more limited goal that can be expanded. To address these differences in objectives, the One Plus model encompasses multiple outcomes.

Basic Coverage

Basic coverage comprises the EL-embedded teacher preparation courses, field/clinical experiences, and assessments that are part of an EL-infused program. We recommend that, at a minimum, basic coverage include embedding the majority of foundational and discipline-specific courses, observations and interviews of English learners in instructional settings, and a reflective portfolio of each candidate's compiled EL-focused assignments. A critical component of all EL-infused program outcomes, basic coverage can be augmented by the other elements that lead to EL-qualified credentials, but may be an end in itself in some contexts.

For various reasons, colleges of education that pursue EL infusion may end up with certain programs whose outcomes do not include a credential in teaching ELs. This result may stem from limited resources or particular noninstructional disciplines whose contact with preK–12 English learners is minimal (for example, exercise physiology). In other cases, faculty from certain degree areas may express a strong commitment to developing an infused program but faculty from other areas are not interested in allocating resources to EL-specific courses. Another obstacle to seeking a credential is low EL enrollment in the local schools, which makes tutoring or practice teaching impractical.

Degree programs that opt to pursue infusion generally count on the EL content embedded in common core or foundations courses. These courses often form the

Figure 3.1   **One Plus Model Program Outcomes and Elements**

Program elements	Basic coverage	*plus* EL-qualified for academic subjects	*plus* EL-qualified for language arts	*plus* ESL endorsement or certification
			Program outcomes	
EL-embedded courses	Various teacher education courses are EL embedded	Majority of teacher education courses are EL embedded (category 1+ and 2+ courses)	Majority of teacher education courses are EL embedded and language arts (category 3+) courses are broadly embedded	Majority of teacher education courses are EL embedded with targeted courses more thoroughly embedded
EL specific courses		One EL-specific course on adapting curriculum, instruction, and assessment for ELs including assignments linked to early field experiences or student teaching in certification area	One additional EL-specific course on second language development and educational linguistics applied to language arts instruction for ELs including assignments linked to student teaching/internship in language arts certification area	Additional EL-specific courses on teaching ESL (e.g., L2 grammar instruction, designing EL-specific language development curricula) linked to internship/student teaching
Field/clinical experiences	Observation or interview of adult or child EL(s) in instructional setting (virtual or face-to-face experiences)	Tutoring or practice teaching EL(s) as part of early field experiences or student teaching in certification area	Teaching one or more ELs throughout student teaching/internship in language arts certification area	Internship/student teaching ELs exclusively in self-contained, sheltered setting or as an ESL specialist in other program models
Assessment	Portfolio of assignments addressing ELs from embedded teacher education courses	Additional portfolio assignments from second EL-specific course, evaluation of teaching one or more ELs throughout student teaching/internship in language arts certification area	Additional portfolio assignments from 2nd EL-specific course, evaluation of teaching one or more ELs throughout student teaching/internship in language arts certification area	Additional portfolio assignments from EL-specific courses, evaluation of teaching ELs exclusively in self-contained, sheltered setting or as an ESL specialist in other program models and completion of state ESL licensure exam

nucleus of multiple degree programs and therefore are an important element in basic coverage. When these courses have been embedded for one program that develops an EL-qualified credential, other programs that share the courses benefit, even though they may not establish the additional elements required for a credential. Candidates' increased awareness about ELs and their families, communities, and educational experiences, which are common embedded topics in foundational courses, can give them advantages once they begin teaching. Although this basic coverage makes no claims to preparing candidates for teaching and assessing ELs, it can result in greater empathy and understanding of these students.

With basic coverage solidly in place, programs can build up to two credentials that prepare educators to teach and assess ELs in mainstream classrooms: EL-qualified for teaching academic subjects and EL-qualified for teaching language arts and literacy, with the second credential encompassing the general elements of the first. In other words, the second credential adds curricular components to those of the first, with each credential including the same component types, but which are specific to their disciplines.

EL-Qualified for Teaching Academic Subjects

Increasingly, teachers of academic subjects are asked to consider the language demands of their disciplines for native speakers of English and ELs alike. Although language development can be an important part of learning about a subject such as mathematics, most academic subject instructors are primarily concerned with teaching the concepts, facts, and skills of their disciplines. Language focus can be facilitative of these ends but should not overshadow them in mainstream academic subject classes. Moreover, many academic subjects lend themselves to other types of presentation, exploration, and assessment of their concepts, facts, and skills than just verbal discussion and explanation. For this reason, accommodations in instructing and assessing these subjects can be more feasible than in subjects that focus specifically on building English language skills.

An example from science can provide details about the nature of these accommodations.[1] When teaching the phases of the moon, science teachers can use a hands-on, minds-on approach that immerses learners in visuals and actions that show the process as it is being explained verbally. English learners can then associate new terms with their illustrative visuals or actions and can record the terms in science notebooks for later reinforcement. Likewise, assessments can be enhanced with graphic organizers, clip art, and other accommodations to enable ELs to demonstrate what they know and can do.

Teacher candidates need exposure to strong examples of this type of comprehensible instruction and need practice in developing adaptations for ELs in curriculum, instruction, and assessment that embody these principles and practices. The EL-qualified for teaching academic subjects credential prepares candidates in general linguistic and contextual adaptations and accommodations for ELs at multiple levels of English proficiency in the areas of curriculum, instruction, and assessment; it further develops candidates' application of comprehensible instruction and assessment to their particular disciplines. Chapter 1 outlined how academic subject teachers can promote ELs' academic achievement as well as language development in a collaborative instructional model for ELs. To do so effectively, teacher candidates in these disciplines need substantial preparation, which we believe can be achieved through the components of the EL-qualified for academic subjects credential.

EL-Qualified for Teaching Language Arts and Literacy

Language arts and literacy teacher candidates also benefit from learning and practicing general linguistic and contextual adaptations for ELs at multiple levels of English proficiency. For example, in teaching secondary literature such as *Romeo and Juliet*, language arts instructors teach facts and concepts that can be made clearer to ELs through contextual and linguistic support such as story diagrams and summary outlines with definitions or translations of difficult terms. In addition, many language arts and literacy teachers support students' development of knowledge and skills in various academic subjects through a focus on reading and writing in the content areas, so understanding how these subjects are made comprehensible is important for that reason as well.

However, in addition to their roles in teaching and supporting development in academic subject areas, language arts and literacy teachers have the weighty responsibility for language skill development. Knowing how to support ELs' development of listening, speaking, reading, and writing skills in English requires a deeper knowledge about language and SLA and more specialized, in-depth clinical experiences and supervision by school district cooperating teachers with expertise in teaching ELs.

Even in bilingual and ESL program models where ESL specialists teach language arts and literacy to ELs, mainstream language arts teachers and literacy specialists often interact with ELs for at least part of the instructional day. Where the critical mass of ELs necessary to obtain funding for ESL or bilingual support is not met, mainstream language arts teachers may be the only instructors of ELs in this vital area. The important role of these teachers in ELs' language development cannot be overstated, and their preparation would not be complete without knowledge and skills for teaching ELs. Whether supported (ideally) in a collaborative instructional model of EL-qualified teachers partnering with ESL specialists or required to serve as sole providers of language arts instruction to ELs, EL-qualified language arts and literacy teachers require greater depth of preparation than teachers of other subjects.

ESL Endorsement or Certification

Although the One Plus model is intended to prepare mainstream teachers for instructing and assessing ELs, its stackable nature permits the possibility of building up to the ESL endorsement or certification. This can be accomplished by adding more EL-specific courses as well as more in-depth and specialized clinical experiences with ELs and more rigorous and comprehensive assessments of the ESL endorsement standards. The Florida ESOL infusion model described in chapter 2 affords program completers the full ESL endorsement, but we are skeptical of the equivalence of that ESOL infusion model's minimal criteria with a stand-alone fifteen-credit specialization in ESL. Accordingly, we recommend at least three or four EL-specific courses, a full internship working exclusively with ELs and specialists, and completion of state licensure exams in ESL in addition to any EL-embedded courses, field/clinical experiences, and formative and summative assessments that form the EL-qualified for language arts and literacy credential. The additional EL-specific courses allow for greater concentration on language development issues for ELs, including second language grammar instruction and designing language development curricula for ELs at different levels of English proficiency.

In terms of additional resources, offering a full endorsement or certification requires faculty to teach the additional EL-specific courses as well as means for candidates to complete the ESL internship. For those who elect to pursue the credential, the additional costs involve tuition, travel to internship site (and lodging if the site is remote to the program), as well as licensure examination fees. Since this book focuses on the preparation of mainstream academic subject area and language arts and literacy teachers to instruct and assess ELs, the issue of resources will not be further explored.

One Plus Model: Program Components

There are a number of components essential to EL-infused programs without which the qualities of interconnectedness, cohesion, and interdisciplinarity are less likely to be achieved. Our experience indicates that a combination of program components, including EL-embedded and EL-specific courses with associated field/clinical experiences and systematic formative and summative candidate evaluation improve the quality and impact of the infusion effort.

Embedding Teacher Preparation Courses and Field Experiences:
1+2+3+ Framework

Concurrent with the stackable nature of the program outcomes supported by the One Plus model, the term *one plus* also applies to the EL-embedded courses that form part of the infused curriculum. We have found that teacher preparation faculty who are experts in disciplines other than ESL benefit from a structure that provides a starting point for embedding EL content into their courses. Moreover, establishing minimal requirements for embedding maintains a degree of consistency across courses and fairness in the expectations placed on faculty. Lest these minimal requirements be construed as limited expectations of quality or depth, we affixed a plus to each category to indicate that more—even much more—can be incorporated. If there were no *plus*, the goal would be no more than compliance.

Because many teacher preparation curricula include foundational courses that focus on the learner and learning context, and because the courses are often placed in the beginning of the coursework sequence in the major, they lend themselves to certain types of embedded EL content. Courses such as Psychological and Social Foundations, Child Development, Educational Policy, Parent-Child Relations, and Multicultural Education expose teacher candidates to concepts and constructs regarding teaching and learning and involve reading, discussing, reflecting on, and writing about these topics.

In many cases, these courses also require an initial field experience, often involving classroom observations or interviews or other types of interactions with individual students. A good starting point for embedding these types of courses is to identify at least one topic that has implications for ELs. For example, in a child development course, expanding the existing course topic of child language development to include a reading, website, and/or video about bilingual language development is a simple first step. Adding such materials grounds the embedded content in the literature on ELs and provides information to support candidates' reflections and growing awareness about the effect of linguistic and cultural backgrounds on ELs' education. The task of infusing a 1+ course goes beyond simply adding this EL-focused information: candidates should do something with it, perhaps by participating in a class discussion (online or face-to-face), writing a reflection paper, or completing a quiz or test that includes the information. In addition, if the course includes an observation of children at a preschool, ideally this might include ELs and could lead to expanded reflections about their bilingual development.

So, for 1+ courses, the minimum added content is an article, chapter, website, video, or other form of information about ELs relevant to at least one course topic. If this embedded content contributes to documentation of standards for credentials in teaching ELs, then there should be some means of assessing candidates' comprehension or application of the information. For 1+ courses, this commonly is achieved through written reflections or discussions. Since the *plus* in 1+ appeals to faculty to go beyond the minimum, they are encouraged to consider using multiple EL-focused materials for the relevant course topic. In addition, the *plus* indicates that more than one course topic may be expanded to include EL content.

The second category of EL-embedded courses, 2+, requires application of candidates' developing knowledge and skills in planning and implementing curriculum, instruction, and assessment. These courses may be general, such as Measurement and Assessment, or specific to a particular academic subject, such as Methods of Teaching Social Studies. In addition, many of these courses involve field experiences that include preliminary instructional interactions with individual or small groups of students. Building on 1+ courses, 2+ courses include 1+ requirements, namely the addition of at least one EL-focused article, chapter, website, or video, as well as some form of assessment of candidates' comprehension of the added content. However, since 2+ courses typically include assignments involving planning and implementing curriculum, instruction, and assessment, candidates apply the added EL-focused information to making adaptations and accommodations for ELs in at least one course assignment.

An example of a 2+ course assignment could be developing a lesson plan that includes adaptations and accommodations for ELs in a Methods of Teaching Social Studies course. After candidates have read and discussed an article about adaptations and accommodations for teaching social studies to ELs, they then incorporate them into the lesson plan they develop. Again, in keeping with the *plus* in 2+ courses, additional articles, chapters, websites, and videos can be incorporated, and additional course assignments can add an EL focus.

Figure 3.2

Categories of EL Embedded Courses: The 1+2+3+ Framework

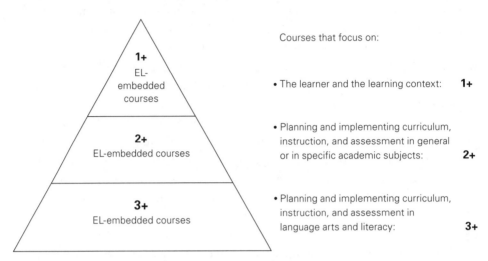

The most deeply and broadly embedded courses, 3+ courses, include all 1+ and 2+embedded elements but their emphasis is on teaching and assessing language arts and literacy. Because nearly every topic regarding teaching language skills has a specific variation for ELs, 3+ courses add an EL focus to most of the course content and elements. This means that there are multiple readings, websites, and videos regarding aspects of teaching listening, speaking, reading, and writing to ELs as well as assignments requiring candidates to demonstrate competence in differentiating planning and implementing curriculum, instruction, and assessment of language arts and literacy for ELs. Additionally, many courses in the 3+ category include field/clinical experiences that may be expanded to include ELs. Those who teach language arts and literacy in the mainstream classroom have a special responsibility for supporting ELs' language development, and embedding 3+ course elements with substantial and plentiful EL content recognizes their key role. Figure 3.2 and table 3.1 summarize the 1+2+3+ framework for embedding EL content in teacher preparation courses.

EL-Specific Courses and Field/Clinical Experiences

In accordance with the program outcomes presented in table 3.1, we recommend at least one EL-specific course (or its equivalent) for programs granting the EL-qualified for teaching academic subjects credential, and at least two EL-specific courses (or their equivalent) for programs granting the EL-qualified for teaching language arts and literacy credential. What follows is a general overview of the content and sequence of these courses (detailed examples are described in chapter 10).

Those designing EL-specific courses may elect to develop variations of one course (Adapting Curriculum, Instruction, and Assessment for English Learners) that is part of both of these credentials, depending on the program and primary certification areas.

Table 3.1

Added content of EL-embedded course categories

Course elements	Embedded EL content		
	1+ course	*2+ course*	*3+ course*
Added EL-focused information, instructional material, or media	At least one per course	At least one per course	At least one for most of the existing course topics
Added EL-focused class or online activity	At least one per course	At least one per course	At least one for most of the existing course activities
	or	*and*	*and*
Added EL-focused assessment	At least one (if course is designated as a source of documentation for EL standards)	At least one that focuses on planning or delivering curriculum, instruction or assessment to address ELs' needs at three levels of English proficiency	Most of the existing course assessments that focus on planning or delivering curriculum, instruction or assessment to address ELs' needs at three levels of English proficiency

For programs leading to the EL-qualified for teaching language arts and literacy credential, designers may also elect to develop the second EL-specific course with variations by program and certification areas. Both of the EL-specific courses may be offered in different configurations, either as two 3-credit courses, three 2-credit courses, or even a series of 1-credit seminars that can be corequisite with certain teacher preparation courses. These courses also typically include a field-based or clinical application of their content with ELs at the grade level the candidates are preparing to teach. Table 3.2 summarizes possible variations of the two courses by program areas.

Candidate Assessment

Candidate assessment is especially critical for EL-infused programs, both at the formative and summative stages. Because the EL content is distributed across a variety and multitude of curricular elements, a sound candidate assessment plan can serve as a coordinating structure and a measure of program effectiveness. Tracking candidate work samples, tests, course assignments, periodic reflections in electronic or paper portfolios, or other types of assessment systems can all be used. Assessment of candidates' attainment of EL standards may take place in 1+, 2+, and 3+ EL-embedded courses; in all EL-specific courses; in field, clinical, and internship experiences; and in culminating formal exams, and should be tracked and reviewed for any remediation needs at regular intervals.

Table 3.2

EL-specific courses and their variations by program area

	EL-specific course content	
Variations by program	*Adapting curriculum, instruction, and assessment for English learners (at multiple levels of English proficiency)*	*Second language development and applied linguistics*
Early childhood and elementary education	Academic subjects	Early second language and literacy development
Secondary language arts	Language arts and literature	Adolescent second language and literacy development
Secondary academic subjects	Academic subjects	

Teaching Cases

We have found that using common teaching cases to represent ELs at three levels of English proficiency has helped cement across-course connections. According to Colbert, Trimble, and Desberg, case method instruction provides context for teaching about research and theory.[2] Building a shared context is a powerful means of strengthening the cohesion of infusion. At the University of Central Florida, for example, three cases (representing beginning, intermediate, and advanced levels of proficiency; see chapter 7 for the student profiles) are introduced in the first EL-specific course and reinforced and expanded in EL-embedded courses. Each case presents the subject's story and includes a stock photo of a child of the same gender, age, and culture as the student profile. In addition, sound files of interviews and read-alouds of all three are presented, along with writing samples for the intermediate and advanced students. These cases illuminate issues in English proficiency–based instructional and assessment differentiation at the upper elementary, middle school, and high school levels, and they also raise common issues that ELs and their families' experience. When teacher candidates learn to develop a lesson plan in the general methods course, for example, they are asked to review the three online cases they first viewed in the EL-specific course, which is a corequisite to the EL-embedded general methods course. Candidates then develop lesson plans that include instructional differentiation and assessment accommodations for the cases. As this cross-course connection has been further developed, a lesson plan differentiation and accommodation template has been established for use in both courses. The cases and lesson plan template are used in other EL-embedded courses as well.

There are many additional components of the One Plus model that pertain to the process of infusion, such as faculty development and mentoring. Those will be briefly described in the instructional design section of this chapter and discussed in detail in chapters 4 and 5.

Conceptual Foundations of the One Plus Model

Three pillars support the One Plus model. The theoretical orientation guiding curriculum development efforts is *interdisciplinarity*, the content is based on the literature on *effective instruction and assessment* of ELs in preK–12 mainstream classrooms, and the operationalization is informed by *instructional design*. In the following sections, we describe the structural underpinnings and curricular elements of the model in detail.

Interdisciplinarity

American postsecondary educational institutions have grappled with rigid disciplinary boundaries for decades, exploring ways of softening, or what Klein terms *blurring*, traditional disciplinary borders in faculty scholarship and academic degree areas.[3] Ernest Boyer of the Carnegie Foundation for the Advancement of Teaching described a "sea change" in the trend toward interdisciplinary and integrative scholarly activity: "Today, interdisciplinary and integrative studies, long on the edges of academic life, are moving toward the center, responding both to new intellectual questions and to pressing human problems."[4] Continuing in the spirit of Boyer's groundbreaking work, William Newell, editor of a seminal collection of scholarly essays on the subject, noted that interdisciplinarity involves curriculum and instruction that "critically draw on two or more disciplines and . . . lead to an integration of disciplinary insights."[5] are typically organized around a theme, problem, or issue. Interdisciplinary courses require the collaboration of faculty from two or more disciplines, and a new synthesis of information should result. More recent scholarship on postsecondary interdisciplinary curriculum design identifies four core elements: (a) focusing on a problem, such as illegal immigration, or a question, such as "What is family?" that cannot be solved by one discipline; (b) incorporating insights within and across disciplines as well as nondisciplinary knowledge (this means that the disciplinary knowledge bases and research approaches are the starting point for addressing the problem, but their perspectives are not placed side by side but rather are integrated and connected); (c) following an integrative or holistic process that creatively combines diverse perspectives and views the relationship between the parts and the whole; and (d) constructing an interdisciplinary understanding of the problem or question, which entails coming to a conclusion or solution that would not have been reachable through employing the insights and tools of one discipline alone.[6]

While it may seem overreaching to attribute interdisciplinarity to two fields within the same realm of education, research and practice in ESL education have traditionally progressed rather peripherally to other pedagogical content areas, such as math education. There are certainly underlying commonalities, based primarily on general learning theory, but the focus areas, emphases, and assumptions are often markedly different. Research and theory in ESL education have drawn from linguistics, and more specifically the field of applied linguistics, to frame questions, employ research methodologies and tools, and situate findings in theory. Following traditions in these fields, a good deal of research on second language learning has taken place outside of the classroom or laboratory setting. After all, learning a second language, unlike learning math, can take place with or without instruction, as was discussed in the introduction. Moreover, the ESL education field encompasses substantial postsecondary research (often conducted at university-based intensive English programs for international students) and examines not only learning English in English-speaking countries but also in foreign language environments, such as Saudi Arabia. This is all quite different from applied research in learning math, for example.

Even if the two fields of ESL and math education may be considered part of the general discipline of educational theory and practice, interdisciplinarity scholars suggest that focusing on the subdisciplinary level of neighboring disciplines can highlight over-lapping interests, conflicts in perspectives on the same phenomena, and apparent or undetected divisions in acceptable areas or types of work.[7] Interdisciplinary exploration can lead to the identification of gaps in addressing a problem or answering a question sufficiently complex to defy resolution through the knowledge base and research focus of one discipline alone.

If we consider, for argument's sake, that the significant gap between ELs' and native speakers' math achievement is an interdisciplinary issue, we ground our efforts in certain principles.[8] First, we affirm that the knowledge bases of math education and ESL education are both valuable in addressing the issue of teaching math to ELs: no one discipline owns that issue. From an ESL education faculty perspective, developing knowledge about how math is learned in general is a key step in the process, as is situating teaching ELs within the content area and among all other math learners—native speakers and ELs alike. From a math educator perspective, a key step involves learning about SLA, the demands placed on ELs by typical English discourse and literacy practices in the math classroom, and differences in math curricula and in teaching math from one culture to another. Acknowledging that the expert in each discipline needs to learn more about the other discipline is a crucial first step. Collaborating around the issue of promoting ELs' achievement in math is the problem or issue that can be best solved through a commitment to interdisciplinarity.

EL infusion is decidedly smaller in scale than the most notable interdisciplinary efforts across the general education curriculum. Nonetheless, the construct of interdis-ciplinarity provides a solid grounding on which to build EL-infused teacher preparation programs. Beyond the rationale for taking on the issue of improving EL achievement as an interdisciplinary effort, an interdisciplinary outlook enables participants in the EL infusion effort to collaborate on an equal footing. The process of EL infusion involves integrating, in a connected and holistic way, EL content to teacher preparation curri-cula. This requires the expertise of ESL education faculty or subject matter experts, but should not privilege their knowledge above that of their colleagues in other disci-plines. All teacher preparation faculty are credentialed scholars with substantial general pedagogy and pedagogical content knowledge, so extending that knowledge to sup-porting the academic achievement of ELs should not involve reverting these faculty to student or beginner status. Establishing this collaborative mindset at the inception of the infusion process can reduce the risk of lack of engagement and commitment in non–ESL education faculty. We have observed numerous examples of interdisciplinary scholarship around ELs' academic achievement that emerged from EL infusion initiatives grounded in this inclusive philosophical perspective (discussed in more detail in chapter 5).

Effective Instruction and Assessment of ELs

In 2003, the professional organization Teachers of English to Speakers of Other Languages (TESOL) and the National Council for the Accreditation of Teacher Education (NCATE) issued standards for preK–12 ESL teacher education.[9] Revised in 2009, the standards are similar to those of the American Council on the Teaching of Foreign Languages in their focus on preparing second or foreign language teachers to instruct and assess language as a subject matter, albeit for different purposes. For example, while both foreign language and ESL teachers teach syntactic structures needed for social and academic communication, the foreign language teacher would do so to prepare students to apply these skills in other countries or communities, while the ESL teacher would prepare students to use them in other classes at the school they are enrolled in. Nevertheless, the TESOL/NCATE standards are intended for ESL teachers, not teachers of subjects other than ESL whose classes include ELs among a majority of native speakers of English. We refer to the latter as *teachers of English learners* to distinguish them from *ESL teachers*, TESOL's term for those who specialize in teaching ESL or ESOL.

In the absence of national standards for teachers of ELs, teacher preparation programs can consider various sources to guide EL infusion. Ideally, the knowledge, skills, and dispositions to be developed in teacher candidates should be derived from a solid theoretical and research base. As the small but growing knowledge base in EL teacher preparation becomes more established, we suggest that institutions consider the recommendations of a National Clearinghouse for English Language Acquisition (NCELA) Roundtable Report as the basis of their broad goals, or what we term *EL curricular competencies*, that organize the elements of the EL-infused curriculum.[10] Funded by the OELA, NCELA organizes and disseminates research and resources that support an inclusive approach to educating English learners. The NCELA recommendations are divided into five general areas, each of which includes a number of specific criteria for the mainstream teacher of ELs: (a) language acquisition and communicative competence; (b) curriculum and instruction; (c) assessment and accommodations; (d) culture and education; and (e) school and home communities. These recommendations are shown in appendix 3.a. The following examples illustrate specific knowledge and skills related to each that successful teachers of ELs apply in the mainstream classroom:

- Understanding *language acquisition and communicative competence*, the process that learners progress through in becoming proficient in a second language as well as their ability to use it appropriately, would enable teachers of ELs to:
    - Comprehend how ELs move through a process of becoming proficient in listening, speaking, reading, and writing English.
    - Determine which classroom practices support language development.

  – Foster successful communication so that ELs comprehend and express information and ideas related to the content of instruction.
  – Understand when it is appropriate to provide bilingual assistants and materials in instruction and assessment.
  – Analyze how different levels of English proficiency affect the types of tasks ELs can complete, such as writing an essay or creating a concept map.

• In the area of *curriculum and instruction*, teachers of ELs should be able to:
  – Analyze instructional materials and provide alternate or supplementary ones based on students' levels of English proficiency.
  – Individualize instruction to support ELs' academic language development and mastery of subject matter with instructional technology and other media.
  – Discern which teaching and learning strategies work better for ELs at beginning, intermediate, or advanced levels of English proficiency and why.
  – Know what aspects of general teaching practices are equally effective with ELs and what additional teaching strategies should be targeted to their specific needs.
  – Follow best practices in partnering with ESL specialists and other personnel.

• For *assessment and accommodations*, teachers of ELs should be able to:
  – Determine what parts of tests evaluate knowledge of English rather than knowledge of the subject matter.
  – Analyze whether tests require cultural background knowledge that ELs may lack.
  – Compose assessments that provide multiple ways to demonstrate mastery of the subject, including tasks that do not rely primarily on language to express comprehension of the concepts (e.g., drawing a diagram) for students at beginning levels of English proficiency, who struggle to answer simple questions in English.

• In learning about *culture and education*, teachers of ELs should:
  – Have basic knowledge of the cultural background of each student and how it affects performance and behavior at school.
  – Know how recently arrived students typically adjust to their new environment, which could help shed light on behavioral issues.
  – Understand that ELs bring a breadth of cross-cultural experiences to the classroom and capitalize on their funds of knowledge and develop culturally responsive lessons that benefit all students.[11]

• Lastly, in *school and home communities*, teachers of ELs should:
  – Become familiar with educational practices and perspectives of different parts of the world. For immigrant families, consider how prior educational experiences in the EL's native country shape expectations and affect achievement at school.
  – Develop an array of resources and strategies for connecting with parents and guardians who are not proficient in English and involve members of the local language minority communities in activities in and out of the classroom.

In addition to these broad areas of general knowledge and skills, we recommend using research-based best practices for teaching and assessing ELs in each content area in the absence of specific criteria promulgated by professional organizations such as TESOL or the National Council of Teachers of Mathematics. Highlights of some of these best practices are also featured in the NCELA Roundtable Report and are included in sample EL-embedded course summaries in chapters 6 through 9.

Institutions seeking to infuse may adapt the NCELA recommendations or develop their own EL curricular competencies derived from the most applicable performance descriptors for teachers of ELs noted in the TESOL/NCATE standards, the NCELA recommendations, or state ESL teacher endorsement or certification standards. The coauthors of chapter 11, the EL infusion team from Miami University, developed four domains from these various sources for their candidates, which are presented in appendix 3.b.

Programs that operate in states that mandate EL teacher preparation can use state standards as their EL competencies or can choose to augment the state standards by adding other emphases and details. The Florida Department of Education requires that teacher preparation institutions offering initial certification degrees in early childhood, elementary, English language arts, and exceptional education include a full endorsement in ESL. Because the credential is intended to prepare ESL teachers/ESL specialists, the standards are derived from the TESOL/NCATE standards and are more extensive, rigorous, and detailed than the NCELA guidelines, which apply to teachers of all subjects and grade levels with one or more ELs in their mainstream classes. Twelve standards serve as the EL competencies for most EL-infused programs leading to the ESL endorsement in Florida.[12] These standards are reproduced in appendix 3.c.

Establishing program outcomes and adopting standards or developing broad EL curricular competencies to reach them is a collaborative process that helps participants in the EL infusion process understand the desired end results.[13] Program outcomes and standards, what we term *EL curricular competencies*, should be established in the early phases of infusion and are an essential element of the curriculum mapping process, but they should not be prematurely assigned or ascribed in a cursory manner to different curricular components, such as EL-embedded courses or field experiences. Each existing course and field or clinical experience is the starting point for collaborative, interdisciplinary dialogue to explore connecting points between the current course content and the literature on the SLA process and best practices in teaching and assessing preK–12 EL students. These connecting points are then further developed into EL-embedded content in courses and field experiences. The identification of individual EL curricular competencies supported by the embedded content should occur once the products of this collaborative, interdisciplinary process are well defined.

Instructional Design

Just as the individual contributors to this book bring multiple disciplinary perspectives to the infusion effort, we the editors also draw on our backgrounds in different disciplines. Because of our preparation in instructional design, we applied established principles of this field to the overall curriculum infusion process as well as to the many components of the curriculum that incorporated EL-infused content. In other words, the instructional design cycle applies to two levels of our model, a macro or curriculum-wide level (discussed in more detail below), and a micro level that specifies each element of the infused curriculum. Instructional design is a systematic process of developing, implementing, and evaluating instructional materials, activities, and assessments. Because the One Plus model is intended to expand and enhance the *existing* elements of the teacher preparation curriculum, instructional design facilitates this incremental, additive process more effectively than broad conceptual models of curriculum design. Instructional design offers a practical means of bounding and directing what could otherwise become a nebulous, ultimately unrealized endeavor. As each task is completed, the infusion project is propelled forward, steadily rewarding collaborators with small accomplishments that accumulate and result in comprehensive enhancement.

Before the infusion process begins, a task force including all decision makers and stakeholders should be formed. We recommend that colleges or schools of education begin the infusion process by piloting one degree/certification program before expanding to other programs that share core courses with it. Once the degree program is chosen, an infusion team, as suggested in figure 3.3, can be convened.

While it is possible for multiple members to coordinate the team's efforts, it is helpful to have one point person who is responsible for moving the project along. This *EL infusion coordinator* position is essential for keeping a big-picture view of the infusion process and connecting all the collaborators, maintaining communication, and organizing information so it is accessible to all. The coordinator typically is an ESL faculty member who works closely with a college administrator, or vice versa. Institutions that do not have ESL education programs may choose to bring on an ESL subject matter expert as a consultant during the infusion process and then hire permanent ESL education faculty at the point of offering EL-specific courses. Waiting until EL-specific courses are offered to justify the expense of one or more full-time faculty positions is sometimes necessary, although it is preferable to involve experienced, qualified ESL education instructors who are full members of the faculty from the earliest stages of infusion.

The team should include members whose roles are external to the college, collegewide, and program-specific. As shown in figure 3.3, the base team includes external partners, such as local school district administrators and teachers as well as EL advocacy group leaders. In addition, collegewide administrators are key members, as infusion efforts may require the establishment of new policies and procedures that affect faculty, advisers, and candidates, may necessitate internal and external funding, and may involve seeking approval from state educational agencies that recognize infusion as a pathway to a credential for teaching ELs. Of course, the expertise of one or more ESL education experts is paramount to ensure that the focus on ELs retains its centrality and salience in the process. Finally, faculty who teach common core subjects or courses that cut across different programs of study are a critical element in the foundation of any EL-infused degree programs.

Figure 3.3

EL infusion team members

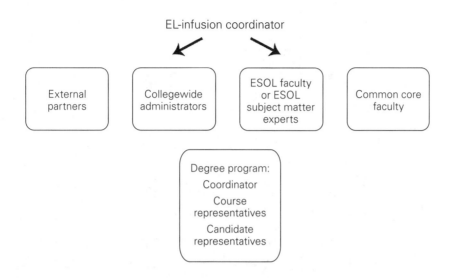

With the base team in place, individual programs can form their subcommittee of impacted faculty and personnel and connect it to the broader team. As noted previously, we recommend that institutions begin with one program area and then add programs once the collegewide EL-infused curricular elements are in place. Typically, there is a coordinator for each program area whose general responsibilities include collecting and presenting information required for continuing approval, and this individual can head up the program area infusion team. Along with the coordinator, program faculty often are designated as lead or coordinating instructors for courses that have multiple sections, so these representatives are important for ensuring that there is consistency among the courses that may embed EL content. Other critical program area contributors are teacher candidate representatives, who can provide the candidate perspective when issues that impact scheduling, additional costs, and such are considered.

After the EL infusion team is in place, the process generally moves forward according to the phases of the instructional design cycle. Numerous variations of the phases in the cycle exist, with a different number of steps or subphases between the major stages of the process. For clarity's sake, we have adopted the straightforward and widely accepted ADDIE (analysis, design, development, implementation, and evaluation) model (see figure 3.4), but institutions may choose to employ any number of variations to guide their process.[14]

Analysis

Beginning a project without carefully analyzing the context and environment, stakeholder needs, existing knowledge, faculty and administration relationships and culture, available resources, and the end goals will undoubtedly lead to missteps. Analysis

Figure 3.4
The ADDIE model of instructional design

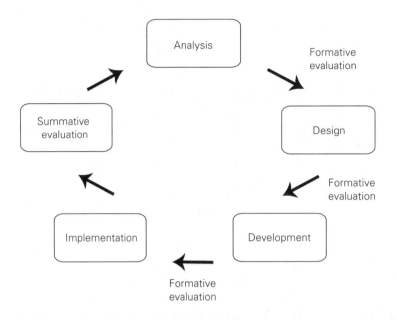

involves the systematic collection and analysis of data that orient the project design. As can be seen in table 3.3, analysis is directed toward many different individuals who would be affected by or who might contribute to developing an EL-infused teacher preparation curriculum. Such stakeholders might include the teacher preparation faculty; school district partners; current teacher candidates; college administrators such as associate deans, department chairs, internship directors, and program advisers; members of the EL community from local preK–12 schools; and state education agency personnel. In addition, the internal and external environments, including available resources, must be considered. Internally, it is important to examine the current degree of standardization of the teacher preparation curriculum; if courses have a common basic syllabus that individual faculty may add to, if there is a comprehensive map of the content of the current curriculum, and if there is an assessment system in place, infusion efforts will be facilitated by these curricular consistencies. Programs that need to institute some of these structures to support infusion will face issues extending well beyond the addition of EL content into the curriculum. Other types of facilitative resources or structures for infusion include university-wide faculty development centers and online course design support. A major part of the analysis involves assessing teacher preparation faculty's background knowledge on teaching and assessing ELs. There may be individuals who have previous coursework in or experience with teaching ELs who could serve as "early adopters" for their colleagues. Conversely, if no teacher preparation faculty have any background in teaching ELs, a more complex faculty development process may be necessary. The importance of external resources cannot be neglected. These include access to ELs in local schools with classroom teachers who are skilled and knowledgeable in supporting their academic achievement and literacy development.

Materials we developed for the analysis phase are presented in chapter 4 and can be a springboard for institutions to develop their own versions. Once the data are collected and analyzed, the EL infusion team will use the findings to set the design phase in motion.

Design

After analysis, the EL infusion team determines the scope and the goal of infusion. Will all degree programs pursue infusion? If more than one program chooses to do so, which program should pilot the process? Will the program that elects to infuse seek a credential for completers? If so, will it be solely an institution-granted credential or is state recognition a goal? The answers to these questions inform the program design and the selection or development of the EL curricular competencies or standards. If mastery of state standards for teaching ELs is the goal for program completers, then all curricular elements will contribute to this goal. Alternatively, if a program opts not to seek a state-approved credential, it can elect to develop EL curricular competencies based on the NCELA guidelines.

From these standards and broad EL curricular competencies, specific objectives, such as the examples presented in the previous discussion of the NCELA guidelines, are established that will be distributed across various elements of the curriculum. As the objectives are being defined, teacher preparation faculty without substantial knowledge and skills in teaching and assessing ELs should be immersed in faculty development that prepares them to effectively embed EL content into their courses. Programs that wish to create faculty development in-house rather than use existing materials and resources must take an additional step of completing an instructional design cycle for materials development between the program analysis and design phases of the overall curriculum infusion. More detailed information on faculty development is presented in chapter 5.

The next step in the design phase is perhaps the most important. Embedding EL content into teacher preparation courses and field and clinical experiences requires meaningful, sustained interdisciplinary collaboration between ESL faculty (or ESL expert consultants) and teacher preparation faculty. To support this collaboration, we have developed a mentoring protocol and criteria for identifying topics, objectives, and assessments for EL-embedded content, both of which are highlighted in chapter 4. During the process of identifying potential EL-embedded content, the faculty who will teach the embedded teacher preparation courses begin individualized faculty development. Chapter 5 discusses options for using existing materials and media as well as developing materials tailored to institutions' needs.

Once the preliminary EL-focused topics, objectives, and assessments are identified, they should be mapped across the curriculum and the program-established EL curricular competencies. At the design stage, this would involve simply marking potential

Table 3.3

ADDIE at the macro level: Infusion of overall teacher preparation program

For each EL-qualified degree/area of certification (e.g., Early Childhood Education, Elementary Education, or Math Education, etc.) the following steps apply:	Analyze	Evaluate	Design	Evaluate	Develop	Evaluate	Implement	Evaluate
	Needs assessment survey: teacher preparation faculty	Infusion team members evaluate and oversee the design phase steps given the analysis results	Establish purpose and EL curricular competencies: nationally informed, state or program specific	Infusion team members evaluate the EL-infused curricular objectives, assessments and field and clinical experiences to determine if design needs adjustment	Produce embedded EL content and assessment modules	Infusion team members evaluate course syllabi, materials, assessment and delivery mode media	Co-teach EL-embedded courses the first time course is offered	Review course evaluations
	Needs assessment survey: Clinical education partners		Establish faculty development plan and outcomes		Develop coordinated instructional platforms, formats, and resources		Co-evaluate EL-embedded assessments the 1st time course is offered	Review inter-rater agreement on assignment evaluations
	Needs assessment survey: Current teacher candidates		Identify topics, objectives, and assessments for embedded EL content		Develop syllabi and materials for EL-specific courses and seek approval		Collect assessment system data continually	Review candidate performance and remediation plans
	Interview: College administrators		Map embedded EL topics, objectives, and assessments across EL curricular competencies		Develop candidate assessment instruments for EL field and clinical experiences		Offer first EL-specific course in program sequence	Review course evaluations
	Interview: State certification office		Identify and map EL embedded field and clinical experiences across EL curricular competencies		Develop field and clinical experiences placement procedures		Place candidates in field experiences with ELs	Review field experience evaluations and survey cooperating teachers

Interview: EL student advocacy group representatives	Identify and map candidate assessment and program evaluation data from EL embedded courses and field/clinical experiences	Map EL-embedded and EL-specific course content in elaborated curriculum map and adjust courses as necessary	Collect and compile candidate observation and interview notes and reflections on field experiences
			Analyze sample of candidate field and interview notes and reflections
Environmental scan: Internal and external resources	Identify and map EL topics, objectives, and assessments for EL-specific courses across EL curricular competencies	Develop advising materials and faculty and candidate notification plan	Offer second EL-specific course in program sequence (if applicable)
			Review course evaluations
	Determine EL-specific courses' placement in curriculum	Develop EL-qualified candidate assessment system, including rubrics	Offer repeated EL-embedded courses without coteaching support
			Review course evaluations
	Offer faculty development options	Develop EL-qualified program evaluation system, including rubrics	Place candidates in internships with ELs (if applicable)
			Interview clinical education partners on placement process and candidate preparation
			Observe and evaluate candidates in internships and teacher work samples
			Review clinical educators' observation instrument results

EL curricular competencies that could be addressed or assessed in each course, which would provide a landscape view of the distribution of potential EL curricular competencies, and institutions can do so with a simple spreadsheet. As an early picture of the EL-embedded content emerges, the EL infusion team should assess which EL curricular competencies are not adequately supported through the embedded content and which ones would be better addressed or assessed, or would benefit from reinforcement, by ESL experts in EL-specific courses. From this point, the EL-specific course objectives, topics, and assessments can be identified and the courses' placement in the sequence of courses can be determined.

Development

After the program curriculum components have been targeted for the integration of EL content, the infusion plan is in place, and the infusion team has completed a formative evaluation of the results of the design phase, the development phase begins. This phase is very labor-intensive, since the course materials and syllabi require faculty and other professionals with knowledge and skills in EL content as well as in materials and media production. The development of the EL content in embedded teacher preparation courses, EL-specific courses, field/clinical experiences with ELs, and candidate assessment/program evaluation data collection and organization systems requires substantial time and coordination.

Chapters 6 through 9 offer examples of EL-embedded content from an array of teacher preparation courses. Production of this content continues the interdisciplinary collaboration between ESL experts and teacher preparation faculty from multiple fields. Because the EL-focused content must interconnect with the existing course content in a logical and stable way, there is a cycle of give-and-take between the two disciplinary experts. Does the added EL content overtake the subject with which it is integrated? Conversely, is the added EL content nearly invisible because it is treated as an unmentioned or merely cursory part of a larger course issue, such as cultural diversity? Alternatively, does the added EL content appear tacked on, as an add-on requirement with no connection to existing course content? Other issues include whether the teacher preparation faculty member feels comfortable and confident in implementing the EL content and whether the content should be online or technology enhanced.

Also during the development phase, ESL faculty work with other teacher preparation faculty to design the EL-specific courses. Chapter 10 offers suggestions for the content and process of developing these courses, but each program's needs will shape the elements of the EL-specific courses. Although these courses' main focus is on teaching and assessing ELs and second language development and applied linguistics, the specific course topics, objectives, and assignments are also addressed in an interdisciplinary manner. Just as the ESL experts consult with teacher preparation faculty to develop EL-focused modules for embedded courses, they also confer with their colleagues from different disciplines to ensure that the EL-specific courses address EL achievement in all subject areas of focus in an accurate, authentic way.

As the EL-embedded and EL-specific course syllabi and materials are developed, procedures for placement in field/clinical experiences with ELs can be determined. These experiences may be associated with various courses, such as EL-specific or EL-embedded, or they may be full-time or part-time internships. Depending on the extent and context of the field/clinical experiences, observation instruments and evaluation criteria will also need to be developed.

Once the courses are developed, the initial spreadsheet gives way to a more detailed curriculum map, which should include summaries of the EL-focused content in all courses, mapped by course and EL curricular competencies. The infusion team can then review the map, making some adjustments and tweaking as needed to strengthen EL-embedded and EL-specific course content. The elaborated curriculum map also serves to display the EL-focused content for faculty who will teach the courses and students who will be assessed by their completion of the assignments described in the summaries. EL infusion team members at Miami University and the University of Central Florida developed an online database system that is easily populated and revised and can give a landscape view of how many EL curricular competencies are assessed in each program course. In addition, course cells include hyperlinks to summaries of each of the tracked EL-focused course assignments. For an example of the online elaborated curriculum maps, see http://www.esolinfusion.org.

In addition to curriculum and assessment development, numerous tasks must be completed during this phase before implementation can begin, such as disseminating information about new requirements to candidates and faculty, revising advising documents, and formalizing approval of new courses. Finally, there is one last formative evaluation step to ensure that all development outcomes support implementation.

Implementation

Implementation of an EL-integrated curriculum occurs in stages. Since EL-specific courses ground much of the embedded content in deeper, more comprehensive study of SLA theory and best practices in teaching and assessing ELs, we recommend that the first EL-specific course in a language arts teacher preparation program (whichever of the two EL-specific courses whose content fits better into the beginning semester of the program curriculum), or what would be the only EL-specific course in an academic subject area teacher preparation program, be offered the first semester of the catalog year that includes the new requirements.

We also recommend that, where possible, ESL education faculty coteach and coevaluate the EL-embedded content the first time teacher preparation faculty teach EL-embedded courses or supervise embedded field/clinical experiences. Implementing EL-embedded content created during the development phase could lead to discussions or questions that the teacher preparation or clinical faculty may not be prepared to adequately address because they lack depth of knowledge or skills in SLA or best practices in teaching and assessing ELs. Presenting, demonstrating, or evaluating the added EL content can be daunting for teacher preparation or clinical faculty even after faculty development. Coteaching and co-assessing the EL-embedded content the first time the enhanced course or clinical experience is offered can alleviate hesitations and ensure that assessment of the EL content is rigorous, yet realistic. For more consistency and facility in grading, formal rubrics may be codeveloped as well.

For language arts programs, a timeline should be put in place to begin offering the second EL-specific course as well as full-time internships including ELs. After the first semester of implementation, EL-embedded courses can be offered without coteaching and co-assessing, if desired. During the implementation phase, data from multiple sources are collected and will be analyzed in the evaluation phase.

Evaluation

Although formative evaluation takes place at three intervals during the instructional design process, summative evaluation tied to the data generated from implementation is also essential. For EL-infused programs, such project evaluation occurs on multiple levels. The EL infusion process and outcomes must be evaluated to determine where improvements can be made. The final column in table 3.3 shows data that may be gathered for this kind of evaluation. Each component of curriculum implementation is linked to a corresponding evaluation task, which provides clear data to inform decisions about necessary changes. Our approach to evaluating the infusion process and outcomes is guided by culturally responsive evaluation, which is described in chapter 11.

In addition to evaluation of the infusion process and outcomes, infusion team members assess teacher candidates for their mastery of the EL curricular competencies and evaluate programs for their effectiveness in preparing teachers to instruct and assess ELs. To demarcate these two types of review, we use the term *evaluation* to refer to the review of program quality measured against accreditation targets, and *assessment* to refer to the appraisal of candidates' knowledge, skills, and dispositions in teaching ELs. EL-focused assessments embedded in teacher preparation courses, cumulative exams on teaching and assessing ELs in EL-specific courses, teacher work samples and observation instruments from field/clinical experiences and internships with ELs, and self-selected, reflective compilations of candidate artifacts from any of these categories are rich sources of assessment data that can be tracked and used for verification of candidates' attainment of EL competencies, or for individualized remediation when necessary.

It is important to mention that EL-infused program evaluation can support unit accreditation. Although the obvious standard that relates to ELs is diversity, data generated from most elements of the EL-infused curriculum can contribute to documentation for all six NCATE Standards.[15] These standards and examples of how EL-infused programs can support them are offered in appendix 3.d.

Timeline for Implementing the One Plus Model

Depending on institutional resources and priorities as well as faculty background and workloads, among other issues, the timeline for completing the infusion process can vary. In our experience, the curriculum-wide process of analyzing, designing, developing, and implementing infusion takes a minimum of three academic years, with a staggered rollout of various infused elements, according to the sequence of courses in the program of studies. In the first semester of year one, the analysis should be completed and the design should be well under way. During the second semester, the development phase should be completed for all infused elements that will be implemented the first semester of year two. This development timeline can be repeated for each new element that is implemented the first time, which could extend the implementation phase to a period of two years. Alternatively, for institutions with substantial resources, such as external funding, development for all infused elements could occur simultaneously, which would make them ready for implementation at the same time, although some of them would not be implemented for up to a year and a half later. Upon completion of implementation of all elements of the infused curriculum, the evaluation and revision phase begins. As this is taking place, research that follows program completers into classrooms with ELs should be initiated.

In summary, table 3.3 shows each phase in the instructional design cycle, listing comprehensive tasks or steps necessary for applying the One Plus model of EL infusion at the curriculum level. The process of planning, implementing, and evaluating each of the components of the EL-infused curriculum also follows the five-phase cycle.

Each column (phase) of the ADDIE cycle may be plotted on a timeline, from the top of the column to the bottom. In other words, the sequence of steps within each column (phase) begins at the top and ends at the bottom. Formative evaluation takes place in between the analyze and design, the design and development, and the development and implementation phases. Each step of the implementation phase is linked to a summative evaluation step.

Promoting EL Infusion That Is Interconnected, Cohesive, and Interdisciplinary

As discussed in chapter 1, we define EL infusion by three qualities that permeate the EL-infused curriculum: interconnectedness, cohesion, and interdisciplinarity. Because our infusion model is comprehensive and curriculum-wide, it offers multiple means of ensuring that these qualities are present. In our description of the three pillars, we discussed how the process of embedding courses, field/clinical experiences, and assessment with EL content interconnects their pre-infusion topics of focus to intersecting issues pertaining to ELs. These interconnected course elements are a hallmark of infusion, because they align and integrate the EL-focused content with related content in teacher preparation courses. We also explained how interdisciplinarity is realized through collaboration across disciplines to address the issues of ELs' achievement in academic subjects and development of English literacy skills. In addition, we have also presented components that promote program cohesion—how to bring all these curricular elements together in an articulated, unified system. Because there are so many EL-focused instructional materials and media, class activities and assignments, field/clinical experiences, and other EL content distributed across the curriculum, a number of measures are necessary to unite them in what the teacher candidate perceives as a cohesive whole. It is especially critical to be mindful of cohesion in EL-infused programs precisely because of this distributed nature, which is in sharp contrast to providing the extensive EL-focused content exclusively through four or five EL-specific courses. By using common contextual and structural features across EL-specific and EL-embedded courses and field/clinical experiences as well as by establishing an overarching portfolio assessment system for candidates to collect and synthesize the distributed elements, curricular cohesion and integrity can be promoted. Cohesion can also be furthered by thematic unity in the curriculum, such as the common thread of the teaching cases of ELs at three levels of English proficiency.

This chapter has provided details on the One Plus model, which is a systematic, comprehensive form of EL infusion—a promising approach to the preparation of all teachers to instruct and assess ELs. Expanding on the overview of the One Plus model provided in this chapter, subsequent chapters discuss in detail the curricular elements that are part of the One Plus model:

1. The process of embedding EL content and faculty development and scholarship to support EL-embedded courses and clinical/field experiences (chapters 4 and 5)
2. EL-embedded courses and field and clinical experiences (chapters 6 through 9)
3. EL-specific courses and field and clinical experiences (chapter 10)
4. Program evaluation (chapter 11)

Each of these chapters will also present common challenges and how the model addresses them.

Appendix 3.a

NCELA Roundtable Report Recommendations*

Language Acquisition and Communicative Competence

The Interplay of First and Second Language Acquisition

Teacher Performance Criterion: Teachers will be able to demonstrate the effective use of first language in the classroom.

Second Language Acquisition Process

Teacher Performance Criterion: Teachers will be able to recognize the signs of progressing second language acquisition.

Curriculum and Instruction

Coordinating Standards through Teacher Collaboration

Teacher Performance Criterion: Through professional collaboration, teachers will be able to coordinate their content standards with English language standards to develop appropriate learning objectives.

Access to the Subject Matter Content

Teacher Performance Criterion: Teachers will be able to routinely use effective, research-based methods to teach ELLs while contextualizing the content in meaningful ways.

Differentiation

Teacher Performance Criterion: Teachers will be able to increase student engagement by identifying language challenges in a text, differentiating material, and grouping students in purposeful and meaningful ways.

Academic Vocabulary and Oral Language

Teacher Performance Criterion: Teachers will be able to explicitly teach academic vocabulary in context and provide ample opportunity for students to use these words, leading to mastery.

Reading

Teacher Performance Criterion: Teachers will be able to demonstrate and monitor effective reading strategies.

Teacher Performance Criterion: Teachers will be able to identify texts that amplify rather than simplify language to facilitate ELLs' reading comprehension.

Writing

Teacher Performance Criterion: Teachers will be able to demonstrate and monitor effective writing strategies.

Technology

Teacher Performance Criterion: Teachers will be able to identify appropriate technology to support learning.

Content Assessment

Teacher Performance Criterion: Teachers will be able to select assessments that test content or design statistically valid and reliable assessments that assess content mastery while students are learning English.

Culture and Education

Teacher Performance Criterion: Teachers will be able to interpret student behavior in light of different cultural beliefs.

School and Home Communities

Teacher Performance Criterion: Teachers will be able to compile community resources and be aware of translation efforts for school-home communication.

*From http://www.ncela.gwu.edu/files/uploads/3/EducatingELLsBuildingTeacherCapacityVol1.pdf.

Appendix 3.b

Miami University School of Education, Health, and Society TELLs Certificate Competencies

Second/New Language Learning:

Candidates understand:

- The major concepts, theories, and research that facilitate second/new language learning
- That language is a system comprised of phonology, morphology, syntax, semantics, pragmatics, etc. and apply this knowledge to assist ELs to communicate in English
- The ways in which languages are similar and different
- How to provide appropriate language input and tasks
- The long-term nature of second/new language development

Language and Culture of ELs

Candidates understand:

- The nature of the role of culture in second/new language development and academic achievement
- How ELs' cultural identifications affect language learning
- That language and culture interact and form the EL's identity as well as his/her sense of self-worth and how these are tied to academic achievement

Planning, Implementing, and Managing Instruction for ELs

Candidates:

- Know and apply concepts, research and best practices as well as create standards-based instruction for ELs
- Are familiar with available resources and technologies to adapt and use with ELs to teach content

Assessment and ELs

Candidates understand:

- Issues with assessment of and for ELs
- Language proficiency assessments
- Use of a variety of assessments and techniques in the classroom for ELs

---

Appendix 3.c

Florida Teacher Standards for ESOL Endorsement*

Domain 1: Culture (Cross-Cultural Communications)

Standard 1: Culture as a Factor in ELLs' Learning. Teachers will know and apply understanding of theories related to the effect of culture in language learning and school achievement for ELLs from diverse backgrounds. Teachers will identify and understand the nature and role of culture, cultural groups, and individual cultural identities.

Domain 2: Language and Literacy (Applied Linguistics)

Standard 1: Language as a System. Teachers will demonstrate understanding of language as a system, including phonology, morphology, syntax, semantics and pragmatics; support ELLs' acquisition of English in order to learn and to read, write, and communicate orally in English.

Standard 2: Language Acquisition and Development. Teachers will understand and apply theories and research on second language acquisition and development to support ELLs' learning.

Standard 3: Second Language Literacy Development. Teachers will demonstrate an understanding of the components of literacy, and will understand and apply theories of second language literacy development to support ELLs' learning.

Domain 3: Methods of Teaching English to Speakers of Other Languages (ESOL)

Standard 1: ESL/ESOL Research and History. Teachers will demonstrate knowledge of history, public policy, research and current practices in the field of ESL/ESOL teaching and apply this knowledge to improve teaching and learning for ELLs.

Standard 2: Standards-Based ESL and Content Instruction. Teachers will know, manage, and implement a variety of teaching strategies and techniques for developing and integrating ELLs' English listening, speaking, reading, and writing skills. The teacher will support ELLs' access to the core curriculum by teaching language through academic content.

Standard 3: Effective Use of Resources and Technologies. Teachers will be familiar with and be able to select, adapt and use a wide range of standards-based materials, resources, and technologies.

Domain 4: ESOL Curriculum and Materials Development

Standard 1: Planning for Standards-Based Instruction of ELLs. Teachers will know, understand, and apply concepts, research, best practices, and evidenced-based strategies to plan classroom instruction in a supportive learning environment for ELLs. The teacher will plan for multilevel classrooms with learners from diverse backgrounds using a standards-based ESOL curriculum.

Standard 2: Instructional Resources and Technology. Teachers will know, select, and adapt a wide range of standards-based materials, resources, and technologies.

Domain 5: Assessment (ESOL Testing and Evaluation)

Standard 1: Assessment Issues for ELLs. Teachers will understand and apply knowledge of assessment issues as they affect the learning of ELLs from diverse backgrounds and at varying English proficiency levels. Examples include cultural and linguistic bias; testing in two languages; sociopolitical and psychological factors; special education testing and assessing giftedness; the importance of standards; the difference between formative and summative assessment; and the difference between language proficiency and other types of assessment (e.g., standardized achievement tests). Teachers will also understand issues around accountability. This includes the implications of standardized assessment as opposed to performance-based assessments, and issues of accommodations in formal testing situations.

Standard 2: Language Proficiency Assessment. Teachers will appropriately use and interpret a variety of language proficiency assessment instruments to meet district, state, and federal guidelines, and to inform their instruction. Teachers will understand their uses for identification, placement, and demonstration of language growth of ELLs from diverse backgrounds and at varying English proficiency levels. Teachers will articulate the appropriateness of ELL assessments to stakeholders.

Standard 3: Classroom-Based Assessment for ELLs. Teachers will identify, develop, and use a variety of standards- and performance-based, formative and summative assessment tools and techniques to inform instruction and assess student learning. Teachers will understand their uses for identification, placement, and demonstration of language growth of ELLs from diverse backgrounds and at varying English proficiency levels. Teachers will articulate the appropriateness of ELL assessments to stakeholders.

*From http://www.fldoe.org/aala/pdf/ApprovedTeacherStandards.pdf

Appendix 3.d

Examples of How EL Infusion Can Support NCATE Standards

Standard 1: Candidate Knowledge, Skills, and Professional Dispositions. The added value of knowledge, skills, and dispositions required to teach and assess English learners in the candidates' areas of certification support this standard.

Standard 2: Assessment System and Unit Evaluation. Data collected as part of EL infusion can feed into the general assessment system and can also contribute to meeting federal data reporting requirements such as Title II.

Standard 3: Field Experiences and Clinical Practice. The added dimension of EL-focused field and clinical experiences provides data for substantiating diversity of field experiences and clinical practice.

Standard 4: Diversity. Of course, the exposure to linguistically and culturally diverse learners and to instructional and assessment practices that further their achievement supports efforts to prepare teachers for diversity.

Standard 5: Faculty Qualifications, Performance, and Development. The faculty development necessary for teaching EL-embedded courses contributes to professional qualifications and continuing education standards.

Standard 6: Unit Governance and Resources. It could be argued that the coordination and resources dedicated to infusion are one form of evidence for satisfactory or adequate governance and resources.

CHAPTER 4

The Process of
EL Content Infusion

This chapter describes how teacher preparation programs infuse existing curricula with EL content. This process spans the design, delivery, implementation, and evaluation phases of the instructional design cycle. The distinct steps for embedding the EL content are explained in detail, and forms that have been developed as a resource for consultation or as starting points for infusion teams that desire to create their own instruments are described throughout (the forms themselves are reproduced in appendices 4.a, 4.b, 4.c, and 4.d).

The Role of ESL Faculty Mentors

For the design and development phases, during which EL content is embedded into courses, we propose a mentorship framework that engages the faculty with ESL expertise and the teacher preparation faculty whose courses are infused in deliberate and sustained collaborations. Mentoring has a long history in various settings where a novice or less experienced professional learns from an expert. In higher education, mentoring most often occurs when a faculty member mentors a promising student. As Sands, Parson, and Duane point out, past faculty-faculty mentoring efforts generally took place in informal and interpersonal ways; for example, a senior faculty or administrator served as guide for a junior member navigating the new culture of the institution in pursuit of promotion and tenure.[1] This customary structure has been depicted as a dyad of unequal power and status in which the mentor transmits knowledge to the mentee in a protective or paternalistic partnership, focusing on the development of professional skills or career advancement.[2]

While operationalizing the embedding process that reflects the theoretical and philosophical orientations of the One Plus model, we first drew on our past experiences assisting with initial EL infusion efforts, designing faculty development in EL content, and our current work in Florida, where existing EL-infused programs are being updated with a new set of state teacher standards for ESOL endorsement. Each discussion resulting from these experiences brought us to reach the same conclusion: it is preferable to embed courses with EL content parallel to offering faculty development in the new content.[3] The literature on infusing teacher preparation curricula presented in chapter 1 confirms not only that simultaneous faculty development and curricular revisions are possible, but also that it can indeed lead to deep conversations among the faculty and a shared understanding of the knowledge and skills the candidates develop as a result of the infusion efforts. What struck us in consulting those publications was the consistent use of professional learning communities in which one or several experts assumed responsibility for presenting new knowledge or practices to the teacher preparation faculty tasked with the integration of the additional content into their courses. Instead of finding traditional one-way relationships built on what Mullen terms a "compensatory" mentoring practice, we encountered many descriptions of a different paradigm—*collaborative* mentoring models.[4] In these models, mentors act as facilitators and teacher preparation faculty engage in reflective practices, sharing their experiences, and supporting each other's personal and professional growth.[5]

This practice of developing partners or "professionals as colleagues who are equal but different" through learning relationships is reflected in the interdisciplinary orientation of the One Plus model.[6] The acquisition of knowledge and best practices regarding EL content by teacher preparation faculty need not resemble the education of teacher candidates. After all, the ESL faculty and the teacher preparation faculty are peers—both grounded in general theory and practice of human development, teaching, and learning. The specific knowledge bases only differ as a result of the respective disciplines. In other words, the EL content is separate, on top of the content and the content pedagogies of a social studies educator, just as the social studies content pedagogies are typically not part of ESL faculty's knowledge and expertise. With these insights in mind, we constructed the mentoring protocol and the process of embedding EL content to go hand in hand with faculty development.[7] For clarity, despite our promotion of a collaborative relationship for the EL content embedding process, the term *mentor* will be used for the ESL faculty (or the ESL expert consultant). However, we use the term *teacher preparation faculty*, rather than *mentee*, when referring to the faculty who embed the EL content in their courses, thus moving away from the expert-novice dyad modeled in other mentoring practices.

The literature identifies several factors that influence success in mentoring and collaborative efforts. Kram and Isabella describe peer relationships along a continuum on which professionals find themselves at various career stages, and these relationships and their primary functions touch on several roles that the mentor in the One Plus mentoring protocol assumes along the embedding process.[8] For example, in the function of *information peer*, the mentor shares information on SLA, culture, legal matters, communication, and effective instructional practices related to ELs with the teacher preparation faculty. As a *collegial peer*, the mentor provides feedback on the teacher preparation faculty's attempts to translate the new knowledge into practice in their courses. Finally, as a *special peer*, the ESL mentor provides emotional support, validates concerns, confirms progress, and offers solutions and general collegiality to the educators engaged in the embedding process. Similarly, three of the four main functions of a mentor delineated by Sands, Parson, and Duane, apply to the role of the mentor envisioned in our protocol: (a) a friend who provides social interaction and emotional support, (b) a source of

information, and (c) an intellectual guide who provides constructive feedback and promotes collaboration among the faculty.[9] Reflecting on their experience with EL infusion, Verkler and Hutchinson report developing necessary mentorship skills along the
way through trial and error.[10] Among these skills, they list being a good listener, being
an open communicator during feedback sessions, and being sensitive to the needs of
infusing faculty, skills they suggest mentors may acquire through formal preparation in
the supervision of clinical experiences. We believe that the above qualities and skill sets
facilitate the creation of an environment that motivates and energizes the teacher preparation faculty who are learning about and embedding EL content in their courses. In
so doing, the ESL faculty mentor invites all partners to try out and share new practices
with peers and increases their confidence that at the end of the project they will have
gained professionally and personally.

   The ESL faculty mentor-teacher preparation faculty relationship also speaks to
staffing considerations for providing faculty development, mentoring, and teaching the
EL-specific courses. Successful use of graduate assistants in providing faculty development has been reported.[11] However, this practice was employed for the training aspect
of the faculty development where graduate students taught the faculty members new
technical skills, conducted workshops during which new content was introduced, and
provided in-class lectures on the new content the first time it was delivered in the
teacher candidate courses. The graduate students did not mentor the teacher preparation faculty through the embedding process by facilitating learning circles or faculty
seminars in which faculty reflected deeply on their own practices. Such activities were
conducted by a faculty member.[12] We recommend a similar separation of duties for
those institutions that have the opportunity to draw on graduate students enrolled in
bilingual education or ESL degree programs. General formal training sessions in which
information is presented can be conducted by graduate students.[13] Graduate students
can also be of great assistance in identifying resources that the infusing faculty can use
for their own study or for presenting the EL content to their teacher candidates. On
the other hand, sessions during which pedagogical practices are explored and where
conversations about the embedded content are likely to take place should be conducted by a peer of the teacher preparation faculty. Likewise, the person who assumes
primary responsibility for teaching the EL-specific courses should have the same level
of preparation as those faculty members who coordinate and teach other courses in
the program. If the unit faculty typically hold a terminal degree, the lead ESL faculty
should also hold such a degree.

The Process of Embedding EL Content

The process of embedding the EL content in individual courses is a labor-intensive
endeavor consisting of seven steps that take place in two phases, which correspond
to the design and development phases of the ADDIE model presented in chapter
3.[14] These steps are depicted in figures 4.1 (shown next) and 4.3 (shown later in this
chapter), respectively.

Figure 4.1

The design phase of embedding EL content

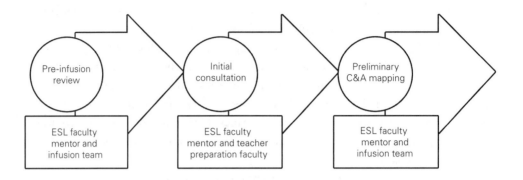

Design Phase

A first critical component of the design phase is the decision of what standards or EL curricular competencies the candidates are expected to master while going through the infused program. This decision is prerequisite to starting the embedding process, as it affects the planning for faculty development, the development of the embedded content elements, and the development of the candidate assessment system.

As we have noted, EL infusion is a collaborative effort between a faculty member with ESL expertise who serves as the mentor and a faculty member or a team of faculty who typically teach the courses into which the EL content is to be embedded. This collaboration should start shortly after the EL infusion team conducts a needs assessment of all faculty involved in the project and holds an infusion launch event. Detailed descriptions of these components are provided in chapter 5. However, we must point out here that the One Plus model, including the explanation of the 1+2+3+ course categories and the minimum required course elements for each category, should be presented during the launch event. This gives the faculty member an opportunity to better anticipate the amount of work embedding their course will demand.

Pre-infusion Review

The first step in the embedding process that involves the courses to be modified is the *pre-infusion review*, which consists of two tasks. The ESL faculty mentor—with the aid of the infusion team to accelerate this first task—examines each course syllabus in the program to determine the level of infusion warranted based on the 1+2+3+ framework. This determination is accomplished by completing the first page of the EL Content Consultation form (appendix 4.a), which derived from the flow chart shown in figure 4.2. The first question in the flow chart—whether the course focuses on planning or delivering curriculum, instruction, or assessment—is represented in the form by the question, "Does this course require candidates to develop or implement any: instructional materials, plans, activities, assessments, or demonstration?" If none of

Figure 4.2

Course category determination flow chart

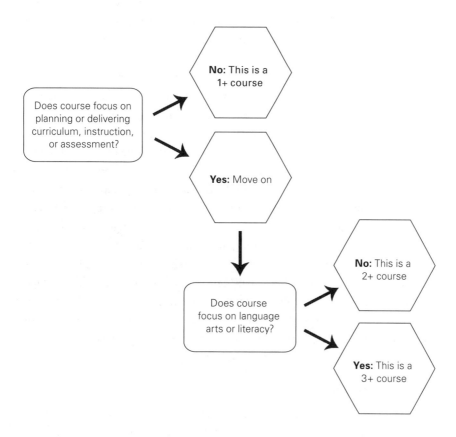

these options is answered in the negative, the reviewer can establish that the course is a 1+ course. If any of the options are answered in the affirmative and the course does focus on planning or delivering curriculum, instruction, or assessment, it must be established whether the focus of the course is on language arts or literacy. If not, and the focus is on teaching art, science, or life skills, for instance, the course is a 2+ course. If the focus is on teaching language arts or literacy, the course is a 3+ course.

This determination of course category impacts the mentoring assignment and scheduling. The minimum number of added EL-focused elements required for each category (as shown in table 3.1) means that infusing a 1+ course typically takes less time and effort on the part of the course instructor and requires less support on the part of the mentor than infusing a 2+ course, and so on.[15] The necessary effort also varies depending on the individual faculty member's prior coursework in ESL and experience working with ELs. If more than one mentor is available, each mentor should be assigned approximately the same number of 1+, 2+ and 3+ course faculty with a mix of professional development needs, and every group can commence the embedding process at the same time. If the institution has only one mentor for the entire body of infusing faculty, the embedding process should start gradually, with new groups starting every month. This staggering is intended to avoid bottleneck times where more intensive interactions occur, such as during initial consultations, during small-group or individualized professional development, and when assistance with EL content design is required.

Once the mentor assignment and scheduling are completed, the mentor carries out the second task of the pre-infusion review: a close examination of the syllabus. To see whether the course already contains any elements that address EL content, we recommend completing the left columns under each question in the subsequent pages of the EL Content Consultation form in a first pass (Appendix 4.a).[16] The questions follow instructional design principles that align topics or objectives with content, activities, and assignments, as well as assessments. In a second pass through the syllabus, the mentor completes the right columns, noting where connections between existing course elements and EL content could be made (or strengthened), drafting suggestions for EL-specific information to be added to the existing materials, activities or assignments, and assessments. The EL content in the modified course must be clear and explicit. Tacking a notation such as "including English learners" onto a course topic and reflective paper does not constitute *meaningful* EL content inclusion that prepares the candidates to work with ELs.[17] Therefore, whenever the existing course activities and assignments do not lend themselves to adding the EL content in a substantive and explicit manner, other options, such as a stand-alone EL module, should be explored.

Initial Consultation Meeting

The second step of the embedding process consists of an *initial consultation* meeting between the ESL mentor and the teacher preparation faculty who is embedding the course with EL content.[18] This meeting marks the beginning of both formal and informal individual face-to-face mentoring meetings that should occur at intervals throughout the embedding process. It presents an opportunity to set expectations, to discuss options for embedding the EL content, and to establish a roadmap for faculty development. More importantly, however, the initial consultation should be seen as a point of departure for building the collaborative relationship between the two peers. Even if both parties have previously served together on committees or have a personal friendship, the mentor should be sensitive to the fact that the nature of the established relationship is bound to change as a result of collaborative mentoring during the embedding process. To accomplish this mission, the ESL mentor should request between an hour and an hour and a half of the teacher preparation faculty's time and, if possible, propose that the meeting take place in the teacher preparation faculty member's office because this gesture shows the mentor's willingness to meet outside her "territory." Selecting this meeting space also gives the teacher preparation faculty easy access to materials for explaining the course to the mentor, an important step during the initial consultation.

To open the consultation, we suggest that the mentor ask whether the partner has any questions in regards to EL infusion or the One Plus model that were not answered during the launch event or that have emerged since then. Rather than going into great detail about the model or EL content, the mentor should keep the information general, possibly referring to later steps in the process when providing detailed information would be more appropriate. Next, the mentor should ask about the teacher preparation faculty's experience working with ELs and/or what kind of courses in ESL content or related to SLA he or she may have taken in academic preparation. The third discussion point focuses on the course to be infused. The teacher preparation partner is invited to explain the overall objective of the course and where in the sequence of courses the majority of candidates enroll in it. This part of the conversation offers the mentor a rapid self-check whether the syllabus was correctly interpreted during the pre-infusion review. The mentor then goes over each finding and drafted suggestion in the EL Content Consultation form, checking along the way whether the course instructor or designer agrees with the mentor's assessment. It is possible that the course already contains individual EL content components that are not explicitly stated in the syllabus and would therefore have been invisible to the mentor during the initial review.

In our experience, this is the time when the codevelopment of a plan commences. Faculty who have recognized the need for this substantive curricular revision and who embrace the challenge of delving into new, uncharted territories in the process will show their eagerness to move forward (an example can be seen in Cynthia Hutchinson's reflection about her infused course, in chapter 7). In such a situation, the two partners confer on the EL curricular competencies that might be addressed and assessed through the modified objectives, topics, activities, or assignments and assessments. At the conclusion of the meeting, the faculty mentor suggests a few readings for knowledge development, offering to put copies into the partner's mailbox within a few days.

Not all colleagues acknowledge the need for the level of revisions that the One Plus model puts into motion, however. Some may argue that their course already includes discussions on cultural sensitivity or the need for differentiation in instruction for all learners, and thus contains adequate treatment of the specific needs of ELs. Others, overwhelmed by the numerous obligations of academic life, may have the attitude, "Just tell me what you want me to do, and I'll put it into the syllabus." These two reactions present a pivotal moment for the mentoring relationship. The mentor, while needing to maintain that EL-focused content is relevant and to lead the candidates to understand how it impacts their future practice, should bear in mind that in order to bring about sustainable program change, the embedding process must be undertaken through collaborative authoring. EL infusion cannot be prescriptive, but must occur through interdisciplinary discussions in which each discipline informs the practice of the other within the institution's context. Protocols and instruments designed to provide guidance in the mentoring and embedding process should not be used as the yardstick against which each action is measured.

In moments of possible impasse, the mentor has to show that the faculty's points of view are heard, but also needs to keep them in balance with the commitment to excellence that the infusion aspires to. During the infusion process, the mentor is going to see different levels of engagement and attention to detail in embedding EL content, and must find ways to make the needs of ELs visible in what is being embedded. In the case of the faculty member who deems the course sufficiently infused without the explicit focus on educating ELs, the mentor should validate that there is some consideration of the needs of ELs while explaining why in its current form the treatment does not quite hit the mark of EL content infusion. Next, the course designer could be encouraged to add a brief EL-focused lecture to the material used for discussion, thereby adding another dimension to the course and expanding the treatment of EL issues by making these issues more explicit. An offer to assist the faculty in finding the material to inform the lecture construction or to identify an appropriate practice-oriented article for the candidates is typically well received and opens the door for collaboration.

When faculty members appear unable or unwilling to work in this collaborative way, the EL mentor should find out whether they would agree to make room in class meetings to discuss EL-focused topics if ready-made content were available. If so, the mentor has found an opening. Agreeing to work on identifying and developing the content, the mentor asks the partner to explain the foci of the course so as to identify topics and activities to which the EL content can be attached. Educators typically like to talk about their content area and their courses. As the teacher preparation faculty describes, for instance, developing connections between the school and the home, the ESL mentor could interject that this brings to mind a recent policy brief listing barriers that make it difficult for parents of ELs to fully engage in their children's schooling, then offer to put a copy in the faculty mailbox and to meet over a cup of coffee a few days later to discuss how this may fit into the lecture and action plan assignment. If the partner appears uncertain of whether it is possible to make room in the course for EL-focused discussions and activities during class meetings, the mentor should suggest the option of a stand-alone online module that the candidates complete for a grade as part of the course requirements. The tactic would be the same: asking the partner to talk in detail about the course topics and assignments, remarking on possible connections, and offering resources. By adjusting the amount of support provided to reluctant partners, the ESL mentor can find ways to plant the EL content in courses. However, for EL infusion to be more than a cursory treatment of EL-focused topics, it is important that all teacher preparation partners come to claim it as an integral part of their courses.

To prepare teacher candidates for teaching ELs to the fullest extent possible, programs that infuse EL content must provide several opportunities for candidates to observe and work with ELs through field experiences and clinical/internship placements. In many instances, courses that already have a field-based activity can expand the experience to include an EL component. This discussion obviously presents an important part of the initial consultation between the ESL faculty mentor and the teacher preparation faculty whose course contains a preexisting field experience. Some faculty who may have been thinking about incorporating a field experience into their course may take advantage of the infusion project to modify or augment their course in this vein and tailor the experience to contain an EL content component. Options for experiences tied to EL-specific courses are described in chapter 10. Teacher preparation programs that want to stamp their candidates' diploma with an institutional indication that they are EL-qualified for language arts must also make plans for internship placements in classes with one or more ELs. Naturally, discussions need to be held with school district personnel or within the individual schools where candidates typically fulfill their internship requirements to find collaborating teachers whose classes include one or more ELs. This gathered information impacts the placement procedures at the clinical experiences office.

In terms of the EL-content embedding process, designing internship experiences that include instruction and assessment of ELs means that clinical supervision instruments must be revised to adequately evaluate candidates' performance. Therefore, we recommend that the head of the internship office and a group of clinical supervision faculty meet with the ESL faculty mentor during this step of the EL embedding process to plan for changes in placement procedures, and that clinical supervision faculty obtain faculty development at the 2+ or 3+ course level, depending on their typical assignments.

Preliminary Curriculum and Assessment Mapping

In the third step of the design phase, the ESL faculty mentor reports the findings of the initial consultations to the infusion team. Relative to the design phase, this step helps to identify objectives for group and individual faculty development sessions. Additionally, the potential standards or EL curricular competencies that may be met through the embedding of the identified EL-focused material, activities, assignments, or assessment are placed in a *preliminary curriculum map*. At this stage, the map consists of nothing more than check marks for each EL curricular competency that could be addressed and/or assessed in each course in the program. The infusion team must keep in mind that the landscape of how the selected competencies are being distributed across the program is highly fluid in the early stages. If teacher preparation faculty and the ESL faculty mentor discover in the course of embedding the content that different or additional topics should be addressed, the distribution of competencies may change. This is a positive occurrence because it shows active involvement and ownership of the embedded content on part of the infusing faculty. Therefore, the map should not drive the subsequent integration of EL content by dictating which standards should be addressed or assessed; rather, it should be used as a planning tool for designing the EL-specific course and may contribute to the planning of the eventual assessment system.

The ESL faculty who will be developing the EL-specific courses can use this map to gain a general idea of which standards or competencies may need to be introduced, which ones need to be reinforced in some detail, and which ones can be touched on in less explicit ways because they have already sufficient coverage throughout the program. This information also helps in planning the placement of the EL-specific courses in the course sequence. As will be explained below, this draft curriculum map can initiate questions for assessment system planning. Should the embedded content be integrated into the existing candidate portfolio, or would it make more sense to have a separate collection of artifacts? Are there any existing key assessments that the program collects for quality assurance or state and accreditation reporting to which EL content will be added? Because the EL curricular competencies the institution intends to use have been identified during the early stages of the design phase (as described in chapter 3), the assessment director can request the addition of these competencies into the database of the assessment system.

Development Phase

Figure 4.3 depicts the four steps of the development phase. It opens with the concurrent faculty development and the development of the EL content with which each course is enhanced. While this first step demands significant time and labor, and thus takes several months to carry out, the subsequent three steps—the mentor's EL content review, the elaborated curriculum and assessment mapping of the EL-embedded content, and the post-infusion review—are typically completed in quick succession. Once the development phase is completed, the implementation of the embedded content and the EL-specific courses can begin.

Faculty Development and EL-Focused Course Modifications

During the first step of this phase, *faculty development and EL-focused content modification*, collaboration between the teacher preparation faculty and the ESL faculty mentor is highly intensive. We therefore recommend that each ESL faculty mentor conduct a group informational and working session to launch this step. Several identical sessions may need to be held to accommodate the various class schedules of the collaborating

Figure 4.3

The development phase of embedding EL content

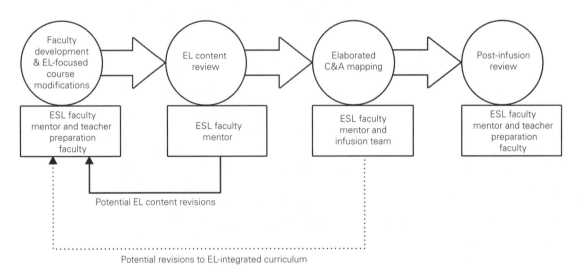

faculty. Because the information shared in group sessions is applicable to all who infuse, the mentor thus economizes the time it would take to meet individually with each faculty member. More importantly, group sessions present an opportunity to foster collaboration among all teacher preparation faculty who are tasked with adding EL content to their courses. The overall layout and sequence of activities in this session consists of four parts: (a) an EL content presentation such as language, language acquisition, or culture that is general enough to present an overview of the topic and applicable to 1+, 2+, and 3+ course content; (b) a brief introduction to the EL Content Description form (appendix 4.b), which individual teacher preparation faculty members complete as they develop EL-embedded content; (c) a semistructured activity during which small groups of faculty first discuss how the presented EL content information could be translated into activities or assignments in a course of their choosing and then apply their findings to the EL Content Description form; and (d) a question-and-answer segment that focuses on the general process rather than on specific faculty's courses. In closing out the session, the mentor asks each participant to complete the Follow-Up Request form (appendix 4.c), which is designed to solicit the type and the amount of support teacher preparation faculty think they may need from the ESL mentor at this point. Some faculty view the entire embedding process as part of their own professional growth and duties as course developers and opt to undertake most of this task on their own; others prefer a few sample articles to use as a springboard for building their knowledge base or for potential use in their course; while yet another group of faculty may request more hands-on involvement for the development of the EL-content activity or assignment. The infusion team can use the form to further identify faculty development needs. More importantly, the form restates the ESL mentor's commitment to supporting the teacher preparation faculty in the embedding process while it informs the mentor about each partner's perceived needs to move the project forward. It is obviously vital that the mentor fulfill the requests for assistance in a timely manner.

As busy professionals and experienced learners, many faculty prefer to work through professional development material at their own pace. This can be accommodated through online modules and individualized reading lists. However, in the spirit of creating a collaborative environment in which teacher preparation faculty not only support each other's learning but become thoroughly familiar with how their candidates develop competencies throughout the program, we recommend that small-group meetings be scheduled on a regular basis. We will discuss options for such meetings in chapter 5.

Because coursework that prepares candidates to work with ELs leads to the ultimate practical application during internship, the internship coordinator and at least one clinical faculty member should be involved in these sessions. The shared information and ensuing conversations assist them in mapping out the revision of observation forms and in designing requirements of candidate-created internship documentations, such as lesson plans that include modification for ELs at multiple levels of English proficiency or teacher work samples in which the candidates purposefully reflect on the learning of the ELs within the unit of instruction.

In addition to holding small-group sessions, ESL faculty mentors should maintain frequent formal and informal interactions with each faculty member whom they assist. Formal interactions should be regularly scheduled, with an established agenda that is constructed at the close of each prior meeting. Informal interactions consist of e-mail messages or brief visits to the collaborator's office. Both forms of interaction are intended to move the project forward, but informal check-ins can also be employed to clarify how a specific theory translates into practice in the teacher preparation faculty's discipline, to offer assistance in locating additional resources, or to lend a sympathetic ear.

As previously explained, 2+ and 3+ courses, by definition, require considerably more work on the part of the teacher preparation faculty than 1+ courses. Coaching teacher candidates who have little experience in designing and delivering curriculum and instruction on how to differentiate the curriculum, instruction, and assessment for ELs at multiple levels of English proficiency (we recommend differentiating for beginning, intermediate, and advanced ELs) is no easy task, even for a seasoned ESL specialist. Therefore, the mentor has to make extra efforts to provide continued, tailored support to the 2+ and 3+ course faculty as they develop knowledge and skills in using and modeling instructional strategies that make content comprehensible to ELs and move their academic language development forward.

EL Content Review

The purpose of this second step is quality control of the embedded content. Depending on individual work schedules and the category of course that teacher preparation faculty infuse, the completed EL Content Description forms are typically turned in over an extended period of time. As each form arrives, the mentor conducts an *EL content review* of the course elements that contain the added EL content, evaluating the readings or other content information, activities and/or assignments for breadth and depth. Appendix 4.d contains the EL Content Evaluation form designed for this task. Our proposed minimal requirements of added course elements, which are highlighted in table 3.1, are a determining factor of the evaluation. Other criteria are: whether the EL-focused readings or other materials is current and whether this information supports the meaningful application of the content based on the course category. For example, if the EL-focused article in a 2+ course concentrates on cultural differences in immigrant populations, then candidates would not have adequate guidance for adapting curriculum, instruction, and assessment for ELs' language proficiency levels. The mentor either approves the integrated EL content and assigns the appropriate EL curricular competencies, or requests revisions of the course elements that fall short. If revisions are required, the ESL mentor should return the form to the teacher preparation faculty in person and discuss specific areas that need improvement. As always, an offer to assist the collaborating partner in this task is advised.

The arrow in figure 4.3 that leads from the EL content review step back to the EL-focused course modification step is a solid line to indicate that revisions are highly likely to be needed. This happens mostly with 2+ and 3+ category courses, given the added complexity of application of the EL-focused content. Once the embedded elements are revised, the mentor completes a new evaluation form. As the courses containing the new EL focus are approved and EL curricular competencies assigned, the preliminary curriculum map is adjusted to reflect the changes. We recommend that different colors be used to identify those courses whose EL content has been approved, those that are undergoing revisions, and those in which EL content embedding has not yet been completed. This color coding helps the infusion team to keep track of the progress.

Ideally, a representative sample of clinical supervisors would field-test the revised internship observation forms at the beginning of step two. Since none of the candidates placed in internship during this time have taken any of the embedded courses, arrangements should be made for a number of observations to take place in mainstream classrooms of practicing teachers who have at least one EL. This field-test can help determine if the revised forms allow for meaningful assessment of the differentiated instructional practices the institution would like their candidates to exhibit once the EL infusion is completed and fully implemented. If the clinical faculty are not satisfied with the findings, additional revisions to the observation protocol need to be made, just as revisions to the EL-embedded content in courses may be necessary.

Elaborated Curriculum and Assessment Mapping

As soon as the first few EL-infused courses are approved and the associated EL curricular competencies are assigned, the third step, compilation of summaries of the EL-embedded content for each course, can begin. A separate summary based on the information provided in the EL Content Description forms should be completed for each activity and each assignment in the course, as the two do not necessarily address the same competencies. Figure 4.4 depicts the shell of such a summary. These summaries expand the preliminary curriculum map into an *elaborated curriculum and assessment map*. It is important to note that when the infusion team members review the final curriculum map, after all modifications to courses have been evaluated as meeting the minimum requirements of EL content infusion, they may discover that coverage of individual standards or EL curricular competencies is too concentrated or lacking. This finding may necessitate additional modifications from some course faculty; for example, if there is too much coverage of some competencies, the infusion team can tell the developers of one or two courses with multiple assessments that they may take out one of the overage assessments. In the case of insufficient coverage, the infusion team members need to decide whether it is reasonable to request certain faculty to address the missing competency by making a change that would result in a different activity or assignment (going back to step one), or whether the EL-specific course(s) could fill the gaps. This potential revision, because it is less likely to occur, is expressed by the dashed appearance of the arrow line in figure 4.2. With the distribution of curricular competencies across the program confirmed, the objectives of the EL-specific course can be finalized, and the EL faculty can begin course development in earnest.

Figure 4.4

EL content summary

Course element	Description
EL curricular competency(ies)	
EL-focused information, instructional materials, or media	
Activity or assignment objective	Activity: Assignment:
Activity or assignment description	Activity: Assignment:
Official assessment artifact?	_____ Yes _____ No

Post-Infusion Review

In the forth and final step of embedding EL content, the ESL faculty mentor performs a brief check of the infused syllabus with the teacher preparation faculty to ensure that all elements listed in the elaborated curriculum and assessment map are also represented in the syllabus. Together they look for evidence that the embedded EL content is explicitly stated in objectives, topics, standards, readings or other informational materials, activities and/or assignment descriptions, and assessments. The intent of this *post-infusion review* is twofold. First, the detailed record of EL-embedded course elements in the syllabus serves as a reminder to the faculty that the new content is indeed an integral part of the course, reducing the likelihood that its coverage is overlooked. Second, this step facilitates quality control and documentation in view of accreditation and program approval. National bodies and specialized professional associations that grant program accreditation and state departments of education that grant initial or continued program approval typically require significant documentary evidence that standards and curricular competencies are being met. The detailed matrices composed of content summaries and syllabus descriptions greatly aid compilation of documentation for program coordinators and those responsible for program assessment reporting.

With the embedded elements developed and approved, the EL-specific courses developed and going through the institution's curriculum approval process, the infusion team can turn its attention to the final phases of infusing the curriculum.

Implementation and Evaluation

After investing extensive efforts in designing and developing the EL-embedded content, many faculty are eager to roll out the modified course. While, to a large extent, their work is done, the infusion team has to ensure that the implementation runs as smoothly as possible. It also has to finalize procedures and/or policies, and look toward the evaluation of the infusion effort.

Implementation

Faculty who embed the EL content into their courses need not wait until the EL-infused curriculum is included in a new catalog year before implementing the modified course discussions, activities, and/or assignments. As discussed in chapter 3, implementing the full program can take several semesters. Indeed, a gradual rollout as each course is infused is warranted for several reasons. From an administrative point of view, offering separate sections of EL-embedded courses for those candidates who start their studies under the newly approved program and for those who are already on their way to graduation is not practical. More important, although the candidates who are going to graduate from the old program will not have the benefit of the full picture of working with ELs, they will at least have an opportunity to gain some knowledge and skills that would otherwise have been altogether absent.

The transition time is likely to extend several semesters into the official start of the new EL-embedded program, especially in programs that do not use a cohort system where all candidates take the same courses at the same time. Provisions should be made for the level of performance in EL-focused assignments expected of the candidates who have not gone through the prerequisite courses after infusion. Additionally, the infusion team should coordinate the dissemination of information regarding the EL infusion to candidates, teacher preparation faculty, and staff through targeted newsletters and question-and-answer sheets as well as handbooks.

When the embedded EL content is delivered for the first time, we recommend that the ESL faculty mentor be present. The level of involvement of the mentor will depend on teacher preparation faculty preference. Some faculty members prefer to introduce the content on their own, even if they supply it through a lecture rather than through a print or media resource. In this case, the ESL faculty mentor would be present to assist in the class discussion, adding comments or responding to questions only if the faculty requests assistance in form of coteaching. Other faculty favor observing the ESL faculty model the lecture and discussion during the first semester before they assume responsibility the next time the course is offered. In terms of evaluating assignments, we also recommend collaborative sessions during which the ESL faculty mentor and the teacher preparation faculty member discuss the depth of the candidates' products, closing the instructional design loop of the embedded content.

Candidate input obtained during the implementation phase can assist the instructor in assessing how the content was received, opening space for reflection on whether the first delivery achieved the intent of the discussion, activity, and /or assignment. This information can be gathered through a brief questionnaire administered to the candidates at the end of the EL-focused module or semester. Areas to investigate could include the candidates' knowledge of ELs and beliefs about ELs and their responsibility to teach ELs before and after the EL module, as well as the most important points about the EL content addressed in the course that the candidates took away. A sample four-question student questionnaire can be found in Meskill's description of the embedding process at the University of Albany.[19] In addition to providing data for the purpose of formative evaluation to be used for the next delivery of the embedded content, the collected data can also be useful for scholarship for those teacher preparation faculty who engage in inquiry and self-reflection during the EL infusion process.

Evaluation

As described in chapter 3, infusing teacher preparation programs with EL content entails processes at both the macro and the micro level. The content embedding process that has been the topic of this chapter can be examined in terms of: (a) the process, and (b) the product, or outcome. In view of the current climate of accountability and measures of institutional effectiveness, we focus here on the outcome of candidate knowledge, skills, and beliefs and describe a system designed to facilitate stability in the delivery of the created EL-infused curriculum.

Assessment System

Outcome data on the effectiveness of the embedded EL content can easily be gathered through established candidate assessment systems that are designed to show mastery of institutional, state, and national competencies and standards. In those course assignments that already contribute data to measure program effectiveness in form of key assessments, the added EL focus necessitates the addition of at least one evaluative criterion aligned with the associated EL curricular competencies. To obtain a full view of program effectiveness, however, additional assessments will likely need to be added. Questions the infusion team and the person responsible for the assessment system have to consider include, but are not limited to:

- What is the purpose of the assessment system related to the EL-infused curriculum? Is its purpose accountability regarding internal or external credentialing? Is it intended for accreditation purposes to show candidate attainment of knowledge, skills, and dispositions and efforts of continuing improvement? Is it designed for internal measures of quality control?
- Which EL-embedded assignments are most suited for the purpose of demonstrating growth in candidate knowledge and skills or change in dispositions over time?
- Will the candidates be required to compile a separate portfolio from that currently required for graduation in which they focus on the EL-embedded content?
- How many data points are necessary to show solid grounding in the planning and delivery of instruction for ELs?

Institutional context obviously drives the details of the assessment system. However, we suggest that candidates who obtain a credential at the end of their program, whether an institutional stamp of EL-qualified or a state-approved credential, should be required to assemble a portfolio. The portfolio, in binder form or, preferably, in electronic format, should show a candidate's gradual progression toward becoming an effective teacher of ELs and contain proof of EL content mastery through a collection of artifacts produced in EL-focused assignments, as well as cumulative reflections at established benchmark points in the program. As with portfolios that many institutions already require, the EL portfolio can be showcased by candidates interviewing for a teaching position. Possessing evidence of experience in planning and delivering curriculum, instruction, and assessment to address the needs of ELs in states that currently do not require any EL qualifications makes the candidate stand out among a pool of applicants who have not completed an EL-infused teacher preparation program. Table 4.1 offers a summary of the instructional design cycle tasks for embedding EL content into the teacher preparation courses described earlier in this chapter.

The Dangers of Slippage

The return on investment expended in form of financial resources, time effort, and human capital that goes into the EL infusion effort throughout every phase of the embedding process can quickly diminish and eventually become meaningless if no provisions for maintaining program quality are made. The greatest danger to program quality is through *slippage*—EL-focused content that is no longer delivered as it was developed and appears in the curriculum map. Slippage can occur for several reasons. The most common "culprit" is a teacher preparation faculty member's desire to improve a course. Teachers often make adjustments, either in substantive fashion by undertaking a general overhaul of the content or, more commonly, in more subtle ways when changing informational material or tweaking activities, assignments, and assessments. Often this tweaking takes place over several semesters. Even minor changes in EL-focused elements, however, especially when they happen repeatedly, may have the unintended consequence that the original intent and purpose of the content is no longer met. Therefore, institutions should develop a policy that whenever faculty who teach EL-embedded courses want to make changes, they have to first consult with the ESL coordinator who is responsible for program integrity.

Several potential triggers for slippage are related to personnel. First, if the teacher preparation faculty member who originally infused the course is replaced by someone who does not possess the theoretical knowledge and practical skills of working with of ELs, the embedded EL content cannot be effectively delivered. To prevent this from happening, the institution has to institute policies for faculty development.

Slippage also stems from individual instructors making changes to the EL-embedded activities and assessments. For example, a new faculty member who, unfamiliar with the EL-infused curriculum but who may possess the necessary knowledge and skills related to the EL content, might decide to modify the EL-focused content to better fit his or her teaching style. Similar danger exists with multisection courses that have a generic syllabus but are taught by a number of full- and part-time faculty members who were not involved with the embedding process or who are unfamiliar with the EL-infused curriculum. Such changes result in uneven coverage of the EL curricular competencies; some candidates receive the EL content as planned, while others receive different coverage or none at all. Again, institutional policies need to be implemented to keep this from taking place.

At the University of Central Florida, we have created an online curriculum map that is intended to prevent slippage of the EL content. The map resembles a traditional matrix that lists the courses in the program along the top row and the ESOL

Table 4.1

ADDIE at the micro-level: Infusion of individual components of teacher preparation programs—EL-embedded courses

Component	Analyze	Evaluate	Design	Evaluate	Develop	Evaluate	Implement	Evaluate
EL-specific courses	Review faculty needs assessment completed during macro level analysis	Infusion team members participate in continuous evaluation, as described in Table 3.3	Determine standards or EL curricular competencies for each program	Infusion team members evaluate the EL-embedded courses' preliminary EL content across all program courses	Offer group and individualized faculty development linked to embedded content of each course	Infusion team members evaluate breadth and depth of embedded EL content across program curricula	Co-teach and co-evaluate embedded EL content the first semester and keep reflections on outcome	Review faculty reflections
			Review program syllabi for course category to match mentors to teacher preparation faculty		Follow up on any requests for EL content resources or support		Collect candidate evaluations of EL content	Review candidates' evaluations
			Draft suggestions for topics, objectives, and assessments with EL connections in syllabi		Review teacher preparation faculty's EL content description		Monitor student reflections and field and clinical partners' correspondence	Review reflections and correspondence
			Hold initial consultations between mentors and teacher preparation faculty		Revise EL content as necessary		Monitor student progress and adjust instruction as needed	Review grade distribution and number of attempts to meet the assessment criteria
			Establish procedures for embedded field and clinical experiences with ELs		Adjust preliminary curriculum map to ensure that curricular competencies are well addressed and assessed		Track candidate assessments in portfolio	Review candidate assessment data for attainment of curricular competencies
			Plot embedded content on preliminary curriculum map		Revise field/clinical experience forms to include EL focus			Based on all evaluations completed (all of the above), adjust EL content, assessments, and delivery
			Launch faculty development		Complete elaborated curriculum map			
					Adjust EL content for adequacy in addressing and assessing curricular competencies			
					Begin EL-specific course development			
					Complete post infusion review of course syllabi			

performance standards vertically in the first column. However, instead of the traditional "X" placed at the intersection of courses and assigned standards that represent an EL-focused assessment, there is a hyperlink that takes the user to a new page holding the assignment summaries for that particular course. This detailed map is a recent addition to our toolbox for disseminating EL infusion information to our faculty and teacher candidates. We have made it publicly accessible at http://www.esolinfusion/org both as a resource for other institutions that look to infuse their programs with EL content and to actively prevent the issue of slippage.

In our depiction of the EL content embedding process, we referred on several occasions to the need for teacher preparation faculty development in EL content. The content for, amount of content needed, and modes of delivery, as well as resources for faculty development, are described in chapter 5.

Appendix 4.a

EL Content Consultation Form

EL Content Consultation

Faculty Name: _____ Date of Meeting: _____

E-mail:_____ Mentor Name: _____

Course Prefix & #:_____ Course Title: _____

Degree programs that require this course:_____

****

Does this course require candidates to develop or implement any instructional:

Materials	_____ Yes _____ No
Plans	_____ Yes _____ No
Activities	_____ Yes _____ No
Assessments	_____ Yes _____ No
Demonstration	_____ Yes _____ No

If any of the above apply, does this course require candidates to develop or implement instructional materials, plans, activities, demonstrations, and/or assessments in the area of Language Arts/Literacy?

_____ Yes _____ No

Course Category: _____ 1+ _____ 2+ _____ 3+

Complete the appropriate pages for 1+ <u>or</u> 2+ and 3+ courses.

Note follow-up steps on last page.

1+ course syllabus

1. Is there at least one objective and/or a topic that explicitly links to EL-specific information identified?

Yes	*No*
Specify objective(s) and/or topic(s):	Suggested natural connection with course to objective(s) and/or topic(s):

2. Is there a Reading or a Content Presentation that provides EL-specific information identified?

Yes	No
Check material or media of EL-specific information: ____ Journal article ____ Textbook ____ Video content ____ Web Content ____ Instructor lecture/presentation ____ Guest lecture/presentation ____ Other Specify checked material or media of EL-specific information (URL, bibliographical information, etc.):	Suggested keywords for locating EL-specific information, suggested sources, and/or suggested EL-specific material or media:

3. Is there an activity and/or an assignment that connects to the EL-specific information described?

Yes	No
Specify activity(ies) or assignment(s):	Suggested activity(ies) or assignment(s):

4. Is there an assessment of mastery of EL-specific information based on activity and/or assignment?

Yes	No
Specify assessment(s)(check all that apply): ____ Reflective paper ____ Quiz/test ____ Presentation ____ Project ____ Research paper/article review ____ Field-based observation notes ____ Other (specify)	Suggested assessment(s):

5. Potential EL curricular competencies:

    a. _____

    b. _____

    c. _____

    d. _____

Appendix 4.b

EL Content Description Form

EL Content Description

Faculty Name: _____   Mentor Name: _____

Course Prefix & #:_____   Course Title: _____

Course Category: ___ 1+ ___ 2+ ___ 3+

****

1. Please describe how the activity and/or the assignment connects to the course (e.g., objective(s), topic(s)).

   _____

   _____

2. Please list the objective(s) of each activity and/or assignment.

   _____

   _____

3. Is the EL-focused information and assignment provided as a stand-alone online module?

   _____ Yes _____ No

a. Please indicate how the EL-focused information is provided to the candidates:

   _____ Journal article _____ Textbook _____ Video content

   _____ Web content   _____ Instructor lecture/presentation

   _____ Guest lecture/presentation   _____ Other (specify)

   _____

b. Please specify the content of *each* EL-focused information (attach text/content or give link to source, if applicable):

   _____ Copy of text (article, textbook) attached   _____ URL:

   _____ Detailed description of content (if presentation/guest lecture):

   _____

   _____

4. Please describe how the EL-focused information is applied in the activity(ies) and/ or the assignment(s). (The description should be sufficiently specific for the mentor to evaluate the depth of EL-content application. Include the instructions to students/ formal activity description if desired.)

   _____

   _____

_____

_____

5. Please describe how the EL-focused information in the activity(ies) and/or the assignment(s) is assessed. (Attach rubric, where appropriate).

_____

_____

_____

_____

6. Please provide any other information that would assist the mentor in evaluating the EL-focused course elements.

_____

_____

_____

_____

Appendix 4.c

Follow-Up Request Form

Follow-Up Request

Faculty Name: _____   E-mail:_____

Course Prefix & #:_____   Course Title: _____

Best days & times to meet: _____

****

Please note the type of assistance you most need from your ESL mentor:

_____ Professional readings on SLA, teaching ELs for my own background building;
Specify _____

_____ Possible resources (information, material, readings) for use with my teacher candidates;
Specify _____

_____ Activity or assignment development;
Specify _____

ML_

Appendix 4.d
EL Content Evaluation Form

EL Content Evaluation

Faculty Name: _____ Mentor Name: _____
Course Prefix & #:_____ Course Title: _____
Course Category: Course Category: _____ 1+ _____ 2+ _____ 3+

****

1. How many topics and/or objectives does the modified syllabus contain?
       _____ 1 _____ 2 _____ 3 _____ 4+

===> Is this sufficient for the category of course?   _____Yes _____No

2. How many EL-focused information, instructional materials, or media does the modified syllabus contain?
       _____ 1 _____ 2 _____ 3 _____ 4+

===> Is this sufficient for the category of course?   _____Yes _____No
===> Is the information current?   _____Yes _____No

3. How many activities with assessments does the modified syllabus contain?
       _____ 1 _____ 2 _____ 3 _____ 4+

===> Is this sufficient for the category of course?*   _____Yes _____No
===> Is each activity linked to information identified?   _____Yes _____No
===> Does each activity allow for meaningful application of
       the information by the candidate?   _____Yes _____No

4. How many assignments with assessment does the modified syllabus contain?
       _____ 1 _____ 2 _____ 3 _____ 4+

===> Is this sufficient for the category of course?*   ____Yes _____No
===> Is each assignment linked to information identified?   ____Yes _____No
===> Does each activity allow for meaningful application of
       the information by the candidate?   ____Yes _____No

Based on the EL embedded elements, the following EL curricular competencies about ELs apply:

_____
_____
_____
_____

*1+ courses must contain either an activity or an assignment. 2+ courses must contain at least one of each, 3+ courses must contain at least one activity and several assignments with assessments.

CHAPTER 5

Faculty Development

In chapter 4 we described the process of embedding EL content, which runs concurrently with faculty development. In this chapter we consider the time requirements, content, and options for providing the content. We also provide resources ESL faculty mentors can offer their colleagues who are embedding their courses, either for their own learning or for consideration as the EL-focused instructional information, material, or media that serve as the springboard for activities and assignments.

Considerations for Faculty Development

Following instructional design principles, faculty development for EL infusion starts with an analysis of the situation. A number of key questions focus the analysis, such as: What is the information to be provided? Who needs to receive the information? Who puts the training together? What delivery options are available? Responses to these and other questions guide the design, development, implementation, and evaluation phases of the faculty development. The answer to the first question is evident. Teacher preparation faculty tasked with embedding the EL content during the EL infusion project must themselves be informed about the theories and best practices they will be adding to their existing courses. Although teacher preparation institutions are increasingly sensitive to the need to incorporate EL issues into all programs, these additions typically take place in initial certification programs. Terminal degree programs that prepare for the professoriate in teacher preparation focus on specialization in various disciplines, with little or no coursework in or focused studies of EL content. Furthermore, many teacher educators, especially if their prior preK–12 experience took place in an area with few ELs, may have had little or no practical experience in working with this population. Therefore, before designing the content of the faculty development effort, the infusion team must first determine the needs of the teacher preparation faculty as a whole.

None of the published reports on EL infusion contain samples of needs assessments conducted with their participants. However, Levine and Howard, conducting research on their infusion effort at the University of Connecticut, describe two versions of a self-efficacy instrument designed to elicit the perceptions of their teacher preparation faculty and their candidates' knowledge, skills, and beliefs to teach ELs.[1] Our colleagues at Miami University developed a multisection needs assessment. The first part comprises eleven questions designed to elicit the teacher preparation faculty members' familiarity with EL content such as levels of English language proficiency, Ohio's

English language proficiency standards, cultural issues, and theories and research on bilingual language and literacy development. A second section contains fourteen items derived from Woolfolk-Hoy's Teachers' Sense of Efficacy scale but tailored to reflect the EL focus.[2] Finally, the instrument contains an eleven-question section on attitudes and beliefs regarding immigrants and U.S. societal norms, the added value of immigrants and refugees to American schools and society, and the use of heritage language, among others. This assessment, which was developed to determine faculty development needs for ESOL MIAMI, has since been adapted for use with teacher candidates, including aspiring school leaders, in furtherance of research on the effectiveness of the EL-embedded content.[3]

While such assessments furnish important information on faculty's differing knowledge about ELs and SLA and their self-efficacy reports regarding preparing candidates for teaching ELs, it is not the sole source of information for determining how faculty learning should be constructed. The One Plus model's framework for faculty development can be illustrated with the following formula:

EL infusion faculty development = Time considerations +
Content considerations +
Delivery considerations

Each factor is now explained in detail.

Time Considerations

In Florida, where the preparation of preservice teachers to teach ELs is highly prescriptive (see chapter 2), faculty development in EL content is equally regulated. The state requires all faculty who teach EL-infused courses, regardless of the types of courses they teach, to fulfill a minimum of forty-five contact hours surveying the five areas required for the ESOL endorsement.[4] However, we believe that a one-size-fits-all approach to faculty development does not adequately prepare all faculty to teach the EL content in the embedded courses.

Institutions that adopt the One Plus model to infuse programs have to consider two factors when designing faculty development: the knowledge of EL topics along the 1+, 2+, 3+ course continuum and the number of embedded elements required for each course category. All faculty require the background knowledge of the content addressed in the 1+ course category, but faculty who teach 2+ and 3+ courses need to acquire increasingly specialized knowledge of what instructing ELs in academic content areas entails. The stackable nature of knowledge required at each of the three course categories in the One Plus model is represented in table 5.1.

The increasing number of elements with an EL focus in the progression from 1+ to 3+ courses (see table 3.1) directly impacts the workload for the teacher preparation faculty who embed EL content at each of these levels. Adding an EL focus to multiple course topics, most course activities, and most course assignments and assessments related to instruction or assessment for teaching language arts or literacy (3+ course), is obviously much more time consuming than infusing a 1+ course with one or more

Table 5.1

Suggested distribution of faculty development hours

Faculty development components	1+ Course	2+ Course	3+ Course
Launch event	√	√	√
Group sessions (1+ level information)	√	√	√
Group sessions (2+ level information)		√	√
Group sessions (3+ level information)			√
Mentor discussions (including initial consultation)	Approximately 3-4 hours	Approximately 8–10 hours	Approximately 12–15 hours
Individualized learning (including embedding of EL content)	Approximately 5–6 hours	Approximately 12–14 hours	Approximately 18–20 hours
Approximate total hours of faculty development	20–25	40–45	60–65

EL-focused reading or media element followed up with an EL-focused activity or assignment. Furthermore, the 3+ course instructor must acquire sufficient knowledge of the English learner, effective general instructional practices in differentiating instruction for ELs at multiple levels of English proficiency, and teaching language arts and literacy to ELs before embedding the required elements can even commence. The efforts faculty expend to develop the necessary background knowledge to embed EL content and the actual development of the content vary depending on the instructor's prior knowledge and practical experience. Consequently, these factors impact the number of hours needed for individualized learning and the amount of time spent in discussions with the ESL mentor. The range of hours needed for these two components in the faculty development effort, as well as the approximate total hours invested for each course category are also shown in table 5.1.

As professionals, those who prepare teacher candidates continuously engage in professional development by attending conferences, conducting research, and interacting with school district personnel within their discipline. The fact that faculty development is necessary for an infusion project to reach its intended goal is indisputable. However, it is done within a short but intensive period of time and forces the faculty to navigate unfamiliar territory. Subject matter experts in ESL and second language acquisition should be cognizant of the fact that colleagues from other fields do not share ESL experts' fascination with and enthusiasm for their discipline, and faculty are terribly busy with their own disciplinary obligations as well as institutional demands on their time, such as participation in faculty governance. They should not be discouraged by teacher preparation faculty's giving priority to tasks other than embedding their courses with EL content. It is, however, important that those leading the infusion efforts avoid giving the impression that this task is one more institutional request for information or nothing more than checking off evidence of compliance with external regulations.

Conversely, the process should not be perceived as an endless series of discussions that don't lead to any stable outcomes.

Content Considerations

The ESL community is building consensus regarding the knowledge, skills, and dispositions teachers should possess to engage ELs with the content of their lessons and the general curriculum. We described various standards and broad topics identified by professional organizations and expert panels in chapter 3. Because EL-infused programs are designed to develop these competencies in their teacher candidates, teacher preparation faculty should also develop them.

Our experience suggests that topics for faculty development be organized according to course category. For 1+ courses, which typically focus on the learner and learning context, for 2+ courses, which typically focus on planning and implementing curriculum, instruction and assessment in general or in specific academic subjects, and for 3+ courses, which typically focus on planning and implementing curriculum, instruction and assessment in language arts and literacy, we offer the following suggested topics:

1+ courses
- SLA
- EL legal issues
- EL program options, including instructional models
- EL cultural issues and acculturation
- EL policy issues
- EL family issues
- EL exceptional education issues
- EL demographics
- EL support services

2+ courses: 1+ course topics and
- Content-based instruction
- Specific content area research and best practices for ELs
- Curricular adaptations for ELs by English proficiency level
- Instructional modifications for ELs by English proficiency level
- Assessment accommodations for ELs by English proficiency level
- Academic language demands

3+ courses: 2+ course topics and
- Interlanguage data analysis
- Common phonological, morphological, semantic/lexical, and syntactic development patterns
- First language/second language contrasts for major EL first languages and English
- Contrastive rhetoric
- Differences and commonalities in first language/second language reading and in first language/second language writing
- Error correction in SLA

Delivery

When the Florida Department of Education started to require the forty-five hours of faculty development in the five areas of the ESOL endorsement, institutions were allowed to choose how they would deliver the content. Faculty could complete the traditional coursework or acquire the knowledge by attending colloquia or workshops, engaging in field experiences, watching videotaped modules, participating in team planning and coteaching with ESL faculty, or any combination thereof. Reports from infusion efforts in New York, Connecticut, and Massachusetts describe some of the same options and also portray the formation of faculty learning communities in which some of the content was acquired through joint readings of professional literature, followed by a series of deep conversations among the participants.[5]

As we explained in chapter 4, we see the collaborative relationship between the ESL faculty mentor (or ESL expert consultant) and each teacher preparation faculty member as an essential component of faculty development. The mentor not only makes the content available through a variety of delivery options, but acts as resource by providing guidance in the development of EL-embedded course elements. Faculty development should consist of a launch event, followed by a combination of group sessions, individual discussion meetings, and individualized learning. We believe that this combination of learning opportunities enables the faculty to engage in a dialogue that can lead to a meaningful and sustainable infused program.

The Launch Event

The purpose of the launch event, which takes approximately half a day, is to bring together all teacher preparation faculty whose courses are part of the program to be infused.[6] It is important for the dean of the college or the director of the school and department chairs to be present, to demonstrate administrative support. The adopted infusion model (specifically program outcomes), the 1+2+3+ course framework, and the minimum required course elements for each course category should be explained so that all faculty have a clear understanding of the institution's vision of the end result.[7] Another central component of the launch event is providing participants with a general overview of what working with ELs entails. We have found that a simulation that puts the faculty in the situation of a language learner who is expected to comprehend academic content instruction in an unfamiliar language is an effective way to start out.[8] By demonstrating a social studies lesson in, for example, Swiss-German, while employing very few strategies to make the content comprehensible, the teacher preparation faculty find themselves in the position of ELs in mainstream classrooms where the teacher is not prepared to support their learning. After a second pass of the lesson, this time facilitating general understanding of the content through rich verbal and nonverbal support, the participants discuss their feelings of the two experiences and compare the two instructional practices. In the final part of the launch event, the infusion team announces the matching of the ESL mentors with their group of faculty, and some time should be spent in the individual groups. This small-group session presents a good opportunity to determine each member's course category and to start building the group identity.

Group Sessions

Periodic group sessions introduce the faculty to the content consideration topics listed above. They enable the ESL mentors to use their time efficiently, since all faculty benefit from the same information.[9] Faculty members' teaching schedules shape the frequency and duration of the times the majority of the group members can meet. If there is relatively little overlap in members' course schedules and only short meetings are possible, more frequent sessions will need to be scheduled. Shorter meetings may also mean that the faculty complete reading assignments prior to each session.

Although the number of topics addressed in each session can vary, we recommend that the initial session include a general overview of what makes working with ELs different from working with native English speaking students before the first topic is treated. Thereafter, we suggest that each group session contain a presentation of content, followed by ample time for the teacher preparation faculty to discuss how this information applies to their respective disciplines. Faculty with some background in ESL or prior experience teaching ELs present a valuable resource here, as they can share stories and talk about how they overcame perceived hurdles. If at all possible, time should be allocated for faculty to work on their infusion activities in pairs or small groups. During this time, the ESL mentor can be available to answer specific questions. These small-group segments can be fruitful for the production of scholarship, as faculty may discover commonalities across their courses or discipline that they could further investigate through research. Following instructional design principles, each group session should conclude with a brief questionnaire that gives participants a chance to reflect on what they understood well enough to apply it to their embedding activities and what they would like to see expanded on or have reinforced, either through additional reading material or a personal conversation with the ESL mentor. We suggest that the infusion team arrange for videotaping of the group sessions for those faculty members who miss a session. Furthermore, some of the information in this video archive might be converted into self-paced, online learning modules to support ongoing development for adjunct faculty who start to teach embedded courses after the original faculty development and infusion process are completed.

Individual Meetings

Individual discussion meetings offer the opportunity to move from the general view of the faculty development topics to the specific view of how the information connects with the faculty member's course. They also help move the project forward. The items on the agenda depend greatly on the faculty member's motivation. When working with highly motivated partners, the ESL faculty mentor can supply additional resources or critique early drafts of the infused activities or assignments. Alternatively, the ESL mentor may need to prime each step to keep the embedding process moving forward while keeping less-motivated faculty members engaged at a level appropriate to their commitment to infusing—perhaps by supplying a small set of preselected articles or creating first drafts of embedded assignments that teacher preparation faculty can tweak and make their own. Such help may also be applicable for those who are overwhelmed with too many tasks and too little time. For the ESL mentor working with faculty between these extremes, offering an increasing amount of ready-made content for approval or adaptation can facilitate positive results. In all cases, the mentor's goal is to obtain the broadest participation of faculty while supporting the most substantial contribution that each individual can dedicate to the process, and individual discussion meetings lend themselves very well to this outcome.

Independent Learning

The faculty development activity that rounds out the package is independent learning. It is perhaps the most important component, in that it encompasses both the deepening of the knowledge gained through group sessions and individual meetings and the application of the new knowledge and skills through the development of the EL-embedded activities, assignments, and assessments. Despite its importance, however, it is also the component that allows for the most freedom for both ESL mentor and faculty member. Independent learning, which is largely self-directed, should be tailored to the individual's needs and background. For instance, a 3+ course faculty member whose formal preparation includes some coursework in linguistics does not need to relearn this content through self-study. Instead, this person and the mentor can hold conversations of how phonological or morphological patterns in English connect to developing language skills in mainstream classrooms, and move on to the next topic. The more extensive the prior formal training or the practical experience is, the smaller the need for independent learning, which also reduces the total number of hours of faculty development needed.[10]

Independent learning is also impacted by personal motivation. A motivated faculty member is likely to embrace this mode and use it as an opportunity to engage the ESL mentor and colleagues in rich discussions. Less-motivated individuals can be supported and nudged along by the ESL mentor's suggestions of materials for reflection. Sample activities for this mode can include viewing available online resources such as the ones on the TAPESTRY website (see appendices 5.a and 5.b), reading research on any of the topics linked to their course category, visiting schools to observe ELs in mainstream classrooms, or producing a manuscript on teaching a specific academic subject to ELs. Since independent learning leads to engagement with discipline-specific information and practices, it is closely linked to the individual discussion meetings. Insights gained through reading articles or viewing online resources, whether they were discovered by the faculty member or suggested by the ESL mentor, can form the basis for many fruitful discussions, and the consulted resources may end up being used as the informational material on which an EL-focused activity or assignment is constructed.

Evidence of Faculty Engagement

Some institutions may opt to keep records of the faculty members' engagement in various aspects of acquiring knowledge and skills about teaching ELs and infusing their courses. Such record keeping may be prompted by: (a) a mandate that requires it, as is the case in Florida; (b) whether the infusion effort is funded through sources that expect such measures of accountability; or (c) whether detailed documentation is simply part of the infusing institution's culture. Whatever the reason, and whatever the required level of formality, we recommend that the infusion team put into place a system whereby the ESL faculty mentor and the teacher preparation faculty members can track progress toward the end goal. This system may consist of an agreement that lists dates by which various components of the faculty development should be completed and when drafts or final versions of the EL-embedded course are expected to be delivered.[11] As each part of the agreement is fulfilled, the ESL mentor confirms progress toward the agreed-on outcome.

Resources for Faculty Development

As we argued in chapters 3 and 4, all teacher educators already possess solid grounding in learning theory, child development, as well as instructional practices. The EL content they need to acquire through faculty development to embed their courses builds on this knowledge base. We believe that the use of textbooks designed to be used in an EL-specific course for faculty development purposes is inappropriate as these books typically include detailed descriptions of the type of knowledge our peers already possess. While there are excellent professional texts on individual topics related to ELs available, no textbook of the EL content to be infused throughout teacher preparation has been written for teacher educators. Therefore, EL infusion teams need to design the content for faculty development by assembling professional resources from a variety of sources.

When the Florida State Department of Education mandated the infusion of EL content into its initial teacher preparation programs in the 1990s, the University of South Florida sought and obtained funding from the U.S. Department of Education Office of English Language Acquisition (OELA) to support the professional development of teacher preparation faculty who were tasked with the development and delivery of EL content. As the principal investigator of ESOL TAPESTRY (ESOL Training for All Pre-service Educators Stressing Technology-Based Resources), Joyce Nutta collaborated with leading experts in the field of TESOL to identify and to design flexible professional development options around critical issues regarding the education of ELs in the mainstream classroom.[12] The resulting product was TAPESTRY (http://tapestry. usf.edu), a website dedicated to support EL infusion for teacher preparation programs. The original website has been updated and enhanced with new content over the past few years, mainly with the aid of an OELA National Professional Development grant, ESOL MIAMI, housed at Miami University[13]. It currently contains three main facets: video tutorial modules, web-based and print-based resources, and a multidisciplinary journal. An overview of the main purpose or function of each of these components and a description of content is contained in appendices 5.a, 5.b, and 5.c, respectively.

Making Faculty Development Ongoing and Self-Sustainable

The need for faculty development in view of EL-infused programs does not finish when the infusion project is completed and the new curriculum is implemented. Although the resources expended during the infusion process typically become unavailable when the ESL faculty mentor assumes full teaching duties, personnel changes, as explained in chapter 4 and mentioned above, necessitate the continuing availability of faculty development. Each new faculty member who teaches an infused course has to acquire the knowledge and skills required to teach the embedded content. EL infusion teams should plan for this situation during the infusion project.

One way to sustain development for new faculty is through the creation of online modules that mirror the 1+ 2+ 3+ framework of faculty development. Information provided during the launch event and during group sessions can be converted to text-based tutorials. Suggestions for background reading can be organized by 1+ 2+ 3+ course category content topics and also included in these tutorials. If a regulatory body or the institution requires proof of completion of the faculty development, quizzes or other outcome products, such as reflections, can be aligned with the online tutorials. However, we maintain that face-to-face sessions with an ESL faculty member continue to be necessary so that the EL-focused activities and assignments and the embedded content can be discussed. Ideally, this should happen before the new faculty member teaches the embedded content for the first time, even if all portions of the online tutorials are not completed by that point.[14] Regardless of how far into EL content knowledge building the new faculty member is by the time the embedded content is taught for the first time, we strongly recommend that the ESL expert assists in the delivery. This assistance is even more important in this case than it was with the faculty who originally embedded the content, because the new faculty member is given the embedded content and does not know why it was incorporated in the course in this manner. Since new faculty members teach already-embedded content, they do not need to complete the same total hours of faculty development as those faculty who initially infused the course.[15] However, should they later decide to add an EL-embedded course, possibly as a result of a substantive program revisions that require the design of new courses which have to be embedded, the institution should make provisions for reinstituting more intensive faculty development options.

Pros and Cons of Faculty Development Incentives

If infusion is compulsory, whether through state or institutional mandates, some, or all, of the teacher preparation faculty will need to embed EL content into their courses. When participation is required, there is wide variability in faculty involvement and engagement in embedding their courses. In other cases, institutions may voluntarily begin the process of infusion without a determined outcome, only to find during implementation that the best intentions of teacher preparation faculty were not transformed into meaningful participation resulting in embedded content of substance. This shortcoming in outcome begs the question, what motivates educators to develop the knowledge and skills necessary to expand their course focus to include ELs? If the motivation is not intrinsic, then what sorts of incentives have successfully engaged faculty in the dual process of faculty development and course expansion?

The answers to these questions vary according to the circumstances prompting EL infusion as well as the preferences of faculty called to infuse. No matter the context of infusion, faculty invest time in embedding their courses and developing knowledge and skills related to ELs in their particular discipline. Some will relish the opportunity to learn something new and will be early adopters. Others may have a deep commitment to equity and inclusiveness and will come to view the issue of EL achievement as an area that offers them a new way to put their convictions into action. A certain number will go along with the infusion initiative but will not dedicate the same care and enthusiasm that they reserve for work in their own discipline. They may be willing to do what is expected of everyone, but they seek the easiest, least burdensome route. Alternatively, some faculty may be hesitant to embed EL content into their courses because they are uncomfortable teaching about a topic outside of their expertise. A minority may view the infusion efforts as a form of regulation of their academic freedom and may be passively or openly resistant, especially if the decision to infuse or the process of infusing did not begin in an inclusive or collaborative manner.

Our experiences with faculty from numerous disciplines and with institutions operating with and without a mandate can provide insights into the many options for encouraging faculty to participate in infusion. It would be difficult to find a teacher educator who does not agree in principle that all teacher candidates should be prepared to teach and assess ELs. For this reason, it is paramount to keep that overarching goal constantly visible as the outcome of this collaborative endeavor. When the logistics of infusion tax the optimistic and disaffected alike, a reminder of each individual's crucial contribution to the curricular change can mitigate the propensity to withdraw. As with any shared principle, however, operationalizing it presents both expected and unanticipated difficulties.

Because there are varying levels of engagement in the course-embedding process, different strategies for encouraging faculty to invest their time and talents can be tried. Of course, in most cases intrinsic incentives, extrinsic incentives, or a combination thereof influence faculty engagement, depending on both the individual and the context.

Intrinsic Incentives

Intrinsic incentives involve teacher preparation faculty's perception of the potential for personal and professional advancement and growth inherent in the process or product of infusing and do not lead directly to immediate, tangible returns. They may include, among others, the opportunity to further educational equity and excellence for ELs, professional growth through faculty development in new area (the pleasure and professional advantages of lifelong learning), reinvigorated teaching through new content and presentation, and personal connections with colleagues and associated benefits of collaboration. In addition, intrinsic rewards may also be gained by the individual's expanded perspective of her or his contribution to the teacher preparation curriculum. Many faculty lack the big picture of how their courses fit at a level of detail beyond a list of required courses and their prerequisites for a given degree program. Although this should not be the case, involvement in infusion is the first time some faculty have interacted with colleagues about commonalities and contrasts in their courses. New collaborations on other projects such as grants or academic articles may be the unplanned result of these encounters.

Two forms of potential intrinsic benefits of the process and product of infusion include what Ernest Boyer terms the *scholarship of integration* and the *scholarship of teaching*.[16] As discussed in chapter 3, the philosophical underpinnings of the One Plus model are based on interdisciplinarity—what William Newell refers to as curriculum and instruction that "critically draw upon two or more disciplines and . . . lead to an integration of disciplinary insights."[17] Boyer describes the scholarship of integration as "doing research at the boundaries where fields converge" and advocates for increased attention to this sort of scholarship, which brings faculty together "toward a shared vision of intellectual and social possibilities."[18] This has broad implications for collaborative scholarship regarding ELs' achievement in various school subjects. Whether planned as part of the infusion process or emerging from interactions along the way, interdisciplinary scholarship around ELs holds potential for advancing the knowledge base in multiple disciplines and for improving instruction and assessment for ELs preK–12. Ideally, this sort of integrative scholarship should be encouraged from the onset of an infusion effort, with sufficient resources available to support faculty initiatives. Faculty involvement in this type of interdisciplinary scholarship should also be celebrated and made public as an example of collaborative engagement with issues that impact children in schools.

Similar to the scholarship of integration is the scholarship of teaching and learning, which Huber, Hutchings, and Shulman describe as ranging from formal research design and implementation to action research involving inquiry into one's own classroom practice.[19] They go on to discuss its variations, such as reflection on teaching and learning and cross-disciplinary collaborations. Infusing curricula and embedding courses with EL content is in many ways a cutting-edge approach to instruction at the postsecondary level and merits study and review by the scholarly community. Certainly the literature of the ESL education field as well as of the discipline in which the EL content is embedded would benefit from the publication of new insights into interdisciplinary teaching that infusing prompts. The teacher preparation literature likewise benefits from publishing integrated scholarship. Additionally, in higher education there are numerous publications that focus on the scholarship of teaching and learning from a broad perspective that transcends specific disciplines. These are all appropriate venues for action research by faculty who have reworked their courses to embed a focus on the English learner. A number of publications by faculty in ESL and other disciplines during the past decade point to the benefit of incorporating an action research agenda into infusion efforts.[20] This book, too, is a testament to the value of the scholarship of teaching and learning in the EL infusion process.

Extrinsic Incentives

Institutions can offer extrinsic incentives along with the intrinsic incentives. They should be featured at the outset of the infusion process. Where possible, stipends for completing faculty development can make participants feel that their time is valued. In lieu of monetary compensation, materials or travel may be provided. Similarly, stipends for completing embedded content according to a contract agreed on by the infusion mentor and teacher preparation faculty member can be effective incentives, especially when the institution wants or needs to move the process along as quickly as possible. Not everyone is motivated to complete work in order to receive a check, but this motivation has been very effective with some faculty. For faculty who are interested in taking on infusion more deeply than completing the basic embedding process with a mentor, mini-grants for faculty-proposed projects regarding preparing candidates to teach and assess ELs can be a great incentive for excellence. Faculty have designed projects to support their own intensive second language learning experiences in order to incorporate them into their classes; develop community-based service learning opportunities for candidates to work with immigrant families who are ELs; and use technology in innovative ways to support infusion. Some of these examples and their results can be found in the EL-embedded course summaries presented in chapters 6 through 9.

Most faculty prioritize their time and tasks according to their institution's standards for promotion and tenure and annual review. Perhaps nothing will make the work of EL infusion more important that recognizing it for these important elements of the academic reward system. As the definition of scholarship broadens to include the scholarship of integration and the scholarship of teaching and learning, and to the extent that an institution values innovation and excellence in teaching, the EL infusion process is facilitated. In a higher education report, Braxton, Luckey, and Helland present an inventory of scholarship according to Boyer's four domains, which includes specific scholarly outcomes and publications. They assert that "advancements in knowledge and understanding of the human condition may result from structural, procedural, and incorporation level institutionalization of the scholarships of application, integration, and teaching."[21] They appeal to university presidents, provosts, deans, tenure and promotion committees, and other faculty and administrators to build this form of scholarship into their reward systems. We concur with their argument and extend it to the specific instance of EL infusion, which if supported and valued in academic reward systems can lead to far-reaching impacts not only for individual faculty and the institution, but for the EL community as a whole.

With this chapter, we conclude the presentation of the components of One Plus model and the descriptions of the infusion effort. The next part of the book shows how faculty from four institutions have successfully embedded EL content into their courses in order to prepare their candidates to reach all ELs in mainstream classrooms and in non-instructional settings.

Appendix 5.a

The ESOL TAPESTRY Website: Expert Video Series

Each video tutorial centers on an issue identified by experts as essential to the provision of comprehensive and thoughtful instruction for ELs. The topic is presented by a prominent expert through lecture or interview, or as a workshop. This part, which lasts approximately one hour, is accompanied by either talking points or a PowerPoint slideshow. Each presentation is supplemented by web-based resources that provide the opportunity for in-depth self-study. All modules begin with a pre-viewing activity for brainstorming and activating the prior knowledge of the viewer, and ends with a self-reflective post-viewing activity designed to synthesize and verify and document module completion. The contents of each module at the time of publication are:

First module: "Teacher Education and ESOL" is a lecture by Jodi Crandall and is the recommended introduction to the video tutorials. In this module, Crandall introduces the background and history of various models for preparing teachers to provide effective instruction to language minority students. Additionally, she presents a rationale for including ESL in teacher training programs thereby serving as a good introduction to the EL infusion model.

Second module: Attorney Peter Roos discusses the various programs and legal provisions for the education of language minority students nationwide. He speaks in depth about the Florida Consent Decree and addresses the concerns that universities and teacher training programs have with the infusion process. This module is ideal for those instructors teaching social foundations or school law courses.

Third module: Sandra Fradd discusses the issues surrounding exceptional student education and ESL. She stresses the importance of literacy and providing appropriate instructional assessments and explores how these two issues relate to theoretical perspectives. She provides context for her argument by contrasting the literacy development of two children and the opportunities they are afforded to foster these skills. The cases represent different populations of children: those with and without prior exposure to literacy skills. She stresses the importance of classroom conditions and reaching a diverse student population through the use of technology.

Fourth module: Deborah Short addresses the area of sheltered content instruction for ELs. She gives an overview and explanation the eight components of the Sheltered Instruction Observation Protocol (SIOP) Model: preparation, building of background, comprehensible input, strategies, interaction, practice/application, lesson delivery, and review/assessment. She discusses the benefits of collaboration among educators from different fields of specialization and concludes with information on what teacher candidates need to know in order to provide appropriate and effective instruction for culturally and linguistically diverse students. This tutorial module is ideal for methods courses in math, science, social studies, and literature.

Fifth module: This module is of particular importance for English education faculty members. It focuses on the relationship of the various English language dialects to the teaching of ESL. Walt Wolfram dispels the myths surrounding dialects and ESL that often lead to the discouragement of including dialectal information in programs for ELs. Wolfram instead discusses the benefits of teaching ELs about dialects that they may encounter and provides sample teaching approaches for the teaching of dialect awareness.

Sixth module: Joyce Nutta presents two experiential language activities taught entirely in Italian. Each of the two video modules shows the activities as they were presented to groups of teachers followed by a full screen presentation intended for use in a class or workshop as an immersive experience, where the viewer casts students into the role of a language learner attempting to comprehend text and instruction in a foreign language. Module 1, "L'Arancia" demonstrates strategies for comprehensible instruction, and Module 2, "Buccheri" involves participants in different strategies for comprehending text in a second language.

Seventh module: The module comprises two parts: a lecture on second language literacy by Neil Anderson and a discussion between Anderson and Vassiliki Zygouris-Coe. Anderson's lecture covers the important influences on how ELs learn to read and analyze text, including age, first language literacy, English language proficiency level, and grade level. Anderson and Zygouris-Coe then discuss these factors' impact on literacy skills. They also reveal what mainstream teachers should know to better serve all students in preK–12 mainstream classes.

Eighth module: This module on EL infusion breaks with the original design to provide EL content for faculty development due to the growing need for EL infusion. Joyce Nutta and Carine Strebel first present the One Plus model in a lecture, describing how EL teams continuously zoom in and zoom out to look at the micro and macro aspects of infusing teacher preparation curricula with EL content. Nutta is then joined by Bruce Perry for a discussion on how the One Plus model was adapted for the creation of the Teaching English Language Learners (TELLs) certificate at Miami University.

Ninth module: Currently the most recent video, "EL Assessment Issues" features Jamal Abedi and Florin Mihai who examine testing accommodations for ELs in standardized testing through three increasingly focused lenses. Starting with a general introduction, they provide examples of the most commonly used forms of test accommodations. They then discuss critical issues such as validity and reliability, especially in the comparison of results of ELs based on accommodated versus nonaccommodated assessments. In the third part, they turn their attention to the use of language in testing and associated recommendations for reducing the linguistic load in content area assessments for ELs.

Appendix 5.b
The ESOL TAPESTRY Website: ESOL Resources

As a supplement to the video modules, the ESOL TAPESTRY website also contains a large, routinely updated compilation of web-based and print-based resources relating to the education of ELs. These resources can be used with teacher preparation faculty in constructing theoretical and practical knowledge in EL content and in teacher education courses as instructional information, material, or media. The resources, divided into online resources and print-based resources, are organized by subject area in alphabetical order according to author name in full APA citation format. Icons are placed next to each citation, indicating whether the resource is recommended for faculty development or for use as instructional information or material in EL-embedded courses. Examples of the resources used as EL content in courses can be found in chapters 6 through 9 within the examples of infused course elements.

The categories are:

- Art for English Learners
- Music for English Learners
- Physical Education for English Learners
- Content Area Reading for English Learners
- Early Childhood Education for English Learners
- Language Arts for English Learners
- Literacy Development of English Learners
- Literature for English Learners
- Math for English Learners
- Methods and Curriculum for English Learners
- Psychological Foundations for English Learners
- Reading for English Learners
- Research and Theory for English Learners
- Science for English Learners
- Social Foundations for English Learners
- Social Studies for English Learners
- Special Education for English Learners
- Teacher Training for Working with English Learners
- Testing for English Learners
- Writing for English Learners

We invite visitors of this part of the website to assist us in expanding and augmenting the existing resources by notifying us when they find a valuable resource not yet listed by sending an e-mail with this information to: tapestry@ucf.edu.

Appendix 5.c

The ESOL TAPESTRY Website: *The Tapestry Journal*

The Tapestry Journal's inaugural issue was published in winter 2009 and the journal now publishes biannually in June and December. It accepts articles, commentaries, and book reviews with the goal of integrating research and best practices into a variety of subjects relating to ELs' academic achievement and English language development. Topics in the archive range from case studies into ELs' social, emotional, and language growth within schools to practical methods for teachers to incorporate explicit linguistic and cultural instruction in mainstream classrooms. The journal invites manuscript submissions in the following three categories: research and theory, effective field practices, and commentaries. Additionally, a supplementary blog functions as an informal forum for discussing issues, controversies, and viewpoints relating to the education of ELs and SLA.

Submission guidelines can be accessed at http://tapestry.usf.edu/journal/submissions.php. For inquiries, manuscript submissions, and blog entries, please e-mail tapestry@ucf.edu.

PART II

Application of the One Plus Model Across Selected Disciplines

CHAPTER 6

Infusing EL Content into Category 1+ Courses

The Learner and Learning Context

In this section, four teacher preparation faculty affiliated with three U.S. higher education institutions in two states share how they have infused EL content into their category 1+ courses with the goal of preparing teacher candidates to effectively support the education of English learners. The sample course summaries also include a reflection from these course instructors in which they delineate some of the ways in which the EL-infused course assignments and activities have enhanced their practices as well teacher candidates' preparation to teach ELs.

Sociocultural Studies in Education: For this multisection course, which is required of all education licensure students but also satisfies a humanities requirement in the university's liberal education plan, Professor Richard Quantz, in the Department of Educational Leadership at Miami University (Oxford, Ohio), codesigned a set of EL-infused activities and assignments aimed at engaging teacher candidates in discussions on issues pertaining to the education of ELs. For instance, in the Text Interpretation Activity, candidates discuss how theories of assimilation and pluralism impact the dominant ideologies at the basis of current instructional models for ELs and how teachers' personal philosophies affect their work with this particular student population. For the larger Democracy and Dialogue Project, at least one group of candidates delves deeper into the topic of ELs by engaging in discussions on how schools can assist *all students* to form their democratic voices. Teacher candidates then share the gist of their deliberations and learning via an online discussion board and audio recordings of face-to-face meetings, and produce a final paper. In a reflection on the implementation of the activity and the assignment in the course, Lauren Isaac, a doctoral candidate who teaches one section, describes how her experience as a former high school ESL specialist impacted her approach to introducing the EL-embedded course elements.

Human Development and Learning in Social and Educational Contexts: In this course, Assistant Professor Darrel Davis at Miami University incorporates an EL focus that "challenges students to gain an understanding of the individual differences that affect development patterns, rates of change, and effectiveness of learning in typical and exceptional individuals, within the context of cultural, ethnic, gender, and racial inter-actions." Working closely with his ESL mentor, Davis describes the development, pilot-ing, and refinement of a multistep EL-focused module designed to challenge teacher candidates to think deeply about language, culture, and schooling and to apply that knowledge to how ELs are taught and assessed. The module epitomizes the *plus* of minimal EL-focused elements suggested in a category 1+ course by including a schol-arly article on language, culture, and schooling as well as an instructor-created chart, personal reflections, class discussions, a mini-ethnographic project, a quiz, and a group reflection paper. Reflecting on his experience, Davis reminds us that once designed, ESL-focused content need not be static; rather, he and his colleagues look at the module each semester and tweak it to strengthen weaker areas.

Parent-Child Relations: This third sample is a new course that focuses on review of research on childrearing and parent-child relationships. By adding objectives linked to existing course goals, Judith Levin, Instructor and the Coordinator for Early Childhood Development and Education programs at the University of Central Florida, addresses the cultural and linguistic influences that affect how parents interact with their chil-dren, and how these factors impact the interactions between school and home. Levin, who developed the course, opens her reflection with the rationale for needing to infuse after the first semester of teaching it. She shares her "ah-ha!" moment when she real-ized how one candidate who had self-elected to develop a parent-training program for parents whose primary language was other than English had ignored considerations for cultural differences in child-rearing and, other than providing handouts in Spanish, had neglected to add strategies that would have supported the parents' understanding. Taking us through each step of how she revisited the entire course for missed opportu-nities to discuss culturally and linguistically diverse families, Levin then discusses her own research into the topic, and the resulting activities and assignments.

The ESE Learner: Kim Stoddard, Associate Professor and Coordinator for the Special Education program at the University of South Florida, St. Petersburg, shares a course designed for non–special education majors. She embedded EL content by expanding an existing key objective to include the treatment of ELs and added an objective aimed at helping teacher candidates recognize and use appropriate accommodations and com-munication strategies for mainstreamed ELs with exceptionalities and their families. In one assignment, Stoddard requires her teacher candidates to attend three multidis-ciplinary or family conferences and write a reflection regarding best practices. As they work with an English learner with exceptionalities in at least one of the conferences, they focus on identifying effective communication strategies, including accommoda-tions for exceptionalities and cultural and linguistic modifications for ELs and their non-English speaking parents. Stoddard reflects on how rich conversations with her faculty mentor enabled her to better understand how the concept of diversity extends beyond the cultural differences and encompasses linguistic concerns and how strate-gies can be used to differentiate instruction for students at different levels of English proficiency.

The sample EL-infused course syllabi described herein provide suggestions and guidelines for infusing EL-content into category 1+ courses with the goal of enhancing teacher candidates' preparation to effectively teach ELs in the mainstream classrooms. We encourage teacher educators to consider incorporating versions of these assignments and activities into their pre-service teacher education programs or identify other, providing their teacher candidates with a beginning repertoire for teaching ELs, whom they are increasingly likely to have in their classes.

Sociocultural Studies in Education

Lauren B. Isaac and Richard A. Quantz
Miami University

Course Description

Required of all education licensure students as well as speech and hearing students, this course is nonetheless *not* a professional education course. Rather, it fulfills a humanities requirement in the Miami Plan (the university's liberal education plan). As a humanities liberal education course, its focus is on the analysis, interpretation, and critique of educational texts. It is a reading and writing course designed to help students understand the debates around education and democracy that appear in publications and media. As such it directly addresses controversial issues, especially issues around diversity.

This is a multisection course where each semester we offer approximately 22 sections for over 400 students on three different campuses and from every school at the university. Instructors are primarily Teaching Associates and adjuncts who have their degrees from our department. All instructors must spend a year in a co-instructor mentoring program to learn how to teach this complex course.

Course Topics

1. The various understandings of the meaning and purpose of education in a democratic society.
2. The range of different philosophies of education and economic-political ideologies that provide a context for understanding educational texts.
3. How education has been represented in educational texts throughout United States history.
4. How specific sociocultural identities such as race, English Learners, gender, sexuality, and social class are revealed and addressed in educational texts.

Course Objectives

Students will be able to:

1. Analyze, interpret, and critique educational texts including written, visual, and social texts.
2. Identify the basic philosophical and ideological influences on public debate of educational issues, particularly issues related to diversity including race, English Learners, gender, sexuality, and social class.

3. Write a clear and coherent essay that advances a particular position on at least one contemporary educational topic.

EL-Focused Materials

Abowitz, K.K. (Ed.). (2006). *Readings in sociocultural studies in education* (6th ed.)
 Boston: McGraw-Hill Learning Solutions.

    a. Chapter 50: A Call for the Americanization of Mexican-American Children (1928) by Merton Hill, 319–321.

    b. Thinking Box: Theories of Assimilation, 322.

Clark, K. (2009). The case for structured English immersion. *Educational Leadership, 66*(7), 42-46.

López Estrada, V., Gómez, L., & Ruiz-Escalante, J.A. (2009). Let's make dual language the norm. *Educational Leadership, 66*(7), 54-58.

Mora, J.K. (2009). From the ballot box to the classroom. *Educational Leadership, 66(7)*, 14-19.

Quantz, R., & Abowitz, K.K. (2010). *Background essay #4: Educational and political-economic ideologies.* (Unpublished manuscript). Miami University, Oxford, OH.

In-Class Activity

Background Readings: Students are assigned four articles to read in preparation for this in-class activity. The first three articles describe some contemporary approaches of English Learner education (Clark, 2009; López Estrada, 2009; Mora, 2009). The fourth article is an excerpt from a 1928 Merton Hill article, which mandates an "Americanization" program in public schools in response to the growing Mexican population.[1] Part of the "Americanization" program is the rapid acquisition of the English language, American patriotism, and an adoption of Anglo culture and history.

Text Interpretation Activity: Students are divided into four groups, and each group is assigned one of the four above articles. Students are assigned the tasks of conducting a text interpretation where they discuss their assigned article in light of the two theories of assimilation and one of pluralism found in the "Thinking Box: Theories of Assimilation" reading in the course textbook.[2] These theories are "Anglo-conformity," "melting pot," and "cultural pluralism." The instructor explains to the students that these are three dominant ideologies underlying approaches to teaching English Learners. In groups, students use the theories of assimilation and pluralism as interpretive tools to gain a deeper insight into the EL teaching approaches discussed in the articles. Students are required to share their interpretation of their assigned article. After all four groups have presented their text interpretation, the instructor facilitates a class discussion with the goal of connecting the topic of English Learners back to previous course units on educational philosophies and political-economic ideologies. Some discussion questions posed to the students are the following:

1. For what would a progressive educational philosophy advocate in regard to English Learners?
2. What role does an essentialist educational philosophy play in the current education of English Learners?
3. Since the education of English Learners has been put in the hands of the voting public, how have the political-economic ideologies appeared in the public debate?
4. In what ways could the ideology or philosophy of teachers affect the education of English Learners?

Assignments

Description of Democracy and Dialogue Project: Students are given the opportunity to explore in depth the topic of English Learners in the course's long-term assignment, called the Democracy and Dialogue Project. In this assignment, students participate with four or five classmates in study and dialogue around one educational topic, such as Sexuality in U.S. schools, Parental Involvement, or English Learners. Each course section is required to have at least one group explore the English Learner topic. The central question for the project is the following: How should schools teach to form the democratic voices of students? For six weeks, students collaboratively read, analyze, and interpret texts from a diversity of perspectives on their assigned topic. These ongoing dialogues occur via online discussion boards as well as face-to-face meetings. At the end of their long-term group dialogue, individual students identify a claim that each will argue in his or her own individual final 6–8 page paper. The claim must speak to how schools should develop democratic voice among its students given their assigned topic.

English Learner Topic: The English Learners group(s) explores what types of programs, if any, are best suited to helping English Learners fully develop their democratic voice in U.S. society. Some believe that the best way to both promote ELs' learning of content and of English is to provide bilingual education, in which they continue to learn content in their first or primary language, while they develop fluency in English. Others believe that these students will develop fluency faster and more effectively if they are pushed to learn English more quickly by immersing them in English-only classes. Still others reject both exclusively bilingual and exclusively immersion programs and advocate a variety of alternative approaches. Some of the questions that the EL group explores are: Which approaches or combination of approaches seems best for advancing the interests of English Learners and the interest of promoting a democracy that is inclusive of all its citizens? While everyone agrees that EL students should learn standard American English, should they be required to do so in a manner that forces or encourages them to give up their native language, or should they be taught in a manner that purposively works to maintain their native language while acquiring English? What are the public interests in this debate? What kind of regulations should government place on schools regarding EL students?

Students in the English Learner group are required to read the following EL-focused articles and are also encouraged to find outside resources.

Adams, M., Kellie M., & Jones, K. (2005, Winter). Unmasking the myths of structured English immersion: Why we still need bilingual educators, native language instruction, and incorporation of home culture. *Radical Teacher*. Retrieved from http://findarticles.com/p/articles/mi_m0JVP/is_75/ai_n16439994/

Associated Free Press (2007, September 4). New York's first Arabic school opens under police guard. *Associated Free Press*. Retrieved from http://afp.google.com/article/ALeqM5gguNcON4AgCQ4Jf-KmUJANEYWbZQ

EPE Research Center. (2004, September 21). *English language learners*. Retrieved from http://www.edweek.org/rc/issues/english-language-learners/

Fox News (2007, April 1). Newt Gingrich decries "ghetto" nature of bilingual education. Retrieved from http://www.foxnews.com/story/0,2933,263038,00.html

Lewin, T. (2009, June 26). Supreme Court sides with Arizona in language case. *The New York Times*. Retrieved from http://www.nytimes.com/2009/06/26/education/26educ.html?_r=1

Maceri, D. (1999, June 24). The pros of bilingual education. *Denver Business Journal*. Retrieved from http://denver.bizjournals.com/denver/stories/1999/06/07/editorial4.html

National Council of Teachers of English (2008). English language learners: A policy research brief produced by the National Council of Teachers of English. (NCTE: Urbana, IL). Retrieved from http://www.ncte.org/library/NCTEFiles/Resources/PolicyResearch/ELLResearchBrief.pdf

Assessments

Democracy and Dialogue Project Assessment

All students are assessed on both the quality of the dialogue through examination of discussion board and audio recordings of face-to-face meetings, as well as the individual paper as the final exam. For example, the English Learner group's dialogue is assessed based on: (1) how well students identify, evaluate, and differentiate the various arguments of the assigned texts; (2) how well students locate any implicit or explicit concepts of democracy assumed in the texts; (3) how well students identify the rhetorical strategies used in the texts; (4) how well students interpret the texts through different political, philosophical, historical, or sociocultural lenses.

The individual students then draw from the texts and group dialogues to write their final paper. The final paper is assessed based on: (1) the strength of their argument, which must relate an EL educational approach (or combination of approaches) to the development of EL's democratic voices; (2) their definition of democracy in relation to the education of ELs; (3) their integration of the readings in support of their argument; (4) evidence that their participation in group dialogue has informed their argument and/or their understanding of the debate; and (5) the overall quality and creativity in their writing.

Reflection

Beginnings

When I (Richard Quantz) was approached by my colleague Dr. Martha Castañeda, ESL/ foreign language education specialist, about infusing the topic of English Learners into the course, I was eager to participate. EL students have been discussed irregularly in the course, and institutionalizing the topic into the course seemed like a natural next step. However, since the course is already packed with different topics, finding a way to integrate it without shortchanging another topic became the central problem. In thinking about the curriculum, however, I thought one good way to integrate it would be to use the topic of EL students as the example for when the course introduces social text and performance of identity. After all, one's language is a central part of identity performance. Another problem existed in the fact that this is a humanities liberal education course and not a professional course or a social science course, which requires us to find texts that reveal different contexts that inform texts on the topic rather than using texts that are based on claims of efficacy—especially reports on research. After discussing the possibilities with Dr. Castañeda, she kindly did some research and located several articles that could fit our needs. Taking her recommendations and locating some texts ourselves, the readings and the topics were inserted into the master syllabus which all sections must model their section after. All instructors were required to integrate the topic into the section on social text and performance using the designated readings.

A second way of integrating the topic was to include it in the large project in the course, which we call the Democracy and Dialogue (D&D) Project. This project organizes the students' work for the second half of the course. Students are assigned to dialogue groups of four or five that address a topic of some controversy in education. Students may select from one of six topics covering such areas as sexuality, race, discipline, social class, gender, and now, English Learners. To develop the new EL topic, I recruited some of the other instructors to research and create the topic for the D&D Project. The basic topic problem and readings have evolved since the initial offering of the topic in fall 2009. What follows is a discussion of one of the instructors of the course over her experience in implementing these two aspects of the course.

Implementation

For me (Lauren Isaac), the prospect of infusing English Learner content into this course was met with nothing but enthusiasm. I thought of it as a great opportunity to draw from my own experience as a high school ESL specialist. While working with ELs and content teachers, I learned that schools not only present ELs with linguistic challenges, but also that there are enormous social and cultural barriers that inhibit ELs from fully participating in the schooling process. So a sociocultural studies in education course, for obvious reasons, provided many chances to infuse EL content. Here I reflect on a discussion of English Learners connected with social text and performance of identity as well as the final Democracy and Dialogue Project.

As Richard Quantz says above, language is a central part of how people construct and perform their identity. In scholarship and practice, English Learners, by their very label, are primarily constructed as deficient of an essential skill to succeed in U.S. schools: the English language. For this course, I wanted the undergraduates to think about the asset-versus-deficiency dichotomy and relate it to how English Learners may experience school. I struggled with how to get this idea across for some time. Then, I decided to ask the undergraduates, all monolingual English speakers, to think of all the ways that their K–12 teachers considered them "assets" to the classroom. The students had an easy time with this task. Students shared that they were assets because they participated frequently in class, always did their homework, or volunteered to tutor classmates. Then, I asked the students to think of all the ways that their teachers considered them "deficits" to the classroom. My second request prompted an eruption of devious laughter. Many students responded with the ways in which they disrupted the teacher's lesson through cracking jokes, throwing pencils, showing up late, or constantly talking to their classmates. Perfect. At this point, I began to realize this thought exercise, as I call it, might actually be quite useful in driving my point home. I knew the next step in the exercise was crucial. I then asked the students to describe all the ways they were considered "deficits" to the classroom by virtue of some fundamental aspect of their identity, such as language, culture, ethnicity, or religion. Silence. The jovial mood in the room shifted. After a bit of time, a student shared how she hadn't thought about ELs in terms of giving up parts of their identity to become members of the classroom. To avoid ending on this note, we then discussed how EL students, by the virtue of their linguistic and cultural identity, are actually assets to a school community. This exercise was very meaningful for the students because, even with all the linguistic modification strategies in the world, EL students could remain "problems" in the classroom. In reflection, I think this exercise provided students with a chance to reflect on the relationship between identity and schooling.

When I worked with the Democracy and Dialogue EL group, I noticed their struggles in connecting the notion of democracy to the public debate over what programs are most suitable for EL students. Students began to see that the debate between bilingual education and English immersion is steeped in strong ideological notions of citizenship, the politics of immigration, and connections between language and patriotism. In other words, students began to realize that the issue is quite complex. In this assignment, however, the students are supposed to think about which model (or combination of models) is most appropriate to develop the democratic voice of the EL students. Students began to think about schools and communities as potential democratic spaces, and thus, connected a student's "voice" to their ability to speak for themselves in the language that they feel most comfortable. Consistently, when put in these terms, the students in the EL group became critical of the "sink or swim" models of English immersion because of the model's potential to hinder the democratic voices of the students. Also, the students begin to think about the political and practical complexity of implementing bilingual education. Overall, this project frames the EL topic around the central question for the entire course: What does it mean to educate for a democratic society? Thinking about educating English Learners raises many important questions about the purposes of schools, the role of community in the classroom, and how schools can play a part in strengthening or weakening democratic life. In my experience, this project does an excellent job in giving undergraduates the opportunity to grapple with these questions.

Human Development and Learning in Social and Educational Contexts

Darrel R. Davis
Miami University

Course Description

In-depth examination of theoretical issues and principles of human development and learning, including developmental changes, motivational and learning processes, exceptionalities and other individual differences, and dynamics of social groups. Various ways human development and learning can be fostered within diverse social and educational contexts and the interactive influences of contextual differences on the direction and nature of these processes will be a major focus for systematic inquiry.

Course Topics

The course focuses on the major theories of human learning and development and the various social and educational factors that affect these processes. Inherent to this goal is knowledge of the contexts that influence social interactions with peers, parents, teachers, and others in the human community. The course challenges students to gain an understanding of the individual differences that affect development patterns, rates of change, and effectiveness of learning in typical and exceptional individuals, within the context of cultural, ethnic, gender, and racial interactions.

Course Objectives

Of the eight existing course objectives, four were identified as candidates for making connections to ESL content because they already touch on cultural diversity and social interactions or contexts.

1. Gain an understanding of the intellectual, social, moral, personality, and physical/motor processes of human development and the effects of various social and educational contexts of these processes, especially as they affect early childhood, middle childhood, and adolescent development.
2. Evaluate factors such as intrinsic/extrinsic loci, attributions, motivational hierarchies, goal structuring, and processes by which these factors interact with racial, gender, ethnic, and cultural barriers present in contextual systems, especially as they influence the motivational achievement of individuals during early childhood, middle childhood, and adolescence.

3. Explore individual differences that affect development patterns, rates of change, and effectiveness of learning in typical and exceptional individuals, within the context of cultural, ethnic, gender, and racial interactions, especially during early childhood, middle childhood, and adolescence.
4. Critically analyze the contexts that influence social interactions with peers, parents, teachers, and others in the human community, such as peer interactions, group decision-making processes, competition and cooperation in learning, and interpersonal communication, especially in relation to the family/school community contexts present in early childhood, middle childhood, and adolescence.

EL-Focused Module Objectives

The EL module was designed to be a step-by-step process that guided student groups through the experience. The collaborative approach afforded each student the opportunity to gain maximum experience via the distribution of tasks and working together to complete the tasks. Four objectives of what the students would be able to do after the module guided the development:

1. To make connections between the immigrant experience and language.
2. To identify, compare, and contrast the similarities and differences between learning a first (native) and a second (new) language.
3. To apply the content of learning a first (native) and a second (new) language to real world examples.
4. To connect the characteristics of language learning to educational psychology.

EL-Focused Standards

Ohio TESOL Endorsement Standards

1. Candidates demonstrate knowledge and understanding of students of diverse cultural and language backgrounds.
    1.1. Candidates know and use information relating to different cultural and language groups in U.S. and Ohio.
    1.2. Candidates understand the student's culture and the impact on learning and performance in the classroom.
3. Candidates demonstrate knowledge and understanding of the process of language learning.
    3.1. Candidates demonstrate and know similarities and differences between first and second (new) language acquisition across age/grade levels.

EL-Focused Materials

McKeon, D. (1994). Language, culture and schooling. In F. Genesee (Ed.), *Educating second language children* (pp. 15–32). New York: Cambridge University Press.
    a. Chart derived from Richard-Amato (2003) and Cook (n.d.) comparing the characteristics of first and second language learners.

b. Cook, V. (n.d.). First and second language acquisition. Retrieved from http://
homepage.ntlworld.com/vivian.c/SLA/L1%20and%20L2.htm
Richard-Amato, P. (2003). The classroom as an environment for language acquisition. In
Making it happen: From interactive to participatory language teaching (pp. 29-48).
White Plains, NY: Pearson.
a. Introductory video—provides an introduction to the module.
b. Sample interview questions.

In-Class Activity

Class time is used to both open and close the module. The module is introduced on the
day that we begin the Culture and Diversity section of the course. Sample videos are
used as discussion anchors, and students are encouraged to reflect on the experiences
they had during the process of completing the module.

Assignment

To complete the EL module, follow these six steps:

1. Watch the introduction video. This video introduces the module, provides the rationale and importance for the content, and provides an overview of what is required to
complete the module.
2. Complete the pre-reading questions on your family history, previous interaction with
language and language learners.
3. Read the McKeon (1994) article, which provides a critical look at language, culture,
and schooling.
4. Connect the reading with the chart, which provides a comparison of the characteristics of first and second language learners and provides additional resources for
further inquiry. The combination of the chart and the article provides the required
practical and theoretical content background.
5. Complete the quiz.
6. Complete the mini-ethnography project, consisting of:

   Part 1—Create a video:
   a. Generate a plan of action, decide group roles, and secure any required
   technology.
   b. Review the sample interview items provided and add at least eight additional
   items.
   c. Locate a language learner who fits the criteria provided.
   d. Conduct the interview. Written consent is required, and the interview is
   recorded.
   e. Edit the video to include the following sections: an introduction of the language learner, a presentation of the best example of the language learner
   demonstrating one of the characteristics on the comparison chart, and a
   description of how the selected highlight is an example of the chosen characteristics on the chart.

Part 2—Write a group reflection paper:

    a. Reflect on the experience focusing on the knowledge gained; the applicability of this knowledge to different settings; the relationship between this knowledge and course content; and, if any, myths/misconceptions that were dispelled.

Assessments

1. Quiz containing multiple-choice, true/false, and fill-in-the-blank items
2. Group reflection paper

Reflection

Personally, I must admit that the EL infusion could not have come at a better time for us. We were in the process of redesigning the course to foster greater student inquiry and content mastery. This redesign was a university initiative, and this course was eligible because it is one of the twenty-five courses at the institution with the highest enrollment. I rationalized that the "dust" from the redesign activities would provide cover for the EL infusion. If ever there was a time to try something new, this was the time. My infusion process did not start with the question of whether or not I should infuse. That ESL should be infused was unquestionable in my mind, especially given my connection to individuals within the field. Instead, the question was: How can I get the most value in terms of initial and continuing resource investments and the resulting student and faculty experiences? This question had to be considered within several constraints. The experience had to: (1) connect seamlessly with the course content, (2) be meaningful for students, (3) be applicable in a hybrid-online setting, (4) scale to large-enrollment classes, and (5) be sustainable over time. My fundamental question and the identified constraints provided a sense of focus that guided the infusion process.

Getting a mentor was the first task. Although I did not "chance upon" my mentor, I must say that he was indeed very wise. From the beginning we decided that we would create something special for students, something that would add value to the course and also exemplify our redesign efforts. We were fortunate that the course content readily lent itself to the EL themes, and we were determined to ensure that ESL would be explicitly presented at some point during the course and also that the ESL themes would be infused in other topic areas when possible. My mentor and I decided that our best course of action was to start small and then gradually expand the ESL experience. We used the existing collaborative structure of the course to our advantage and converted one of the two required group tasks from a general culture task, to an ESL task with cultural components. Immigration was the central theme for the ESL task. Students were required to read an article that connects the 1982 U.S. Supreme Court *Plyler v. Doe* decision to today's immigration debate, and also use a provided textual timeline of events to more deeply research the Irish Immigration of the 1840s. These two activities were the basis for a paper that would be a reflection of the group's cooperation, collaboration, and ability to form consensus. The reflection paper topics were focused on Ohio, thus providing additional opportunities for students to personally connect with the content. After papers were graded, we had a class discussion covering the article, students' research, and general reactions.

Response to the ESL task was extremely positive. The in-class debriefing discussions were always lively, and students were able to proficiently articulate positions and perspectives in part because of their prior group discussions. I had many positive conversations with students regarding the task, but in my mind the definitive proof of the effectiveness of the task was the number of groups that chose to do their final project on an ESL-related topic. The task had generated such interest and passion that I had to limit the number of groups that could focus on ESL themes. This was sufficient evidence for me that the EL infusion was on the right path.

After the successful pilot, we decided to repeat the task for the second semester and begin preparations for the eventual expansion of the task. We used the lessons learned from the first semester and made small changes to the task. The second semester response was as overwhelmingly positive as the first semester's. In-class discussions were rich and engaging, and once again many groups wanted to do ESL related final projects. At this point I was extremely relieved to see that the first semester's results were more than luck.

After the second semester, I was assigned a new mentor who, by luck or by design, happened to be as wise as my first mentor and more importantly, shared the same infusion vision. This was very good news because it ensured that we would continue with the original infusion approach. We started this new phase by reevaluating the ESL task and reflecting on the ESL themes that I was able to infuse throughout the course. It was clear that students wanted to learn this content and that they were making personal connections during the learning process. It seemed that students wanted more, and were capable of more. That summer, fortune smiled on us once again. As a part of our redesign efforts, we were implementing significant additions to the course, focusing on increased workload, increased individual and group accountability, and increased use of technology. We thought, "Why not?!" This seemed to be the perfect opportunity to really expand the ESL task by increasing workload, accountability, and technology. Perfect! This was the perfect time to develop a comprehensive module that contained all the elements that we thought would make the task more interesting and meaningful. We decided to start from the basics and examined both our course objectives and the Ohio TESOL Endorsement Standards. We decided on a course of action and then slowly began to build an experience that we thought would be effective and one that students would enjoy.

Our new module had five sections. The first section required students to reflect on their past, focusing on their family history and their experiences with language and language learners. This we felt would provide an opportunity for students to embed themselves in the task and begin the process of creating a personal connection with the content. The second section focused on the McKeon article (1994, listed in Materials section). This article was an important part of the content, and it was chosen because it is a scholarly investigation of the interplay between language, culture, and schooling. For the third section, we created a chart comparing learning a first language to learning a second language. The chart provided additional content and, when combined with the article, gave students a holistic look at the field and research within the field. The fourth section was focused on individual accountability. Students were required to complete an online quiz covering both the article and the chart. The fifth and final section was designed to bring students in contact with others who have access to different perspectives and realities. Groups had to interview a Miami University student with specified characteristics. Before starting the interview, groups were required to create a set of interview questions that would complement the questions we provided. Our aim was to get our students to reflect on what they truly wanted to find out from the person they were interviewing. Next, groups had to create a video based on the interview, and then write a group reflection paper highlighting both the scholarly and personal aspects of their interview experience.

The first semester we introduced the module was amazing. The module was a perfect fit for our evolving course. Students embraced the opportunity to explore, and this was demonstrated by every metric we used. In my opinion, the videos and the reflection paper were true showcases of students' reaction to the module. The videos were of high quality and students were able to use the content to correctly identify language characteristics seen during the interview. The reflection papers were amazing as well. It was very common to read about students' transformation as they described how they either learned something new, or how a myth or stereotype was removed as they conducted the interview.

After grading the submissions, I was very excited to talk about the results in class. As was scheduled, the topic for that week was culture and diversity, and I expected to discuss the ESL task at some point during the class. To my surprise, however, the moment I entered the classroom students were asking about the ESL task. We proceeded to the content for the day, and at every possible occasion, students would link our discussion to their ESL experience. This was extremely exciting for me because students were making connections far beyond what I had hoped. At that point I realized that I would need to expand the post-task discussion to give students more opportunity to debrief their experiences.

The second and third semesters were as successful as the first. We made minor changes to the module itself, but perhaps the biggest change occurred in the post-task discussions. I now use the module as an anchor for the class discussions for that week. I share exemplary videos with the class and encourage students to talk about what happened during the interviews. These personal reflections enhance our class discussions and the students are able to link their experiences to the topics covered in class.

We currently use the module but we are constantly trying to improve it. At the end of every semester we take a step back and look critically at our module. We try to enhance what works and modify weak areas. This process, we hope, will help us keep the module fresh and relevant. I will admit, however, that there has been a decline in the amount of groups that chose an ESL-related topic for their final project. I would like to think that the scope of the module has something to do with that.

I am not sure if my EL infusion is typical or not, but I am glad that I had a great course to infuse, great mentors to work with, and a professional atmosphere where I was free to experiment. If I had one piece of advice to put forward, I would neither offer a specific strategy nor make an appeal as to why you should infuse ESL. My strategy worked because of my circumstances, and if you need still need a rationale, then you should return to the beginning of the book :) My advice would be, "Set high expectations and provide support. Students will rise to the occasion." I know you have heard it before, but I believe that it is true. Students hunger for this type of knowledge because it applies to all areas of life. Students will more than likely rise to the height of the bar you place, so go ahead and set the bar high, create experiences that are rich and meaningful, don't be afraid to increase both breadth and depth of EL content in your infused assignments. Students will appreciate this and they will show it in their words and their actions.

Parent-Child Relations

Judith N. Levin
University of Central Florida

Course Description

The course is a review of research on childrearing and parent-child relationships using case studies to explore influences of personality, developmental stages, family structure, as well as ethnic and cultural factors on parenting. It is recommended to be taken during the semester prior to the Practicum in the Early Childhood Development and Education BS program.

This course focuses on the relationship between parents and children. Students need to be aware of their interactions with adults and children alike who are ELs. These pre-professionals also need to develop an understanding of how language can be a barrier for parents in supporting their children's learning needs.

Course Objectives

Although the course has a total of six goals, only two of them were chosen for infusing EL-focused materials and assignments. Following are the original course goals and the objectives that were added when revising the course to better address the needs of ELs and their families:

Goal 4: Understand cultural influences on families and parenting.
1. Understand how parents' lack of English language proficiency influences their lack of involvement in their child's school.
2. Examine how the attitudes of school officials towards parents who lack English language proficiency impact the parents' involvement in the school.
3. Examine successful models which bridge the disconnect between school and home culture.

Goal 6: Apply course concepts to real-world situations.
   Identify practices that may improve EL parental involvement.

EL-Focused Materials

1. Selected required course readings (included in Assignment description below).
2. School websites and individual teachers' websites to review for evidence and examples of a targeted goal to include families of ELs.

Assignment

The course has four main assignments. Assignment 3, the Issue Comparison Paper, was revised to focus on understanding ELs. In addition to including requirements for identified readings, the assignment description was changed to emphasize a focus in the paper reflecting how the selected issue impacts parents and families whose first language is not English.

The purpose of this assignment is:

1. To familiarize students with a current issue in parent-child relations.
2. To familiarize students with the manner in which a parenting issue is treated by professional sources.
3. To enable students to compare and analyze a parenting issue's significance through an understanding of different cultures.

Read a minimum of four selected professional journal articles [listed below]. At least two articles must be selected from the included list of articles that address issues faced by parents and families of ELs. After reading the selected articles, you will write a paper analyzing and evaluating each article and then summarizing them, comparing how the issue is treated by each of the sources.

Some things to consider are: the purpose of the article, who the target audience is, qualifications of the author(s), evidence presented for any claims made in the articles, how language is used, theoretical viewpoint of the author(s), what kind of outside sources are cited, whether or not the information and findings in each article are logical, what is your opinion of the findings in each article, and any other information that is relevant.

Offer an analysis and evaluation of each article you read, explain similarities and differences in how the articles are written, and make a determination as to how valid the information is in each article. Be sure to include a summary of your findings at the end of the paper. This summary should sum up each of the articles and then compare each one to the others as they relate to the issue. What are the implications of this compiled research on ELs and their families? As part of your Implications section, include how the research guides your thinking of supporting ELs and their families.

Sources

A minimum of two of the readings must be selected from this EL-focused reading list:

Arias, M.B., & Morillo-Campbell, M. (2008). Promoting ELL parental involvement: Challenges in contested times. *Education Policy Research Unit*, 1-22.

Cho, E.K., Chen, D.W., & Shin, S. (2010). Supporting transnational families. *Young Children, 65*(1), 30-37.

Kauffman, E., Perry, A., & Prentiss, D. (2001). Reasons for and solutions to lack of parent involvement in parents of second language learners. ERIC: ED458956. Retrieved from http://www.eric.ed.gov/PDFS/ED458956.pdf.

Panferov, S. (2010). Increasing ELL parental involvement in our schools: Learning from parents. *Theory into Practice, 49*(1), 106-112.

Stagg-Peterson, S., & Ladky, M. (2007). A survey of teacher' and principals practices and challenges in fostering new immigrant parent involvement. *Canadian Journal of Education, 30*(2), 881-910.

Thao, M. (2009). Parent involvement in school: Engaging immigrant parents. *Snaphot, Wilder Research,* 1-4.

Waterman, R., & Harry, B. (2008). Building collaboration between schools and parents of English language learners: Transcending barriers, creating opportunities. *The National Center for Culturally Responsive Educational Systems.*

List of Academic Journals targeting issues on ELs and their families:

TESOL Quarterly
TESOL Journal
The Tapestry Journal
TESL Canada Journal

The following journals are not specifically focused on ELs, but often contain articles that address ELs and their needs:

Child Development
Childhood Education
Child Study Journal
Childhood Education
Early Child Development & Care
Journal of Marriage and Family
Journal of Family Issues
Young Children

Assessment

The student's work will be assessed by rubric.

Reflection

Since this was a new course in our program and I was the instructor who developed the course, I was exceptionally sensitive to ongoing assessment of the course content, my teaching practices, and the students' learning outcomes. One of my "ah-ha!" moments came while I was grading the final assignment, Parent-Training Program. A student developed a curriculum for parents whose primary language is not English. This student wrote lesson plans, PowerPoints, and handouts in both English and Spanish. Other than these accommodations, there were no additional strategies infused in the parent-training curriculum. The student's lack of consideration and failure to implement a variety of successful strategies for supporting parents with limited English proficiency was the encouragement I needed to reexamine the entire course. Through this review, I was able to see how many opportunities to teach an understanding of the diverse cultural and language needs of families were missing in this course. Before I revised the course, I reviewed literature related to the challenges parents whose primary language is not English face in supporting the needs of their children. These readings, in combination with interviews I conducted on five undergraduate ELs, provided me with a strong sense of what to include in the revised syllabus.

This course was a newly developed course that included objectives related to diverse families. It was taught for one semester to undergraduate students. At the conclusion of the course, explicit ESL components were added to an assignment to better prepare practitioners for working with ELs. There were also objectives added to two of the course's six goals to include an awareness of how schools can sabotage parent involvement with parents whose first language is not English and the role professionals can play in providing better support to families of ELs.

In initial course development, the first steps are to write a course description and course goals and objectives. These serve as a guide to all instructors, ensuring adherence to the intent of the course. When making changes in a course, there is a domino effect. Each change impacts other course components (goals, objectives, learning modules, readings, assignments, assessments). Careful alignment of each component is imperative. All revisions must be aligned throughout the course.

As I developed revisions for this course with the intent to increase my students' knowledge and understanding of families of ELs, I followed a step-by-step approach in revising this course to include ESL content:

- My first step was to review the course goals and objectives and determine where EL infusion would match. I did not make any changes in the course goals; instead I added to objectives under goals 4 and 6.
- The next step was to review the modules for goals 4 and 6 and include ESL teachings within these modules' readings.
- The third step was to revise an assignment with the intent of adding an understanding of ESL knowledge and to provide the students with a more comprehensive perspective of ELs and their families.

I am a firm believer that I learn from my students at least as much as they learn from me. The anecdote regarding the parent-child (bilingual) class assignment was all the encouragement I needed to revise the course, learning every step of the way. If this learning can be used by other instructors, then it will serve not only the students in my pre-professional Early Childhood Development and Education Program, but other students and families alike. For me, the process proved to be a valuable experience, giving me the opportunity (push) to include ESL knowledge in this course.

The Exceptional Student Education (ESE) Learner

Kim Stoddard
University of South Florida, St. Petersburg

Course Description

Designed for non–special education majors. Includes basic identification techniques and strategies to promote academic and social integration and interaction of "mainstreamed" exceptional students. Concurrent field experience projects are included.

Course Topics

1. Discerning typical language development (first and second) from language disabilities or other exceptionalities.
2. Recognizing appropriate accommodations/communication strategies for mainstreamed ELs with exceptionalities and their families.

Course Objectives

Teacher candidates will be able to:

1. Describe the identification procedures used with students suspected of learning and behavior exceptionalities; and discuss the research that focuses on both the efficacy and validity of these procedures, paying particular attention to issues related to the over and under representation of minorities, including English learners.
2. Demonstrate an understanding of the techniques for improving the home and school partnership, including reducing cultural and linguistic barriers ELs face.
3. Identify the modifications appropriate for various EL proficiency levels for different exceptionalities.

Standards

Florida ESOL Performance Standard 25: Recognize indicators of learning disabilities.

EL-Focused Materials

Several readings were added at different points in the course where it was necessary to provide the perspective of working with ELs with special needs and their families. As a whole, they aided in giving the foundation for the Assignment. One of these articles became the basis for supporting the modified In-Class Activity. EL-focused readings include the following:

Artiles, A.J., & Ortiz, A.A. (2002). English language learners with special needs: Contexts and possibilities. In A. J. Artiles & A.A. Ortiz (Eds.), *English language learners
with special needs: Identification, assessment, and instruction* (pp. 3-27). McHenry,
IL: Delta Systems.

Baca, L.M., & Cervantes, H.T. (1991). Bilingual special education. (ERIC Digest No.
ED333618). Retrieved from http://www.ericdigests.org/pre-9219/education.htm

Figueroa, R.A., & Newsome, P. (2006). The diagnosis of LD in English learners: Is it non-
discriminatory? *Journal of Learning Disabilities, 39*(3), 206-214.

Garcia, S. B., & Tyler, B. (2010). Meeting the needs of English language learners with
learning disabilities in the general curriculum. *Theory into Practice, 49*(2), 113-120.
doi:10.1080/00405841003626585

Lozano-Rodriguez, J.R., & Castellano, J.A. (1999). Assessing LEP migrant students for
special education services. (ERIC Digest No. ED425892). Retrieved from http://
www.ericdigests.org/1999-3/lep.htm

Wilkinson, C.Y., Ortiz, A.A., Robertsib, P.M., & Kushner, M.I. (2006). English language
learners with reading-related LD: Linking data from multiple sources to make eligibility determinations. *Journal of Learning Disabilities, 29*(2), 129-141.

In-Class Activity

Teaching Case Responses: In-class discussion in response to selected teaching cases
involving ethical dilemmas related to special education. One case will present a situation involving a child of migrant farm workers who may have limited English proficiency.
Read the Baca and Cervantes and the Lozano-Rodriguez and Castellano ERIC digests
prior to reading the case.

Assignment

The candidate will attend three multidisciplinary or family conferences and write a
reflection regarding best practices observed. Candidate must work with an EL student
with exceptionalities in at least one of the conferences.

The candidate will focus on identifying effective communication strategies, including accommodations for exceptionalities and cultural and linguistic modifications for ELs
and their non-English speaking parents. Candidate will document date, setting, participants in attendance and length of the meeting.

Final submission requirements are as follows:

Comprehensive reflections
Identification of best practices
Accommodations noted

Assessment

Final exam will include the following question: Describe the typical process of identifying ELs with exceptionalities. Provide examples of normal second language acquisition
processes and characteristics that may be mistaken for exceptionalities.

Reflection

I resisted and avoided the process of infusing ESL requirements into my teaching repertoire. I never questioned the importance of gaining more insight into working with students from ESL backgrounds or the infusion of ESL practices within the curriculum. I've always been interested in learning new techniques and new perspectives regarding "best practices" in teaching, including cultural diversity and the theoretical perspective of cultural differences. However, at first I believed that since I was already aware of individual differences, including how to implement strategies for diversity, why did I need professional development and why was it necessary for me to change my course?

Despite my resistance and avoidance, I reluctantly became involved in the training, completed the requirements, and provided the necessary documentation. The information offered by the facilitators was informative and enlightening, and over time, the discussions that occurred during the eventual curriculum revision process caused both the ESL faculty and the Exceptional Education faculty to rethink how the two disciplines intersect. Different gatherings of ESL and ESE faculty chatted informally at the bookstore coffee shop or at the picnic tables by the harbor, going around in circles sometimes and reaching a solid conclusion now and then.

After a few dozen cups of coffee, we had our first breakthrough. We noticed that we meant different things when we used the same terms. For example, the terms *modification* and *accommodation* are used very precisely in Exceptional Education. With an *accommodation*, the teacher requires the students to master the same objective; however, the process for learning the objective or the process for demonstrating mastery of the objective might be different than for traditional students. In a *modification*, the teacher changes the objective of the lesson. The learning objective for the student with a disability is different than the other students in the general education classroom when a modification occurs. The ESL faculty often referred to modifying a lesson plan for English learners at different levels of proficiency, when only the lowest levels of proficiency required a true modification. This small point of distinction continued, unnoticed, until two of us sat down with a paper and pencil and starting listing terms in the field and defining them. Once we got started, we added basic assumptions and conditions of each field to our list: goals for the students, duration of services, predictability of progression, and teaching strategies. We noted contrasts in each of these areas, which eventually led to a published article.[3] More important, we affirmed our overarching commitment in both fields—treating each child as an individual and assessing and adapting instruction to her/his needs. These are the hallmarks of ESL and Special Education teachers.

Once these issues were clarified, I began to see that I could offer many more specifics to my teacher candidates enrolled in my courses when we focused on EL issues. Whereas I previously thought of ESL as another facet of "diversity," I had developed a more complete concept of diversity for ELs that went beyond cultural differences alone to specific linguistic concerns. When I considered an instructional strategy, such as graphic organizers, that is effective for both English learners and students with exceptionalities, I had a theoretical and practical understanding of how the strategy supported comprehensibility for ELs at different levels of English proficiency.

After our discussions and additions to my syllabus, the ESL faculty member and I planned the debut of the ESL-infused course. For our first discussion based on the ESL readings, I had prepared a PowerPoint and asked the ESL faculty member to attend to field any questions that went beyond my developing knowledge about ELs. I felt uncertain about presenting a topic that I was not an expert in, but having my colleague there alleviated some of my apprehensions. Actually, having a colleague from another field co-present a topic in my class was an entirely new experience for me. I had invited guest speakers many times, but this was different. I knew my colleague would be considerate of my instructor role, but what if I made a misstatement?

The lecture was well received, and my colleague only interrupted to amplify or expand issues I addressed. We began to build a back and forth exchange of insights and details, and the teacher candidates were engaged and asked pointed questions that we both responded to. I took some notes of terms, researchers, and other information to have ready for next semester's solo lecture.

My ESL colleague suggested that we both grade a sample of teacher candidates' first EL-focused assignment. Although coordinating our efforts was more time consuming than just grading everything myself, I appreciated the chance to compare our evaluations of the work and for me to be perhaps a bit more discerning on EL issues. We were surprisingly close on many points, but one in particular set us apart. When teacher candidates addressed accommodations for ELs, they often identified ESE accommodations and noted that they were also appropriate for ELs. My colleague demanded more details and differentiation than I thought necessary, but our discussions led to a greater depth of understanding and application, and we went on to informally establish interrater reliability.

I still find that some of the teacher candidates enrolled in my ESE courses struggle with the issue of identifying ELs who need special education services, and I continue to look for better ways to clarify this and other issues for them. One approach that has helped has been to work with the ESL faculty member to crosslink the topic in her course (an EL-specific course) and mine, requiring teacher candidates to work with ELs needing special education services and connecting these field-based assignments across the two courses. We see promise in this integrated approach.

CHAPTER 7

Infusing EL Content into Category 2+ Courses

Developing and Implementing Curriculum, Instruction, and Assessment

In this chapter, six teacher preparation faculty, affiliated with three U.S. higher education institutions in two states, share how they have infused EL content into their category 2+ courses with the goal of preparing teacher candidates to effectively support the education of English learners. In addition to the embedded EL-focused content, the 2+ courses include assignments involving planning and implementing curriculum, instruction, and assessment. They also require candidates to apply the added EL-focused content to making adaptations and accommodations for English learners in at least one assignment. The sample course summaries include a reflection delineating some of the ways in which the EL-embedded course assignments and activities have enhanced instructor practices as well teacher candidates' preparation to teach ELs.

Teaching Strategies and Classroom Management: In this course, Associate Professor Cynthia J. Hutchinson, University of Central Florida, engages her teacher candidates in exploring strategies for planning, organizing, and managing effective learning environments for all students, including English learners. In a one assignment, Hutchinson's teacher candidates develop a lesson plan for a microteaching experience with peers. In the lesson plan, they are expected to apply what they have learned about effective instructional planning to accommodate the needs of three English learners with varying language proficiency levels and needs. In reflecting about her experience teaching her teacher candidates to adapt instruction to student needs, Hutchinson highlights the importance of team work and collaboration among general education and ESL faculty. In the end, Hutchinson felt good about what she was able to accomplish and felt that her general methods students would be better prepared for the EL challenges that lay ahead of them.

Social Studies in the Elementary School: Associate Professor Will Russell, University of Central Florida, focuses on the identification and examination of appropriate and effective teaching strategies for all learners, including ELs. In one assignment, teacher candidates develop a social studies lesson plan that could be taught within a K–6 classroom. Emphasis is placed on adjusting instruction to accommodate the learning needs of English learners in a heterogeneous classroom. In reflecting about preparing teacher candidates to teach English learners, Russell provides a positive yet cautious report about the progress made.

Middle School Science: In this course, Assistant Professor Nazan Bautista, Miami University, engages her teacher candidates in planning and implementing effective science instruction for all students, including English learners. Particular emphasis is placed on adapting instruction to meet the language and content needs of English learners in middle school science classroom. In a major project, Full Circle Interdisciplinary Lesson Plans, teacher candidates work in teams in developing an interdisciplinary unit that provides evidence of planning for instruction incorporating multiple content areas of licensure. They are evaluated on various criteria, including evidence for differentiation of instruction for ELs with varying proficiency levels. Bautista uses her own experience as a non-native speaker of English to help her teacher candidates experience learning science in a second language.

Adolescent Mathematics II: Associate Professor Todd Edwards, Miami University, engages his teacher candidates in creating innovative mathematics problem-solving materials that support the learning needs of English learners in public school classrooms. In one key assignment, Rich Problem Planning Project, teacher candidates use the open-source Learning Management System (LMS), Moodle (modular object-oriented dynamic learning environment), and Google Docs to coteach a series of online "short-courses" offered to area high school students in diverse settings. As Edwards' class members develop instructional materials in consultation with a practicing classroom teacher, they carefully consider issues associated with language acquisition, communication, and reading comprehension—all within the context of curriculum design. In his reflection on the course, Edwards notes how using multimedia technologies such as Moodle provided a valuable tool for developing and delivering instruction to students in rural schools.

The final two course summaries differ from the first four. These two courses are not traditional three-credit classes with embedded EL content; rather, they have integrated an EL focus in a different manner.

ESOL for Physical Education Teachers: This is a one-credit course codeveloped by the ESL and Physical Education faculty. The course is a corequisite with a three-credit Methods of Teaching Physical Education course offered immediately afterward in the same classroom. It is linked to the three-credit course in much the same way as a lab credit, and its weekly focus coordinates with the topics of its corequisite. Professor Keith Folse, University of Central Florida, is the only ESL expert featured in the embedded course samples. Because of the codesign, development, and instruction of this course by both ESL and Physical Education faculty, it represents a novel approach to embedding EL content. Folse addresses issues English learners face in a regular classroom setting, including cultural, linguistic, and educational obstacles, as well as strategies for teaching PE to these students. In addition to planning and evaluating instruction, teacher candidates also engage in activities aimed at helping them make language more comprehensible to English learners. In related assignments, Folse's teacher candidates read selected articles on issues facing ELs in an English-speaking environment, then interview and interact with ELs. They also participate in an activity that compels them to modify their language to make content more comprehensible for these students. Folse feels that assignments such as these help his teacher candidates better understand the language needs of ELs.

Math for All Students: In this course the embedding of EL content is taken to a deeper and broader level of integration than other 2+ courses. University of South Florida, St. Petersburg, offers an innovative bachelor's degree in teaching all elementary students. Each course in the curriculum was designed around four integrated pillars—the standards or competencies of the content area (in this sample course, mathematics) and related competencies for teaching ELs, students with exceptionalities, and literacy skills. Faculty in each area codesigned, developed, and teach the courses, with some shared sessions, some online instructional modules, and some individual-led instruction. All faculty are involved in courses shared with colleagues from other disciplines and collaborate in instruction in an interdisciplinary manner. Candidates graduate with certification in elementary and exceptional education and endorsements in ESL and reading. In Math for All Students, Associate Professor Kim Stoddard, USF, St. Petersburg, focuses on making mathematics comprehensible to all students, including English learners. In one assignment, teacher candidates develop a lesson that demonstrates the ability to teach mathematical problem solving effectively, and includes writing or modifying objectives for English learners, describing how content vocabulary will be taught, describing alternative instructional strategies, anticipating student responses to the problem, describing how to assess student thinking, and including EL modifications. In her reflection, Kim comments on the progress she made as she infused EL-content through this course with respect to her own professional learning and helping prepare teacher candidates to teach English learners.

The sample EL-infused course syllabi described herein provide suggestions and guidelines for infusing EL-content into category 2+ courses with the goal of enhancing teacher candidates' preparation to effectively teach English learners in the mainstream classrooms. We encourage teacher educators to consider incorporating some of these assignments and activities, and others, into their pre-service teacher education programs, which should provide their teacher candidates with a beginning repertoire for teaching English learners whom they are increasingly likely to have in their classes.

Teaching Strategies and Classroom Management

Cynthia J. Hutchinson
University of Central Florida

Course Description

Students will explore instructional, organization, and classroom management strategies to create effective learning environments. There is a fifteen-hour service-learning requirement. There is a fingerprinting requirement in various counties.

Course Topics

1. Lesson planning that includes goals for instruction, assessment options and ESL strategies.
2. Analyzing recorded delivery of microteaching experience for evidence of ESL strategies that address three levels of language proficiency in the students and proposing additional ESL strategies that could have been used.

Course Objectives

Teacher candidates will be able to: Recognize, select, write, and clarify behavioral objectives using cognitive, affective, and psychomotor taxonomies and the Florida state standards.

- Develop instructional plans, which meet the needs of diverse learners (ESOL 13, 16).
- Develop instructional plans appropriate to learner's socialization and communication (ESOL 13).
- Develop a repertoire of teaching strategies for diverse populations (ESOL 13).
- Explain the advantages and disadvantages of various instructional strategies relative to the age of student, content being taught, limitation, etc. (ESOL 13).
- Understand and recognize social and cultural experience implicit in all instructional objectives (ESOL 13, 16).
- Understand and recognize exceptional abilities and special needs implicit in all student populations (ESOL 13, 16).

Program, State, or National Standards

Florida ESOL Performance Standard 13: Evaluate, design, and employ appropriate instructional methods and techniques appropriate to learner's socialization and communication.

Florida ESOL Performance Standard 16: Design and implement effective unit plans and daily plans, which meet the needs of ESOL students within the context of the regular classroom.

Materials

Jacobsen, D., Eggen, P., and Kauchak, D. (2009). Building on learning differences: Instruction strategies. In *Methods for teaching: Promoting student learning in K–12* classrooms (8th Ed.). Upper Saddle River, NJ: Prentice Hall.

ESL module online at http://education.ucf.edu/es/edg4410New.cfm.

SLIDE and TREAD handouts prepared by TESOL faculty (see the appendix at the end of this chapter for a fuller description of the SLIDE and TREAD strategies).

Case studies for Edith, Edgar, and Tasir prepared by TESOL faculty (see the appendix at the end of this chapter for a profile of these case studies).

In-Class Activities

1. Students participate in an EL simulation where they attempt to learn how to make orange juice with instructions given in an unfamiliar language (Swiss, Dutch, or Italian) using nonverbal (represented by the acronym SLIDE) and verbal (represented by the acronym TREAD) strategies.

2. Students view a film, *Victor*, about a fifth-grade student who is experiencing a disconnect between his school experiences, where everyone speaks English, and his home life, where the family speaks Spanish. After viewing the film, students make a list of the modifications the teacher in the film made for Victor and a separate list of the EL modifications they would have made. In small groups, students discuss the two lists.

Assignments

Microteach Lesson Plan: Students investigate several online resources that explain various graphic organizers. They create a lesson plan for a microteaching experience with their peers that is recorded for viewing later. Taking into consideration how they are going to teach their content-specific terminology, they select an appropriate graphic organizer. As they create the procedures section of the lesson plan, they incorporate SLIDE and TREAD strategies appropriate for each of the case study students, Edith, Edgar, and Tasir in bold, capital letters.

Professional Development Plan: Students view the recordings of their microteaching to analyze for evidence of SLIDE and TREAD strategies that addressed each level of language proficiency. They describe the strategy, how it was used in the lesson, and whether or not they were successful. They explain why the SLIDE or TREAD strategy would help each case study student at his/her level of language proficiency. They recommend additional strategies that could have been incorporated.

Reflection

At the dawn of the new millennium, I was quite proud to be associated with a teacher preparation program that enjoyed a reputation for preparing a well-qualified beginning teacher. The surveys completed by principals at the end of our graduates' first year of teaching gave us feedback that was positive and encouraging. However, Florida's school population was changing, and the piece that was missing was preparing our teacher candidates to work with English learners (ELs). Our college reacted as all good educators react; we created a committee to address this concern. I was invited to serve on the TESOL Advisory Committee and a decision was made that the college would adopt the infusion model.

Although I am known for my willingness to participate and carry my fair share of the load, I found myself wondering, "What can I contribute? What do I know about ELs?" My personal associations with ELs were my maternal and paternal grandparents, who emigrated to the United States from Russia and Czechoslovakia. They learned English through the school of hard knocks—being charged penalties for missing important deadlines because of their limited English proficiency or being bypassed for jobs they desired. They made sure that my collective group of thirteen aunts and uncles were required to speak only English in their homes, denying the next generation an opportunity to be bilingual.

As a college, we had outstanding faculty but many of us lacked TESOL preparation. Our experiences with ELs were very limited. The first order of business for the committee was our *own* professional development. But the challenging question was, "How will we inspire our colleagues to embrace this idea?" College of Education faculty *present* professional development opportunities to other educators, they do not generally *participate* in them. The TESOL professional development was appropriately titled Jericho, because the walls needed to come tumbling down!

A dedicated English language arts professor created a forty-five-hour professional development TESOL course for the faculty. It was a series of online modules we could master independently, combined with a smattering of whole-group experiences. The whole-group sessions featured knowledgeable guest speakers with many hands-on experiences. All journeys have a beginning, and this was ours.

I am an early adopter. When computers were new in the early 1990s, I received an Apple grant that brought the first eight computers to the college and introduced Hyper-Studio to my teacher candidates, who then taught it to third-, fourth-, and fifth-graders at a local elementary school. I participated in the first class to receive training to create online courses. I jump into my training feet first. In terms of ESL knowledge, skills, and dispositions, I was consciously incompetent. I knew that I didn't know and I was eager to learn. I finished my Jericho modules, passed all of the quizzes, got my certificate, and was ready to take on the world. But as I began the next phase in the process of infusion—modifying courses—I was slow to understand what my teacher candidates would need to be successful. As the course shepherd for the general methods class, I was responsible for the curriculum revision.

Because our college is large and there are many sections of every course offered each semester, the educational foundations faculty chose to create online TESOL modules for teacher candidates that could be used in all course sections, insuring that regular faculty as well as our adjunct instructors would provide the same experiences. Using faculty development opportunities offered through the Faculty Center for Teaching and Learning, we spent a summer conference creating the initial ESL modules. Hindsight is always 20/20. I realize now that I had wonderful resources in the College of Arts and Humanities who would have been happy to participate with us, and eventually did in later years adding richness to our modules. But I digress.

The first year using the revised courses was disappointing. Our initial TESOL module lacked depth. We exposed students to the literature and online resources but we were new to the TESOL standards and misinterpreted some of them. Each year we would analyze our success and weaknesses. We found the modules difficult to grade. We noticed a large understanding difference between students who had completed one or both of the stand-alone TESOL classes and students who had not yet attempted these classes. Finally, at the suggestion from our TESOL coordinator, we participated in another revision. This time we had the assistance of faculty from the College of Arts and Sciences. This revision was much closer to the mark we were aiming for, but we were still off-center. Our teacher candidates created lesson plans with lists of ESL modifications that could be used, but they were unable to suggest specific modifications for individual learner needs.

The most powerful lesson learned during my TESOL journey is teamwork. During this academic year, the TESOL faculty offered to partner with each infused course shepherd. My partner helped me analyze the teacher candidates' individual lesson plans for their incompleteness. She created three case studies that our teacher candidates will encounter in several classes. She offered to come into my classes and simulate an EL experience for my students before they wrote their lesson plans. Bang! This time I knew we were really onto something. The students' work was much improved, demonstrating a richer understanding of how to meet the needs of each level of language development—especially the beginning level—after participating in the simulation. They finally got it. Next came their professional development plans, based on their lesson plans. Another direct hit! The students were much more successful justifying modifications they made and suggesting additional modifications when they were needed. I experienced fewer desperate middle-of-the-night e-mail messages from students confused about the assignments.

I realize that we're not home free yet. It's not realistic for the ESL faculty to conduct ten to fourteen EL simulations each semester in all of the general methods classes. We plan to redesign the template and rubric for the professional development plan. We need to create sample lesson plans that address the case studies that have been added to the ESL module. But I feel that I can truthfully say that my general methods students are better prepared for the EL challenges that lie ahead in their future classrooms.

Social Studies in the Elementary School

William B. Russell III
University of Central Florida

Course Description

Designed for elementary education majors. Includes strategies, methods, materials, and technologies for teaching social studies in the elementary schools. Concurrent field experience projects are included.

Course Topics

Identification and examination of appropriate and effective teaching strategies for all learners, including English learners at beginning, intermediate, and advanced levels of proficiency.

Course Objectives

Upon successful completion of the requirements of this course, teacher candidates will be able to:

1. Discuss the impact of diversity, including differences due to culture, ethnicity, native language, socioeconomic status, gender, and exceptionalities.
2. Utilize appropriate and creative use of instructional technology, media, and materials as tools to enhance student learning as well as select, evaluate, and use educational software for social studies.
3. Apply a variety of instructional strategies for the teaching of elementary social studies to diverse learners, including English learners at beginning, intermediate, and advanced levels of proficiency.

Program, State, or National Standards

Florida ESOL Performance Standards 2, 6, 7, 12, 14, 16, 18, and 20

EL-Focused Materials

Brown, C.L. (2007). Strategies for making social studies texts more comprehensible for English language learners. *Social Studies, 98*(5), 185-188.

Cruz, B., Nutta, J., O'Brien, J., Feyten, C., & Govoni, J. (2003). *Passport to Learning, Teaching Social Studies to ESL Students*, National Council for the Social Studies.

Olmedo, I. M. (1993). Junior historians: Doing oral history with ESL and bilingual students. *TESOL Journal, 2* (4), 7-10.

Weisman, E., & Hansen, L.E. (2007). Strategies for teaching social studies to English-language learners at the elementary level. *Social Studies, 98*(5), 180-184.

Lecture notes via a PowerPoint addressing EL instruction and assessment.

In-Class Activity

1. *ESL Responses:* In-class discussion in response to the required reading titled, Junior Historians: Doing Oral History with ESL and Bilingual Students.
2. *Class Discussion:* In-class discussion based on the ELs PowerPoint

Assignments

1. Candidates will read an article by Olmedo (1993) entitled: "Junior Historians: Doing Oral History with ESL and Bilingual Students." They will then write a two-page reflective response to the reading (not a summary). Candidates should include a reaction to the article, a discussion of the article's relevance to social studies instruction, and a discussion of how the insights gained will impact candidates' ability to work with EL students in mainstream classrooms. (ESOL Standards 2, 7).
2. Lesson plan: Candidates will create a social studies lesson plan that could be taught within a K–6 classroom. Candidates may use the grade level of choice, while assuming that the lesson would be taught to twenty to thirty students from a heterogeneous population, which includes ELs. Lesson plan should indicate how instruction and assessment will be adjusted to accommodate the learning needs of Edith, Edgar, and Tasir. (ESOL Standards 6, 12, 14, 16, 18, 20).

Lesson Plan Components

- *Title page:* Include title, grade level, discipline, and topic.
- *Content summary:* Provide a description of the content that will be covered.
- *Standards:* List national and state standards that will be covered.
- *Objectives:* What should the students gain from this lesson?
- *Materials:* List all the items needed to complete the lesson (e.g., handouts, books, artifacts, technological devices, software)
- *Procedures:* List in chronological order the steps needed throughout the lesson, including all activities and materials. Be specific! Be sure to make specific accommodations for ELs and other students with individual needs.
- *Evaluation and assessment:* Explain how you plan on assessing the effectiveness of the lesson and your teaching and the knowledge gained by the students.
- *ESL accommodations:* Describe how your lesson was adapted or modified for ELs at various levels of proficiency.
- *Resources:* Provide resources other than those provided in the lesson for extension or modification.
- *Reflection:* Write a brief reflection on the lesson module for your portfolio.

Reflection

My outlook on infusing ESL strategies into my teaching is unique. I was trained in my undergraduate teacher preparation program to adapt my lesson plans to meet the needs of all learners, including ELs. So developing lessons that were adapted for EL students was the only way I knew. Nonetheless, that does not mean I was not cautious when it came to ESOL infusion.

My educational background and teaching experiences had provided me with only one perspective toward ESOL infusion. Simply—it is a requirement. Teaching in Florida and attending state universities, there was always a district, university, or state requirement to adapt lessons to meet the needs of individuals. So I always attempted to approach all my teaching to meet the needs of all students (ESL, special needs, etc.). I would even add a section in my lessons explaining how I would adapt my curriculum and instruction to meet the needs of all learners, including EL students.

These techniques carried over into my college classrooms. I remember when I first become a professor. A week into my first semester, my department chair called a meeting with faculty. She needed me and my colleagues to add an ESL-related assignment to our syllabi. We were going through NCATE accreditation, and we needed to demonstrate that were providing ESL training. Luckily, I already had a required ESL component in my unit plan assignment because my students would not have been too pleased if I added an additional assignment after the semester started.

As time went on, I noticed that many professors saw ESOL infusion as a hassle and/ or additional work. This was problematic and troublesome. What I realized is that I knew more than the average educator about infusing ESL, but not enough to truly feel comfortable to effectively train future educators and encourage other professors to do so. At this point, I was in need of help. I examined various articles and books related to ESL and social studies.

I began to explore new teaching activities and assignments. I became aware that I needed to do more than have students add an EL accommodations/modifications section to a lesson plan: I needed to have them understand the importance of meeting the needs of all learners with relation to their content. I needed to have them understand and appreciate all learners and learning styles.

So I decided to expand my EL-related course requirements. In addition to the EL modification section of a lesson plan, I started requiring the procedure section to have a detailed step-by-step list of lesson procedures including how and what modifications were going to be made for EL students. Additionally, during a lesson on teaching history, I expanded my discussion of oral histories and included a reading titled, "Junior Historians: Doing Oral History with ESOL and Bilingual Students." At this point, my students truly started to appreciate the concept and embrace the idea of teaching EL students. It was finally more than just an additional section on a unit or lesson plan.

The lesson accommodation requirements, the ESL discussion, and the EL readings all helped better prepare my pre-service teachers for actual ESOL infusion. However, I still find that some of the pre-service teachers enrolled in my social studies methods course struggle with the idea of meeting the needs of all learners. They often can be closed-minded and content driven, isolating themselves and the content from the student and the learning process. This apathy toward effective instruction and meeting student needs is disheartening, but it is also reality. Therefore, I continue to explore new opportunities and learning activities that may improve my instruction.

One of the most valuable assets that I have found for all of my EL questions and concerns has been the ESL faculty member at my university. She has been more than encouraging and nonjudgmental. She has provided me with tremendous feedback and opportunities to expand my knowledge base on EL education.

With such a support for ESOL infusion, I feel I have helped many pre-service teachers understand the need for EL awareness in schools and EL accommodations in the classroom.

Middle School Science

Nazan U. Bautista
Miami University

Course Description

Middle School Science is a science methods course with a focus on basic principles, methods, and materials for teaching science to children, grades 4 through 9. Field experiences with children are integral to meeting course objectives.

Course Topics

1. Nature of science and scientific literacy
2. Misconceptions and conceptual change
3. Inquiry-based learning and learning cycle
4. Informal science teaching
5. Technological/engineering design
6. Teaching science to English learners

Course Goals and Objectives

The overall goal of this course is to prepare candidates to successfully complete student teaching in a middle childhood science classroom (grades 4 through 9). Emphasis will be placed on planning for instruction, teaching, and learning; technology; and adaptation of instruction for various student populations, including ELs. Candidates will be actively engaged in constructivist learning experiences, including demonstrations; problem solving activities, individual and group presentations; and field-based teaching experiences.

By completing the course activities, teacher candidates will be able to accomplish the following objectives:

- Examine personal beliefs and attitudes and engage in metacognitive reflections regarding the learning and teaching of science in the middle school.
- Explore the implications of constructivist instructional activities that integrate science across curricular areas, that are developmentally appropriate, that are differentiated for culturally and linguistically diverse student populations, and that display understanding and application of the National Science Education Standards (NSES) and Ohio Academic Content Standards (ACS) as they relate to science teaching.
- Construct, apply, and differentiate various assessment strategies (formative, alternative, informal, and formal) for evaluation of science knowledge and process skills of students who are linguistically and culturally diverse.

Materials

Course packet: Collection of book chapters and current articles that focus on the concepts listed under course topics. The reading materials related to ELs are listed below:

Bautista, N.U., & Castañeda, M. (2011). Teaching science to ELLs, Part I: Key strategies every science teacher should know. *The Science Teacher, 78*(3), 35-39.

Castañeda, M., & Bautista, N. U. (2011). Teaching science to ELLs, Part II: Classroom-based assessment strategies for science teachers. *The Science Teacher, 78*(3), 40-44.

Nutta, J.W., Bautista, N.U., & Butler, M.B. (2010). Part 2. What we know from research. In J.W. Nutta, N.U. Bautista, & M.B. Butler, (Eds.) *Teaching science to English language learners,* (pp. 38-56). New York, Routledge.

In-Class Activity

The course instructor engages teacher candidates in an activity in which candidates are at prefunctional level in the instructional language used. The main goal of this lesson is to demonstrate how to effectively modify a science lesson to meet the needs of English learners at various language proficiency levels through a lesson titled, "What causes seasons?" In this lesson, the instructor models two different instructional approaches to teaching about seasons. In the first, she lectures on the causes of seasons in Turkish, which is her native language, without providing any scaffolding or modifications. She then asks candidates if they can predict what the lesson was about. Then, the instructor implements the second approach, in which the lesson is modified for beginning and prefunctional-level ELs. At the end of the activity, teacher candidates reflect on their experiences, review key strategies that need to be considered while planning a lesson for EL students at various proficiency levels, and discuss the course reading materials regarding teaching science to ELs. Candidates are provided with copies of modified and nonmodified versions of the activity along with visual aids.

Course Assignments

Modifying a lesson: After participating in an activity modified for EL students at beginning and prefunctional levels modeled by the course instruction, candidates will modify a lesson plan on "Day and night" and associated handouts provided by the course instructor to make the content more attainable and accessible for EL students.

Inquiry-based lesson plans and peer teaching: The purpose of this project is to provide the candidates with experience in planning and teaching inquiry-based and student-centered lessons. Students work in pairs and select from a list of concepts provided by the instructor. Once pairs pick their topic, they identify the grade level they want to focus on and the specific benchmark and indicator(s) (grade levels 4 through 9) in the state standards. Then, each pair will prepare a lesson plan, targeting the indicator(s) at the chosen grade level, and teach them in class during one of our regular meeting times. Integration of other content is not required, but encouraged when possible. Candidates will also provide differentiations for EL students with varying proficiency levels in their lesson plan (objectives, instruction, and assessment). They *cannot* submit and present a lesson plan they planned for another course or assignment.

Full Circle Interdisciplinary Lesson Plans (NCATE key assessment): Teams of candidates will select an area and develop an interdisciplinary unit that provides evidence of planning for instruction incorporating multiple content areas of licensure. Candidates are expected to provide differentiations for EL students with varying proficiency levels in their lesson plans (objectives, instruction, and assessment).

Assessments

1. A rubric is used to evaluate the candidates' performance on modification of the lesson plan and handouts about "Day and night." This assignment counts for 10 percent of their overall grade.
2. A rubric is used to evaluate candidates' performance on inquiry-based lesson plans and peer teaching. This assignment is worth 40 points and candidates can earn maximum of 10 points (25 percent of the assignment grade) based on their performance on the differentiations they provide for the EL students.

Reflection

Being an English language learner myself, I quickly bought into the idea of embedding teaching ELs into my science methods courses. Although I learned English ten years before I came to the United States, most of my language development took place while I actually practiced speaking, listening, writing, and reading in English in the eleven years I've lived in the United States. I was able to relate to the experiences of many EL students, though my experience was at the advanced and intermediate levels of language proficiency. I know, for instance, how easy it can be to block out a language that is different from yours while attending a class, unless the instructional materials are modified for students like you. Although these personal experiences have helped me relate to the experiences of growing number of EL students in the United States, I have come to understand through the EL infusion process that I was too naive to think that I knew how to go about accommodating ELs in science classrooms.

As a former physics and science teacher and as a science teacher educator, I believe in the importance of students' constructing their own knowledge through inquiry-based activities. Inquiry-based science instruction can be structured, guided, or open-ended, but regardless of its structure, it has to be student-centered, hands-on, and open-ended (meaning students do not know what the result is before they begin the activity). Thus, inquiry-based teaching is the centerpiece of the two science methods courses I teach. I create inquiry lesson plans, model how to teach them in my courses, and require teacher candidates to plan and teach inquiry lessons while they are in the field as well as in the class. This style of teaching is appropriate for both native English-speaking students and ELs. The literature about teaching science to ELs reveals that hands-on instruction and inquiry are effective ways to convey content to this population.[1] But the question is how this can be done effectively. Teaching science through inquiry requires teachers to facilitate student learning through effective open-ended questioning. *How could this be possibly accomplished with students who do not have access to the language?* This was the question I had to answer in my class and show my students that it could be done.

I decided to modify a fifth-grade astronomy lesson plan, titled "What causes seasons?" This is an activity that I use to model how to teach through guided inquiry in my middle school science methods course. At the beginning of this activity, I give the students the question that they will investigate: What causes seasons? I then provide them with materials and open-ended questions and show them how to set up the materials. Through answering questions, students discover these two important concepts: (1) seasons are in opposite order in the southern and northern hemispheres, and (2) seasons don't have anything to do with the distance between Earth and the sun.

I shared this activity with an EL infusion mentor at my institution. While we reviewed the activity, she constantly challenged me to think about the things I said I would do in the procedure section of my lesson plan. For instance, when she ran into statements like "ask students," she asked me *how* I was going to *ask* the ELs to do that particular action. This meant that I had to carefully think about every action I would take in the class and determine exactly *how* I or ELs would do that. Also, through this process I realized that teaching the related academic vocabulary would not give enough information for ELs to understand what the concept was. Thus, besides the words such as *sun*, *Earth*, *rotation*, *night*, and *year*, I would also have to teach words such as *long*, *short*, *same*, *direct*, *indirect*, *seasons*. My mentor suggested that I should prepare a cheat sheet containing the important vocabulary and visual representation of all of these words, along with their definitions. She also emphasized that the visuals should be culturally relevant. For instance, if I put the word *winter* in the cheat sheet, the picture representing winter should be familiar to the ELs who would receive this cheat sheet, possibly a picture of winter season in their native country.

In the following weeks, I modified my lesson to make the content more attainable and accessible to ELs, especially at the beginning and prefunctional proficiency levels. I prepared a cheat sheet that included *all* vocabulary that an EL needs to know to understand this particular concept. Finally, I revised the format of the activity from guided inquiry to a very structured inquiry. Instead of asking students to follow the questions to reach to a conclusion on their own, I, as the teacher, planned to assist ELs by showing them what to do. For instance, I planned that I would show ELs the intensity of the sunlight hitting the surface of the Earth (globe) *directly* and *indirectly* by using a flashlight and reflecting on the surface of the table directly and indirectly.

I shared the modified activity with my EL infusion mentor once again to receive her final feedback before I shared the plan with my students. I planned to provide both *before* and *after* versions of the activity to help them understand the key points they had to consider while revising their lessons for this particular group of students. After reviewing the modified version of the activity, my mentor suggested that I should teach both before and after versions in my class, but in my native language, Turkish. Since none of my students knew Turkish and since Turkish was very different from English, all students could be considered as prefunctional in such a situation. With the help of my mentor, I created a Turkish version of the cheat sheet and the activity. I considered Ohio as the students' native land and selected visuals that are representative of Ohio, such as the picture of seasons in Ohio.

I did not inform my students about my plan, and went into my class speaking Turkish. While I was telling them that they would be learning what causes seasons, they were smiling but surprised to hear me speaking another language. I took advantage of the situation and lectured about the cause of seasons in Turkish. After I was done lecturing, I stopped and asked them in English if they knew what I was talking about. Then I started implementing the modified version of the lesson. First, I gave each of them the cheat sheet and helped them learn the vocabulary by using a PowerPoint presentation that had the same images on their sheets. I would say the word aloud and by using my hands and body made them understand that I wanted them to repeat the words after me. The most interesting part was where I was explaining what the North Star was and where it was located, and how the Earth's axis always pointed toward the North Star although it would be toward or away from and sometimes neither toward nor away from the sun.

At the end of the lesson, I asked the candidates what the lesson was about and reviewed everything they learned. We compared the two-modeled instruction and talked about how they felt during the first versus the second one. This modeling activity was a great way to start a discussion about issues regarding ESL. With the help of my mentor, who observed my modeling, we discussed several key points that every science teacher needs to know, such as focusing on discipline-specific language and considering language proficiency levels of ELs prior to planning or modifying a lesson.

Nevertheless, I had to make sure the candidates understood that since I knew the language they were speaking (English), I could easily monitor whether they were getting it or not, without actually giving them a chance to communicate their understanding to me (e.g., by nodding). They may not have the same advantage; thus, we emphasized that they have to stop at times during the instruction to check whether students are following and grasping the concept.

Although I find the infusion of EL content into my middle school science methods course successful, I don't claim to be an expert in teaching science to ELs. In my experience, my mentor's comments and feedback were right on target, and I actually experienced some of the situations she described to me while I was modeling. Thus, having a mentor whom I can trust makes me believe that this infusion will be effective and will work. I know it because more than 75 percent of this class applied to get the ESL certificate at my institution.

Adolescent Mathematics II

Michael Todd Edwards, Suzanne R. Harper, Nicholas Shay,
and Jennifer Flory Edwards
Miami University

Course Description

Second semester mathematics methods course for future high school mathematics teachers; the third in a four-course sequence of classes.

Course Topics

Designing mathematics tasks, lesson planning, assessing student work for diverse learners, including English language learners.

Course Objectives

Demonstrate their knowledge of NCTM Content and Process Standards and apply them teaching English learners at different levels of English proficiency.

Materials

Borgioli, G. (2008). Equity for English language learners in mathematics classrooms. *Teaching Children Mathematics, 15*(3), 185-191.

Carpenter, T., & Lehrer, R. (1999). Teaching and learning mathematics with understanding. In E. Fennema & T.A. Romberg (Eds.), *Mathematics classrooms that promote understanding* (pp. 33-42). Mahwah, NJ: Lawrence Erlbaum Associates.

Murrey, D. (2008). Differentiating instruction in mathematics for the English language learner. *Mathematics Teaching in the Middle School, 14*(3), 146-153.

Course Assignment

This assignment, which we refer to as the Rich Problem Planning Project, was implemented in Adolescent Mathematics II (EDT 430). Candidates coteach online "short courses" offered to area high school students in diverse settings. Using the open-source Learning Management System (LMS), Moodle [modular object-oriented dynamic learning environment], and Google Docs, candidates author a series of mathematics tasks and activities for a diverse group of high school students, including ELs. As candidates construct materials in consultation with a practicing classroom teacher, they carefully consider issues associated with language acquisition, communication, and reading comprehension—all within the context of curriculum design.

The project aims to provide candidates with opportunities to gain proficiency in the following areas: (1) writing lesson materials/activities in small groups using Google Docs; (2) constructing online assessments for a diverse student population (including ELs) within Moodle; and (3) using standardized testing data to inform the construction of lesson materials/activities and assessments. Candidates create teaching materials for Angela Roth (pseudonym), a mathematics teacher with five or more years of teaching experience in the Midvale City Schools, an urban district serving approximately 7,000 students in 11 schools in grades preK–12. The Midvale City School District serves a small but growing EL population, with 3 percent of its population designated English Learners. Roth teaches three classes of students who are struggling to pass the Ohio Graduation Test. Roth's challenge is to present content in innovative, engaging ways that make the mathematics seem new and interesting (and more readily understood by ELs).

In an effort to provide teacher candidates with a better sense of Roth's students, individual student test data was provided to candidates. The EDT 430 methods instructor (Edwards, a coauthor of this paper) observed, cotaught, and videotaped approximately one week's worth of instruction in Roth's target classes—fifth-, sixth-, and seventh-period geometry classrooms. In particular, Edwards and Roth cotaught several lessons that utilized Moodle questionnaires and quizzes. Videos of these teaching sessions were made available to teacher candidates through the EDT 430 Moodle site. In addition, several teacher candidates physically visited the classroom.

Sample district tests (and accompanying student data) provided candidates with an initial framework for modeling their own tasks for students. Unfortunately, as Solorzano notes "high stakes tests as currently constructed are inappropriate for ELs, and most disturbing is their continued use for high stakes decisions that have adverse consequences."[2]

In groups of two or three, candidates construct three weeks' worth of cohesive, engaging teaching materials for Roth's students using this data. The materials were made available for Roth to use with her students following their collection in EDT 430.

The initial rubric guiding the construction of teaching materials made no mention of ELs. Not surprisingly, tasks initially constructed by teacher candidates—although mathematically sound—failed to address the needs of EL students. For instance, Moodle quiz items were predominantly text-based. Graphical elements that would likely benefit all students (including, but not limited to ELs) were noticeably lacking. In fact, of the over 60 tasks initially created, not one included embedded graphics or other visual information. Furthermore, tasks were written in an impersonal style closely mimicking items from standardized district tests. For the most part, items were not tailored to students' backgrounds and interests. Lastly, many items contained dense, technical language written at a level inappropriate for high schools students; for example, "Using the information below, calculate the average height of a group of people: 5 ft. 7 in; 5 ft. 3 in.; 6 ft.; 6 ft. 1 in., 5 ft. 1 in.; etc." and "Determine the slope of the line passing through the following ordered pairs: P = (2,3) and Q = (5,7). Type your final answer as a fraction in the space provided in a/b form."

To assist candidates in the creation of teaching materials and rich tasks that support ELs, teacher educators at Miami University constructed the Teaching English Language Learners (TELL) rubric in consultation with area EL teachers and Roth. Constructed based on recommendations presented by Carpenter and Lehrer and Borgioli, the TELL rubric explicitly organizes assessment criteria into two dimensions: tasks and tools.[3] There are five dimensions to each task: (a) keys, (b) connection to theme, (c) relevance, (d) solution strategies, and (e) cognitive demand. Each of these dimensions is evaluated as exceptional, satisfactory, or revision required. There are three tools: (a) visual cues, (b) representation choice, and (c) tool choice, each of which also is evaluated as exceptional, satisfactory, or revision required. After candidates had constructed initial tasks, they were provided with the TELL rubric.

During subsequent EDT 430 class meetings, candidates continued to work on Moodle tasks, using the TELL rubric to guide their revisions. The acronym VIP (*visual* and *varied*, *interactive*, *personal*) was coined by several candidates to remind classmates of essential ideas from the TELL rubric. The following bulleted list was posted on the main Moodle page to remind candidates of the needs of the Midvale students:

- Vary problem types (multiple choice, true-false, open-ended)
- Make tasks visual (include graphics)
- Make tasks interactive (embed GeoGebra applets, links to websites, etc.)
- Personalize tasks (include names of students, area landmarks, teachers, local sports teams, etc.)

Following the introduction of the TELL rubric, teacher candidates were more mindful of the contexts they provided in their tasks. A revised Moodle quiz item illustrates ways that candidates made use of students' backgrounds, experiences, and interests—as well as Moodle's multimedia capabilities—in revisions to initial quiz items.

The revised item includes a context familiar to Midvale High School students—namely, their school and surrounding community. A Google map embedded within the item includes a driving route that many students take at the end of the school day. In addition to embedded graphics, the item includes embedded audio content to further support ELs as they make sense of the task. Clicking on the embedded audio player positioned at either side of problem text plays an audio recording of the text to the student. The audio can be played repeatedly by students as they consider the task. As ELs listen to the audio recordings, they focus on deciphering meanings rather than struggling to sound out written words.[4] Building on students' real-world understanding of miles per hour as a rate of change of distance and time, the physical scenario depicted in the Google map is connected to a more formal mathematical representation—namely a graph of time-distance ordered pairs.

Reflection

Too often, university faculty who work with pre-service teachers struggle to bring authentic classroom experiences to teacher candidates. As the number and percentage of ELs in secondary school classrooms continue to grow, systematic treatment of practical issues concerning ELs becomes a necessary component of any mathematics methods course. Yet, when one's campus is located in rural Ohio—in the middle of a cornfield, nearly an hour away from large urban school districts—how does one provide an authentic EL experience for teacher candidates? This was the instructional hurdle we faced as we began to conceive the Rich Problem Planning Project.

We desired a mechanism that would allow urban high school students and their teacher to collaborate with undergraduates in our teacher preparation program. For EDT 430, a course focused on curriculum design and implementation, we needed a way to collaborate with classroom teachers to construct lesson materials and rich mathematics tasks for students in a way that would be convenient and timely. A solution that didn't require long car rides on icy roads was a must, as was one that would provide high school students with easy access to rich mathematics tasks and teachers with easy access to student assessment data. For us, Moodle provided a nearly ideal solution. While Moodle didn't provide teacher candidates and students with opportunities to talk face-to-face, the platform—when used in conjunction with multi-media components—provided pre-service teachers and students with a way to interact meaningfully. Perhaps most important, Moodle provided candidates with a context for meaningful construction of teaching materials for ELs. Using Moodle as a platform for the mathematical tasks allowed the teacher candidates more options for different interactive representations, whether an embedded graph or an audio file reading the task to the student. While the Moodle website aids the teacher candidate to provide richer mathematical tasks for ELs, it also benefits the EL students as they solve the task, too.

Rather than constructing tasks and lessons for hypothetical students, candidates authored materials to be implemented in a real classroom. Because candidates knew that their materials had the potential to impact student understanding of mathematics and because candidates knew that an actual classroom teacher would evaluate the materials, candidates took the assignment far more seriously than typical lesson-planning assignments. ELs were enrolled in the high school classroom, thus constructing materials that addressed the needs of those learning English was paramount. The TELL rubric that we created—using earlier EL research as a starting point—provided candidates with a framework for adapting their materials. The multimedia capabilities of Moodle provided candidates with a means for producing tasks that engaged ELs and native speakers alike.

ESOL for Physical Education Teachers

Keith Folse
University of Central Florida

Course Description

Designed for physical education majors. Includes an overview of issues ELs face in a regular classroom setting, including cultural, linguistic, and educational obstacles as well as strategies for teaching physical education to ELs.

Course Topics

1. Who are our ELs?
2. Language problems faced by your ELs
3. Cultural differences between ELs and non-ELs
4. Teaching strategies for physical education classes with ELs
5. Modifying your lesson plans to meet state ESOL standards

Course Objectives

Teacher candidates will be able to:

1. Design a physical education lesson plan with appropriate modifications for ELs.
2. Recognize ELs' common difficulties of English, including pronunciation, vocabulary, and syntax, that can impact communication in the context of a physical education class.
3. Paraphrase their own language to make it more comprehensible for ELs, including basic directions for playing a game or other classroom activity.
4. Apply knowledge of games and physical activities found outside the US in a physical education class.

Program, State, or National Standards

- *Florida ESOL Performance Standard 12:* Apply content-based ESOL approaches to instruction.
- *Florida ESOL Performance Standard 16:* Design and implement effective unit plans and daily lesson plans, which meet the needs of ESOL students within the context of the regular classroom.
- *Florida ESOL Performance Standard 17:* Evaluate, adapt, and employ appropriate instructional materials, media, and technology for ESOL in the content areas at the elementary, middle, and high school levels.
- *Florida ESOL Performance Standard 18:* Create a positive classroom environment to accommodate the various learning styles and cultural backgrounds of students.

EL-Focused Materials

Bell, N. & Lorenzi, D. (2004). Facilitating second language acquisition in elementary and secondary physical education classes. *Journal of Physical Education, Recreation, and Dance, 75*(6), 46-52.

Clancy, M., & Hruska, B. (2005). Developing objectives for English language learners in physical education lessons. *Journal of Physical Education, Recreation, and Dance, 76*(4), 30-35.

Florida Department of Education Bureau of Student Achievement through Language Acquisition (1995). Some issues regarding the education of language enriched pupils (LEP) in the state of Florida: A Restatement. Tallahassee, FL: Florida Department of Education. Retrieved from http://www.fldoe.org/aala/restatem. asp?style=print.

Folse, K. (2009). What K–12 content teachers should know about ESL grammar. *Essential Teacher, 6*(3-4). Retrieved from http://www.tesol.org/s_tesol/secet. asp?CID=2037&DID=12753

Gil, G. & Gil, R. (1993). LEP students and PE: Overcoming the language barrier. *Journal of Physical Education, Recreation & Dance, 60*(6), 10.

Glakas, B. (1993). Teaching secondary physical education to ESL students. *Journal of Physical Education, Recreation and Dance, 64*(7), 20-24.

In-Class Activities

1. *Modifying your teacher language:* Explaining a culturally specific activity (tic-tac-toe)
2. *EL Interviews:* In-class interviews with non-native speakers studying English at our university's intensive English program

Assignments

Assignment #1: Explaining a Culturally Specific Activity

The purpose of this activity is to demonstrate how important language is in explaining directions for a common activity. Candidates will understand how imprecise teacher directions can be when both the teacher and the student share a common cultural background.

1. The teacher is at the board with a marker in hand. Ask your students to imagine that you are from a different county where tic-tac-toe is not played.
2. Candidates will call out directions on how to start the game, with the first step being the drawing of the tic-tac-toe grid. This step is actually the entire activity. The problem is that, because of shared cultural knowledge, both the teacher and the candidates know what the grid looks like and, in the real world, they would never verbalize drawing the grid. One of the two game players would simply and quickly draw the grid.
3. Since the teacher has no idea what the grid looks like, the students must call out the first step. The teacher will intentionally mis-draw the grid but will follow the students' directions.

Figure 7.1 shows some common directions native U.S. English speakers often call out during this activity, with accompanying intentional but accurate mis-drawing responses by the teacher in order to demonstrate misunderstandings when we go only by the teacher's exact words.

As a follow-up assignment, have candidates work in groups of three to go through the process of pretending to explain the directions for playing checkers, a simple game that is not as simple as we might expect when one person has never played the game.

Assignment #2: Interviews with ELs

The purpose of this activity is for teacher candidates to gain familiarity with ELs and their language issues, including pronunciation, vocabulary, and syntax, in communicating in English.

Almost every college or university has on its campus an intensive English program. These programs attract international students who aspire to attend a U.S. college or university but lack the requisite English skills, often as demonstrated on the TOEFL (Test of English as a Foreign Language). These non-native speakers come from all over the globe and represent many different countries, languages, and cultures. Typically, they study English five hours a day for five days a week in an intensive English language program. They usually range in age from 18 to 30, with a few older students.

These students crave an opportunity to practice their English with a native speaker, and the administrators of these programs are usually actively seeking native speaking volunteers to do "conversation hour" programs with their students. If you contact the director of this program at your institution, the director will more than likely be extremely eager to have your students work with the English learners. The best arrangement is for your entire class of teacher candidates to work with a class or a few classes of English learners at the same time. In many programs, there is a conversation or communication skills class, which is the most natural class to pair up with your teacher preparation class.

It is possible to have ELs and candidates work one on one, but you may wish to have two candidates interview one English learner at the same time but submit separate original interview reports.

The candidates will focus on cultural, linguistic, and educational differences or difficulties. Candidates will document date, setting, participants in attendance, and length of the meeting.

Possible questions that teacher candidates should be given in advance include: What is your name? Where are you from? How long have you been here in the United States? Why are you here? Specifically, why did you come to this school? How long have you been studying English? What were English classes like in your country? Does everyone in your country study English? What are the most difficult parts of English for you? What are you doing to work on these areas? If I were to study your language, what do you think are the 3 most difficult areas of your language? Since you have been here, have you had any cultural problems? What things are the most different between

Figure 7.1

Possible errors based on exact directions given

Direction given	Accompanying mis-drawing
Draw a tic-tac-toe grid.	No action. Blank stare. "What?"
Draw 2 lines.	Draw 2 lines: _____ and _____
No, draw 2 parallel lines.	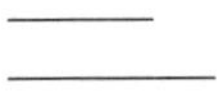 _____ _____
No, the 2 lines have to be the same length.	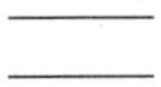 _____ _____
No, they should be longer.	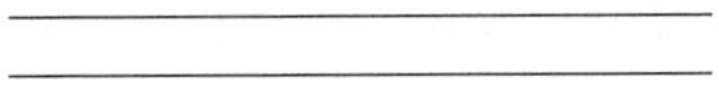 _____ _____
No, about half as long.	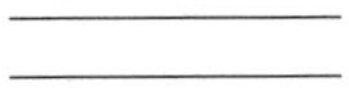 _____ _____
Yes, but you need more space in between.	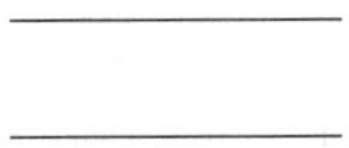 _____ _____
Ok, now add two vertical lines.	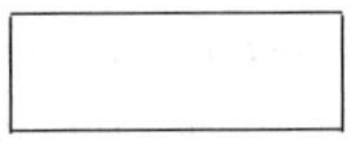 [rectangle box drawing]
No, don't make a box.	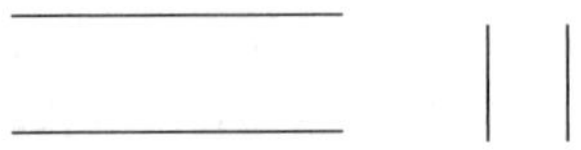 [two horizontal lines and two separate vertical lines drawing]
No, the 2 vertical lines need to cross the first two lines. Make them longer.	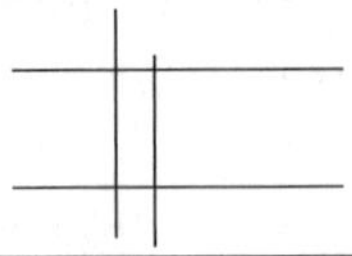 [grid drawing with crossing lines]
No, the 2 vertical lines should be the same length.	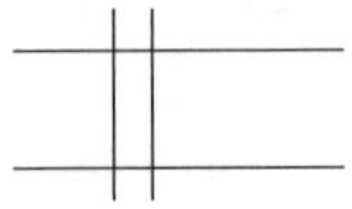 [grid drawing]
No, open them up so that they cut the two horizontal lines into 3 more or less equal parts.	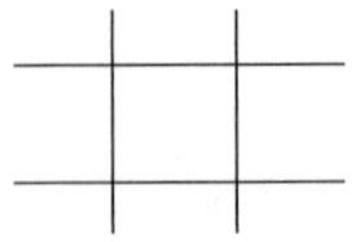 [tic-tac-toe grid drawing]

your country and the United States? If I went to your country, what might be difficult for me? Did you have a class in your school where you studied physical education? What kinds of sports are the most popular in your country?

You can set up your candidates' final reports in many ways, but one possibility is that they include this information:

1. Background information of the EL.
2. Summary of cultural problems that the EL has faced in the United States; for example, differences in U.S. culture that caused the EL confusion or hardship.
3. Summary of linguistic difficulties that the EL has faced in the United States; for example, pronunciation problems, vocabulary issues, grammar obstacles.
4. Summary of educational difficulties that the EL has faced in the United States; for example classroom atmosphere and/or teacher expectations that the EL found problematic.
5. List of possible accommodations that a physical education teacher could make to avoid or overcome any of the issues presented in items 2, 3, or 4.

Reflection

Unlike the other contributors in this area of the book, I am an ESL specialist. My training is in TESOL, and my main research area is second language vocabulary acquisition. I am secondary language arts certified, and I have taught languages for more than 30 years to people from second grade to seventy years old. I have taught in the United States, Saudi Arabia, Malaysia, Japan, and Kuwait, and I speak a few different languages.

Before I explain the actual course, I think it is extremely important to note the very important role that the physical education (PE) class and the physical education teacher can play in the acculturation of an English learner, especially one who has recently arrived in the United States and does not speak much English yet.

I have several colleagues who came to the United States as young non-native English speakers and found themselves confused, alone, and even ostracized because of the language barrier. Years later, many of them now tell similar stories in which they remember how much they enjoyed their PE class time because it was the one time during the day when they were not lost linguistically. This is not to say that you don't need language for communication in this class, but in a PE class, there are many activities and it is possible to function well by just doing what everyone else is doing. Clearly, the PE class and the teacher can be instrumental in the EL developing a positive attitude toward the new school experience and U.S. culture as well as self. All of these play a very important role in the ELs' ultimate educational success.

This course was designed especially for PE teacher candidates, most of whom have had little to no experience working with ELs. It was a one-credit course that was taken concurrently with a PE methods class.

I was asked to teach this course because of my experience working with ELs and, I think, because of my love of tennis. I had no experience working with PE teacher candidates, and I have to admit that I was anxious about working with this audience. My only experience with PE teachers was many years ago when I was in junior high and high school, and I initially had apprehensions about how I would be able to get across strategies for teaching ELs.

When I walked into the first class meeting, I met my 36 teacher candidates. More than half of them were athletes on the university's football, basketball, baseball, or softball teams. None of them was a tennis player, let alone on the tennis team. Teachers are always a little nervous on the first day of class, but I just did not know what to expect from this group of students and was out of my element.

In the assignment described here, the PE teachers had to interview an EL. Although I could have set this up as an out-of-class activity, I decided to arrange it during a regularly scheduled class to make sure that everyone had this opportunity at the same time. Over the years, I have found that the best way for a teacher candidate to learn about ELs is to meet one. People will remember people long after they have forgotten a textbook description or a lecture. I wanted to put the face and name of a real person to this label *EL* that the candidates kept hearing about in their teacher preparation courses.

To accomplish this, I contacted our intensive English program. Almost all universities and colleges have such a program—where international students aged 18 to 50 come to learn academic English. Many of these ELs intend to matriculate into an American university or college but first need to demonstrate their English proficiency on an exam such as the TOEFL.

I obtained a list of the instructors who were teaching any type of conversation, speaking, or communications skills class at the intermediate level and explained that I wanted their students to participate in an interview with native-speaking university students who were in a teacher education program. Because intensive English program students want to practice their English with native speakers, especially native speakers of a similar age and academic background, the teachers quickly agreed to my request.

I had 36 teacher candidates and could have easily matched them up with 36 ELs. However, I chose to have my candidates work in pairs with one English learner, so I needed only 18 ELs. I used pairs for the interview because I wanted my candidates to work together to form their interview questions around the three summary areas in the assignment. I knew my candidates would be nervous meeting an English learner, and I wanted them to be able to make solid observations about the English learner. In pairs, the candidates could take turns asking questions and taking notes on the ELs' responses.

The results of this assignment were phenomenal, and the activity was a great success. It was interesting to read comments from physically daunting football players such as, "I was nervous meeting Peng from China. I didn't know what to expect. She was really nice, but I was scared working with an English learner. By the end of our meeting, everything was going well, and I wasn't so nervous anymore." Observing these interviews, it was hard to tell who was more nervous—the English learner or the native speakers.

This single meeting with an English learner is not sufficient for teacher candidates to become knowledgeable about EL teaching strategies, but it is a great way for them to have a better understanding of the problems that ELs face in a regular classroom taught by a teacher who is not familiar with EL issues.

Math for All Students

Kim Stoddard
University of South Florida, St. Petersburg

Course Description

Designed for all education majors. Overview of mathematical concepts in elementary mathematics. Implementation of mathematics learning strategies, teaching methodology, content, and accommodations/modifications for ESE and EL learners.

Course Topics

1. Whole number operations: basic meanings, basic facts, developing number and operation sense, place value.
2. Addition and subtraction algorithms and related cultural issues.
3. Multiplication and division algorithms and related cultural issues.
4. The implementation of RTI practices, IFSP, IEP, and ITP in classroom instruction including the English learner.[5]
5. Accommodations, modifications including technology to provide instruction for a wide range of abilities/disabilities, age ranges, and cultural and language differences.
6. Differentiated grouping for instruction to accommodate a wide range of abilities/disabilities, age ranges, cultural and language differences.

Course Objectives

Teacher candidates will be able to:

1. Learn how to differentiate instruction to meet the needs of all of their students including EL students at varying levels of English language proficiency.
2. Learn how to differentiate instruction to meet the needs of all of their students, including EL students at varying levels of English language proficiency.
3. Demonstrate knowledge of numbers, number relationships, and numeration systems for whole numbers and fractions, including notation systems for different cultures.
4. Demonstrate knowledge of the meanings of operations and how they relate to each other and to EL students.
5. Create appropriate objectives for instruction, including accommodations for EL students.
6. Include alternative strategies and use manipulative, technology, and other classroom tools in instruction and modify strategies using content-specific ESL strategies, materials, and technology.

7. Assess students' mathematical thinking and problem solving processes, with modifications for EL students at various proficiency levels.

ESOL Standards

Florida ESOL Performance Standards 2, 3, 4, 5, 6, 7, 12, 14, 16, 17, 18, 19, 21

EL-Focused Materials

Artiles, A.J., & Ortiz, A.A. (2002). English language learners with special needs: Contexts and possibilities. In A.J. Artiles & A.A. Ortiz (Eds.), *English language learners with special needs: Identification, assessment, and instruction.* McHenry, IL: Delta Systems.

Bresser, R. (2003). Helping English language learners develop computational fluency, *Teaching Children Mathematics 9*(6), 294-299.

Recommended English Learner Readings

Anstrom, K., & Dicerbo, P. (Eds.) (1999). *Preparing secondary education teachers to work with English language learners: MATHEMATICS.* Center for the Study of Language and Education, Graduate School of Education & Human Development. The George Washington University: Washington, DC. Available at http://www.ncela.gwu.edu/ncbepubs/resource/ells/math.htm

Crandall, J., Spanos, G., Christian, D., Simich-Dudgeon, C., & Willetts, K. (1987). *Integrating language and content instruction for language minority students.* Wheaton, MD: National Clearinghouse for Bilingual Education.

Garcia, S. B., & Tyler, B. (2010). Meeting the needs of English language learners with learning disabilities in the general curriculum. *Theory into Practice, 49*(2), 113-120.

Ortiz, A. (2001). English language learners with special needs: Effective instructional strategies. *ERIC Digest.* Washington, DC: ERIC Clearinghouse on Languages and Linguistics. Retrieved from http://www.cal.org/resources/digest/0108ortiz.html

In-Class Activity

Discussion of the Bresser article and how it applies to the classrooms in which the candidates are working as part of their field experience.

Assignments

1. As a teacher candidate, your task is to develop a lesson that demonstrates the ability to teach mathematical problem solving effectively. You will write/modify objectives for the ESL (including EL students and students in ESE), describe how content vocabulary will be introduced and taught, describe alternative instructional strategies, include the use of manipulative or other instructional tools, anticipate student responses to the problem, describe how to assess student thinking, and include EL modifications. The product consists of the lesson objectives, the procedure for conducting the lesson (including alternative strategies for EL students), the materials

necessary, the anticipated student reaction, and the analysis of anticipated student responses.

2. You are expected to turn in an end-of-term paper on a topic of your interest that relates to mathematics (e.g., function machines). Paper includes review of pertinent literature and plans on how to accommodate for cultural and language differences.

Reflection

The faculty on our campus infused EL strategies into many courses. Through the workshops provided by the ESL faculty, the entire faculty in the College of Education began to move to a greater understanding of infusing ESL into our courses. We moved beyond an understanding of cultural differences with EL students and had developed a better understanding of the critical role that linguistics plays in EL students' understanding of concepts. Most faculty were now familiar with the levels of language development that occurs for EL students.

As faculty in our different disciplines, we began to include within our specific content area the importance of exploring teacher differentiation in pacing. Additionally, we began to emphasize with our preservice teachers the awareness of context as a critical issue in teaching EL students. The further exploration of the differences in a language learning disability and the role that native language plays in the development of learning began to be emphasized throughout our course content. Faculty continued to address the issue of the disproportionate number of ethnically diverse students receiving special education services. However, now in discussions with pre-service teachers, faculty had a greater understanding of how language differences, along with cultural differences, can result in the appearance of a disability.

In the process, the faculty's understanding of the differences, similarities, and relationships between ESL and ESE took time and followed an evolutionary process of assimilation into each faculty member's teaching repertoire. As the process continued to evolve, all the faculty began to realize that perhaps the best teacher education program for our pre-service teachers is one that embraces a perspective that all teachers should begin their professional careers believing that diversity of differences in language, culture and process of learning should be valued and an expected part of every teacher's classroom. Infusing the various strategies into each content area was a first step, and total integration of our different programs seemed to be the next evolutionary step in the process. The faculty voted to move forward and take the next step. We didn't exactly know where we would end up, but we had a commitment and passion for moving beyond separate education entities to an integrated program. Our new Bachelor of Education degree would be an integrated Elementary Education, English for Speakers of Other Languages, Exceptional Education, and Reading Initial Certification program.

The process to get to the implementation of the new degree took considerable time, cooperation, and collaboration on the part of many different people. We met in small subgroups to design our vision of the competencies that needed to be covered, including all state, national, and professional standards of each area of certification and/or endorsement in elementary education, ESL, ESE, and reading. Once the competencies were designed, we collected them into meaningful groups to develop the specific courses. This took thoughtful consideration and discussions across disciplines as the competencies grew into courses and the courses and practical experiences merged into a new integrated program.

The model of implementation for each course was designed by the faculty members responsible for delivering the course. Faculty members implemented various models of instruction for the courses. There were four basic models of instruction and a few combinations of several different models were implemented in the first year of the new program:

- In one model the two faculty members taught together in each class meeting for the entire period of the class.
- A second model of instruction had one faculty member teaching solo for the first half of the semester and the other faculty member teaching solo for the second half of the semester.
- A third model of instruction had the instructors teaching alternating weeks throughout the semester.
- In a fourth model one faculty member provided the students with in class instruction while the second faculty member taught the students through an online component.

The model of instruction selected for the first course I taught in the new program was a combination of several different models. The syllabus for this course is noted earlier. Although the course was designed to be co-taught by both an ESE and content area specialist, the implementation of the coteach model was left to the discretion of the two faculty members assigned to teach the course. This four-credit course was designed to be taught two days a week. The content specialist was responsible for three credit hours of the instruction, thus meeting with the class for three hours one day a week and an additional one hour and thirty minutes of instruction every other week. I, as the ESE specialist, was responsible for one hour credit of the instruction, thus meeting with the class for one hour and thirty minutes every other week. I also added an online component for work groups, PowerPoint slides, and additional useful resources.

Because this was the first semester of implementation of the new program and the new course, we wanted to be very clear to the pre-service teachers on the responsibility of each instructor teaching the course along with expectations for the course. It was decided that the assignments for my section of the course would be graded as S or U, with the understanding that the student must pass with a grade of S in my section of the course to earn any type of grade in the content area specialist's section of the course. This made it very clear for the students on grading expectations and the responsibility for each instructor. This also assisted the students in understanding to whom a question or clarification of assignment would be directed.

I taught this first course a little unsure if I was going to be able to deliver all the needed components and how to integrate all four certification areas covered in my section of the course. One of the first lessons I learned is how important it is to reiterate to our teacher candidates the different needs for students receiving services for ESE and those students receiving services for ESL. I had learned a great deal from my work with the ESL faculty, and in one of the first courses of the first semester the students are enrolled in our teacher education program. I spent a great deal of time detailing the similarities and uniqueness of ESE and EL students. I provided many examples, and we discussed in class what the teacher candidates observed while out in their teaching settings. I even shared the story of how ESL and ESE faculty learned from each other and discovered that each faculty member had a different understanding of the term *modification*. I provided several examples in the first class and then assumed the teacher candidates would have a good understanding of the concepts. I believed that the concentrated effort on my part would give the teacher candidates a thorough understanding of the terminology, needs, characteristics, and effective strategies that are similar and unique to ESE and EL students. I thought that the teacher candidates would have a good foundation to continue on in our teacher education program.

I was thus quite surprised when a teacher candidate who had the first course with me submitted his reflection on one of the projects for the course. I learned that despite my concentrated effort, there continued to be some confusion. This confusion was clearly demonstrated to me as I graded journal entries by one of our teacher candidates in which the assignment was to work with a student receiving services for Exceptional Student Education. The teacher candidate discussed the needs of the student with whom he was working—and there wasn't any mention of any type of disability. He discussed the student's cultural background and the accommodations he made to address the linguistic needs of the student. However, there was no mention of an Individualized Education Program (IEP). I followed up with the teacher candidate and questioned him about the student with whom he was working. During my questioning, I realized that the student was not in ESE and was receiving services for ESL. When I again explained the differences of ESE and ESL, it was as if a light bulb went off as he listened and then couldn't believe that he didn't see the differences earlier. I was reminded again that our teacher candidates need more than one lecture or one class to recognize and correct the misinformation they have already assimilated into their teaching repertoire. The concepts need to be reinforced as many times as possible in many different settings.

This course allowed the students to develop a lesson plan (Assignment #1) based on the information on ESL and ESE that they had learned in their previous coursework and apply this information in a practical teaching lesson plan. It was a wonderful way to determine if the information was truly assimilated. In this assignment, the teacher candidates had to demonstrate their knowledge of mathematical concepts and their understanding of the needs of EL and ESE students. For example, in developing their lesson plans for math, the teacher candidates had to assess each student's mathematical thinking and problem-solving ability with modifications for the level of language proficiency for the EL students and processing abilities of the students in ESE. Once assessment was complete, the next step for the teacher candidates was to develop teaching objectives. In creating the objectives, the teacher candidates had to demonstrate their understanding of numeration systems along with demonstrating their understanding of notation systems for various cultures. In teaching the objectives, the teacher candidates also had to consider how each student related to the meanings of the mathematical operations and if the students related different meaning to various operations based on their culture.

This type of thinking and organizing required a real merging of mathematical concepts and an understanding of the unique needs of EL and ESE students. It was exciting to see the overlay of the different concepts they had learned in their content area of mathematics while also considering the unique needs of each student. What was even better is that in our new program, the teacher candidates receive this same type of overlay practice in each of their content courses throughout the program. This practice also helped me, as a faculty member, practice what I preach.

Appendix 7.a

Synopsis of EL Differentiation Resources Developed

Joyce W. Nutta

Highlights of SLIDE and TREAD Analysis

When analyzing and developing lesson plans or descriptions, watch for the following verbs, which indicate a non-verbal (SLIDE) or verbal (TREAD) act or task of the teacher or students:

S   Show (also watch, pantomime, model, display)

L   Look (also smell, taste, feel, and other nonverbal use of senses)

I   Investigate (also measure, weigh, categorize, classify, connect)

D   Demonstrate (also draw, design, act out)

E   Experience (also act, move, do, make, create)

T   Tell (also present information, lecture, narrate, recount)

R   Read (also, skim, scan, review)

E   Explain (also listen)

A   Ask/answer (also write, respond)

D   Discuss (also describe, define)

Instructional and assessment descriptions with what J. Cummins terms "contextual support" often include SLIDE verbs (or their synonyms), and those that are language intensive often include TREAD verbs.[6] Language intensive instruction, in particular, needs substantial differentiated support for English learners. Specific differentiation strategies by level of English proficiency are demonstrated and described in course materials. The three levels of English proficiency for which instruction and assessment must be differentiated are represented by the following cases. Additional information about each English learner, including sound files of interviews and read-alouds and copies of the intermediate and advanced students' written work, are provided in course materials.

Highlights of Teaching Cases

We have found that using common teaching cases to represent English learners at three levels of English proficiency has helped cement across-course connections. At the University of Central Florida, these three cases are introduced in the first EL-specific course and reinforced and expanded in EL-embedded courses, such as the general methods and social studies methods courses. The beginning level of English proficiency is represented by the case of Edith, the intermediate level is represented by Edgar, and the advanced level is portrayed by Tasir. The learners' names are pseudonyms.

Edith Rodriguez — available at http://engage.ucf.edu/v/p/6uUmfrL

- Arrived in the United States one month ago from the Hidalgo region of Mexico
- Now in the sixth grade
- Tested in English and Spanish—beginning level of English proficiency and poor literacy skills in Spanish
- Never volunteers to answer the teacher's questions, but not disruptive
- When the teacher asks her if she understands, she smiles and nods
- Struggles to answer even the simplest yes/no questions in English
- In small group work, does not participate in a meaningful way
- When there is a quiz or test, turns in a blank page

Edgar Ponce — available at http://engage.ucf.edu/v/p/WTkQHQD

- Moved from Puerto Rico to the U.S. mainland eight months ago
- Now in the eighth grade
- Recent English proficiency test placed Edgar at a low intermediate level
- Hesitatingly conversant in everyday English, speaking in simple sentences with frequent grammatical errors
- Comprehends more than he is able to express
- Has difficulty understanding academic discussions and teacher presentations
- Often refuses to turn in written work, since he says he cannot write well in English
- English reading skills are very weak, and Spanish reading and writing skills are below grade level, according to bilingual testing results

Tasir Barad — available at http://engage.ucf.edu/v/p/WCUP5WC

- Came to the United States from Egypt when she was in the third grade.
- Now in the seventh grade
- No traces of foreign accent in speech
- Her teachers are skeptical of her categorization as an EL since she sounds like a native speaker
- Some teachers believe that Tasir doesn't try hard enough and that she does not warrant extra help or accommodations
- Seems to keep up in class most of the time but struggles with tasks involving writing and reading
- When reading aloud, lacks fluency, and when writing, makes frequent spelling and syntactic errors
- Diagnostic testing placed her at the advanced level of English proficiency in listening and speaking but below grade level in reading and writing

CHAPTER 8

Infusing EL Content
into Category 3+ Courses

*Developing and Implementing Curriculum, Instruction,
and Assessment for Language Arts and Literacy*

In this chapter, three literacy education professionals, who are affiliated with three U.S. higher education institutions in three states, share how they have infused EL content into four category 3+ language arts and literacy courses, with the goal of preparing teacher leaders to effectively support the education of ELs in schools settings. In addition to a description of EL-embedded content, each of the course summaries also includes a reflection from the respective course instructors delineating some of the ways in which the infused course assignments and activities have enhanced teacher educator practices as well as their teacher candidate preparation to teach ELs.

Teaching the Reading of Young Adult Literature: This is the first of a sequence of two courses that address children and young adult literature, in which Associate Professor Donna Niday, Iowa State University, shows how she engages her pre-service English Education majors in (a) understanding the language and culture of ELs, and (b) using linguistically and culturally responsive practices to enhance student learning and engagement. In this first course, Niday provides an opportunity for her teacher candidates to read a professional educational text about ELs, and then work within a group to plan and teach the rest of the class the information they have gained. She also requires students to create a unit in which they describe universal design strategies, as well as accommodations specifically for English learners, including use of visual aids, written directions, and step-by-step directions.

Practice and Theory of Teaching Literature in the Secondary Schools: In this second course of the series, Niday requires her teacher candidates to participate in a field-based practicum, which gives them the opportunity to apply the strategies learned in the course as they work with English learners in a real-world classroom setting.

Foundations of Reading, Language and Literacy: In this course, Assistant Professor Melissa Schulz, Miami University (Oxford, Ohio), shows her early childhood education majors how to plan, implement, and evaluate instruction for all students, including students who are from linguistically and culturally diverse backgrounds. In addition to engaging her teacher candidates in reading and discussion of various reading materials aimed at promoting a deeper understanding of students from cultural and linguistically diverse backgrounds, Schulz requires her teacher candidates to connect with ELs and their families through a modified literacy bag activity for an English learner. In this activity, students prepare four language and literacy learning activities for a preschool English learner child, which are then used with a parent or caregiver at home to foster language and literacy development.

Developmental Reading: In this course, Associate Professor Vassiliki Zygouris-Coe, University of Central Florida, shows how instruction can be adjusted to support the language and literacy needs of English learners in a course designed for a wide-ranging audience of preK–12 teacher candidates from fields including language arts, exceptional education, and counselor education. In this course, she engages her teacher candidates in various activities designed to challenge their knowledge, perceptions, beliefs, and attitudes about English learners. For instance, she requires students to participate in a set of carefully guided literacy logs through which they discuss how they view English learners; what they think and expect of culturally and linguistically diverse students in their classrooms; what they think they should do to maximize students' academic success in language, literacy, and content learning; what experiences they have had with these students; what they would do to differentiate instruction; and how they would monitor student progress and adjust instruction to support their learning needs. Zygouris-Coe believes that assignments such as the literacy logs activity, as well as other ESOL-infused course assignments and assessments, "will help to first make [students'] thinking processes and reflections more visible and secondly, will also illustrate some of the processes they are involved in as they grow in their knowledge and understanding of EL-related issues."

The sample category 3+ EL-infused course syllabi described herein provide suggestions and guidelines for adapting literacy courses and programs with the goal of enhancing teacher candidates' preparation to effectively teach English learners in the mainstream classrooms. We encourage teacher educators to consider incorporating some of these assignments and activities, and others, into their pre-service teacher education programs, which should provide their teacher candidates with a beginning repertoire for teaching English learners whom they are increasingly likely to have in their classes.

Practice and Theory of Teaching Literature in the Secondary Schools

Donna Niday
Iowa State University

Course Description

Current theories and practices in the teaching of literature to secondary school students. Integrating literary study and writing. Preparation and selection of materials. Classroom presentation. Unit planning. Portfolio review. (Taken concurrently with a two-hour practicum experience in the schools.)

Course Audience

This course is required for English Education majors and serves as the methods course taken in the junior or senior year prior to student teaching. A few students may be working toward an ESL endorsement in addition to their English education licensure. All students in the course would have previously taken Teaching the Reading of Young Adult Literature, in which they read two novels about English learners and devised a teaching unit with EL accommodations. Therefore, these skills are scaffolded into higher expectations for the teaching unit and for EL accommodations. This methods course includes the opportunity to read a professional education text about either English learners, students who are talented and gifted, or students with disabilities and then work within a group to plan and teach the rest of the class the information they have learned. The course also requires pre-service teachers to create a unit in which they are to describe universal design strategies, as well as accommodations specifically for ELs.

Course Objectives

Upon successful completion of the requirements of this course, teacher candidates will have an opportunity to:

1. Read a wide range of literature (fiction and nonfiction).
2. Select appropriate literature for a specific audience (considering reading abilities, multicultural literature, and balance of male and female protagonists).
3. Prepare a unit based on a theme, including demographic analysis, rationale for novel selection, 15 lesson plans with handouts including strategies using universal design and accommodations for English learners and students with exceptionalities, a range of assessments, etc.

4. Provide commentaries and artifacts documenting that teacher candidates have met the minimum program and state standards to teach all students, including English learners.

Program and state standards expect that teacher candidates are prepared to teach linguistically and culturally diverse students. Candidates are expected to "[demonstrate] an understanding of how students differ in their approaches to learning and [create] instructional opportunities that are equitable and adaptable to diverse learners."

Materials

See Student Resources for Projects and Works cited at end of the syllabus. The annotated bibliography provides a list of resources that can be used as a basis for class discussions, activities, and projects for analyzing effective strategies in teaching English learners including language acquisition, reading, and writing skills, as well as literature analysis.

Assignments

The following sample assignments are designed to contribute in different, yet complementary, ways to the objectives of this course. These sample assignments provide an example of EL-infused activities and projects aimed at preparing English Education teacher candidates to address the language and literacy needs of ELs in mainstream K–12 classrooms.

Reading/perusing one of the texts: The class is divided into three research groups: English learners, diverse learners, talented and gifted learners. The students in the English learners group each read an individual text and prepare a handout. Then they work together on how they will present the information to the class—see the Reflection section for more information.

Unit plan: In the inclusion section of the unit plan, students must describe how they used universal design practices to aid all learners and what strategies they used to assist English learners—see sample lesson plans attached.

Assessments

A teacher-designed rubric will be used to evaluate the teacher candidates' performance on the following course assignments:

1. Performance in presentations
2. Performance in representing course content: midterm/writings
3. Performance in unit planning
4. Performance on unit commentary
5. Performance in the unit presentation
6. Performance in crafting your portfolio as "reflective practice"

Reflection

In the fifteen years that I have taught teacher education classes, I have tried to integrate working with English learners into the English Education methods class. In my first years, I asked an ESL professor to be a guest speaker, but she spent the hour lecturing on theoretical principles, and the teacher education students were still uncertain how to apply these principles to the classroom.

Another year, my class and the ESL methods class used a roving conference model in which for the first half of the period, my English Education students sat at tables and explained handouts of lesson planning and other materials for the ESL pre-service teachers, and during the second half of the period, the ESL methods students staffed the tables and discussed ways to work with English learners. This process seemed more helpful, but scheduling the two classes at the same time never reoccurred, making the method unsustainable.

I have also sought texts to use with my English Education students, but most of them focus on working with the ELs in an ESL classroom or on tutoring an English learner in a one-on-one experience. Rarely could I find information on infusing ELs into a regular classroom. Last year I had an opportunity to apply for a state grant to help teacher education students meet state standards. I used this grant to purchase professional education books on ELs, talented and gifted students, and students with disabilities. I then divided the class into three research groups, made each student responsible for one text, and asked students to read their text and compose a handout. Then the group met to determine how best to teach their peers what they had learned about teaching this special population, and we used the next three class periods for students to teach their peers about best practices for working with these special populations.

In teaching about integrating ELs into the classroom, I stress the need to view these students as opportunities rather than problems. English learners are wonderful human resources who can share their culture, opinions, and perspectives, and they can broaden other students' global views. For instance, as a former high school English and journalism teacher, I would often ask ELs and international exchange students to describe journalistic freedoms in their home countries, which were usually much more restrictive than freedoms in the United States, giving my native students a more global concept of journalistic freedom. In my high school literature classes, I would ask the ELs to talk about authors from their home countries. English learners in my high school composition classes often wrote about their experiences in coming to the United States or differences in traditions, schools, foods, and other factors in the two countries, and once a classroom had gelled into a shared community, the students would usually feel comfortable in allowing peers to read and respond to these writings. I share these past experiences with my teacher education students and encourage them to take advantage of the "expertise" that ELs bring to the classroom.

After community acceptance, I work with my methods students on universal design instructional strategies, best practices for all students (National Universal Design for

Learning Task Force).[1] Visual aids, written directions, and step-by-step directions can assist not only English learners but also students who are visual learners, students struggling academically (often with a lack of organizational skills), students with audio impairments, students with learning disabilities, and many others, including absentees or tardy students. Next, we discuss alternative texts including films, graphic novels, picture books, bilingual texts, CDs, modern language texts (with current slang), and others (see Examples of Alternative Texts below). We talk about making these texts available to all students, not just those who are English learners or who are academically struggling. Finally, I allow students to choose their group (English learners, students who are talented and gifted, or students with disabilities) and then to choose a text within that group. I've found that making students responsible for their own learning and then teaching others is often the key to providing both theoretical and practical knowledge for students soon to be in a student teaching environment.

After the teaching presentations, I collate their ideas with tips from Jeff Wilhelm and Jim Burke and provide a handout (see below).[2] Most of this advice has already been provided by the teaching groups, but this provides a summary of down-to-earth teaching strategies for helping ELs be successful in the classroom. This combination of letting ELs describe their cultures, discussing universal design strategies, giving teacher education students research and teaching projects, and then providing an encapsulated list of helpful tips can help teacher education students become more prepared to welcome ELs into their classroom.

Handout—Teaching Tips:
Helping Students Succeed Using *Universal Design Strategies*

- Use a variety of instructional strategies to meet the needs of diverse learners.
- Use visuals as often as possible (write on the board; use overheads, film clips, posters, PowerPoint presentations, etc.).
- Use drama as a visual aid—students can experience and see the plot, characterizations, situations, etc.
- Use art (drawings, collages, posters, mobiles, dioramas, etc.) as a visual aid—(e.g., posters of the Capulet family on one wall and the Montague family on the other wall).
- Use interactive technology (Smart Boards, etc.).
- Use course management software (Blackboard, WebCT, Moodle) so students can recheck assignments, due dates, etc.
- Use small-group work so students can be more interactive with the content and their peers and learn from others; use partner reading (one partner reads a short passage and then is questioned by the partner; then the other partner reads and is questioned).
- Use graphic organizers so students can create a plot line or character tree.
- Employ a variety of multiple intelligences.
- Ask students to state their opinions and then provide supporting literature text.
- Make connections to contemporary events or students' lives.

- Give a print copy of all directions.
- Give directions in sequenced, numbered order.
- Ask students to repeat the directions or explain a concept (hearing a peer's language may make the meaning more comprehensible).
- Consider alternative or supplemental texts (see list below).
- Use teacher think-alouds to help students see the reading process in action and recognize that questioning and rereading are good reading strategies.
- Teach making annotated notes such as sticky notes.
- Provide choices, especially for individualized reading, writing topics, and projects.
- Ask, "How can I structure my classroom to accommodate all students and help them be successful?"
- Ask students, "What can I do to help you be successful?"

English Learners

- Respect and honor the student's expertise by asking him/her to share about his/her country, culture, traditions, or talents and make connections to literature unit.
- Seat ELs in the middle of the classroom so they can observe other students' actions (such as taking out paper, opening a textbook, jotting notes, etc.).
- Use multimodal communication, especially a combination of visual and audio (see visual possibilities above).
- Allow additional time for assignments (compositions, tests, etc.).
- Ask students individually to repeat the assignment directions or give a summary of the reading.
- Allow students to conduct interviews and take notes in a first language and then compose the essay in English. (*Note:* It is usually better not to allow students to compose an essay in a first language and then translate it because English learners need practice in thinking and composing in English).
- Consider the learning needs of the individual student to decide whether to provide a text in the first language or an alternative text (see list below).

Examples of Alternative Texts (e.g., Romeo and Juliet)
Providing an alternative text can help students read and understand the text. They must understand the plot and action before they can begin to analyze characterization, symbols, themes, etc. One or a combination of the texts below can be a starting point for students in comprehending the text.

- Entire text in student's first language
- Bilingual text (e.g., English on left page, other language on right page)
- Audio text (audiotapes, CDs)
- Text in modern translation
- Text in Elizabethan English on the left and modern translation on the right
- Abridged version
- Summary text (read a summary such as Charles and Mary Lamb's *Tales from Shakespeare* before reading the actual text)

- Graphic novel
- Film version
- YouTube clips
- Picture book
- Large-print text
- Text with accompanying genres (novel, short stories, poetry, etc.) to fit a thematic unit (e.g., family conflicts for *Romeo and Juliet*)
- Class-, group-, or individual-created text using teen slang

Unit Directions for Accommodations for English Learners

Compose 15 days of lesson plans for your thematic unit and include a rationale, corresponding state standards, appropriate handouts and assessments, bibliography, etc. (see items on rubric below). Also provide an analysis of how you will accommodate or meet the needs of English learners, gifted learners, students with learning disabilities, and students with physical special needs.

Sample Lesson Plan Using *Walk Two Moons*

Objectives

- Students will analyze *Walk Two Moons* using physical, emotional, and spiritual journeys.
- Students will apply symbols to portray a character's emotional journey and their own reader's journey during the novel.
- Students will discuss and apply the "mystery" quotes to the entire novel and to their own lives.
- Students will apply inductive thinking to realize their use of literary theories: cultural (analysis of Native American subtle references in novel), feminist (analysis of Sal's mother's leaving and Phoebe's mother's leaving), and reader response (portrait of own reader's journey).

Materials

- Text: *Walk Two Moons*
- Collection of Native American–related literature
- Equipment: CD player, ELMO projector, LCD projector, laptop computer
- CD of Native American flute music
- Map of United States shown on ELMO
- Printed copy of small-group directions
- Poster paper
- Markers
- Cups with dried fruit and nuts (label bottom of cups 1–6 for group formation)
- Quotes from book shown on ELMO—leaf border
- Large-group discussion questions on PowerPoint

Motivation
- Play Native American flute music as students enter.
- Show table display of books on Native American literature—ask "What generalities can be made from viewing these books?" (e.g., many books about Native Americans are written by non-native authors).

Activities

Introduce journey theme of physical, emotional, and spiritual journeys.

a. Physical journeys:
   - Students plot Sal's physical journey from Kentucky to Idaho on U.S. map.
   - Students list subtle connections to Native Americans during the physical journey (students write these on the board during brainstorming).

b. Emotional journeys:
   - Emotional journey of characters:
      - Students are in groups (group numbers are on bottom of dried fruit cups). Groups: 1—Sal, 2—Sal's mom, 3—Sal's dad, 4—Phoebe's mom, 5—Grandma, 6—Grandpa
      - Teacher distributes poster paper and markers for groups.
      - Groups brainstorm possible symbols and create poster showing symbols for particular character.
      - Small group sharing.
   - Emotional journey of readers:
      - Teacher discusses ways students can think about their journey as readers (e.g., vote taken of time when readers learned of Sal's mother's death—at beginning, middle, or end of book?).
      - Individuals create own posters to show personal reader journey in reading this text.
      - Individuals voluntarily share posters with whole group.

c. Spiritual journey:
   - Teacher explains that *spiritual journey* in this case refers to nature and how spirituality lies at the core of Native American beliefs.
   - Teacher refers to cups with dried fruit and nuts as traditional natural foods.
   - Quotes from "mystery" writer—groups discuss connection to the story.
   - Small groups share meanings of quotes.
   - Large-group general discussion of other parts of the story.

Closure

Groups analyze the three types of journeys used in today's lesson (physical, emotional, and spiritual) and the literary theory (cultural, feminist, and reader response).

Assessment
- Amount of students' participation in individual, small-group, and whole-class activities
- Quality of students' responses in individual, small group, and whole class activities
- Quality of symbolism in individual and small group posters

Potential Problems/Solutions

Due to the large number of activities, we may not have time to finish all of them. If so, the individual posters of the reader's journey could be changed to a brief large-group discussion. Part of the lesson could be carried over to the next class period (such as the mystery quotes).

Sample Universal Design Strategies or Accommodations for English Learners from Lesson Plan on *Walk Two Moons*

The English learners in the class will see many visuals (a universal design strategy) during this lesson: U.S. map, character posters, the quotes on the screen, printed copies of small-group directions, food, and large-group questions on PowerPoint. They will also have audio learning through the native music, small-group discussions, and large-group discussions. English learners may also have an alternative text, such as an audio book on CD or the film in DVD form.

Rubric for Unit Plan

Category	Instructor Comments	Points (1–5, 5 being high)
Demographics of student population		
Rationale for unit, texts		
State standards employed		
General unit objectives		
Calendar of lesson plans		
Lesson plans: Objectives		
Lesson plans: Materials		
Lesson plans: Variety of activities		
Lesson plans: Daily assessments		
Accommodations for students with exceptionalities (ELs, gifted, students with disabilities, etc.)		
Unit assessments		
Handouts		
Bibliography		
Reflection		

Directions for Individual Reading and Summarizing

Read one of the texts (see Sources for Student Projects). Then compile a 10-item bullet list of the most important information from the text. Quotes can supplement the ten points, but the ten points must be in your own words. Then compose a 1–2 paragraph reflection on your new realizations or how you hope to adapt these points in your classroom. Later you will work with a small group who will use these points to teach a 30–minute lesson, demonstrating how you would use accommodations for English learners.

Rubric for Bulleted Ten-Point Reading About English Learners

Category	Instructor Comments	Points (1–5, 5 being high)
Gave major, not minor points		
Summarized information and used quotes only as supplementary, if needed		
Reflected on new realizations		
Reflected on adaptations to the classroom		
20 points possible		Total ____ points

Resources for Student Projects

Bouchard, M. (2005). *Comprehension strategies for English language learners*. New York: Scholastic. This book includes teaching strategies, standards, supporting research, prompt reflections, and recommendations for working with young adult English learners (fourth grade through twelfth grade). It especially emphasizes frame sentences, question guides, graphic organizers, reciprocal teaching, cued retelling, signal words, and others.

Fisher, D., Rothenberg, C. & Frey, N. (2007). *Language learners in the English classroom*. Urbana, IL: National Council of Teachers of English. This book, aimed at grades 7–12, analyzes what makes learning in English challenging for adolescent English learners and provides best practices in academic literacy for immigrant secondary school students. It includes research-based strategies to help English learners with vocabulary, comprehension, grammar, and fluency.

Freeman, D., & Freeman, Y. (2009). *Academic language for English language learners and struggling readers*. Portsmouth, NH: Heinemann. This text for teachers of language arts, social studies, science, and math shows how they can use specific strategies to motivate and engage English learners, help make texts more accessible, and develop academic language for their content area.

Freeman, Y., Freeman, D.E., & Mercuri, S.P. (2002). *Closing the achievement gap: How to reach limited-formal-schooling and long-term English learners*. Portsmouth, NH: Heinemann. The authors provide ways for teachers to work with middle school and high school ELs who are either recently arrived (less than five years) students with limited previous formal schooling or long-term English learners who have been in U.S. schools for seven or less years but are below grade level in reading and writing. The authors provide both theory and practice in showing the most effective strategies for working with older English learners.

Freeman, D., & Freeman, Y. (2007). *English language learners: The essential guide.* New York: Scholastic, 2007. This book shows how to support language development, encourage sharing of primary language and culture with classmates, organize curriculum around standards-based themes, focus on ways to help ELs to construct meaning, and increase use of academic language. The book is aimed at grades K–12.

Freeman, Y.S., Freeman, D.E., & Ramirez, R. (2008). *Diverse learners in the mainstream classroom: Strategies for supporting ALL students across content areas: English language learners, students with disabilities, and gifted/talented students.* Portsmouth, NH: Heinemann. Two of the chapters in this text discuss working with ELs. The first chapter discusses differences among ELs, identification policies, school programs, and best teaching practices based on research and theory. The second focuses on bilingual education programs and provides research and theory to support bilingual education.

Gibbons, P.. *English learners, academic literacy, and thinking: Learning in the challenge zone.* (2009). Portsmouth, NH: Heinemann. This book examines effective middle school practices for providing both high expectations for and maximum support to ELs. The author provides examples across the curriculum for ways to scaffold instruction to develop academic literacy, improve reading comprehension, encourage writing independence, and use classroom small-group and large-group discussions to develop reading and writing proficiency.

Works Cited

Burke, J. *The English teacher's companion.* 3rd ed. (2007). Portsmouth, NH: Heinemann.

Lamb, C., & Lamb, M. (2007). *Tales from Shakespeare.* Columbus, OH: Signet Classics.

National Universal Design for Learning Task Force. (2007). Universal Design for Learning. http://www.advocacyinstitute.org/UDL/

Wilhelm, J. (2007). *"You gotta BE the book": Teaching engaged and reflective reading with adolescents.* 2nd ed. 2007. New York: Teachers College Press.

Teaching the Reading of Young Adult Literature

Donna Niday
Iowa State University

Course Description

Critical study and evaluation of the genre; examination of modes and themes found in the literature; strategies of effective reading; study of the relationship of the genre to children's literature and adult literature; discussion techniques for teachers and parents. Evaluation of literature for use in school programs. Restricted to students seeking teacher licensure.

Course Audience

This course is required for English education majors and serves as an elective for elementary education majors and other secondary teacher education majors. A few students may be working toward an ESL endorsement. English Education students usually enroll in the course as sophomores and take the course as their first English Education course. However, many other students who are transferring from another college or have changed their major may enroll as juniors, creating almost an equal number of sophomores and juniors, along with a few seniors. The course is used for English Education requirements and can be used to fulfill a required course for a reading endorsement. This course includes one young adult novel, which shows teen immigrants entering the country, and another depicting a teen adapting as an English learner; these novels provide a contextual background for pre-service teachers in working with English learners. The course also requires pre-service teachers to create a unit in which they are to describe universal design strategies, as well as accommodations specifically for ELs.

Course Objectives

Upon successful completion of the requirements of this course, teacher candidates will have an opportunity to:

1. Read a wide range of young adult literature (fiction and nonfiction).
2. Select appropriate young adult literature for a specific audience (considering reading abilities, multicultural literature, and balance of male and female protagonists in the curriculum).
3. Prepare a unit on one whole-class novel, including: demographic analysis; rationale for text selection; ten lesson plans with handouts, including strategies using univer-

sal design and accommodations for English learners and students with exceptionalities, a range of assessments, etc.

4. Provide commentaries and artifacts proving that they have met the program and state standards for educating all students including ELs.

Program and state standards expect that teacher candidates are prepared to teach linguistically and culturally diverse students. Candidates are expected to "demonstrate an understanding of how students differ in their approaches to learning and create instructional opportunities that are equitable and adaptable to diverse learners."

Materials

The following resources provide a focus for the course and information useful for class discussions, activities, and projects. Of the eight required books, six are taught by groups of students to the class. The following two books, taught by student groups, look at the lives of ELs. The first book, *La Línea*, demonstrates code switching, in which each page contains both English and Spanish words and phrases, as well as the cultural situation of attempting to cross into the United States. The second book, *A Step from Heaven*, shows Young Ju's experience in the schools as an English learner and how visual cues and peer assistance (her friend Amanda) help her grow in her language acquisition and usage. After reading each book, students can discuss cultural situations, universal design strategies, and accommodations for ELs.

Jaramillo, A. (2008). *La Línea*. New York: Square Fish.
> Miguel and Elena desire the American dream and wish to join their parents in the United States by crossing *la línea*, the line or boundary between Mexico and the United States. Part of their journey includes riding atop a freight train, or "people killer." (The author teaches ESL at a middle school in California and asked for students' input while writing the book.)

Na, A. (2002). *A Step from Heaven*. New York: Penguin.
> When Young Ju Park and her family move from Korea to California, Young Ju thinks that America must be heaven, but the future is less than angelic when jobs are scarce and the family lives in poverty. Her father becomes depressed and angry, and outwardly shows higher expectations for her younger brother than for her. Young Ju wonders what she can do to change this situation. (The book was a National Book Award nominee.)

Assignments

These sample assignments provide an example of EL-infused activities and projects aimed at preparing English Education teacher candidates to address the language and literacy needs of ELs in mainstream K–12 classrooms.

Book Group Presentations: Students rank their preferences for six whole-class novels (two of which focus on protagonists who are immigrants and ELs). The instructor assembles students into equal numbers among these six groups, and they collaboratively plan how to teach their book with a variety of activities. Each group has one class period to present their book though a variety of activities. Possibilities include small-group discussions or artwork (collage, etc.), large-group discussions, individual work (journaling, etc.), and/or brief presentations by group members. Groups are required to involve their audience in the presentation, use at least one visual, and include interesting and learning-filled (critical thinking) activities. Groups may use a handout, poster, slide presentation, video clip, overhead or Elmo projection, map, costume, artifact, etc., for the visual requirement. Students are given parts of two class periods to meet with their group to plan their presentation and may also meet in person or via e-mail outside of class. Following the presentation, each group member composes a two-page reflection on the teaching experience.

Unit Plan: Students are to locate five books connected by theme, topic, or author. These books need to have a representation of the following: gender of protagonists, diverse reading levels (high, average, low), and multiculturalism. Students then select one of the books for their whole-class book and compose a ten-day unit plan for this one book. Students then list the other four books and explain why they chose them (to be used for a literature circle unit following the whole-class book unit). Requirements for the unit include school demographics, rationale for unit topic and text choices, unit objectives, unit assessment, and analysis of teaching strategies, including universal design and unit accommodations for ELs and students with exceptionalities. Each lesson plan includes objectives, materials, introductory activity, in-class activities, closure activity, assessment, and possible problems/solutions. Each student then gives a five-minute presentation on the unit, which includes interactive activities. Students compose reflections on both the two-week unit plan and on the unit presentation.

Assessments

A teacher-designed rubric is used to evaluate the teacher candidates' performance on the following course assignments.

Book Group Presentations (two of which involve protagonists who are ELs): Students provide a self-assessment (reflection) on their presentations and also assess the contributions of their peers in the small-group work/presentation. The teacher also assesses the presentation.

Unit Plan and Presentation: Students compose a self-assessment (reflection) on both their unit plan and the unit plan presentation. One requirement is assessing how they met the needs of all students in the classroom, including ELs.

Portfolio Commentary and Artifacts for Meeting State Standards: For each of the six state standards incorporated into the course, students must provide a commentary arguing that their artifacts demonstrate their knowledge and application of the standard. For the second standard, they must describe how they have learned to help ELs be successful in the classroom. For the third standard they must include an artifact from their unit plan showing how they use universal design to meet the needs of all students and accommodations to specifically aid ELs.

Reflection

This course often comprises a high percent of Caucasian students who may not have had ELs in their rural or suburban school districts or who may have been in schools in which ELs were not often infused into the regular classroom. Therefore, I wanted to prepare these pre-service teachers for this important group of students. In the last several years, I have included one novel which shows the cultural influences in ELs, usually in merely getting to the United States. This year I decided to incorporate two novels: *La Línea*, in which Mexican teens try to get across the U.S.-Mexico border, and *A Step from Heaven*, which describes a Korean girl's experience as an English learner.[3] For the course to meet the standards for a reading endorsement, the state department of education requires that some of the literature in the course must include linguistic differences, and both of these books interweave words, phrases, or sentences of the first language into the protagonist's speech. These two novels provide students with varying cultural and linguistic situations, creating rich discussions for pre-service teachers.

Novels of Immigrating Teens

The young adult novel *La Línea* provides pre-service teachers with a cultural background of immigrant children trying to cross *La Línea*, the line between Mexico and the United States. The story describes why siblings Miguel and Elena are trying to join their parents in California. Their travels include being sent by police to the southern border of Mexico, getting robbed, riding atop a fast-moving train, and crossing a desert. This action-packed narrative helps pre-service teachers understand the reasons for a family's immigration and their travails.

The book presents a realistic portrayal, since its author, Ann Jaramillo, is an ESL teacher in California who listened to her students' stories and interwove them into one story. She shared portions of the novel with her students to receive their feedback and maintain an accurate depiction. While the two characters do reach the United States, the epilogue provides some realism: the immigrant children feel jealous of their American-born siblings, Elena returns to Mexico after one year, and the grandmother in Mexico dies without the family getting to see her again. On the positive side, Miguel grows up in the United States and graduates from college, adding an element of hope.

Other young adult novels can provide a similar depiction. *The Crossing* (Gary Paulsen) describes a young boy trying to entice an adult American to help him cross the border.[4] *Crossing the Wire* (Will Hobbs) provides an adventure story of fifteen-year-old Victor, who heads north from Mexico to the U.S. border to help prevent his family from starving, and and depicts his adventures jumping trains, stowing away on trucks, and hiking through the desert.[5] Alternatively, *Enrique's Journey* (Sonia Nazario) is a nonfiction, journalistic account in which the author follows Enrique, a seventeen-year-old from Honduras trying to enter the United States.[6] First published as a series in the *Los Angeles Times*, where it received two Pulitzer Prizes, the articles were turned into a book. Although intended for an adult audience, the book couples storytelling with factual information and allows pre-service teachers to view multiple perspectives on immigrant issues.

Having taught all four of these books in recent years, I recommend *La Línea* for several reasons. While all four books feature a male protagonist, only *La Línea* includes a female co-protagonist, who travels across Mexico and across the border with her brother, making the book more appealing to both male and female readers. Female characters serve only as background characters in the other books. While *Enrique's Journey* offers nonfiction, statistical information, and a multilayered perspective, it is much longer and often jumps abruptly from one story to another and vacillates from narrative to essay to persuasive editorial due to its origin as a series of journalistic articles. Pre-service teachers would be more likely to use one of the shorter narratives—*La Línea*, *The Crossing*, or *Crossing the Wire*—with their upper elementary, middle school, or lower high school students or with their ELs. Of the three, *La Línea* contains the most authenticity, since the author's husband's family were Mexican immigrants, whereas the other two authors (Gary Paulsen and Will Hobbs) live in the Southwest but do not have direct family or student connections to border crossings. *La Línea* also contains more authentic language. *The Crossing* and *Crossing the Wire* intertwine occasional Spanish terms, but *La Línea* intersperses entire sentences that are not directly translated and require readers to use context clues to decipher their meanings—in linguistic terms, *code switching* (moving back and forth between languages). This makes the book more welcoming to Spanish speakers and requires native English speakers to decipher the language meaning, replicating on a small scale the struggle that ELs experience in reading English texts.

This text was recommended to me by Kris Peterson, a high school English teacher in Postville, Iowa, a community with a large number of Latino/a students. She wrote, "The glow in the Hispanic students' eyes when they read this book . . . they lived this. The confusion and irritation in some gringo students' conversations when they dealt with the Spanish. It all led to powerful and productive conversations."[7] Peterson said she supplemented the text with the documentary *Which Way Home?* which shows children journeying across Mexico atop trains to immigrate to the United States.[8]

Pre-service teachers can find an array of topics to discuss in *La Línea*—the adventure/survival genre; issues of illegal immigration; language depiction; and themes of family relationships, perseverance, and hope. By reading this text, pre-service teachers can begin to envision the lives of some of their ELs and how they can work beside them to help them become proficient readers and writers.

Novels with English Learners

While *La Línea* portrays entering the United States, other books show the teen protagonist's life after entering the American borders. *A Step from Heaven* (An Na), a 2001 National Book Award finalist and the recipient of the 2002 Michael L. Printz Award, describes the part-autobiographical, part-fictional, first-person narrative of a girl immigrating from Korea with her family. The story begins when Young Ju is six and concludes when she is in her teen years. While Young Ju expects life in the United States to be "a step from heaven," her father struggles with keeping a low-paying job and becomes an alcoholic, physically abusing her and her mother and brother. When the abuse becomes severe, Young Ju calls 911, but after a short jail stay, her father moves in with a mistress, and her mother blames her for breaking up the family. However, the ending offers hope, since her father returns to Korea, her mother realizes that Young Ju saved her life, her brother stops skipping school, and Young Ju earns academic high school honors and looks forward to college life.

Like *La Línea*, *A Step from Heaven* presents an interesting linguistic depiction. While *La Línea* offers entire sentences in Spanish, *A Step from Heaven* incorporates the character's use of Korean words in her thoughts and dialogue. She refers to her papa as *Apa* and her mother as *Uhmma*. In addition, Na gradually moves the protagonist's language from the childish thoughts of a six-year-old to the more mature reflections of a teenager. She organizes the novel as a set of vignettes, which she says in the appendix was inspired by Sandra Cisneros's *The House on Mango Street*.[9]

While *La Línea* concludes with the successful border crossing and an "Afterward" that describes events ten years later, *A Step from Heaven* depicts Young Ju as an English learner. She attempts some American names, "but my mouth does not want to make those words."[10] The family's American helper allows her to mispronounce his name "until my mouth is ready to learn."[11] In showing Young Ju's language struggles, Na provides the sounds Young Ju hears such as the teacher saying "ho ha do" (How do you do?) and "wah ko um" (welcome), but does not provide the translation.[12] The novel shows Young Ju's early language learning through observation. When another child "rubs the red stick on some paper and the color stays there," Young Ju experiments with her own crayon drawing.[13] This incident shows pre-service teachers the importance of peers as models and why seating ELs in the middle of a classroom surrounded by native language speakers (rather than in the front row or corners of the room) can help increase the ELs' participation in classroom activities. The book also depicts the importance of visualization. While the other students are at recess, the teacher sits down by Young Ju, mimics eating from an empty bowl, and says "laanchu" (lunch).[14] When Young Ju repeats the word, the teacher retrieves a bag of goldfish crackers, which Young Ju swims in the air and repeats the teacher's use of "go-do-feesh" (goldfish).[15] Other language depictions are shown when Young Ju does not understand idioms such as "going with a boy" (dating), bilingually speaks Korean at home and English at school, and attends a Korean church in which the minister "uses Korean and English examples to talk about the compassion of God."[16] All of these textual references provide effective discussion topics.

In addition to discussing language use, pre-service teachers can also analyze the portrayal of cultural customs and gender stereotypes. For instance, the birth of Young Ju's brother brings a family celebration in which Young Ju's father openly describes his preference and high expectations for his son, stating, "Someday he could be a doctor or lawyer." Her aunt adds, "Someday he could be president," and her father proclaims, "Someday my son will make me proud." When Young Ju says, "I can be president, Apa," her father points at her, laughs, and says, "You are a girl, Young Ju."[17] Even though her uncle says, "In America, women can do almost anything men can do," Young Ju states, "His words do not make the hurt in my heart go away. The cut of Apa's laugh is still open."[18] Young Ju becomes so jealous of her brother that she fibs during her elementary class's show-and-tell, saying that her brother has died, evoking the sympathy of her teacher, classmates, and entire school. As Young Ju and her brother grow older, the difference in parental treatment continues, and her father upbraids her brother Joon, saying, "You cry like a girl. You whine like a girl. Have I not taught you anything? Be strong. Be a man."[19] He then hits his son and kicks him in the stomach, physically attempting to instill his gender values.

The negative portions of the book—poverty, alcoholism, and physical abuse—can provide an insight into the family lives of students, whether they are native-born speakers or ELs. Pre-service teachers can discuss the connection of school and home, the requirements of mandatory reporting, and the need to work with other school personnel such as guidance counselors, social workers, administrators, ESL teachers, and teachers in regular classrooms.

Other young adult novels also provide a glimpse into the lives of ELs, but sometimes portray incorrect word choices. Jamie Gilson's *Hello, My Name Is Scrambled Eggs* depicts Tian, a boy from Vietnam, moving to Minnesota and the attempts of his next-door neighbor Harvey to initiate him into American traditions such as trick-or-treating, toilet papering, and making snowmen.[20] Henry's efforts sometimes help—and sometimes harm—Tian's endeavors to learn English. As the title indicates, the book is intended to be humorous; however, it often denigrates the English learner.

Similarly, *Children of the River*, by Linda Crew, describes a Cambodian girl adapting to her new school in Oregon.[21] The conflict centers on an immigrant family who try to hold on to traditional values and disapproves when their daughter falls in love with a Caucasian boy. The girl has difficulty pronouncing her boyfriend's name, which he takes to be an endearment. However, both books have been criticized by the Asian American community for deriding ELs in their attempts to learn English by using mispronunciation and lack of cultural knowledge as a means of humor. Both of these books were written in the 1980s, and more recent books, such as *A Step from Heaven*, are less likely to ridicule characters and more likely to show the daily struggles and eventual language empowerment of ELs.

Other books, such as *Esperanza Rising* (Pam Muñoz Ryan) and *American Born Chinese* (Gene Luen Young), also describe teens' lives after they immigrate to the United States, but these books tend to focus more on cultural assimilation than being an English learner.[22] *American Born Chinese* does include school scenes, but they emphasize the bullying the protagonist receives. *The Circuit* and *Breaking Through* (both by Francisco Jiménez) are autobiographical; *The Circuit* depicts Jiménez's elementary experiences, and *Breaking Through* his high school life.[23] Both books contain some school experiences but both tend to emphasize his family life.

Other Novels for English Learners

Young adult novels in verse tend to feature easier reading levels while providing more complex and age-appropriate themes and characters. Recommended books include

What My Mother Doesn't Know, All the Broken Pieces, The Surrender Tree: Poems of Cuba's Struggle for Freedom, Keesha's House, Home of the Brave, and *Becoming Billie Holiday*.[24] These books often incorporate native language and traditions and can help ELs feel more comfortable in learning the English language and understanding American customs. Native English speakers can enlarge their perspectives in these books featuring multicultural settings and protagonists.

Incorporating Universal Design into Lesson Plans

Because this course is a teacher education course (and not just a literature requirement), one of the class activities is for students to work in a group to determine a lesson plan to teach the book to the rest of the class. The five or six students in the group must actively participate in planning and teaching the lesson which must incorporate class participation, visual communication, technology, and a variety of teaching strategies. I encourage the groups teaching *La Línea* and *A Step from Heaven* to include discussion of various EL issues, especially looking at how Young Ju struggles with and eventually masters English language learning.

In addition to discussing two novels—one about coming to the United States and the other about living in America—pre-service teachers can also incorporate universal design or accommodations into their unit lesson plans. Universal design, which encourages best practices for all students (National Universal Design for Learning Task Force), can help all students feel more comfortable in the classroom.[25] For instance, visual communication (electronic slides, Smart Board, white board, posters, objects, YouTube, film clips, etc.) can aid not only ELs but also students with special needs and students who are visual learners. Providing other forms of universal design, such as written directions for daily or long-range assignments, as well as in-class assignments such as quick writes, can benefit a late-arriving student, an absentee, or a student with organizational struggles, in addition to the English learner who needs more time to decipher individual words, distinguish the context of words, follow sequential steps, and meet all requirements of the assignment. Other types of universal design strategies include providing alternative texts to any students wishing to use them: CDs, films, graphic novels, e-books, dual language or interlinear books, or translations into other languages, less complex language, or modern or slang language. Pre-service students can discuss this wide range of universal design options, as well as occasional accommodations (additional time, quiet environment, books read aloud by a teacher or aide, etc.) and can incorporate these into their lesson plans, providing a section of their unit plan which reflects on making the course one in which ELs can be successful.

Through discussion of whole-class novels taught by student groups and through unit plans which incorporate universal design and possible accommodations, pre-service teachers can be more prepared to integrate ELs into the regular classroom. Including novels with ELs in this course has added an extra layer of critical thinking and enrichment for pre-service teachers.

Sample Instructional Accommodation for English Learners Focused on Vocabulary Development

La Línea—Spanish Words and Phrases

Most Important Terms

coyote—person paid to help immigrants cross the border

mata gente—train, called the "people killer" (immigrants ride the train by sitting on top or by hanging on the sides)

la migra—the police

Beginning (basic) Spanish Words (used throughout the book)

amigo—friend	madre—mother
agua—water	hijo—son
café—coffee	niños—children
casita—home	padre—father
donde—where	pesos—money
el Norte—the North	por favor—please
hermano—brother	pronto—fast
hermana—sister	pueblitas—pueblos, towns
hombre—person (human)	rancho—ranch
me llamo—my name is	tío—uncle

Intermediate Spanish Words

abrazo—hug

Dios—Deity or God

llegamos—we arrived

mercado—market

la primaria—primary or elementary school

muerto—dead

nueva—new

quinceañeras—fifteenth birthday

tengo—I have

vamonos—"Let's go!"

Advanced Spanish Words

el alcalde—mayor

chupacabras—legendary animal that supposedly drinks the blood of livestock, especially goats

embustera—liar

fíjate—"Listen!"

levántate "Get up!"

la llorona—weeping woman, a legendary ghost

mujer—woman

menso—easily fooled

pollero—one who keeps chickens or other fowls

pozole—Mexican stew

Deciphering Spanish Words and Expressions

Definition Directly Given

Sometimes the definition of a phrase is provided after the sentence.

- *Example:* "*Tu no eres nadie para juzgar,*" she said. "Who are you to judge?"
- *Example:* "*Si Dios es servido, llegamos,*" she said. She thought it was all in God's hands.
- *Example:* "*Por fin tu súplica se e ha concedido,*" Abuelita finally said. "I know how much this means to you."
- *Example:* "*Esperen,*" I waved my arms wildly above my head. "Wait for me!" Answer: *esperen* = wait

See if you can translate these italicized terms:

- Papá left without me. *Me abandonó.* He couldn't take me with him and he didn't.
- *Fácil.* Everyone told us how easy it was to hop on board the train.
- A snake seemed like a small thing, or just another thing. It seemed neutral, a part of this place. I didn't have enough energy to care about a *culebra*.

Similar Words

Sometimes we can figure out the meanings for Spanish words that resemble English.

- *Example:* "I'm going to *la capital.* My aunt knows the director of a good *preparatoria* there."
- *Meaning:* My aunt knows the director of a good preparatory school in Mexico City, the capital.

See if you can translate these italicized terms:

- "You can't live with both kidneys gone. *No es possible,*" Tio reminded him.
- They said that [Don Clemente] had never lost a single person [in crossing the border]. *Nunca. Ni una persona.*
- He held me for a second, then whispered his blessing into my ear, "*Que Dios te acompañe.*"
- At the far corner of the *mercado*, we found the one and only *botas* stall. The scent of new leather filled the air. Some boots sat displayed on shelves in the back. Others hung from the ceiling, out of reach.

Context

Sometimes we can figure out the meanings by looking at the surrounding words.

- *Example:* Within seconds, Javier had Elena in a giant *abrazo.* He reached out to pull me into the circle. I felt myself resist, but Elena grabbed my waist and tugged me in closer. Answer: *abrazo* = hug

- *Example:* The people on the ground called back . . . One old woman stood unsteadily . . . "Go to your father," she urged. Another old man called out, over and over, "Find your mothers." . . . Javi didn't smile at the *bendiciones* from below. Answer: *bendiciones* = benedictions or blessings (good wishes)

See if you can translate these italicized term.

- Elena wiped her hand across the [dirty] trunk of a parked taxi, then [humorously] wrote *"Lávame"* with her index finger. Note: *lávame* is like two words: _____ me. (Think of "lava" like "lavatory.")

Sample Lesson Plan for *La Línea* (written by a small group)

Objectives:

- Students will analyze why children/teens choose to attempt to cross the U.S.-Mexican border.
- Students will critically think about and discuss controversial issues connected to immigration.
- Students will use context clues and inference to translate Spanish words and phrases.
- Students will analyze the use of code switching of Spanish and English in the novel and how it helps or hinders students' reading.
- Students will discuss characters' motivations and actions in the story.
- Students will debate the pros and cons of teaching this novel in their own future classrooms.

Materials

- DVD projector
- DVD of *Which Way Home?*

Motivation

- Video clip from *Which Way Home?* showing children riding atop trains
- Journal writing: Choice of: (1) What is the most dangerous or hardest decision you have made in your life? or (2) If you had been Miguel or Elena, would you have attempted this trip to the United States?
- Partner share of journal writing
- Large-group voluntary sharing of journal writing
- Large-group discussion of students' response to film clip

Activities

- PowerPoint information on causes of migration to the United States
- Small-group discussion (four members each) of one of the following current controversial topics on immigration and complex social issues:
  - How would your home community change with an influx of immigrants? Would your community be accepting? Why or why not?

- – Should the federal government raid businesses or factories to arrest illegal immigrants? Should illegal immigrants who have children born in the United States be deported to their original country even though their children may remain here, or should the parents be given amnesty? Why or why not?
        - – Should the U.S. government build a wall between Mexico and the United States? What are the pros and cons?
        - – Should signs and directions be given in multiple languages or only in English? Should we become an English-only country? Why or why not?
- Whole-class sharing of small-group discussions
- Small groups given a sentences in Spanish and asked to translate and match with sentences in English. Members are to infer the meaning of unfamiliar words and phrases from context, word origins, and other clues. (Students with a high level of Spanish proficiency are asked to observe other group members and refrain from participating.) After groups share their answers, they may share their level of comfort with activity
- PowerPoint information on language in text, use of code switching, and translations
- Large-group discussion of pros and cons of Spanish-English combination of language in the text
- Large-group analytic discussion of *La Línea* text
    - – Why did Miguel's father not send for Miguel earlier?
    - – At what point in the story do Miguel and Elena bond as family members?
    - – Which part of the journey is the most dangerous for Miguel and Elena? Why?
    - – Is the epilogue, occurring ten years later, helpful in showing readers the future or is it a too-quick resolution to the story? Why?

Closure
- Whole-class debate on pros and cons of teaching this book in the classroom (class divided in half, planning time provided for each group to formulate points and rationales, speakers present pros/cons, speakers give rebuttals to other sides' comments—one or two students will write the pro and con points on the board as the debate progresses).
- Large-group discussion of best strategies for teaching this novel.

Assessment
Student participation in journal writing, small-group discussion, large-group discussion, and debate
- Quality of responses in journal writing, large-group sharing/discussion, debate

Potential Problems/Solutions
- *Problem:* Because some of the discussion topics are controversial, students may not feel comfortable sharing their opinions.
    Solution: If students are reluctant to talk, discuss the text in depth prior to a more personalized discussion.

- *Problem:* The code switching may make the book less appealing to students, since they may be confused if they don't know the Spanish words and phrases.
  Solution: Before assigning the novel, provide the vocabulary exercises (see earlier section) for students to complete individually, as partners, or as a whole class, so students have practice in seeing direct definitions, similarities of English and Spanish, and use of context clues.

Sample Universal Design Strategies or Accommodations for English Learners from Lesson Plan on *La Línea*

English learners who are Spanish speakers may feel more comfortable seeing familiar words and phrases. ELs with other first languages may find the book to be less accessible. The visual learning (a universal design strategy) of the video clip and the PowerPoint presentations may assist students. Audio elements are the small-group and large-group discussions. An audiotape or CD can be provided to accommodate ELs.

A Step from Heaven—*Vocabulary*

Note: Since both pre-service teachers and middle school students often struggle with the Korean names for family members and places, especially in the first pages of the book, a list is provided below:

Korean Names
Ahjimma—a middle-aged or married woman
Apa—dad
Gomo—your father's sister (Young Ju's aunt)
Halmoni—grandmother (Young Ju's father's mother)
Han Gook—Korea
Harabugi—grandfather (Young Ju's father's father—deceased)
Joon—Young Ju's brother
Ju Mi—Young Ju's friend in Korea
Mi Gook—United States
Mi Shi—Young Ju's dog, which stayed in Korea
Sahmchun—your father's brother (Young Ju's uncle)
Uhmma—mom
Uhn-nee—older sister; but in Korean culture girls use this name to call
    older girls from school or social settings
Young Ju—protagonist of story

English Vocabulary Words

The following vocabulary words can be differentiated for readers:

Beginning	*Intermediate*	*Advanced*
camouflage	calloused	billowy
clench	deciphering	bungalow
flare	discreetly	demure
impulse	glower	etched
incredulous	grimaces	glen
linger	guttural	juniper
nubby	intricate	laments
nuggets	luminous	opaque
obligation	profile	scallions
pier	purses her lips	shards
quivers	specious	skewed
utter	tactics	sparse
		wispy

Foundations of Reading, Language, and Literacy

Melissa M. Schulz
Miami University

Description

Designed for early childhood (preK–3) education majors. The course explores the foundations of literacy as content background for effective reading and English language arts instruction, birth to age twenty-one.

Audience

Undergraduate early childhood education teacher candidates enrolled in Foundations of Reading, Language and Literacy are in their sophomore year. This course is the first of four literacy courses the students will take during their undergraduate early childhood education program.

Objectives

This course seeks to develop and/or expand teacher candidates' knowledge of language and literacy development and literacy of early childhood education students (preschool-third grade). Emphasis is placed on understanding and planning instruction for all students, including students who are from linguistically and culturally diverse backgrounds. The course is informed by the National Association for the Education of Young Children (NAEYC) and Ohio Academic Content Standards (ACS) as they relate to literacy instruction for preschool to third-grade students. Upon successful completion of the requirements of this course, teacher candidates will have an opportunity to:

1. Develop and/or expand foundational knowledge of children's language and literacy development as important components for planning and implementing effective instruction for all children in preschool through third grade.
2. Develop an understanding and appreciation for students' cultural and linguistic backgrounds, which impact children's language and literacy development.
3. Apply knowledge gained about children's interests and abilities, as well as language and cultural backgrounds, to differentiate instruction for all students, including English learners.
4. Gain knowledge and skill in developing and implementing research-based strategies for teaching literacy to all students, including ELs.

Materials

The following resources will provide a focus for the course and information useful for class discussions, activities, and projects.

Main Texts

Au, K. (2008). *Multicultural issues and literacy achievement*. New York: Routledge.

Dickinson, D.K. & Tabors, P.O. (Eds.) (2001). *Beginning literacy with language: Young children learning at home and school*. Baltimore, MD: Brookes Publishing.

Schulz, M. & Honchell, B. (Eds.) (2007). *Literacy for diverse learners: Finding common ground in today's classrooms*. Norwood, MA: Christopher-Gordon Publishers.

Additional Readings

Collection of book chapters and journal articles focused on the content outlined in the course objectives. Sample reading materials that focus specifically on EL issues include, but are not limited to, the following.

Avalos, M., Piasencia, A., Chavez, C., & Rascon, J. (2007). Modified guided reading: Gateway to English as a second language and literacy learning. *Reading Teacher, 61*(4), 318-329.

Crafton, L.K., Brennan, M., & Silvers, P. (2007). Critical inquiry and multiliteracies in a first-grade classroom. *Language Arts, 84*(1), 510-518.

Fernandez, R. C. (2003). No hablo Ingles: Bilingualism and multiculturalism in preschool settings. *Early Childhood Education Journal, 27*(3), 159-163.

Ordonez-Jasis, R., & Ortiz, R. W. (2006). Reading their worlds: Working with diverse families to enhance children's early literacy development. *Young Children*, 42-48.

Ordonez-Jasis, R., & Ortiz, R. W. (2006). Reading their worlds: Working with diverse families to enhance children's early literacy development. *Young Children*, 42-48.

Tabors. P.O. (1997). *One child, two languages: A guide for preschool educators of children English as a second language*. Baltimore: Paul H. Brookes Publishing Company.

Assignments and Assessments

The following sample assignments are designed to contribute in different, yet complementary, ways to the objectives of this course. These sample assignments provide an example of EL-infused activities and projects aimed at preparing early childhood teacher candidates to address the language and literacy needs of English learners in the mainstream preK–3 classrooms.

Small-Group Discussion of Language and Literacy Issues for All Learners

In this assignment, teacher candidates have an opportunity to discuss various issues pertaining to the education of English learners. Issues range from identifying the needs of students to designing instruction to accommodate those needs. Teacher candidates are asked to complete specific assigned reading (e.g., chapter 4 and chapter 8 in Au's *Multicultural Issues and Literacy Achievement*) in advance of each class session. In class, the course instructor engages teacher candidates in small-group discussion of the issues in the assigned readings. Sample questions to guide group discussions include:

1. What two kinds of literacy learning experiences must be available in the classroom for students of diverse backgrounds? Why are both kinds of experiences important?
2. How can classroom teachers provide all students with the opportunity to engage in reading and writing for authentic and meaningful purposes?

Teacher candidates use the information gained from small-group discussions to refine their understandings of the issues raised and to ask deeper questions about how to enhance the language and literacy development of students in the classroom. Teacher candidates are evaluated on the level of participation in and contributions to the discussions.

Family Literacy Night

In this assignment, teacher candidates have an opportunity to gain a deeper under-standing of the needs of EL students and their families with respect to language and lit-eracy development. Teacher candidates are asked to complete specific readings (e.g., Ordonez-Jasis and Ortiz's article, "Reading Their Worlds: Working with Diverse Families to Enhance Young Children's Early Literacy Development." In class, the course instruc-tor shares a video clip of a Family Literacy Night held in a second-grade classroom at a local elementary school. The instructor and the teacher candidates brainstorm why Family Literacy Nights are critical for building and sustaining relationships with students and their families. Next, the instructor and the teacher candidates discuss how to plan a Family Literacy Night to ensure parent/caregiver communication about the event is translated into the languages spoken within the homes of the students. The instructor and the teacher candidates create a parent/caregiver handout, drawing on accessible resources online or using translation software. Teacher candidates are evaluated on the quality of the handout prepared for families.

English Learner Vignette

In this assignment, teacher candidates have an opportunity to adjust instruction to accommodate the language and literacy needs of ELs in their classrooms. The instruc-tor shares a vignette of an authentic English learner and her experience attending an American school for a "Meet the Teacher" night before she starts first grade at a new elementary school with her family. In small groups, the students engage in a discus-sion about the English learner (EL) vignette and the how to effectively work with ELs to enhance their literacy skills. Next, the course instructor asks the teacher candidates to look at a literacy bag designed for a *mainstream* preschool student and her family. The following items are included in the literacy bag, and the instructor shows them to the candidates and discusses why they were selected for the preschool student's literacy bag.

1. *Two books* that are appropriate for a child in preschool or in kindergarten. One book should be an *informational text* and one book should be a *fictional or literary form of*

text (e.g., poetry, narrative). Create a "theme" around the two different pieces of children's literature.

2. *Four different activities* from at least four different areas of early literacy (preschool) development:
   – Vocabulary and oral language
   – Phonological awareness
   – Alphabet knowledge
   – Print awareness/concepts of print
   – Writing

   For each activity, the necessary materials for the activity are included in the literacy bag:
   – Alphabet knowledge games
   – Phonological awareness games or texts
   – Ideas for parent/child discussions around the books chosen
   – Journal or story writing/dictation
   – Activities or games to promote print and/or word awareness
   – Letter formation
   – Ideas for vocabulary words for parents to discuss from chosen books

3. A typed *resource guide* to explain the following:
   a. Book titles with a rationale for your choices
   b. Overview each literacy activity including:
      – Your articulation of the instructional purpose/objective for the activity that includes the broadly defined area of early literacy development (above), as well as a more specific purpose of your particular activity (e.g., Alphabet knowledge—Identifying letters M, W, N, Z).
      – Description of each literacy activity and an explanation of how each literacy activity align with your stated instructional purpose.
      – Description of materials included in the literacy bag and an explanation of how the materials align with the literacy activity and stated instructional purpose.

4. Type a *parent or caregiver handout* to provide them with guidance and information about how to help their child use the literacy bag. Describe *all four activities* included in the literacy bag. Use parent/caregiver-friendly language, which will be *different than the language you use in the resource guide*.

After the instructor shares the content of the literacy bag with the teacher candidates, she explains that for their course assignment they are going to design a literacy bag for an EL student. The instructor and the teacher candidates discuss exactly how a literacy bag will need to be modified for an English learner. The modified literacy bag assignment includes the following items:

1. The two books (one fiction and one nonfiction) included in the bag must be published in Spanish or published as bilingual English/Spanish texts.
2. The resource guide needs to clearly explain how each literacy activity they select and include in the literacy bag promotes language and literacy learning and home literacy

connections for ELs. This resource guide is only turned into the instructor; it is not placed in the literacy bag for the ELs and their families.

   c. The parent/caregiver handout will be provided in both English and Spanish, translated to the best of the student's ability, drawing on accessible resources online, in software, or from real Spanish speakers.

Literacy Bag Designed for an English Learner

In this assignment, teacher candidates learn how to prepare a literacy bag, which includes *four* language and literacy learning activities for a preschool child who is an EL student. The preschool student will bring the literacy bag home to use with a parent or caregiver as a means to foster language and literacy development. Within the literacy bag, teacher candidates include a letter to the child and to the parent or caregiver and a resource guide. The letter outlines four literacy activities that the child can do at home. Teacher candidates can purchase, make, or borrow materials for the literacy bag they design for a preschool student. Literacy bags are evaluated on the quality of materials included, and the presentation of the materials.

Assessment

A teacher-designed rubric will be used to evaluate the teacher candidates' performance on the literacy bag for an EL assignment, which is worth 20 percent of the overall course grade.

Reflection

As a former elementary classroom teacher for ten years, I understand and value the importance of working closely with families of ELs I realize how dramatically many elementary classrooms have changed in the last fifteen years due to the growing population of ELs in mainstream classrooms. I know that many teachers, administrators, and researchers continue to search for ways to advance literacy skills of ELs because they want ELs to be academically successful and confident learners. Many teachers, administrators, and researchers realize how important it is for ELs to become proficient readers and writers inside and outside the classroom in order to master the skills needed for grade-level work.

As a professor of teacher educators, I am constantly trying to convey to teacher candidates how diverse our future elementary classrooms will be. I share personal examples of how I have worked hand-in-hand with parents and caregivers of ELs to support the literacy growth of their child. Teacher candidates appreciate the personal stories I share with them but they also want to know practical ways they can advance the literacy skills of ELs they will teach someday. The teacher candidates want to know how they can partner with families of ELs so there is a strong relationship between home and school.

I have been teaching Foundations of Reading, Language, and Literacy for the last five years. The university at which I am employed acquired an OELA grant. The research team invited professors to volunteer to infuse EL content into their undergraduate teacher education courses. I quickly volunteered to infuse the Foundations of Reading, Language and Literacy course. I volunteered because, as a recent elementary teacher, I value the importance of understanding and working closely with ELs and their families. I know that this will be critical for any teacher to be successful in today's classroom. I made two major changes to the Foundations of Reading, Language, and Literacy course. First of all, I added more reading material that focuses on understanding students from culturally and linguistically diverse backgrounds. The second change involved modifying the literacy bag assignment for an EL in preschool. I decided to create a vignette of an actual English learner whom I personally worked with when I was a classroom teacher. The student spoke Spanish as her native language and was learning English as her second language. I believe that the vignette and in-class discussion provide the teacher candidates important background information to understand and contextualize their future work as teachers of ELs.

I believe that by requiring additional reading material which focuses on how to work effectively with culturally and linguistically diverse students and their families and by modifying the literacy bag assignment, I am helping my teacher education students understand the importance of differentiating the literacy curriculum for ELs. Due to the modifications I have made to the Foundations of Reading, Language, and Literacy course, the teacher candidates are learning how to partner with parents and caregivers of ELs on early literacy instruction and how to use translation software to modify letters and written materials that a teacher sends home to families of ELs.

Developmental Reading

Vassiliki I. Zygouris-Coe
University of Central Florida

Description

An investigation of the needs of individual learners in reading instruction across grade levels. The primary foci of the course are on organizational techniques for promoting optimum reading growth, research-based qualities of effective reading instruction, reading techniques, classroom organization, and instructional materials.

Course Audience

This course is designed for pre-service teachers pursuing initial certification, and graduate level education majors in a number of programs (i.e., elementary education, reading education, English language arts, curriculum and instruction [pre-service level], MAT. [pre-service level], communicative disorders, exceptional education, counselor education, and school psychology). Classroom observations are encouraged, but no field experiences are attached to this course. Because of its wide programmatic implications, this course serves many core needs of both the pre-service and in-service teacher education curricula.

Course Objectives

Upon successful completion of the requirements of this course, teacher candidates will have an opportunity to:

1. Develop a reflective attitude and a feeling of confidence toward the teaching of reading to a diverse group of students.
2. Understand how to adapt to needs of pupils in a multicultural classroom; plan instruction to meet diverse needs especially for children learning English for Speakers of Other Languages (ESOL). (Florida ESOL Performance Standards 2, 4, 5, 16, 21, 25)
3. Understand the process of reading as interactive involving reader, text, and contextual factors (Florida ESOL Performance Standard 4).
4. Explain the components of a complete literacy program.
5. Demonstrate knowledge of the content of word identification/decoding (i.e. sight vocabulary, phonics, morphology, and context) (Florida ESOL Performance Standards 8, 9, 10).
6. Explore a variety of instructional approaches including the basal reader, language experience, literature-based, and whole language reading approaches.

7. Teach a guided reading or directed reading activity for a literary or nonfiction text (Florida ESOL Performance Standards 6, 12).
8. Select and evaluate instructional materials, including print, literacy software, and utilize technology to support reading instruction and students' reading development (Florida ESOL Performance Standards 7, 13).
9. Compare various methods of grouping children for reading instruction.

Materials

Allington, R. (2009). *What matters in response to intervention: Research-based designs.* Boston. MA: Pearson.

Florida Department of Education, Office of Multicultural Student Language Education (1990). *Consent decree.* Retrieved from http://www.fldoe.org/aala/rules.asp

Frey, N. & Fisher, D. (2009). *Learning words inside and out, grades 1–6: Vocabulary instruction that boosts achievement in all subject areas.* Portsmouth, NH: Heinemann.

Krashen, S. D. (1988). *Second language acquisition and second language learning.* New York, NY: Prentice-Hall.

Opitz, M., & Rasinski, T. (2008). *Good-bye round robin: 25 effective oral reading strategies.* (Updated edition). Portsmouth, NH: Heinemann.

Rivera, M. O., Moughamian, A. C., Lesaux, N. K., & Francis, D. J. (2008). *Language and reading interventions for English language learners and English language learners with disabilities.* Portsmouth, NH: RMC Research Corporation, Center on Instruction.

Robertson, K. (2009). *Five things teachers can do to improve learning for ELs in the new year.* Retrieved from http://www.readingrockets.org/article/29590

Short, D., & Fitzsimmons, S. (2007). *Double the work: Challenges and solutions to acquiring language and academic literacy for adolescent English language learners —A report to Carnegie Corporation of New York.* Washington, DC: Alliance for Excellent Education.

Teachers of English to Speakers of Other Languages. (2000). *Assessment and accountability of English for speakers of other languages students: A position statement.* Alexandria, VA: Author.

Various additional on-line articles and resources in support of course objectives.

Assignments

The following sample assignments are designed to contribute in different, yet complementary, ways to the objectives of this course. These sample assignments provide an example of EL-infused activities and projects aimed at preparing teacher candidates to address the language and literacy needs of ELs in a mainstream K–12 classroom.

1. Weekly Course Discussion Posts

There are 14 written reflections, each containing a high-quality discussion that illustrates the candidates' personal experiences with, and understanding of, the material.

This discussion assignment is designed to meet course objectives that address building the teacher candidates' knowledge about characteristics and needs of ELs, effective reading instruction for ELs, assessment and monitoring of ELs' progress and needs, and creating an environment that is conducive to learning. Here is an example of a discussion assignment addressing issues relating to EL students.

In this assignment, you will have an opportunity to develop and/or expand your knowledge about the characteristics and needs of EL students, including planning effective reading instruction, assessing and monitoring progress, and creating a classroom environment that is conducive to learning for these learners. To help achieve this goal, you will be asked to review and respond to at least one classmate's posting regarding a specific issue by thoughtfully commenting on his/her suggestions and ideas. There are probably one or more students in your Florida classroom/learning environment that did not grow up speaking English. They were raised in another country, or perhaps even in the United States, where another language was primarily spoken at home. Students who do not speak English at all—or do not speak, understand, and write English with the same capacity as their classmates—are referred to as English Learners (ELs). The EL students in your classroom learning environment may be very different in their background, skills, and past experiences from the other students you are teaching. Using information from this learning module please discuss the following:

- How do you find out what knowledge, experiences, needs, and skills EL students in your classroom/learning environment have? How do you utilize the information you collect about them to plan instructional goals and to build a classroom environment that will enhance learning for all of your students? Please provide a rationale for your response.
- What two insights did you gain from this learning module about the type(s) of instruction, experiences, support, and materials ELs need to succeed? How do you plan to implement this knowledge in your classroom instruction/learning environment? Describe your implementation plan and provide a rationale for your response.

You will be evaluated on your response, the depth of insight provided, and the quality of your writing.

2. Literacy Logs

Teacher candidates are provided with 13 literacy log entries showcasing various reading strategies (e.g., K-W-L-H, Double Entry Diary, Anticipation Guide, Summarization) that address specific literacy needs depending grade levels. The literacy log promotes usage of effective instructional practices to support and develop K–12 students' reading needs. The purpose of the literacy log assignment is to model and scaffold teacher candidates' knowledge about effective reading strategies and provide them with opportunities throughout the course to implement them using course content. This assignment meets course objectives that address teacher candidates' knowledge about how to adapt their instruction to the needs of ELs in a classroom, plan instruction to meet their diverse needs, and select and evaluate instructional materials and practices to support reading instruction and students' reading development. The 13 literacy log entries (or reading strategies) allow teacher candidates to experience each strategy (i.e., its rationale, purpose, step-by-step implementation, benefits for students), reflect on its future use for reading instruction for ELs, and invite metacognitive thinking and behaviors. Here is an example of a literacy log assignment addressing EL-related instructional issues.

> The *"Word Builder"* strategy is a simple way to teach and build students' morphemic analysis, vocabulary knowledge, and skills. The words can be assigned by the teacher before reading, during reading, or after reading. As an alternative, the word builder can be used with whole-class, small group, or individual vocabulary instruction to model how to determine or infer words' meaning by examining word-meaningful parts (i.e., prefixes, suffixes, roots, etc.).

How Does It Work?
  a. Using the Word Builder organizer, choose seven words from the Learning Module on Literacy Instruction and Non-native Speakers of English and write them in the "Word" area of the organizer.
  b. Start "playing" with each word by adding a prefix or suffix in the corresponding area of the organizer.
  c. Write the new word in the "New Word" area of the organizer.
  d. Write the meaning of each word (in your own words) in the "Meaning" area of the organizer.

Reflection: We encourage you to think about how you might use this strategy in your classroom to support your instruction and your students' reading development. You will be evaluated on your response, the depth of insight provided, and the quality of your writing.

3. Reflective Assignment

This "hands-on," problem-solving assignment is designed to invite the candidate to select an instructional challenge that relates to reading and apply principles of effective reading instruction to its implementation for the purpose of improving student learning and achievement. The candidate is expected to use information from course texts and any types of personal experiences to develop a response to a future reading instructional challenge. All candidates are encouraged to implement their plan of action in an actual classroom or work with a student or group of students during the course. Teacher candidates are encouraged to select a research-based and realistic challenge associated with ELs' needs—for example, vocabulary, comprehension, fluency, lack of student engagement with texts, motivation, building a print-rich and language-rich classroom environment, promoting student-student collaboration, assessment of student progress, or working with parents to support ELs' learning at home. This assignment meets course objectives about building teacher candidates' knowledge of learner characteristics, demonstration of knowledge about reading instruction for ELs, assessment, and reflection on instruction and student progress or needs. Here is a detailed description of the reflective assignment:

Part I: Identification and description of an instructional challenge

- Describe the instructional challenge and situate it within your mainstream classroom and/or school.
- Describe the plan of action and the steps taken to address the challenges identified.

Part II: Implementation of a plan of action, reflection, and next steps.

- Describe your plan for implementation including lesson plan, observations, and follow-up questions.
- Assess the impact of the plan of action on all students, including ELs.
- Reflect on your experience implementing the plan of action, along with lessons learned and follow-up questions to be addressed.

You will be evaluated on your response to both parts of the assignment, the depth of insight provided, and the quality of your writing and presentation.

4. Professional Book Groups

The purpose of this assignment is to further develop teacher candidates' knowledge about quality vocabulary instruction for ELs, fluency development and instruction, and intervention models to meet ELs' academic needs. In addition, the professional book groups become a means of modeling about the importance of collaborative learning in a classroom environment. Student-student collaboration is particularly important for ELs; teacher candidates experience the benefits and challenges associated with collaboration and are provided with opportunities to further explore course readings, classroom observations from field or other experiences, exchange ideas, lesson plans and resources, and further their knowledge about reading and reading instruction for all students. Here is an example of what teacher candidates are expected to do as part of this assignment:

> In this assignment, you will have an opportunity to enhance your professional learning and growth by engaging in group discussions of professional books addressing various literacy issues pertaining to all students, including EL students in your classrooms. Your task is to join a group of students who will select and discuss a book of their choice, which may include, but are not limited to: *What Matters in Response to Intervention (Allington, 2009), Learning Words Inside and Out, Grades 1–6 (Fry & Fisher, 2009), Good-bye Round Robin (Opitz & Rasinski, 2008).* You are expected to hold three discussions during the course of the semester and respond in writing to a set of key questions about the topic at hand. Your written responses will be evaluated for clarity of issues identified, the depth of insight provided, and the quality of writing and presentation.

5. Lesson Plan Project

In this assignment, you will have an opportunity to develop skill in creating lesson plans addressing specific components of reading instruction (e.g., phonics, phonemic awareness, fluency, vocabulary, or comprehension) for all students, including ELs. Your task is to develop a lesson plan that addresses one of these critical components and that builds in necessary scaffolds to help make content more comprehensible for your EL students varying in language proficiency levels (e.g., beginning, intermediate, advanced). The instructional adaptations used to make academic content understandable to ELs at different language proficiency levels are frequently referred to in the literature as scaffolds. Some of the ways instruction could be adjusted for EL students in mainstream classrooms include, but are not limited to, giving specific attention to vocabulary development, providing information in multiple ways (e.g., visual clues and physical gestures), presenting ideas verbally and in writing; creating frequent opportunities for meaningful oral language practice, including working with peers, making instructions and expectations very clear (e.g., through modeling a procedure or completing together part of a task); differentiating instruction according to language proficiency or academic skill level; and providing additional opportunities for practice. Your lesson plan will be evaluated for the quality of instruction planned, instructional time allocation, progress monitoring strategies, and the overall quality of writing and presentation.

Reflection

From my perspective, infusing EL content into this course was a given—it fit like a glove. How can we prepare future teacher educators in reading without positioning ELs as an explicit component of reading and reading instruction? In reading, we often use this broad umbrella-type concept of "struggling" readers, under which we place students with varied exceptionalities, ELs, and students who "struggle" with reading in a variety of ways. The main challenge for me lay in how I could position the reading (and other) needs of ELs in a more strategic way in an already comprehensive course. Other challenges included my need to grow in my knowledge of young and older ELs' needs, research-based instruction to meet those needs, ELs and response to intervention (RTI), and how I could balance all of this in the context of reading and in a foundations course for a diverse group of pre-service educators.

I was in the first cohort of faculty at my institution that attended a three-hundred-hour, job-embedded professional development on EL infusion into our curricula. Who wants his or her Fridays to be devoted to professional development that is also followed by "homework"? Well, all of us as faculty have plenty of work on our plate but this professional development not only increased my knowledge about EL-related issues and best practices but also helped to build community among faculty. In addition, it helped to build a "common language" on EL-related issues across programs. Change does not come about easily, nor it is a result of just a professional development program (no matter how effective the program).

As we know, school culture is not a static phenomenon. It is co-constructed through interactions with others (i.e., faculty, students, community, sharing and conversations, and reflections on coursework, academic life, teacher education goals, and outcomes). Our EL professional development initiatives were purposeful, collegial, industrious, relevant, committed, reflective, sustained, measurable, and realistic. These faculty conversations, which were targeted, ongoing, and relevant to our courses, helped to facilitate long-term implementation. For a couple of years following the professional development, the conversations were still present in program-area meetings, in program accreditation meetings, in follow-up smaller workshop opportunities in the summer, as well as in the sharing of resources, ideas, and plans. As a group, we laughed, we dealt with our own cultural misconceptions and assumptions, we role-played, we exchanged feedback, we examined each other's syllabi, and we made strategic decisions about EL infusion in our courses. It is always rewarding, motivating, and engaging to participate in such large-scale efforts when there is minimum risk involved and where support, community, common goals for teacher education program improvements, and resources, for reference and follow-up purposes, are available. Following the aforementioned training, several of us worked collaboratively over the summer to fine-tune courses and examine core accreditation-related tasks about EL infusion in our programs. As a result of this additional follow-up, we were able to showcase specific course and programmatic changes in our college and shared them with faculty across campus.

One of the earliest tasks involved revision of our syllabi. We positioned our syllabi within the conceptual framework of our teacher education program, we set goals and action items about our teacher candidates' knowledge, experiences, and dispositions, and we negotiated on where the infusion should be positioned, what it would look like per course, what outcomes we expected, and how we would assess and demonstrate teacher candidates' knowledge, experiences, and dispositions about EL-related knowledge and practices.

Because of the role this course plays across programs in our institution, it was important to me to not only create an awareness for the participating teacher candidates, but to build their knowledge, invite them to implement that knowledge in meaningful contexts, and be able to reflect about instructional challenges and issues relating to supporting and developing the reading needs of ELs across grade levels. I did not want my students to view EL issues as disjointed instructional add-ons; instead, I wished for them to think critically about their instruction and how students in their class with cultural, linguistic, academic, exceptional, and other needs would respond to, and learn from it. My goal for them was to also think about what they would need to do to differentiate both their instruction and support for ELs. Knowledge is one thing, but what can we do about perceptions, misconceptions, beliefs, and attitudes about ELs? I also wanted to focus on discussions among my students about their own "filters": How did they view, what did they think and expect of culturally and linguistically diverse students in their classrooms? What would they do to maximize their academic success and learning in reading? What experiences did they have with ELs? What would they do to go beyond just having cultural celebrations but also provide an atmosphere of acceptance and differentiated instruction and support? How would they monitor students' progress? With whom would they collaborate (e.g., families, school faculty, professionals, or agencies) to locate resources and provide additional support for ELs? All of these (and many more) are core issues relating to the reading needs of ELs and the future teachers of ELs. One course, of course, will not make anyone an expert but it can set the stage for further learning in the right direction.

Teacher candidates enrolled in my course share common needs across program areas. First and foremost, they have misconceptions about what ELs can or cannot do in reading. Second, they are developing their knowledge about differentiated instruction. Third, they are also on a learning continuum about the role of assessment. Finally, they are expanding their knowledge about RTI and ELs. I believe that the course assignments/assessments in my course help to not only keep these issues in sight throughout the course but they also invite teacher candidates to start implementing theoretical, research, and instructional principles from the get go. Although at times the lack of knowledge and experiences of teacher candidates becomes a barrier (especially at the beginning of the course), the course focus on effective instruction for all students helps to guide them, motivate them, perplex them, and invite them to be reflecting about these issues at all times.

The following are sample course assignments/assessments of student work that will help to first make their thinking processes and reflections more visible and secondly, will also illustrate some of the processes they are involved in as they grow in their knowledge and understanding of EL-related issues. As I continue to grow as an instructor in both my knowledge and experiences with ELs and with teacher candidates I find that the faculty collaborations and sustained dialogue on EL related programmatic issues help me to seek new and improved ways to best prepare my students in reading.

Sample Written Reflections

Student 1

Assessment and instruction are dependent on one another. The information we gain from assessments will help us to better our instruction. Teachers can use various assessments, both formal and informal, to help gauge what their students know. When I begin teaching, I plan on sitting down with my students and their parents for a conference prior to the start of the school year. I will have a translator there, if needed, to discuss their culture, where and how they were raised, and their English proficiency. Other ways that I plan on finding out my students' knowledge, experiences, needs, and skills are to test them both in their first and second language and to have them engage in the writing process, which will include drawings. By understanding where my students are from, I will get a better idea of what information they already know. Also, allowing my students to draw will help my students to express information that they have not acquired the words for yet. I will utilize the information I collect to plan instructional goals for my ELs and to build a classroom environment that will enhance the learning of all students. Once I have an understanding of what my students know, I can differentiate instruction based on my students needs. I also plan on using cooperative learning. My EL students can teach my other students about their cultures. They can share their experiences with their classmates and their classmates can help them to learn English.

I also learned that the use of first language could help students to learn a second language. This insight is contrary to what I have previously learned regarding language. English helped me when I was learning German, but not when I was learning French. I plan on using this insight in my classroom by not limiting my students to only speak in English. I also plan on connecting the grammar of their first language to English to help them learn the structure of the language. Another insight that I gained came from the interactionist theory. It helped me to realize that all my future students have the ability to learn a second language. I plan on creating a classroom environment that shows students that it is okay to make mistakes. I want them to feel comfortable in the classroom so that they participate. To create this feeling of comfort, I plan on creating a community in my classroom. My ELs will have to work with my other students and vice versa to do well. All of my students will have specific tasks to complete individually and together. This will allow all of my students to gain independence and self-esteem, as well as an open and safe environment.

Student 2

I often discover the levels or types of knowledge, experience, needs, and skills present in the classroom through individual surveys/questionnaires, class introductions, class discussions, group work, or individual assignment choice and/or completion. Within each of those situations, strengths and weaknesses often reveal themselves rather quickly and naturally. Levels of confidence, use (and misuse) of grammar, and areas of interest and strength are discovered through personal introductions, topic suggestions, discussions, and assignment choices. In the classroom, I will utilize this information by tailoring the types or levels of projects and/or writing assignments we cover throughout the semester/year. This is one area that provides my subject area with a significant advantage.

One of my favorite progressive assignments is requiring students to find or write a story, fable, or biography from their country of origin and area of interest, which they can translate/interpret and illustrate into a storybook. Within this assignment, students are provided with the opportunity to connect to and share their native language and/or culture with the class, expand their second language acquisition through exploration, and expose the rest of the class to languages and/or cultures previously unknown (hopefully opening doors to additional interest, support, and positive social interaction). Within the field of art, exploring other cultures also opens up opportunities to discuss the various types of artistic processes, color schemes, or subject matter that different cultures favor and reasons as to why.

My first insight is the fact that mainstream children apply deductive reasoning (specific truths are deduced from general propositions), while more diverse groups apply inductive reasoning (fundamental assumptions are inferred from a series of concrete statements). I will implement this knowledge into my instruction by adjusting my expectations accordingly. Before reading this area of the myth about the lack of interest of ELs in learning in detail, I probably would have presumed that my ELs who showed minimum attention spans or levels of persistence either had little to no interest in actual success or had already given up on themselves. This would in turn affect my view of the student and my interpretation of how important their studies are to them. After reading this article entitled "Double the Work: Challenges and Solutions to Acquiring Language and Academic Literacy for Adolescent English Language Learners" by Short & Fitzsimmons (2007), I am more prepared to combat my own presumptions and give the student the benefit of the doubt and do my best to ensure both the student's and my own persistence in regards to their learning. With this knowledge, I will also discover, create, and implement various methodologies to ensure I am reaching my varying student body in as many different ways as possible (visual, auditory, kinetic, etc.) in hopes of additional material sinking in—whether they realize it or not! I also learned that some students are much more likely to pay attention and learn from their peers than from the adults and teachers in their lives. This insight will affect my instruction because I will always keep in mind the degree of peer influence. Within the classroom I will ensure to dedicate significant amounts of time to small group work, cooperative learning, peer discussion and tutoring, etc.

Although these strategies have already proven extremely relevant for all learners (when compared to the outdated methodologies of direct instruction), this newly acquired knowledge will serve as an additional incentive to ensure I integrate peer-to-peer time within my classroom instructional methods. This knowledge also strengthens the importance of finding classroom assignments/topics that connect to and engage my students."

Sample Reflective Assignment with EL Accommodations

Since I do not have a class of my own, I am putting together a plan based on a discussion with my friend who has been teaching elementary school for seven years and is currently teaching fifth grade. She identified her biggest challenge as fluency building for a few low readers and ELs and comprehension building for a couple of readers who read too fast to comprehend. Since fluency and comprehension are linked, the readers struggling with fluency will benefit from fluency and comprehension building. According to Opitz and Rasinski (2008), students who lack fluent reading will spend more effort concentrating on reading each word and not be able to think about what the sentence means. I am designing a plan to help build fluency so that those students can concentrate on comprehension, and then I will focus on comprehension skills for all of the students in the classroom. Therefore, my plan of action is in two parts.

The first part focuses on fluency building for the low readers and the ELs in my friend's classroom. I have chosen to use partner reading of level-appropriate texts to increase successful reading experiences. While making sure that two ELs are not paired together, I will assign the struggling readers to pairs according to ability. Next, I will give an appropriately leveled book to each pair to read together. As part of center time the pairs will read together for a half hour. Reader 1 will read aloud first with reader 2 following along. Then reader 2 will read aloud, and reader 1 will follow along. They will each read for five minutes before changing roles. The readers will be encouraged to help each other with misread words and unknown words. I will model how to help each other with difficult words. When the students can't figure out a word together, they should raise their hands and I will assist them. I think that reading together can help build confidence because the students won't be reading for higher-level readers but for readers at their own level and with a book at their level. I also think that they will build fluency by helping each other. Each student will have a different set of known at-a-glance words to help the other with.

For the second half-hour of center time, the pairs will work on practicing new and difficult words from their reading. They will start by identifying and pronouncing 5 to 10 of the most important and difficult words from their reading. I will model how to choose these words from all the words that they have read by picking words that are difficult and critical for understanding the text. I will have the students write down their list of words. I will pronounce the word and will invite students to examine the context by looking at the sentence the word is in. Next, I will model how to isolate the prefix and separate the suffix. I will give each of the pairs a list of common prefixes and suffixes to use to help them. Next, I will model how to say and examine the stem by looking for meaning in the stem. I will model how they can use each other and dictionaries to help in confirming their work. And last, I will model how to write the correct definition for the word. When this strategy is first introduced, I will not expect the pairs to complete all of their chosen words in one day. But after the students have practiced the strategy for a while, they will need to complete all the words. They should then practice saying the word aloud to each other. I think that this strategy is a good metacognitive strategy that will teach the student how to think about difficult words and learn from them. I think that this will help with fluency by breaking the complex word into segments that are more easily pronounced and understood. Also, by learning how to analyze the word the students will be less likely to skip or stumble on future difficult words.

The second part of my plan focuses on building comprehension skills for the readers who are reading too quickly and lack comprehension. I have chosen to teach the reciprocal teaching strategy in order to help the students struggling with comprehension (see the worksheet at the end of this assignment). Some of my friend's students are reading too quickly and not paying attention to the meaning of what they are reading. I think that reciprocal teaching will show them how to slow down and take note of what the text means. Although this is a during-reading strategy, I will show students the basics before they start to read. Also, since this strategy will benefit the entire class, I will teach it during the thirty minutes of whole-group instruction. I will start by discussing how to make predictions of a text. We will discuss how to look at pictures, graphs, the book title, and any heading that they find as they flip through the book. I will model this with a book that can be read to the class in teaching this strategy. I will write on the board our predictions about the book. Next we will talk about what main ideas are and how to spot them in a book. We will talk about section headings, topic sentences, and chapter themes. I will then read a couple short sections of the book to the class and have them pick out the main ideas of those sections, which will be written, on the board. We will then discuss any questions we have from those sections and write that on the board as well. Next, I will teach the class how to summarize the main ideas we have discussed. I will show them how to eliminate redundant and unnecessary information and connect the ideas together. As a class, we will summarize the sections I had read and write these summaries on the board. Next, we will work on clarifying any difficult vocabulary or anything that confused the students and write that on the board. I will then group the students in pairs and remind them of what they will be looking for in the next sections that we read. I will then read another section of the book to the class. While working in pairs, the students will go through the steps starting with the main idea, using our example on the board for assistance. When they are finished we will discuss their results. After this phase is over, I will let the students use the worksheets during their silent reading time, allowing them to help each other with clarification. I think that this strategy will help the students with low comprehension to slow down their reading and think about the main ideas before proceeding.

After discussing this plan with my friend, I think that my plan will make a difference in the fluency and comprehension skills of her students. The partner reading will allow the students to learn from each other. Partner reading will also increase the confidence of the readers because they will be practicing with readers who are not too advanced for them. I also think that using her suggestions will allow the students to more fully grasp the strategies that were implemented. I think that the reciprocal teaching for comprehension will greatly increase the comprehension skills of the whole class. It will help the students to really understand what they are reading and can be easily transferred to any reading material or content area. Since I haven't been in a classroom yet, it's difficult to get a feel for how long a student can work on one concept, skill, or assignment. Also, I now have a better sense of how much modeling is required as well. It's not enough to model one time. Difficult strategies will require more than one day of modeling and observation of the students as they practice the skills. I also think that tracking the growth of the students at multiple times within the implementation will help me focus my teaching to areas that still need improvement.

The next step would be to actually implement the completed (with improvements from my friend) plan. One day, when I have a class of my own, I will implement this plan and completely evaluate its effectiveness. The biggest unanswered question is how much of an impact this plan actually has. The next unanswered question regards the ELs in the class. Are the ELs in the class benefitting from this plan as much as the native English speakers? Are there other strategies that I should be using to help them more? These questions need further research and implementation."

Sample Group Book Discussions with EL Accommodations

Group discussions from: Allington, R. (2009). *What matters in response to intervention: Research-based designs.* Boston. MA: Pearson.

Effective reading interventions with groups of one to three students can help maximize reader success. One-to-one tutoring works the best; however fewer students are helped each day. Intervention time also needs to be outside of the reading block with 20 minutes of reading leveled texts or rereading texts and 5 minutes of word work and 5 minutes of comprehension skill-building. The most effective interventions are ones in which the reading connects with the general education reading. This is especially true if the student is missing a core class for the intervention. Curriculum coordination helps students by reinforcing and teaching core subjects during the reading intervention. One-to-one tutoring works the best; however fewer students are helped each day. Intervention time also needs to be outside of the reading block with 20 minutes of reading leveled texts or rereading texts and 5 minutes of word work and 5 minutes of comprehensions skills. The most effective interventions are ones in which the reading connects with the general education reading. This is especially true if the student is missing a core class for the intervention. Curriculum coordination helps students by reinforcing and teaching core subjects during the reading intervention."

Group discussions from: Opitz, M., & Rasinski, T. (2008). *Good-bye round robin: 25 effective oral reading strategies*. (Updated edition). Portsmouth, NH: Heinemann.

In our group discussion we talked about radio reading. We discussed procedures of how to carry out the activity found in the book and also suggested some of our own, such as assigning a "versus" activity where the students would be given time to read silently first and then read their selection into the microphone taking turns. We liked the idea of adding a microphone to help engage other students and motivate the reader to do well. We believe the activity to be useful because it allows the reader to practice and allows the listeners to hear another person speak and to process the story through images. We also mentioned how this can be useful for discussion purposes to facilitate collaboration, as well as in assessing students, since it gives each of them an opportunity to read aloud individually. Benefits to repeated readings we discussed are: practice to help the students feel more confident, practicing unfamiliar words to learn to recognize them, and vocabulary expansion from exposure to new words repeatedly. We also noted that assessing students after repeated readings might not provide the teacher with an appropriate representation of the students' skills, since they have had the opportunity to read the text repeatedly.

Other ways we discussed to improve reading fluency were read-alouds, paired reading, and recorded texts. We chose read-alouds for use with whole-class readings of more engaging texts. This helps students with words they don't come across every day, which will increase their reading fluency from expansion of their vocabulary. We chose paired readings to help with a student's confidence in reading and model for reading fluency; however, one member noted how this technique can become problematic when individual students choose poor behavior. Instead of the paired reading, we then discussed recorded texts, since they allow for support through oral reading without the behavior problems. It can aid students' fluency, since it gives the student an opportunity to read along with the recording while hearing it simultaneously. Recorded readings help with word identification abilities.

Sample Lesson Plans with EL Accommodations

1. *Lesson Plan: "I Can Make Words"*

   Grade level: Kindergarten

   Topic: Phonics—The "at" word family

   Goal statement: Students will learn about the short vowel a words in the "at" family.

   Objectives:
   - Students will identify "at" family words
   - Students will classify "at" family words
   - Students will create an "at" family words

   Instructional accommodations for EL students:
   - Provide the students with flashcards of key words/concepts translated in the individual student's first language and in English.
   - During group discussion, encourage the students pronounce the words in their first language.
   - Utilize simple sentences and provide scaffolded support.
   - Provide the students with "at" family words in their first language/English on a graphic organizer with pictures.
   - Provide students with extra time to practice, monitor their progress, and provide them with immediate feedback.

2. *Lesson Plan: "Learning About Prefixes"*

   Grade level: Fifth grade

   Topic: Teaching vocabulary

   Goal statement: Students will be able to identify the prefix "un-" and able to determine if means "not" or "do the opposite."

   Objectives:
   - Students will demonstrate the meaning of "un-" as a prefix.
   - When given an unfamiliar word, students will be able to identify it and understand the meaning with accuracy by using knowledge of the prefix "un-."

   Instructional accommodations for EL students:
   - Several EL strategies will be used throughout this lesson to support student needs.
   - Students will repeat the vocabulary words after the teacher (for the purpose of practicing pronunciation).
   - Teacher will use visual aids, gestures, and nonverbal communication, and provide supplementary explanations and materials as needed to help students understand meaning of words.
   - Teachers will provide feedback on pronunciation of words and also on students' understanding of morphology.

CHAPTER 9

School Leaders, Counselors, and Psychologists

In this chapter, three college of education faculty, affiliated with two U.S. higher education institutions in two states, share how they have infused EL content into a set of courses with the goal of preparing school leaders and other school-based professionals to effectively support the education of English learners in school settings. The three sample course summaries featured are more closely aligned with the 1+ level of infusion, representing the areas of counseling, school psychology, and educational administration. The course summaries also include a reflection delineating some of the ways in which the EL-infused course assignments and activities have enhanced instructor practices as well the preparation of school leaders and professionals to support the education of English learners. Because these courses are outside of the teacher preparation curriculum that is the primary focus of this book, the introduction to this chapter provides a broad view of what these professional roles can contribute to ELs' success at school.

Integration of English Learner Content into the Curriculum for Preparing School Leaders, Counselors, and School Psychologists

Edwidge Crevecoeur-Bryant
University of Central Florida

A tornado whirled through a Spanish-speaking neighborhood in Florida and destroyed everything in its path. Homes, buildings, and schools were destroyed, and family members died. Those whose lives were spared were traumatized by this devastating event; however, they tried to return to a state of normalcy shortly thereafter.

Before the students returned to school, decisions had to be made as to how to proceed with educating these traumatized students. Thus, the principal met with her staff to determine the best course of action. She spoke of the critical need for collaboration within the school, the school psychologist provided information on trauma caused by such environmental occurrences, the school counselor offered ways of speaking and listening to the students, and the teachers revised the curriculum to allow extra time for reviewing all subjects. After extensive discussions, all involved decided that culturally appropriate games, songs, and outdoor activities would take precedence over the regular school curriculum to allow the students to grieve and to build up their morale. It was also decided that the students would determine when they would be ready to return to the regular curriculum and school day. Although no one knew how these decisions would resolve themselves, they were pleased with everyone's involvement in the collaborative decision-making process.

By the end of the school year, even with the month-long disruption, this school's students successfully passed the state standardized test, demonstrating the effectiveness of collaboration among school personnel to attend to the needs of the student body.

In summary, although a devastating event occurred, school personnel collaborated and relied on their individual areas of expertise to focus on the needs of the students. An integrated team of professionals played a critical role in the academic success of these students.

Each of the contributors in the following section has participated in collaborative reflection and analysis with their university colleagues who specialize in teaching English learners. Together they built a common understanding of the knowledge and practices noninstructional school personnel should possess when they work with ELs and their families. The examples of integrated content focused on ELs embody the principle of interdisciplinarity that undergirds the One Plus Model, offering the insights of professionals in multiple fields. This interdisciplinary collaboration between the ESL faculty and the teacher education faculty, when extended to the context of the preK–12 arena, is an example of how an integrated team of educators and other school-based professionals can link the efforts of classroom teachers, ESL specialists, school leaders, counselors, and psychologists in promoting the success of ELs in today's schools.

Faculty preparing professionals in counseling, leadership, and school psychology are in a special category—one that is built on the knowledge and skills comprising the 1+ level of faculty development. Accordingly, the lists in "Knowledge and Skills Needed to Prepare Noninstructional Personnel" presuppose the foundational knowledge and skills listed in chapter 5, which details the content of the 1+ level.

Embedded Topics and Assignments

Integrating topics, information, instructional materials or media, and assignments focused on the instruction of ELs in preK–12 schools may be perceived as an arduous task by many teacher educators who have been recently introduced to the field of second language learning. In many cases, sincere attempts have been made to bring awareness of and engage faculty in discussions on ELs with minimal results. These observations are not a criticism of the curricula of teacher and school-based profes-

Knowledge and Skills Needed to Prepare Noninstructional Personnel

The following lists detail embedded key topics and assignments of school support personnel in leadership, counseling, and school psychology courses to ensure academic success of English learners:

Counseling

- Understand the impact of group processes on the counseling session when linguistic and cultural barriers exist
- Demonstrate appropriate language modification when working with ELs at different proficiency levels
- Show multicultural competence
- Be aware of group leader/facilitator role
- Understand issues of adjustment to a new community (society and school cultures)
- Be capable of developing relationships with members of the students' communities

Leadership

- Demonstrate a genuinely welcoming attitude towards the students and their families
- Provide staff development opportunities for faculty to remain abreast of new research regarding second language learners
- Maintain true collaboration among student support personnel, teachers, and principals
- Provide appropriate assessments to identify gifted as well as ELs who are struggling academically
- Share data to improve instructional decisions
- Be aware of the cultural factors that contribute to academic success of ELs
- Make school professionals (counselors and school psychologists) readily available to assist second language learners
- Be aware of legal issues (identification of ELs, services for ELs, accommodations during high-stakes assessments, reporting/accountability [subgrouping])

School Psychology

- Provide high level of thinking and complexity
- Select appropriate interventions and modifications that are culturally sensitive
- Be knowledgeable of multiple evidence-based interventions
- Hold multidisciplinary evaluation and intervention meetings
- Create formative experiences through interventions
- Possess the ability to reflect on own biases and those of others
- Provide comprehensive evaluation information
- Understand issues of adjustment

sional educators; rather, they are a call for deep reflection and analysis of the many factors that impact the learning abilities of ELs and on how to better prepare school personnel to serve second language learners. The syllabi included in this chapter provide examples of how EL instruction can be infused into curricula once such reflection and analysis have occurred and instructors have become knowledgeable of the many factors that impact ELs through faculty development.

Common Themes

Although each of the following courses focuses on a different subject, four themes are common to all: student achievement, assessment, research, and collaboration.

Student Achievement

Concerns have been expressed regarding the academic success of second language learners. Many teachers have reported that ELs are not performing as well as their native English–speaking peers. Consequently, instructors have been altering classroom instruction to accommodate the students who lack proficiency in reading, writing, listening, and speaking English. English learners are expected to perform in accordance with a standardized curriculum but many of the students are not doing so. What are the factors that contribute to poor educational and linguistic achievement of second language learners in our schools?

To improve student achievement among ELs, it is imperative to identify key factors that contribute to low performance of these students in our schools. In addition, it is necessary to be aware of the achievement gap between native speakers and ELs. Instructors acknowledge this gap; however, they are unsure as to why that occurs even though some have successfully completed teacher preparation programs. Therefore, school leaders need to identify the factors that contribute to student success, failure, or dropout of ELs. School counselors must be ready to assist students in forming positive identities and self-worth. Research states that intentional interactions with ELs may have positive impact on their social-emotional well-being and academic success. School psychologists must employ modifications that are sensitive to and meet the cultural and linguistic needs of ELs.

Assessment

School leaders are responsible for providing an operative learning environment for all students. Therefore, they must address effectiveness of instruction and determine the extent to which Adequate Yearly Progress is achieved among the EL population. Such information is obtained from state accountability test data. In addition, school leaders, psychologists, and counselors should select and use other appropriate evidence-based assessments and interventions that are sensitive to cultural norms. Using appropriate assessments will provide instructors with valuable information to assist in meeting the educational and emotional demands placed on ELs.

Research

Instructors need research data, appropriately analyzed and displayed, to improve their knowledge and provide the most effective instruction in teaching ELs. Providing school leaders, counselors, and psychologists with the opportunities to engage in meaningful data gathering on ELs will enable them to make appropriate changes to interventions. Data-based decision making leads to a more effective selection of multiple modes of assessment for ELs. Activities such as data-sharing meetings and poster sessions are essential for sharing information with teachers and parents.

Collaboration

Instructional leaders are responsible for encouraging and fostering true collaboration among all school personnel to determine the most effective methods for working with ELs. Collaborative exchanges provide effective avenues for gathering of formative feedback and reflections on how to assist ELs to meet the challenges they face. For instructional leaders, collaboration on decision making is key to securing commitments and buy-in toward the implementation of schoolwide research-based systems. In addition, effective use of data chats can enhance the collaboration interaction in effort to select the best instructional interaction for ELs.

Online discussions may be used to share reflections on feedback or to elicit opinions of colleagues regarding second language issues. School counselors believe that collaboration is the key to supporting ELs. School counselors, school leaders, and psychologists must be able to work with everyone, across different ethnicities, races, sexual orientation, cultures, social classes, family types, spiritualties, and exceptionalities. To do so, these education professionals must be able to reflect on how their own biases may influence effective interaction with the students.

In summary, all learners, especially immigrants, face educational and linguistic challenges that require a deeper sense of understanding than in previous years. English learners, as well as native English–speaking students, face the challenges of economic difficulties, leaps in technological advances, housing, poverty, and so forth that will impact their performance in the classroom. Infusing relevant topics and assignments into the curriculum will require a team of professionals composed of school leaders, counselors, and school psychologists to address these factors and assist second language learners to achieve emotionally and academically.

EL-Embedded Course Examples

The following paragraphs summarize the three courses featured in this chapter.

Advanced Practicum in the Diagnostic-Prescriptive Teaching of Exceptional Children and Youth: In this course, Assistant Professor and Educational Psychology Program Coordinator Michael F. Woodin, Miami University, incorporates an array of EL-focused activities aimed at adapting instruction and assessment to the cultural and linguistic needs of ELs. In a sample course assignment, teacher candidates participate in individual tutorials and/or small group instruction contexts with both struggling learners and ELs and write a reflection regarding best practices observed about the instructional process and use of evidence-based interventions, accommodations, and assessment techniques. This, along with several other EL-focused assignments, has helped enhance the content of this course and contribute to the preparation of teacher candidates to teach English learners.

Group Procedures and Theories of Counseling: The infusion of this course with EL content represents a collaborative effort between Associate Professor Glenn Lambie at the University of Central Florida and doctoral candidate Leigh DeLorenzi who is also an Adjunct Instructor at Rollins College. The added EL content focuses on the identification of specific group counseling interventions that school counselors may employ when working with ELs in a group counseling setting. In one assignment, counselor candidates work in groups of two to cofacilitate a twenty- to-twenty-five-minute psycheducational group activity demonstrating how school counselors might facilitate group activities or interventions for ELs in either elementary, middle, or high school. In the reflection, DeLorenzi emphasizes the need for collaboration between school counselors and ESL instructors to provide English learners with the needed support both inside the classroom and in counseling settings.

Organization and Administration of Instructional Programs: In this graduate level course, Associate Professor Rosemarye T. Taylor, University of Central Florida, aspires to help educational leaders develop an awareness of appropriate instructional and intervention practices to promote learning and achievement of ELs in school settings. Taylor uses various strategies to expose class participants to the ways in which EL issues are addressed within schools and districts. For instance, in one assignment, she invites experienced school principals who have been successful in creating systems for improving learning of ELs to achieve Adequate Yearly Progress (AYP) and success on state accountability measures to serve as guest speakers to model their expectations, communication systems, and processes for insuring student success. Taylor notes, "With the strategic scaffolding of candidates' learning through the connected experiences with texts, speakers, classroom practice, and independent practice students develop deeper knowledge of leadership and learning for ELs than before.

The sample EL-infused course syllabi described herein provide suggestions and guidelines for infusing EL content into this special variation of category 1+ courses with the goal of enhancing educational professional preparation to effectively serve English learners.

Advanced Practicum in the Diagnostic-Prescriptive Teaching of Exceptional Children and Youth

Michael F. Woodin
Miami University

Course Description

Designed for graduate students in school psychology and senior teacher education students. Emphasizes didactic coursework and formative practicum experiences in evidence-based assessment and intervention services for struggling learners and English learners in the areas of phonics, reading fluency, reading comprehension, vocabulary, mathematical fluency, and math applications. Simultaneous experiences include one-to-one tutoring, small group instruction, parental and teacher consultation, and production of an accurate and valid response to intervention (RTI) report.

EL-Focused Course Topics

1. Developing competencies in diagnostic-prescriptive teaching, including the selection, administration, and interpretation of educational, evidence-based intervention tools that are designed for use with struggling learners and English learners including intensive 1:1 manualized instruction, group shared inquiry, and individual computer-based interventions in reading and math.

2. Recognize critical elements of student diversity in development and learning by choosing interventions and modifications that are sensitive to and appropriate for meeting the cultural and linguistic needs of English learners as well as those who struggle with academic skills.

3. Understand best practice in the use of evidence-based models of data-based decision making and accountability, including curriculum-based measurement (CBM) and consideration of multiple modes of assessment in working with and differentiating among ELs, struggling learners, and learning-disabled students.

4. Recognizing best practices in working with culturally diverse children and families.

5. Critical use and analysis of published, evidence-based interventions within a modern, RTI context as well as evaluation methods that are empirically validated for children and youth who are English learners as well as those who are struggling or with learning problems.

6. Understanding that language is a system comprising phonology, morphology, syntax, semantics, pragmatics, etc., and that the direct application of this knowledge can

be used to assist ELs to communicate in English and to demonstrate progress in the areas of reading and mathematics.

7. Understanding the ways in which ELs differ and can be distinguished from students with learning disabilities and/or other areas of difference and/or exceptionality.

EL-Focused Course Objectives

1. Students will use, adapt, and/or be discerning regarding the uses of evidence-based reading and/or math interventions with ELs and struggling students based on training provided in class.

2. Students will demonstrate understanding of how language, culture, and self-narratives interact and form the identity and self-worth of all students, including ELs, and how these may impact achievement and progress. Accordingly, they will provide motivational strategies and programmatic incentives during tutoring sessions, and will adapt/adjust lessons based on problem-solving and consideration of student needs in consultation with course materials and the instructor.

3. Students will use course-provided CBM measures of reading fluency, reading comprehension, and/or mathematics as necessary based on the student identified to measure growth and responsiveness to interventions used. Attention to the use of CBM measures with ELs will be reviewed and implemented as needed. The need to change interventions based on results of progress monitoring will be consistently reviewed.

4. Students will understand issues impacting the fair, differential, and valid assessment of and for ELs and struggling learners by using a variety of assessments and techniques in the classroom settings employed.

5. Students will formulate a personalized model of practice in regard to serving the special needs of struggling and/or English learners through guided and reflective journaling. Their journals will be inspected on a weekly basis, and specific commentary will be jointly selected out to be included in a report to be given to parents.

6. Students will learn how to give feedback to varied audiences, as teachers and parents will be invited to sessions in which students give reports and share poster-based data on how their child/student performed during the summer program. These reports will be modified to be in the parent's native language, as we will work through an EL community liaison and linguistic collaborator from the local school district.

Program and National Standards

Program and national standards referenced in creating this course include those related to student diversity and learning, sensitivity to cultural contexts and environments, grounding in professional knowledge, effective instruction, program evaluation, as well as data-based decision making and accountability. The standards referenced and infused include:

- Miami University Division of Education, Health, and Society (EHS) Standards
- National Association of School Psychologists (NASP) Training Standards

EL-Focused Materials

Brown, J. E., & Doolittle, J. (2008). A cultural, linguistic, and ecological framework for response to intervention with English language learners. *Teaching Exceptional Children, 40*(5), 66.

De Ramírez, R. D., & Shapiro, E.S. (2006). Curriculum-based measurement and the evaluation of reading skills of Spanish-speaking English language learners in bilingual education classrooms. *School Psychology Review, 35*(3), 356-369.

Gottlieb, M.H. (2006). *Assessing English language learners: Bridges from language proficiency to academic achievement.* Thousand Oaks, CA: Corwin Press.

Haager, D., Calhoon, B., & Linan-Thompson, S. (2007). English language learners and response to intervention: Introduction to special issue. *Learning Disability Quarterly, 30*(3), 151-152.

Haager, D., Dimino, J. A., & Windmueller, M. P. (2006). *Interventions for reading success.* Baltimore, MD: Brookes Publishing Company.

Haager, D., Klingner, J.K., & Aceves, T.C. (2009). *How to teach English language learners: Effective strategies from outstanding educators, grades K-6.* San Francisco: Jossey-Bass.

Klingner, J.K., Hoover, J., & Baca, L. (2008). *Why do English language learners struggle with reading? Distinguishing language acquisition from learning disabilities.* Thousand Oaks, CA: Corwin Press.

Lau, M., & Blatchley, L.A. (2009). A comprehensive, multidimensional approach to assessment of culturally and linguistically diverse students. In Jones, J., (Ed.). *Psychology of multiculturalism in the schools: A primer for practice, training, and research.* Bethesda, MD: National Association of School Psychologists.

Ortiz, S.O., Flanagan, D.P., & Dynda, A.M. (2008). Best practices in working with culturally diverse children and families. *Best Practices in School Psychology, 5*(1), 1721-1738.

Rinaldi, C., & Samson, J. (2008). English language learners and response to intervention: Referral considerations. *Teaching Exceptional Children, 40*(5), 9.

Sandberg, K.L., & Reschly, A.L. (2010). English learners: Challenges in assessment and the promise of curriculum-based measurement. *Remedial and Special Education,* first published on February 18, 2010, doi:10.1177/0741932510361260.

Vanderwood, M.L., Linklater, D., & Healy, K. (2008). Special topic: Predictive accuracy of nonsense word fluency for English language learners. *School Psychology Review, 37*(1), 5-17.

EL-Focused In-Class Activities

Teaching case rounds: In-class rounds to discuss and highlight salient points regarding teaching cases across differing populations (i.e., ELs, struggling learners, learning disabled), varying instructional contexts (e.g., individual evidence-based interventions and tutorials, small-group instruction, computer-based interventions), assessments, and consultative scenarios based on actual guided experience with students enrolled in the summer program.

Data-sharing meeting and poster session: In-class data-sharing meeting with teachers and parents. Students share posters and RTI reports detailing student progress monitoring data, their responsiveness to interventions used, changes in instruction, and recommendations for use at home and school. Relevant EL readings are assigned as a module before this meeting occurs. Students reflect on the readings through discussion forums. Role-playing scenarios are rehearsed through engagement with the EL Community Liaison through the local school system. In addition, reports and data are made linguistically accessible to parents based on their cultural and linguistic background.

EL-Focused Assignments

1. Students will participate in individual tutorials and/or small-group instruction contexts with both struggling learners and ELs and write a reflection regarding best practices observed about the instructional process and use of evidence-based interventions, accommodations, and assessment techniques. Student must work with ELs either individually and/or in a small-group setting.

2. Students will complete reflective discussion forums and journal entries after reading through online course modules including relevant readings about: (a) use of culturally responsive RTI procedures with ELs, (b) effective assessment procedures for ELs, (c) best practices in working effectively with culturally diverse families, (d) evidence-based interventions and ELs, (e) the linguistic foundations for working with ELs, and (f) effective instructional techniques for ELs. Discussion forums will reflect on the readings and integration of experiences taken from actual work with ELs taught in individualized and/or small group settings.

3. Students will administer, use, and interpret curriculum-based measures, including weekly progress monitoring probes in the areas of reading fluency and reading comprehension. In addition, students will administer other measurements, including a self-efficacy questionnaire about reading, six elements of prosody reading inventory, running records, informal curriculum-based assessments, student charting of their own progress, standardized achievement tests, and teacher questionnaires. Reliability checks for each measurement will be attained at an acceptable level for each graduate student.

4. Students will produce a valid and accurate RTI report detailing the student's progress, instructional program, results, and recommendations. This report will be translated by the community liaison and results will be presented by both this individual and the class student presenting the data. The report will be produced for both audiences (i.e., teacher and parent) but the difference between the two contexts will be mediated through instructor and coordinator commentary as well as reference to the class readings.

EL-Focused Assessments

Instructional assessments: Students are observed by the instructor on a daily basis. Students turn in treatment integrity checklists and reliability tapings once per week for all individual sessions completed with their students. These checklists and reliability tapings are reviewed by the instructor and his graduate assistant for accuracy, consistency, and responsiveness to ELs and struggling learners.

Module responsiveness: Students' responses to modules presented about ELs are graded on a 5-point scale regarding the level of reflection and integration of practical experience indicated.

RTI report: Students' reports are graded according to the rubric used to frame the assignment. Integration of culturally sensitive language/contexts, appropriate review of student progress, and inclusion of effective recommendations is expected.

Participation in data-sharing meeting: Students are assessed as to the quality and accuracy of their posters and in their ability to relate information to teachers and parents. Ratings are created through those given by the instructor, the community liaison, and the students themselves.

Participation in teaching case rounds: Students must present at least two cases during the four-week program that involve ELs. They are graded according to their ability to:

1. Identify the best instructional and management practices for working with their ELs.
2. Reflect and integrate information from readings, knowledge of the interventions, and information about the ELs with whom they work.
3. Identify multiple sources of assessment data (informal teaching assessment, curriculum-based assessment, running records, standardized assessment) and discuss their implications.
4. Link assessment data to evidence-based interventions for ELs.

Reflection

The course represented here has gone through a number of paradigm shifts in school psychology. It was originally intended to reflect the practice of "diagnostic-prescriptive" teaching, much aligned with a medical model of remediation, with the goal of diagnosing and prescribing instruction to "remedy" or "cure" the instructional ailments of the students served. With the advent of the response to intervention (RTI) model of program development and evaluation, the focus of the course has seen a number of significant changes. In an earlier version of the course, students were led primarily through exercises that increased their knowledge, understanding, and use of CBM and brief interventions, such as repeated reading. In its current form, the focus has been placed squarely on the integration of multiple forms of assessment with information designed to inform and potentially change the instruction and evidence-based interventions (EBIs) used with individual students. Such an approach, which actually trains school psychologists and pre-service educators to teach and effectively use a series of six different EBIs, is considered novel and potentially cutting-edge. However, there were no significant ESL requirements. The only activity of record was a didactic, book-based "case study" that students would take on without any interaction with real students, teachers, or contexts.

Having personally taught and practiced in urban environments, and having been exposed to diversity in many of its forms, I was intrigued and compelled to participate in the ESL initiative when it was announced. I was interested in gaining my students' experience with such populations to increase their awareness and multicultural literacy. I also wanted to enable them to be more "marketable" when applying for positions that might demand expertise and prior experience in working with students of cultural and linguistic diversity. So, when the ESL initiative began at Miami University, I attended workshops and met with my mentor at a novice stage of what I would term slightly enlightened but largely uninformed curiosity. I was unclear about how I would integrate such infusion activities and elements within my coursework. In my syllabi, I had always included "progressive" statements about how students of diversity were welcomed within my class. I also set up and included field trips to urban schools where I consulted that provided some limited experience with students of color and linguistic diversity. So, I thought I was fairly well set up to provide the activities needed, with perhaps a bit more flourish and intentionality. After attending the workshops and being given course hyperlinks and resource materials, I curiously explored them but languished in the attempt to forcibly and meaningfully integrate, make room for, and infuse my courses with such content. I often thought that the ESL initiative was an empty gesture. There was so much to get accomplished in my courses already. When push came to shove, there was not enough time or impetus for adding ESL content. Why get rid of other elements? I would just enhance what I already provided.

However, as I reviewed the EL infusion activities and resources I was given, I discovered that there were new articles being written about the need to consider elements of RTI and EBIs in a different light—one that was honoring and respectful of the diversity ELs demonstrate. Through a mentoring grant offered to tenure-eligible faculty, I was also able to coordinate and benefit from consultation with a number of noted leaders in EL instruction and intervention. Their consultation provided a wealth of information and an impetus to further develop the course, syllabus, and appropriate infusion activities. Coincidentally, I also was attempting to broaden the student base of a four-week summer program that was set up for this course with the local school district. I also had had interest in the course—which teaches evidence-based interventions, formative assessment systems, and RTI processes—from undergraduate seniors in teacher education. So the number of potential tutors I had increased, and we therefore could handle the opportunity to serve more children.

Since the summer learning clinic, called the Rocket Summer Learning Program, was very successful in addressing the needs of struggling readers and learners, we welcomed the opportunity to have more students involved and to serve more children from the community. As I discussed our situation with the school superintendent and other representatives, it became clear that while we could continue to serve the struggling learners identified through school-based universal screenings, the EL population could also be served. In the process, we could actually provide formative experiences through individualized interventions, small-group instruction, assessment, consultation, and differentiating activities with these wonderful children of linguistic and cultural diversity. Suddenly, I had a platform from which to provide a unique experience to my students and to have numerous rounds in which we discussed the differential aspects of working with students who are struggling with reading as being distinct from the patterns and growth trajectories of ELs. With this undergirding, the use of relevant articles and readings was made immediately meaningful and applicable. As students are taught to appreciate diversity and difference, they become more culturally literate and informed. In turn, they build the skills to start to become appropriately responsive, questioning, and challenging of their own biases as well as those of others with whom they work and interact within the school setting. Honestly, one of the most remarkable aspects of the training for my students is that which came as a result of having ELs and struggling learners socialize and work together. When reviewing data, it became apparent to the students that the learning trajectories of many of the ELs were far more accelerated than their English-speaking age peers who were struggling with learning and reading. Noticing the difference between the two groups helped to differentiate among the groups and highlight the unique assets that EL children often exhibit. Conversely, it also gave a chance to identify some of the barriers unique to ELs in grasping concepts, vocabulary, and linguistic elements that were not necessarily shared by the struggling readers.

As future school psychologists and educators, the ability to consult, hold multidisciplinary evaluation and intervention meetings, and provide comprehensive evaluation information is critical. To this end, the interaction with parents and school staff has been remarkable. Being able to meet and talk with the parents of ELs and coordinate with the EL director and community liaison of the local school system has given students the ability to benefit from the formative feedback provided by these school personnel members as well as their professor and cohort members. For the undergraduate seniors, the experience added a unique dimension to their pre-service training and competencies not received elsewhere. The data-sharing meeting and poster session gave them practical experience in how to display data to convey the need to make changes in interventions utilized and/or to document an individual student's progress as a result of evidence-based instruction.

In the end, I have been overwhelmingly pleased by the breadth and intentionality offered to me and my students through the infusion of ESL activities and elements within my coursework and syllabi. Effective PowerPoint presentations, course activities, and supportive resource materials have been infused into the course. As a result of this initiative, a school psychology graduate student has been placed in a hybrid graduate assistant position, with the cost being shared by the school district and the university.

The graduate assistant coordinates EL curriculum, provides direct service to ELs, and maintains a consultative link between the school and the university. This position has recently been extended beyond the school year to embrace assistance and work with the Rocket Summer Learning Program. The course content has been made richer, and the actual ability to interact with, teach, assess, consult, and problem-solve issues concerning ELs and struggling learners has been worthwhile.

In the future, we seek to expand the course to include professional development opportunities for teachers and Title I staff members from school districts so that they can engage with students while learning new interventions, assessment systems, and being exposed to work with diverse populations. We anticipate regularly rotating and changing the evidence-based interventions to better meet the needs of the groups served to help participants gain experience and the opportunity to become wise consumers, advocates, and critics of such approaches. I expect that many further epiphanies and paradigm shifts will continue to occur and that lasting change in meeting needs of a diversity of students will occur and be voiced by our new school psychologists and educator as a result of this endeavor in infusion. As Maya Angelou said, "Words mean more than what is set down on paper. It takes the human voice to infuse them with shades of deeper meaning."[1]

Group Procedures and Theories of Counseling

Leigh DeLorenzi and Glenn W. Lambie
University of Central Florida

Course Description

Group Procedures and Theories of Counseling is a course designed to provide gradu-ate school counseling students with an understanding of the role of theory within group counseling as well as the many process applications of groups with student-clients from diverse backgrounds. A variety of instructional strategies are used including: (a) lectures, discussions, and demonstrations by the instructor and class members; (b) demonstration and presentation of group counseling curricula and strategies; (c) and small-group work for the purpose of practicing skills, critiquing other students' perfor-mance, and sharing reactions to the group counseling process.

Course Topics

1. Discerning how student-client age, gender, ethnicity, race, economic status, sexual orientation, social class, spirituality, exceptionality, immigration status, culture, family type, and language of origin can impact group processes and dynamics.
2. Understanding how to navigate challenges associated with language barriers in group counseling, including the impact of translators on group cohesion.
3. Understanding how the basic tenants of group counseling, such as member self-disclosure, sharing of personal problems/concerns, and offering spontaneous feed-back, may be challenging for group members from diverse backgrounds (e.g., culture, language of origin) that discourage these behaviors.

Course Objectives

School counselors-in-training will be able to:
1. Demonstrate their multicultural counseling competencies to support their work as ethical and effective group leaders and educators.
2. Demonstrate their understanding of the influence of diversity (e.g., racial, ethnic, and cultural backgrounds and language proficiencies) on group dynamics and processes.
3. Develop and present a literature review and group curriculum for working with student-clients of diverse cultural backgrounds, exceptionalities, and EL proficiency levels in school settings.
4. Demonstrate an understanding of effective group counseling techniques and strate-gies to support student-clients' academic, career, and social-emotional development.

Identify the group leader modifications appropriate for various EL proficiency levels in a group counseling setting.

Materials

Gladding, S.T. (2008). *Groups: A counseling specialty* (5th ed.). Upper Saddle River, NJ: Prentice Hall.

Goh, M., Wahl, K.H., McDonald, J.K., Brissett, A.A., & Yoon, E. (2007). Working with immigrant students in schools: The role of school counselors in building cross-cultural bridges. *Journal of Multicultural Counseling and Development, 35,* 66-79.

Holcomb-McCoy, C. (2004). Assessing the multicultural competence of school counselors: A checklist. *Professional School Counseling, 7*(3), 178-186.

Malott, K.M., Paone, T.R., Humphreys, K., & Martinez, T. (2010). Use of group counseling to address ethnic identity development: Application of adolescents of Mexican descent. *Professional School Counseling, 13,* 257-267.

McCall-Perez, Z. (2000). The counselor as advocate for English language learners: An action research approach. *Professional School Counseling, 4*(1), 13-23.

Roysircar, G., Gard, G., Hubbell, R., & Ortega, M. (2005). Development of counseling trainees' multicultural awareness through mentoring English as a second language students. *Journal of Multicultural Counseling and Development, 33,* 17-36.

Santos de Barona, M., & Barona, A. (2006). School counselors and school psychologists collaborating to ensure minority students receive appropriate consideration for special education programs. *Professional School Counseling, 10,* 3-13.

Shi, Q., & Steen, S. (2010). Group work with English as second language (ESL) students: Integrating academic and behavior considerations. *Journal of School Counseling, 8*(41). Retrieved from http://www.jsc.montana.edu/articles/v8n41.pdf

The Professional School Counselor and Cultural Diversity. (2010). American School Counselor Association position statement. Retrieved from http://asca2.timberlake publishing.com//files/CulturalDiversity.pdf.

EL-Focused In-Class Activity

Psychoeducation Group Leadership Demonstration

In groups of two, counseling students will cofacilitate a 20–25 minute psycheducational group activity in class, demonstrating how school counselors might facilitate a group activity/intervention for EL students in either elementary, middle, or high school. After the demonstration, counseling students will identify the group counseling modifications used for various EL proficiency levels within their demonstration. Counseling students will also provide the class with a handout that describes the organization of the group, group materials, and process questions appropriate for the activity. For the following class session, the group facilitators will submit an evaluation form to the professor that includes a personal reflection of the counseling student's experience facilitating the group activity.

Assignments

School counselors-in-training write an *American Psychological Association Publication Manual* (6th ed.) style paper that includes a literature review and group counseling curriculum.[2] The students identify a specific student population group and review the research pertaining to the student population group (e.g., English learners in school, or adolescents who self-injure) that would be necessary to facilitate an effective and ethical group counseling intervention. The school counseling students need to construct an empirical rationale for why the chosen student population group necessitates group-based counseling services. In addition, students need to develop an empirically supported six-week group curriculum to utilize with the identified student population group, outlining specific (a) group goals and objectives, (b) group materials, (c) group process questions, and (d) homework assignments for each group session.

EL-Focused Assessment

The final examination (summative course assessment) requires the school counseling students to answer the following question:

> Please describe how working with student-clients with different language proficiencies may influence your role as a group facilitator and leader. List a minimum of three specific group counseling interventions that a school counselor may employ when working with students who are English Learners in a group counseling setting.

Reflection

When I was in school, no other "grown-up" was as loved as Mrs. Ainsely, our school counselor. She was a friendly lady who had an uncanny ability to remember names. Each morning, as we filed up to campus, sleepy-eyed and dragging our feet to homeroom, she was always there to greet us with a big smile and a friendly nod. Students would frequently run to give her a hug or share a few details about the latest quiz that they aced. "Nice job!" she would say energetically, occasionally humoring a student with a high-five.

Today, as a counselor educator, I feel great pride at the helm of a classroom full of future Mrs. Ainsleys. I know now what I didn't fully realize then: school counselors wear many different hats with many different students. To some, Mrs. Ainsley was a group counselor; to others, a vocational counselor; and to a mischievous few, a disciplinarian. Therefore, a school counselor-in-training needs to be prepared to work with students of all ages, ethnicities, races, sexual orientations, cultures, social classes, family types, spiritualties, and exceptionalities.

The goal that is heavily reinforced in most counselor education programs is to produce school counselors who are *multiculturally competent*. To this end, trainees are frequently asked to explore how their personal biases, values, assumptions, and prejudices might influence the way they interact with clients. They are trained to think critically about the style and content of their verbal and nonverbal communication. And, depending on the course, counselor educators are designing assignments that will prepare future school counselors to work with specific populations, including English learners. Unfortunately, although the American School Counselor Association Ethical Standards for School Counselors states that school counselors need to be prepared to work with ELs, research has shown that school counselors are not well equipped to work effectively with them.[3]

A graduate-level group counseling course is an excellent forum for offering school counselors trainees a set of interventions that are specific to ELs, who are at a higher risk for social and emotional problems, and therefore are more dependent on school counselors than other students.[4] Furthermore, research has shown that through intentional interaction with EL students and teachers, school counselors can have a positive impact on the EL student's social-emotional wellbeing and academic success.[5]

While attempting to create a lesson plan that was both useful and appropriate for school counselors working with ELs, I spent several afternoons brainstorming with my TESOL mentor. I found it exciting, yet challenging at times, to come up with ideas that would effectively fuse the fields of school counseling and ESL education. In many ways, our conversations reminded me that counselor educators should be "in the classroom" on their clients as frequently as possible. Thankfully, as in many educational pursuits, the process of slowly and methodically sifting through the tough questions yields the clearest solutions. And in this case, the solution was collaboration.

The most powerful way to meet the needs of EL students is to forge a collaboration between school counselor and ESL instructor. Through this ongoing conversation, school counselors and counselor educators are better able to shape their treatment plans and group curricula in a manner that can be reinforced by ESL instructors in their classroom activities. The goal is for school counselors and ESL instructors to work together in their lesson and group planning, so that EL students can practice what they're learning in both environments, while gaining additional support that may not otherwise be available to them in the classroom setting alone.

In our graduate program, school counselor trainees are required to design a six-week group curriculum for a particular counseling population, which may include ELs. For each session, school counselor trainees are required to provide an objective, materials needed, topics of discussion, appropriate process questions, relevant homework assignments, and an overview of the group leader's role and responsibility. An example session is listed in table 9.1.

Table 9.1

Group session on communication skills with teachers

Objective	To help EL students process their feelings about communicating with their teachers in a school setting.
Materials	Feelings chart with illustrated "emotion" faces; role-plays developed by the school counselor.
Introduction	Session opens with a review of previous group discussion, and students are asked to share whether they were able to practice the skills they learned in the previous group.
Lesson	The group leader introduces the importance of proper communication in a classroom setting. Topics of discussion may include appropriate ways to address the teacher, raising hands before talking, and/or polite classroom behavior.
Role play	Students will role-play different student-teacher scenarios developed by the group leader, such as how to ask to go to the bathroom or how to ask the teacher to borrow a pencil or piece of paper.
Identify feelings	By referring to the feelings chart, students will identify (a) how it felt to practice the skills they learned in group with their peers, and (b) how they have felt in the past when communicating with their teacher in the classroom.
Process questions	Group leaders will ask students: (a) What have you learned about communicating with teachers in the United States? (b) Do you communicate differently with teachers in your home country?
Homework	Practice the skills you learned from group with your ESOL teacher this week and keep a journal of how you felt about the experience using your feelings chart.

School counselors not only play a vital role in the academic success of English learners, they also provide crucial support for ELs who are struggling with common social-emotional developmental factors. Therefore, it is essential for counselor educators to deliver EL-specific lesson plans to their school counseling students so that they are well equipped to work effectively with both EL students and ESL instructors in the field. In summary, if our goal is to support our EL students for success, collaboration is key.

Organization and Administration of Instructional Programs

Rosemarye T. Taylor
University of Central Florida

Course Description

Organization and Administration of Instructional Programs has the focus of leadership theory with the ultimate goal to improve learning for all students. It is required for MEd and EdS students in Educational Leadership, as well as may be taken by EdD students in Educational Leadership and related programs.

Course Topics

1. Developing awareness of appropriate instructional and intervention practices for ELs.
2. Understanding literacy learning preK–12 and expectations for student engagement in research-based instructional practices.
3. Understanding research-based instructional practices across core content, the arts, physical education, technology, and other contents areas.
4. Implementing collaborative decision-making processes for garnering commitment to and fidelity of implementation to research-based systems of curriculum, instruction, assessment, and professional learning.

Course Objectives

Course objectives are Florida Principal Leadership Standard (FPLS) and Florida Educational Leadership Exam (FELE) competencies that follow.

FPLS 2.0 Instructional Leadership: High performing leaders promote a positive learning culture, provide an effective instructional program, and apply best practices to student learning, especially in the area of reading and other foundational skills.

FELE Competency: Knowledge of instructional leadership standard as related to curriculum development and continuous school improvement process.

FELE Competency: Knowledge of instructional leadership standard as related to research-based best practices.

Materials

Florida School Leaders website: http://www.Floridaschoolleaders.net
Reeves, D.B. (2008). Closing the achievement gap [DVD]. In *Leadership and Learning Vol. 1.* Boston, MA: Lead and Learn Press.

Taylor, R.T. (2010). *Leading learning: Change student achievement today!* Thousand Oaks, CA: Corwin Press.

Each chapter has scenarios of leaders who have improved student achievement, with nine scenarios from schools or school districts with an EL student population range of 15 to 52 percent. Two of the scenarios are of principals who were EL students and now are examples of excellence in learning leadership—Jaime Quinones and Gonzalo La Cava. A portion of La Cava's scenario is retold in this section and demonstrates how engaging families in learning about bilingual education improved student achievement.

Taylor, R.T. & Gunter, G.G. (2006). *The K-12 literacy leadership fieldbook.* Thousand Oaks, CA: Corwin Press.

Other reading selections, such as:

Brooks, K. (2010). Creating inclusive learning communities for ELL students: Transforming school principals' perspectives. *Theory into Practice, 49*(2),145-151.

Gandara, P. (2010). Overcoming Triple Segregation. *Educational Leadership, 68,* 60-64.

Himmele, P., & Himmele, W. (2009). Increasing exposure to academic language by speaking It. *ASCD Express, 5.* Retrieved from http://www.ascd.org/ascd_express/vol5/505_himmele.aspx

EL-Focused In-Class Learning Activities

1. Speakers

Principals who have been successful in creating systems for improving learning of ELs to achieve Adequate Yearly Progress (AYP) and success on state accountability measures serve as guest speakers to model their expectations, communication systems, and processes for insuring student success. They model their strategies for addressing instruction for the target students. In 2011, the candidates visited John Wright, principal of Timber Creek High School (TCHS), at his school instead of asking him to come to the class. He shared with candidates how he had determined that most of the EL students take ROTC, in addition to ESL, and how he garnered the commitment of the ROTC instructors to address English language learning within their classes to give the students a learning boost. Through the experience of talking with a creative and committed principal about strategizing beyond the typical, candidates gain awareness of leader actions that improve learning for ELs. Rather than delegating the learning to others, they set expectations, seek solutions beyond what is typical, monitor instruction and learning, and provide feedback to their teachers.

Candidates voice that they enjoy the connection to leadership practice that current principals bring to them. A candidate who does not have a principal who models excellence for ELs, needs to develop a mental model of the commitment and commensurate leadership behavior that works for EL populations.

2. Data-Informed Instructional Decision Making

Principals demonstrate using data management systems to understand and use disaggregated summative student achievement data and monitoring data to identify and monitor improvement in learning. Through data management and monitoring, the principals share how they implement data chats and collaboration of effective teachers with less effective ones to improve learning. Data chats and collaboration are also used to determine the best instructional interventions. Based on EL learning evidence and data, principals model how they intervene with teachers if needed.

It is common for candidates to have principals who do not personally involve themselves with data and how specific monitoring data can be used to change or differentiate instruction immediately based on an individual student's needs. The modeling that principals provide for candidates of using a variety of data and evidence to guide teachers in their instructional decision making assists the students as they develop a data analysis paper in this course.

An EL expert shares with the candidates what leaders should know and do to improve learning for EL students. Myths about EL learning and common incorrect practices are presented along with research-based practices which leaders should expect.

Most of the candidates have experience in teaching EL students in a class with general education students, but only have introductory knowledge on related research. One of the clarifications that students note is that good teaching is not good enough for ELs, but research-based EL instruction is good for all learners. However, they also add that appropriate differentiation for ELs is essential.

3. School Data Analysis

Following the guest principal who shares use of data to make instructional decisions, students are presented with elementary, middle, and high school Florida Comprehensive Achievement Test (FCAT) data and accountability reports from the Florida Department of Education website. In teams, they analyze EL achievement to identify other data needed and to develop potential solutions for addressing the needs of students.

Providing the best learning opportunities for EL students is important for reasons of equity, excellence, and social justice, but school leaders have the additional reason of accountability for each student's learning. Florida has one of the most rigorous accountability assessments of all states, with proficiency set at the 50th percentile for elementary, 60th percentile for middle school, and 70th percentile for high school, with the lowest number (30) of any state to constitute an Adequate Yearly Progress (AYP) student subgroup. Therefore, the activity assists candidates in not only understanding data to inform decision-making, but also seeing how strategically addressing the effectiveness of instruction of ELs impacts the extent to which the school and school district meet AYP.

> *Example:* There may be students who are counted a number of times in the AYP calculation because they are in several student subgroups. One EL student may also be economically disadvantaged (ED) and/or be a racial minority, and/or be a student with a disability (SWD) and count as much as four times in the AYP

formula. Furthermore, if a school does not have thirty EL students (does not have an EL student subgroup), the ELs may still form a student subgroup for the school district AYP calculations and therefore each student's improvement is essential.

4. Understanding Levels of Thinking and Cognitive Complexity

One of the challenges for EL students' success on FCAT is the high percentage of items at a high level of thinking and cognitive complexity. Generally, teachers resist asking students to perform at a high level of thinking or cognitively complex level when their English language skills and academic language are not on grade level. This common teacher behavior is why I give a presentation (which includes their practice) on asking questions, levels of thinking, and cognitive complexity so that the candidates develop greater understanding of questioning concepts and how to provide high level thinking and cognitively complex performance tasks for ELs.

Candidates respond that previously they had little understanding of levels of thinking and of cognitive complexity on which the FCAT items are based. By understanding the need to provide regular opportunities for learning and practice, the candidates express that they will follow through in their own teaching and have the expectation for other teachers when in a leadership position.

Out-of-Class Learning Activities

1. *Research and Exemplar Paper:* After completing their research paper on a narrow content area and grade range (example: bilingual K–1), candidates update others on the research-based practices through engaged learning and modeling of the exemplars found in the research. An exemplar handout is given to all class members that has the title (example: Bilingual K–1), an abstract, and a table comparing nonexemplars (status quo) and exemplars (ideal based on the research), with references. The short, 15-minute presentations are to the point and leave the candidates with a resource file of up to date research-based instructional and curricular practices.

   Candidates tend to think that the typical instructional expectations in their school are research-based. By distinguishing between research-based practice to work towards and the common practice they begin to differentiate between excellence and commercial products and/or accepted practices. Frequently, they will share that they have replicated the presentations and given handouts to their colleagues and grade level teams in their schools.

2. *Data Analysis Paper:* As an independent assignment following the supported learning in class, candidates independently select and complete a data analysis. First, they review the instructional leadership resources on understanding data located on the Florida School Leaders website. Then, they complete the module Data Analysis for Instructional Leaders, which is also on the site. Following the review of data analysis, the candidates analyze at least three pieces of data, including a minimum of one type of achievement data that includes the EL student subgroup. After completing the data analysis, candidates write a potential solution supported by theory/research learned in this course. Solutions should be related to the FPLS and FELE competen-

cies. As an example, a student may review Florida Comprehensive Achievement Test (FCAT) levels 3 (proficient) and above and learning gains for student subgroups. Teacher turnover by teaching assignment may be the third type of data considered in drawing conclusions and crafting a potential solution or perhaps teachers who are out of field. Another student may study FCAT and Scholastic Achievement Test (SAT) performance along with student attendance before drawing conclusions and proposing a potential solution.

Assessments

The midterm and final exams are in-class essays and reflect the application and synthesis learning related to course topics and objectives.

> *Example:* As a school leader, what steps will you take to collaboratively develop a system to address the learning needs of ELs to achieve AYP? Support your response with references, contemporary literature, presentation resources, or speakers from this class.

Reflection

MEd Educational Leadership students typically are classroom teachers or instructional coaches with a narrow experience teaching at a particular grade level or content assignment. While all of the education graduates from the University of Central Florida have met the state's ESL requirement, they may not have deep knowledge of or practice with research-based instructional practices and report relying on the strategies expected and reinforced in their work setting. As an instructor, I strive to change their habits of referring to instructional practices as "in our district" or "at my school" or "the product we use" and change the reference to contemporary literature or research or an expert in the field. My immediate goal is to change their day-to-day instructional practice as teachers, and my long-term goal is for them to be effective school leaders who are knowledgeable in leading learning for ELs. As a result, class reflections and evaluations indicate that they are empowered with knowledge at a higher level than many of the more seasoned faculty within their schools. By initiating data-based discussions and/or professional learning on ELs with colleagues, they create a sense of urgency for change, and respect from those faculties and from their administrators.

Scenarios

Scenarios follow that have taken place in this course. The first showcases a teacher in the class and how she implemented her learning and the results. The second is about Gonzalo La Cava's presentation in class, which follows reading chapter 8 in Taylor.[6] Scenario 3 reflects Principal Wright's presentation on addressing the needs of ELs in a large, comprehensive high school of over three thousand students.

Scenario 1

Erin, a ninth-grade biology teacher, researched strategies for high school support for EL students and began to implement them in her class. She shared with the other candidates that as she scaffolded the learning more, using more visuals and demonstrations, that the EL students responded positively, but so did other students. Science has the most difficult vocabulary of any content area, so she worked with the students to collaboratively create word walls with definitions, nonlinguistic representations, and cognates to use interactively in instruction. In addition to improving day to day learning for ELs, a bonus was that the assistant principal was so impressed that he began to use her teaching as a positive example for the other teachers. As a first-year teacher, she was pleased not only to have success in teaching biology but also to be recognized as an excellent teacher.

Scenario 2

Gonzalo La Cava brought the printed pages to life for the candidates. He was principal of Oakshire Elementary School, with 744 students (Title I, with 77 percent poverty, 52 percent ELs, 13 percent ESE, and 78 percent Hispanic). The school struggled with student achievement until he became principal. By systematically implementing a one-way bilingual program, he created push-in intervention rather than pull out to maximize learning time. Elementary students who knew no English or kindergarten students who only spoke Spanish were placed into Spanish-only classes to develop phonics, phonemic awareness, vocabulary, fluency, and comprehension in Spanish. Other students in grades K–1 had fifty minutes each day of both English and Spanish. As students developed literacy in the primary home language, they were transitioned to English-only classes to develop English literacy—usually by second or third grades.

Beyond the curricular implementation, La Cava also raised expectations for the faculty and staff. He insisted that they be fluent English speakers, readers, and writers themselves. If someone was not willing to implement the bilingual program with fidelity, he counseled them to find a position for which they were better suited.

When La Cava shares with the candidates that he attributes the students' success not only to the curricular and instructional system, but also to engaging the families in the children's learning, they express surprise. By helping families understand the instructional methodology and that children should continue to develop their primary home language literacy while acquiring English literacy, the work that takes place at school is supported in the home.

Further, he shares that he prioritized engaging the families during the school day and providing English literacy learning for the family members. When candidates hear that in three short years the school achieved AYP, they are willing to consider his leadership strategies and high expectations for both the children and the faculty.

Having demonstrated success he was asked to create achievement gains at Liberty Middle School, which mirrors Oakshire's student demographics. During the first year, he had the greatest learning gains on FCAT in the school district through consistent, data-informed, systematic expectations and instructional practices. Most candidates reflect that they have not experienced working in a school culture with high expectations for data-informed instructional decision making and for EL students to have a rigorous on-grade-level curriculum while acquiring English proficiency.

Scenario 3

John Wright, principal of TCHS, exclaimed, "I love our ELL students because they make our data look great! When the school attendance zone was changed to open a new high school, I was afraid that the loss of these students would not only affect our school culture, but also our academic achievement." Candidates are taken aback when he expresses that from a data-informed decision-making perspective, EL students are valued, even though their academic success may be a challenge. Principals like John perceive ELs as eager to learn and supported by families who believe in the value of education. ELs improve quickly in literacy and show learning gains at all grade levels, including high school. Anyone who has worked in a high school with students who do not read on grade level knows how difficult academic achievement is for any student who is not a proficient reader and writer in English. The modeled advocacy for ELs creates motivation and a sense of self-efficacy for candidates to believe in themselves and commit to ensuring rigorous learning opportunities while ELs acquire English proficiency.

Reflective Summary

Many of the MEd students are teacher leaders whose reinforced success has led them to enroll in an educational leadership program. While they learn the legal requirements and accountability for ELs in law and finance classes, they may not know how to do more than comply. Developing awareness of the academic responsibility and how to successfully bring implementation of improved learning for every student to a reality is eye-opening. With the strategic scaffolding of candidates' learning through the connected experiences with texts, speakers, classroom practice, and independent practice, students develop deeper knowledge of leadership and learning for ELs than before. As one student concluded, "Just knowing that there are principals who actually lead significant change in learning for ELLs is empowering. It can be done."

Leadership to improve student achievement and graduation rates of ELs is critical if educational leadership programs are to be grounded in the practice and not just in theoretical understanding. Hawley and James studied educational leadership programs to determine the extent to which diversity-responsive school leadership is present and found that the inclusion was on a surface level—if at all, and that language diversity was rarely identified.[7] Developing future and current school leaders who understand the issues in systematically improving learning for each EL student is essential for graduates of educational leadership programs. Without the learning leadership expertise of the principals, classroom teachers will not have the resources, feedback, support, or accountability to effectively maximize the realization of values of equity, excellence, and social justice for all EL students.

Strengthening the Curriculum by Adding EL-Specific Coursework and Related Field Experiences

Florin M. Mihai, University of Central Florida, and
N. Eleni Pappamihiel, University of North Carolina, Wilmington

In the description of the One Plus model in chapter 3, the book editors highlighted the need to augment the teacher education curriculum by adding EL-specific courses taught by experts in the field of teaching English as a second language (ESL). We concur that while embedding EL content into the teacher education curriculum is understandably necessary, it is not sufficient for preparing teacher candidates to work effectively with ELs in mainstream classrooms. In this chapter, we address the infusion of EL-specific coursework across the conventional teacher education curriculum by focusing on three primary objectives. First, we explain why it is important to require EL-specific courses in addition to EL-embedded courses. Next we describe the course development process unique to infused programs (because of EL-specific courses' close connection with the EL content in embedded courses). Then, we describe two sample EL-specific courses that are designed to expand teacher candidates' foundational knowledge of planning and implementing curriculum, instruction, and assessment for ELs as well as to develop knowledge about second language learning and applied linguistics, which supports ELs' language and literacy development. The first course, EL Instructional and Assessment Methods, introduces all teacher candidates to teaching ELs in mainstream classroom settings. It therefore addresses instructional and assessment approaches, methods, and strategies aimed at scaffolding the content, language, and literacy learning of these learners. The second course, Applied Linguistics and Second Language Development, is designed to develop language arts and literacy teacher candidates' knowledge relative to the nature of language and second language development and applies this specialized knowledge to teaching language and literacy skills for ELs.[1] In the discussion of this course, we provide a rationale for developing teacher candidates' foundational knowledge of applied linguistics and second language development, and why content from this course can help better prepare teacher candidates to address the language and literacy needs of ELs in mainstream classrooms.

Background and Rationale for Incorporating EL-Specific Coursework Across the Curriculum

During the past decade, a growing recognition and consensus among teacher education professionals has emerged in support of the addition of new EL-focused coursework to the teacher preparation curricula. This shift in perspective is driven by several interrelated factors, including but not limited to the changing demographics in public schools, the lack of preparation of teachers to teach ELs, the time it takes to develop teacher candidates' knowledge and skills related to the role of language in learning, and the calls for reform in teacher education aimed at preparing teachers to work with ELs. As a result, several teacher education programs in the United States and Canada have incorporated one or more EL-specific courses into their teacher preparation programs.

A number of teacher preparation programs have attempted to prepare their candidates for teaching ELs solely through embedding teacher preparation courses with EL content, but some teacher educators maintain that adding coursework is simply unavoidable. In a recent article addressing the preparation of teachers to teach ELs, Lucas et al. recommended that teacher education programs add one required course to the teacher education curriculum that is devoted to teaching ELs:

> Although most teacher education programs will have difficulties acting on this suggestion, we see no way around the addition of a course. Given the lack of experience with the education of ELs by most teacher educators and the time that it takes to build substantial knowledge among them, it would be irresponsible to rely on an infusion strategy that requires distributing specialized knowledge and practices for EL education across the faculty. Although such infusion could be a long-term goal, we do not see it as a viable option at present. The new course should address the essential language-related understandings for teaching ELs and the pedagogical practices that flow from them. It should be taught by a faculty member in the program who has the required expertise or by someone recruited for that purpose."[2]

However, while teacher educators assert that additional EL-specific courses are needed, little consensus exists as to how many and to what depth, to help teacher candidates develop sufficient expertise to effectively address the needs of ELs. Suggested additional coursework ranges from one course to as many as seven courses.[3] Consistent with the infusion model presented in this book, which includes a balance of EL-embedded content infused across various programs as well as one or two EL-specific courses, depending on the program area, our position is that because of the idiosyncrasies and constraints of teacher preparation programs, institutions should take into consideration these sorts of internal factors when making decisions about the depth and extent of EL-specific courses. In the following section, we offer insights from our experiences developing EL-specific courses in different institutional contexts.

Developing EL-Specific Courses

To provide an overview of the special considerations in developing EL-specific courses, we first summarize the three instructional design steps of analysis, design, and development of EL-specific courses. Before deciding on the content and format of EL-specific courses, each teacher preparation program should determine the desired outcome of EL infusion. In this chapter, we focus on the two EL-qualified program outcomes that are the focus of this book: EL-qualified for teaching academic subject areas and EL-qualified for teaching language arts (see table 10.1).

Details about the overall program infusion process and how the development of EL-specific courses connects with this curriculum-wide process are found in chapters 3 and 4 (see tables 3.3 and 4.1). In this section, we describe the process of developing the two EL-specific courses presented in the overall infusion model in chapter 3, EL Instructional and Assessment Methods and Applied Linguistics and Second Language Development.

EL Instructional and Assessment Methods, which focuses on adapting curriculum, instruction, and assessment for ELs and introduces academic subject matter, language, and literacy development, is intended for all teacher candidates. The course has three variations for different programs: (a) Early Childhood/Elementary Education, which focuses on teaching and assessing ELs in academic subject matter; (b) Secondary English Language Arts Education, which focuses on teaching and assessing ELs in language arts and literature; and (c) Secondary Academic Subjects (for example, math, science, social studies) Education, which focuses on teaching and assessing ELs in academic subject matter.[4] For Secondary Academic Subjects teacher candidates (option c), EL Instructional and Assessment Methods is the only EL-specific course. For teacher candidates whose certification prepares them to teach and assess language arts, the model includes a second course, Applied Linguistics and Second Language Development. This second course has two variations: (a) Early Childhood and Elementary Education, which examines in detail second language acquisition from birth to adolescence as well as practical applications of applied linguistics for second language literacy development during that phase of the life span; (b) Secondary Education, which examines the same subjects from adolescence through adulthood.[5]

Based on our experience with embedding EL content into general teacher education courses, we have divided the general subjects into these two EL-specific courses. However, the specific course topics, competencies, and prerequisite background knowledge and skills necessary to master the general subjects will differ according to the context of the institution, partially related to how the EL content is embedded in the program, as will the structure and format of each course. Chapter 4 explains how, during the design phase for embedding content, an initial picture of how the EL curricular competencies may become distributed and offers a first glance at how EL-specific courses may need to cover and augment coverage. Although this is a design step for embedded courses, it serves as analysis for EL-specific courses. We now turn to the process of establishing the content of the courses and determining where they should be offered in the curriculum.

Table 10.1

ADDIE at the Micro Level: Infusion of Individual Components of Teacher Preparation Programs—EL-Specific Courses

Component	Analyze	Evaluate	Design	Evaluate	Develop	Evaluate	Implement	Evaluate
EL-specific courses	Review embedded EL courses content curriculum map	Infusion team members evaluate and oversee the design phase steps of the EL-specific course(s) given the analysis results	Determine number of EL-specific courses	Infusion team members evaluate the EL-specific courses' objectives, assessments and field and clinical experiences as well as the EL-embedded content to determine if EL-specific courses need adjustment	Develop EL-specific course syllabi	Infusion team members evaluate EL-specific courses' syllabi, materials, assessments, and delivery modes	EL-specific course instructors collaborate regularly with EL-embedded faculty to reinforce curriculum links	Survey EL-specific and EL-embedded faculty
	Review embedded EL courses clinical experiences map		Establish objectives for EL-specific courses		Select and/or develop instructional materials		Notify field and clinical partners of placements	Survey field and clinical partners
	Review embedded EL courses candidate assessment map		Specify EL-specific course assessments		Develop assessments and rubrics		Monitor student reflections and field and clinical partners' correspondence	Analyze sample of reflections
	Review each program's purpose and outcomes		Identify field and clinical experiences that link to course objectives and assessments		Seek course approval and catalog inclusion		Monitor student progress and adjust instruction as needed	Review candidate assessment data
			Add EL-specific courses to curriculum, field/clinical experiences, and assessment maps		Build courseware sites for online delivery and/or prepare face-to-face instructional media and/or lesson plans			Interview and survey candidates
			Determine delivery modes		Schedule courses according to catalog date			
			Determine staffing needs		Orient course instructors			
					Inform advisers, program faculty, and candidates of new requirements			Based on all evaluations completed (all of the above), adjust course syllabus, assessments, delivery, and placement in the curriculum

Beginning the development process with a needs analysis is essential since each teacher preparation program will be different, with different strengths and weaknesses and operating in different contexts. For example, one program may operate in a fairly homogenous service area, affording students few opportunities to work with diverse students and having few faculty with direct experience with these populations. However, another program may operate in a widely diverse service area where students see ELs on a daily basis in their regular field experiences. Their teacher preparation professors may be quite experienced working with this population through their own work in the schools. Additionally, there should be a strong connection between the content presented and assessed in the EL-specific courses with a field experience component. As field experiences with ELs should occur at multiple points in the curriculum, an analysis of the potential for their inclusion in EL-specific courses is useful. Hence, in terms of context, we provide the following set of preliminary questions that may be helpful for the analysis phase:

- Is there a link between the content presented in class and the educational goals of the field experience?
- Are the assignments connected to the educational goals of the field experience?
- Are there assessment mechanisms in place that will ensure that the educational goals of the field experience have been met?

Each teacher preparation program wanting to infuse EL content must do an individual program examination. For example, how does the program integrate field experiences into the curriculum? If field experiences are to be included in the EL-specific courses, at what point would they come? At what point do students officially enter the teacher education portion of their degree programs (as juniors, sophomores, freshmen)? A freshman or sophomore taking an EL-specific course will need different support and curriculum than a junior or senior taking a course covering similar topics. Here, the EL infusion team examines institutional and programmatic structures that would involve or be impacted by EL-specific courses. Some driving questions for this portion of the preparation stage might consist of the following:

- What are the major gatekeepers in our program?
- How are our university students introduced to and integrated into our cooperating schools? At what point would EL-specific courses best fit into this process?

After these issues have been answered, the EL infusion team can turn to determining the content of the EL-specific courses appropriate for each program. These courses can be structured in multiple ways to address program needs. While EL-specific courses can address a variety of issues, ESL methodology and assessment and second language development and applied linguistics tend to be the most common, since these topics can be difficult for non-ESL professors to address and embed into their coursework. Individual programs can make decisions about what needs to be included in EL-specific courses, bearing in mind the general concepts and skills recommended by the NCELA Roundtable Report:[6]

- Language acquisition and communicative competence
  - Interplay of first and second language acquisition
  - Second language acquisition process
- Curriculum and instruction
  - Coordinating standards through teacher collaboration
  - Access to subject matter content
  - Differentiation
  - Academic vocabulary and oral language
  - Reading
  - Writing
  - Technology
- Content assessment
  - Accommodations
- Culture and education
- School and home communities

Of these categories of ESL expertise, some are easier to reproduce in the regular education classroom and some must almost always be included in an EL-specific course that is taught by an ESL expert. Individual programs must determine how EL-specific courses will be constructed and implemented into the regular teacher preparation program. Some driving questions that could be included at the beginning of this process could include:

- What expertise do we lack in our existing program of studies?
- How many EL-specific courses can we reasonably fit into our current program of studies?
- Will this mean developing new EL-specific courses, or using courses that may already exist within the ESL teacher education program?
- Do we have the resources needed to implement this program?

After beginning to answer some of these questions, programs will need to decide what courses (and concepts and skills) will be most beneficial to their program of studies. In the following section, we provide a brief description of what could be included in each of these categories, some of which may be effectively addressed by faculty who are not ESL experts.

Offering and Putting in Place the EL-Specific Courses

Implementation takes place relatively late in the overall EL infusion process, after integral steps have been taken to determine needs, analyze resources, and determine the best course of action. Ideally, programs that plan to offer a credential in teaching ELs would add one or more EL-specific courses to their degree requirements as soon as these courses are developed and approved. However, catalog change regulations or other internal or external factors may necessitate delaying the requirement of these courses. Additionally, programs must be cognizant of how "old program/new program" advising may alter certain students' programs as the new program is implemented. Most often, confusion can be averted through the use of orientation workshops for both students and faculty. It is critical that all faculty, even those not directly involved in the ESL integration process, be familiar with the new programs so that the students they are advising do not get confused or otherwise off track in their coursework.

In the interim period in which the new program is realized, teacher candidates may elect to complete the EL-specific courses for their degree areas so they may graduate with the EL-qualified designation. In some cases, institutions have decided to make the EL-specific courses optional to avoid adding credits to already lengthy graduation requirements. While this is better than offering no EL-specific courses, we believe that the EL-embedded courses alone cannot adequately prepare candidates to teach their subject to ELs.

During the implementation phase, faculty must consider how closely they want to work together. We have advocated a collaborative model. Hence, we believe that ESL faculty should be considered part of the overall program faculty and included in programmatic administration to the extent possible within their current duties. It would be wrong to think that other program decisions do not impact the ESL faculty and the courses they offer. For example, scheduling changes may severely impact the ESL-specific courses, especially if they create potential conflicts or overloads for students. Even changes that are not so drastic can impact the level of expertise that students enter ESL-specific courses with.

Several factors impact staffing needs. Assuming that the institution requires the EL Instructional and Assessment Methods course of all teacher candidates, multiple sections would need to be offered each semester, regardless of the decision to offer the course in a common-to-all-programs fashion or to differentiate by programs such as Early Childhood/Elementary Education, Secondary English Language Arts Education, and Secondary Academic Subjects described above. For smaller institutions this would mean one full-time ESL instructor. Larger institutions, on the other hand, might require a full-time and a part-time instructor during the first semester. If the institution also decides to implement the two-course option, each semester after the first time EL Instructional and Assessments Methods is offered in multiple sections, Applied Linguistics and Second Language Development would also appear on the course schedule. Since fewer candidates would take that course, fewer sections would be necessary, but it would still increase the need for additional instructors. Of course, the ESL instructors would meet qualifications equal to instructors of other program area courses, following accreditation standards. Now that the key issues of the process of developing and offering the courses have been presented, we turn to a description of the content of the courses.

Description of Two EL-Specific Courses Proposed by the One Plus Model

The following section presents sample course content for the two EL-specific courses included in the One Plus model as well as a rationale for including the study of applied linguistics and second language development.

EL Instructional and Assessment Methods

This course is designed to introduce teacher candidates to EL-focused instructional and assessment approaches, methods, and strategies appropriate to a collaborative instructional approach for ELs. The main goal of this course is to ground teacher candidates in a solid understanding of what ELs can understand and do at three major levels of proficiency and how teachers can differentiate instruction and make accommodations in assessment for each of the three levels in the mainstream classroom. If this course is taken during candidates' first semester in the major, the knowledge and skills acquired can be applied to various EL-embedded courses at the 2+ and 3+ levels.

To ground candidates' developing knowledge and skills in differentiating instruction for ELs, this course introduces pertinent aspects of second language development that will be fully explored in the Applied Linguistics and Second Language Development course and applies this information to realistic teaching and learning contexts. Because the intended audience consists of teacher candidates who are not conventionally prepared for EL-focused specialties, the approaches, methods, and strategies introduced are presented within the context of teaching students in public schools, including classroom, small-group, and one-on-one instructional settings in which language is a source of difficulty.

Although there are various models for organizing and presenting the content of courses such as this one, teacher educators should have the flexibility to plan, deliver, and evaluate the course curriculum and instructional delivery depending on their needs and constraints. We envision an EL instructional and assessment methods course in which teacher candidates learn about prevailing: (a) EL-focused instructional approaches, methods, and strategies designed to enhance language and content learning: (b) EL-focused approaches for assessing the needs of ELs and using that information to inform and differentiate instruction for these students: and (c) EL-focused curriculum materials and resources that support student learning and engagement.

EL Instructional and Assessment Methods is best taught in tandem with general or subject area instructional and assessment methods courses so that students can learn how best to integrate ESL methods with their regular curriculum. Also, because students must develop instruction and assessment using EL and content area standards, the methods are most effective when implemented together. The primary focus of this course is adapting curriculum, instruction, and assessment for ELs at multiple levels of English proficiency. Accordingly, the course should provide introductory information on the stages of SLA, common areas of linguistic difficulty for academic language development, and other SLA and applied linguistics topics that all teacher candidates should know to effectively teach and assess ELs. Candidates then apply this basic knowledge to making appropriate adaptations in teaching and assessing different subjects to ELs.

As teacher educators, we also know that teachers are better positioned to adjust instruction to accommodate student needs when they have an awareness of these students' language backgrounds and abilities, and an understanding of the language demands involved in classroom tasks. The content of our proposed EL Instructional and Assessment Methods course should ideally include methods and strategies for scaffolding ELs' language and literacy development as well as learning and engagement in content area classrooms such as science, mathematics, and social studies. In a course such as this, teacher candidates also learn about strategies for scaffolding and differentiating instruction for ELs based on levels language proficiency, literacy achievement, and other individual differences. Scaffolding strategies could focus on preparing teacher candidates to plan and organize instruction to promote student learning of language and academic content. Examples of scaffolding strategies might include how to present information to students in multiple ways using visual aids as well as verbally and in writing, how to organize instruction so that ELs have opportunities to interact with and learn from each other, and how to differentiate instruction based on students' language proficiency or academic skill levels.

Possible course objectives include:

- Compare and contrast naturalistic (informal) and instructed (formal) second language acquisition (SLA) environments.
- Recognize input, interaction, and output and their role in promoting SLA.
- Identify major stages of second language acquisition and common interlanguage patterns.
- Define and identify social and academic language.
- Identify predominant instruments for assessing English proficiency and descriptors of English proficiency (TESOL standards).
- Recognize how individual variables affect SLA.
- Identify characteristics of beginning, intermediate, and advanced ELs.
- Analyze the language demands and contextual support of instructional or assessment tasks.
- Compare the language demands of a task with the level of English proficiency of beginning, intermediate, and advanced ELs.
- Identify characteristics of the Sheltered Instruction Observation Protocol (SIOP) Model, developed to promote effective instruction for ELs in content areas.
- Analyze math, science, social studies, and other content area lesson plans' language demands and contextual support for ELs.
- Compose content area questions and task descriptions for beginning, intermediate, and advanced ELs.
- Select, adapt, and plan for applying verbal and nonverbal instructional and assessment strategies for ELs at three levels of English proficiency.
- Identify differences in language arts instruction for native speakers and ELs at three levels of English proficiency.
- Recognize the role of native language instruction for language arts development in English.
- Identify the characteristics and benefits of sheltered language arts for ELs (i.e., language arts for ESL).

- Apply knowledge and skills in differentiating instruction for ELs at the beginning, intermediate, and advanced levels of English proficiency to a field experience with one or more ELs in a mainstream classroom setting.

Applied Linguistics and Second Language Development

The following section explores the background and the description of the stand-alone course that explores EL-focused concepts and principles in applied linguistics and second language development that will help pre-service teachers become more effective instructors when working with ELs.

Course Background

Including a course in Applied Linguistics and Second Language Development for teacher candidates obtaining certification in language arts and literacy instruction is broadly supported by a number of teacher education researchers who have suggested that teachers need a basic understanding of applied linguistics, a subfield of linguistics that addresses how key insights about the nature of language impacts teaching and learning, if they are to do their work well.[7] The idea is that key understandings of language and linguistics will help enhance teachers' pedagogical practices, which will in turn impact students' language, literacy, and content learning.[8]

The calls for preparing teacher candidates to effectively teach ELs requires reaching out to disciplines such as applied linguistics, which have traditionally been outside of the realm of teacher education programming. The relevance of applied and theoretical linguistics to literacy development, for instance, can easily be defended on the grounds that the knowledge gained from the field of linguistics (e.g., knowledge of how the various components of language work) incorporates solutions to potential difficulties faced by ELs learning to read and write across languages. Many problems encountered by ELs when learning to read and write in English can be represented as language-related sources of difficulty that can be solved by conceptual understandings found in linguistics.

Language plays an important role in nearly all areas of the curriculum. Literacy and content teachers, for example, intuitively know that a child must understand how to use language to understand and produce written text. Research has shown that effective readers, unlike their less competent peers, have a better understanding of key underlying competencies related to certain key aspects of language having to do with learning the alphabet, making sense of how sounds relate to symbols, how words are formed and used to generate meaning, how sentences are structured, and how larger pieces of discourse are organized.[9] Linguists often divide the underlying competence about these aspects of language development into several components or domains, including, but not limited to, phonology, syntax, and semantics. *Phonology* describes knowledge of the sound structure of a language and of the basic elements that convey differences in meaning, including their internal structure and their relationships to each other. *Syntax* accounts for the descriptive rules of language that specify how to combine different classes of words (e.g., nouns, verbs, adjectives) to form sentences. *Semantics* involves learning the individual meanings of words as well as the meanings of larger segments or text, namely sentences and discourse structures that are typically found in texts that children are expected to read and understand.

Knowledge gained from a course such as Applied Linguistics and Second Language Development provides understandings about language (e.g., knowledge of how sounds combine with symbols to create words) that will enable teacher candidates to assist ELs with difficulties related to word recognition and reading fluency. Teacher candidates working with children experiencing difficulty understanding and producing language will find linguistic insights pertaining to these three key components of language, and others, quite helpful when assisting these children in developing and/or expanding their reading and writing skills and in learning from content areas texts. We know from our experience preparing teachers of reading and writing that teachers who have a basic foundational knowledge of how the sound system of language works are more likely to be better prepared to assist a child experiencing difficulty acquiring the alphabetic principle, which requires an awareness that spoken words are composed of individual sounds or phonemes, that these individual units of sound can change meaning of words, and that phonemes can be substituted and rearranged to create different words.

Teachers who successfully complete an Applied Linguistics and Second Language Development have an opportunity to develop a better understanding of the sources of difficulty children encounter when learning to read and write that are related to other aspects of language development, such as morphology and syntax. It is beneficial for teacher candidates to know that a child needs to understand that languages have rules regarding how words can be combined to form sentences, and that an implicit understanding of the rules of sentence structure is essential to language comprehension and production. This understanding permits teachers to effectively assist ELs to address sources of difficulty emanating from an understanding of English morphology and syntax.

The essential language-related understandings gained from a course such as Applied Linguistics and Second Language Development have important implications and applications for curriculum, instruction, and assessment. While teacher candidates can examine the pedagogical practices that emerge from these understandings, we think it is best for them to examine EL-focused pedagogical methods and practices in more depth in the separate stand-alone methods course such as EL Instructional and Assessment Methods, which is devoted to EL instructional assessment and approaches, methods, and strategies. A course such as this will help teacher candidates organize, implement, and evaluate instruction for ELs in ways that are closely aligned with these students' needs.

Course Description

This course is designed to provide a basic introduction to language and linguistics, with particular emphasis on the role of language in learning and teaching. The content of this course consist of topics pertaining to key aspects of language such as phonology, syntax, and semantics; first and second language acquisition; and language variation. Because this course is designed for teacher candidates who are not conventionally prepared for ESL specialties, a primary focus is placed on the implications and applications of the various issues introduced to real-world educational contexts. These issues will be examined within the contexts of realistic classroom or clinical situations in which language is a source of difficulty.

For instance, when introducing teacher candidates to how the nature and role of phonology in language and literacy development, we would begin by presenting cases of language interference problems that ELs might have with the English sound system. We would introduce key understandings of word formation or morphology by examining writing samples in light of students' developmental spelling stages. When examining SLA, we would begin by addressing developmental aspects of language and literacy, and the acquisition of the morphological knowledge, syntactic structures, and vocabulary required for literacy development and growth.

Possible topics include:

- First language acquisition processes
- Second language acquisition processes
- Phonetics: Exploring the sounds of language
- Phonology: Examining the sound patterns of language
- Morphology: Illustrating word forms and word formation processes
- Grammar: Discussing the patterns of English grammar
- Syntax: Surveying English language syntax
- Semantics: Studying meaning in English
- Pragmatics: Exploring the relationship between meaning and context
- Discourse analysis: Analyzing written and spoken language
- Similarities and differences between L1 and L2 literacy development
- Influences of phonology, morphology, syntax, semantics, and discourse on L2 reading and writing development, covered when each subsystem is addressed individually

Field Experiences and Student Teaching: A Meaningful Merging of Theory and Practice

Theoretical knowledge of language and linguistics is a necessary but not sufficient condition for transforming the practices of teacher candidates in their future interactions with ELs.[10] Without an opportunity to apply linguistics knowledge to meaningful educational interactions with ELs, linguistics courses face numerous challenges. Purmensky investigated pre-service teachers' perceptions before the implementation of a field experience component and found that pre-service teachers learned the linguistics concepts but were unable to make connections to their own future classroom instruction.[11] Moreover, many pre-service teachers communicated that they had never had contact with an EL. Some of them sometimes expressed a certain degree of resentment for having to learn how to teach ELs and questioned the usefulness and necessity of spending so much time learning the challenging content of linguistics just for one particular group of students.

These perceived challenges do not mean that the theoretical knowledge of language acquisition and applied linguistics loses its importance, but rather emphasize the importance of including an opportunity for knowledge application in the form of a field experience or student teaching opportunity. Simply put, the theoretical knowledge of language acquisition and applied linguistics represents the foundation for a meaningful field experience or student teaching opportunity during which the teacher candidates demonstrate that they can use that knowledge to create EL-oriented instructional techniques in their future classrooms.

The field experience/student teaching element is a (if not the) critical component for the Applied Linguistics and Second Language Development course. After theoretical knowledge is presented in class, applying it in their field experience or student teaching environment gives teacher candidates an opportunity to see how linguistics concepts and language development knowledge plays an important role in classroom instruction, especially in developing second language literacy. Additionally, candidates can also use the linguistics concepts to create a variety of instructional tools that are tailored to specific EL language development needs and test the effectiveness in a real-classroom environment.

In addition to insights gained from EL-specific courses, teacher candidates, like ELs, need accommodations and support, which vary depending on their performance in coursework, prior level of exposure to language-related courses, and teaching experience. Consequently, we suggest that EL-specific courses include a field experience component that will allow teacher candidates to apply what they have learned in real-world classroom settings. It is during these field experiences that teacher candidates can gain the most from being exposed to the language-related insights in courses such as Applied Linguistics and Second Language Development or the EL Instructional and Assessment Methods. The insights and practices learned are likely to be most effective once teacher candidates are working regularly with ELs and have a clear understanding of the learning challenges their students face.

To exemplify how to establish a strong connection between theoretical knowledge and field experience–based application, we share a sample field-based course assignment that provides an opportunity for teacher candidates to apply insights gained from an Applied Linguistics and Second Language Development course in a real-world school or clinical setting. Each step of the data collection and analysis process is demonstrated in class, and students practice analyzing a transcript of EL speech for each of the four linguistic subfields as they are presented in the course. After the class codevelops a report of the transcript and audio and print data for the sample student, candidates are placed with an English learner in a preK–12 setting to collect and analyze their own interlanguage data, which is then presented in a report.

Sample Field Experience Project

English Learner Interlanguage Analysis

In this project, you will have an opportunity to apply what you learned about language as a system to scaffold literacy learning for ELs in preK–12 settings.

Guidelines for the Project

Collect oral interlanguage samples from an English learner at the *intermediate level* of English proficiency:

1. Record (audio only) a five-minute conversation with the English learner:
2. Be sure you have several topics (likes, dislikes, hobbies, family, friends, etc.), photos or magazine pictures, toys, etc. on hand to use as props to keep the dialogue going. Use whatever you find will engage the student in language production.

Analyze the data:

3. Transcribe the recordings, including International Phonetic Alphabet transcriptions of words in between forward slash marks to indicate words that are pronounced with notable transfer from the native language
4. Analyze the transcribed data:
   - Look for phonological patterns in the data
   - Look for morphological patterns in the data
   - Look for semantic patterns in the data
   - Look for syntactic patterns in the data
5. Examine the errors the student made. Do you think they are developmental? Do you think they are due to transfer from the native language?
6. Consider if targeted support is needed for the student in each of the four areas. If so, what strategies would you recommend to provide this support?

Your report should include:

Introduction: Who is the student you analyzed? How old is the child? Where does the child come from? How long has s/he been in the US? What language(s) does s/he speak at home? What language(s) is/are spoken at home by the family? At what level of ESL is the child classed? Do you agree with the ESL classification? Why/why not?

Phonology description: Based on your analysis of the data, describe the student's phonological patterns and speculate as to why you think the patterns exist. Be sure to give examples and use the International Phonetic Alphabet to describe the significant phonological data. Issues such as accent (e.g., substitution of one sound for another such as *s* for *th* in *think*), mispronunciations, intonation, etc., should be addressed. If you are able to find information on phonological features of the student's native language and their contrast with English phonology, please include pertinent data.

Morphology description: Based on your analysis of the data, give a detailed description of the student's morphological patterns and speculate as to why you think the pattern exists. Don't forget to give specific examples, such the student's omission of any of the eight inflectional morphemes properly—for example, no -s plural or says "the house of John" instead of "John's house," etc.

- *-s* plural
- *-'s* possessive
- *-s* third-person singular conjugation
- *-ed* past tense
- *-en* past participle (been, given)
- *-ing* present participle
- *-er* comparative
- *-est* superlative

If you are able to find information on morphological features of the student's native language and their contrast with English morphology, please include pertinent data.

Semantics description: Based on your analysis of the data, give a detailed description of the student's semantic patterns and speculate as to why you think the pattern exists. Give examples of the student's lack of vocabulary (if the student gets stuck on a word or doesn't understand a particular work you said) and circumlocution strategies (describing an item that s/he doesn't know the word for). If you are able to find information on semantic features of the student's native language and their contrast with English semantics, please include pertinent data.

Syntax description: Based on your analysis of the data, give a detailed description of the student's syntactical patterns and speculate as to why you believe the pattern to exist. Give examples, such as the use of simple sentences, sentence fragments, avoidance of certain structures (e.g., relative clauses), wrong word order or missing words in negative, interrogative, or relative clauses, etc. If you are able to find information on syntactic features of the student's native language and their contrast with English syntax, please include pertinent data.

Based on your analysis of these four areas, suggest how what you discovered about the student's interlanguage patterns could affect her/his performance in language arts and literacy activities. For example, could some of the pronunciation issues affect the student's spelling? Which issues might impact assessment of the student's reading fluency, for example?

Interview Suggestions

1. Try out a topic that you think will interest the child. If the topic fails to elicit much of a response, move on to something else. Avoid yes-or-no questions. Ask the student to tell you about something (e.g., Tell me what do you like to do for fun. Why? Tell me about your family. What are their favorite things to do? Tell me how school/daily life/

shopping/food is different in the United States than it was back home. Tell me about your favorite teacher. What did you draw here? Who/what is this in your drawing?).

2. If the student fails to respond, or responds with just a smile, don't abandon the topic immediately. Think of a way to rephrase your question. Example:

> Tell me about your daily routine during the week.
> (Blank look)
> What time do you wake up?
> What do you eat for breakfast?
> What time do you get to school?
> What do you do in school?

3. If the student offers a short response, you can attempt to elicit more information—greater detail, greater quantity, longer response (e.g., Tell me more. Can you say more about this? Can you describe . . . for me? What does . . . mean? Can you explain. . . ?).

4. Once you have the student talking, try to take the conversation to a higher cognitive level (compare/contrast, narration about the past, etc.) (e.g. Tell me about a time when . . . Has . . . always been this way?)

5. Keep in mind that what you say will depend on how the student replies, in terms of content and performance level. You'll gauge your next utterance to what the student has just produced.

Excerpt from a Candidate's Interview Transcript

> T (teacher): What is your name?
>
> JN: Javier [pseudonym].
>
> T: What is your last name?
>
> JN: Javier Nuñez [pseudonym].
>
> T: Where are you from?
>
> JN: Puerto Rico.
>
> T: Where in Puerto Rico?
>
> JN: Uhm, Utuado.
>
> T: Can you spell that for me?
>
> JN: Uhm, yeah. U-t-u-a-d-o.
>
> T: What part of Puerto Rico is that in?
>
> JN: Uhm, the /midol/ [middle].
>
> T: How long have you been here?
>
> JN: Like, like, eleven /mons/ [months] /sonsɪŋ/ [something] like /dɜːt/ [that].
>
> T: Did you come here from Puerto Rico to Florida or did you live somewhere else in the U.S.?
>
> JN: No, I /kom/ [come] /fron/ [from] Puerto Rico to Florida.

T: Eleven months! You speak a lot of English for eleven months. I'm impressed.

T: Do you have any brothers or sisters?

JN: Yeah, I have two /brodər/ [brother] and two /sistər/ [sister].

T: What are their names?

JN: My /lidol/ [little] /brodər/ [brother]
/his/ [his] name /is/ [is] Adio, uhm,
my /odər/ [older] /brodər/ [brother]
/his/ [his] name is Mariano, uhm,
my /sistər/ [sister], my /big/ [big] /sistər/ [sister] is 13 year /ol/ [old]
she's name /is/ [is] uhm Diana and
my /lidol/ [little] /sistər/ [sister] her name /is/ [is] Yahira.

Excerpts from a Candidate's Report

Phonological patterns:

Javier substitutes many sounds from Spanish to his pronunciation of English. He consistently substitutes the /i/ phoneme for the /ɪ/ phoneme in English, such as saying /midol/ for *middle*. He also substitutes sounds for both the voiced and voiceless versions of the *th* sound in English. Examples of this are /sonsɪŋ/ for *something* (voiceless th) and /brodər/ for *brother* (voiced th).

Javier deletes phonemes in particular contexts. An example is the deletion of the *th* sound between an /n/ and an /s/ in /mons/ for *months*. He also deletes the /s/ phoneme on the end of many words, such as in *two brother* and *two sister*.

I can see in Javier's writing that these phonological influences from his native language affect his spelling, and I think they could also influence his reading. It's possible that he might mistake the meaning of a word based on how he would pronounce it in Spanish, such as saying *leave* for *live* (as in You should *live* your values) because of his substitution of the /i/ phoneme for the /ɪ/ phoneme in English.

Morphological patterns:

An example of a morphological error is Javier's utterance, "My little brother his name is . . . " which is a substitution for *–s* possessive morpheme, "My little brothe*r's* name is . . . " In cases where Javier omits the final *–s* plural morpheme, although it is technically a morphological error, it more likely is due to Javier's dropping of final /s/ phonemes, which is a feature of his dialect of Spanish.

Again, I can see how this morphological error could affect Javier's writing in English. Not forming the possessive correctly could make Javier lose points in a writing assignment, but he apparently has not acquired that form in English yet.

Syntactical and semantic patterns:

An example of a syntactic error is Javier's statement that, "No they no play football over there," which is a typical stage in the development of negation in English. Another example is, "He gives it me in Spanish," which omits the preposition "to" and may be an instance of transfer from Spanish syntax, "me lo da en español" (me it he gives in Spanish).

Javier uses circumlocution to express concepts when he does not know the English word, such as his statement that when he gets an answer correct, "I feel . . . better . . . because before I didn't do good . . . " to express the word "successful," which he stated in Spanish to clarify.

In both these instances, I can see how the errors might affect reading comprehension. Sentences that have complicated negative structures, such as, "She couldn't have been avoiding junk food while living next to a fast food restaurant . . . " would probably be confusing to Javier at this stage. He also needs more vocabulary development for successful reading in English.

Conclusion

In this chapter, we provided a description of EL-specific courses and a framework for developing and implementing the courses. EL-specific courses are an integral part of teacher preparation programs that aim to give teachers the necessary content and experiential knowledge to help them to address the instructional needs of ELs effectively. The main reason for adding specific EL-focused courses to the curriculum is based on the unique characteristics of ELs. As we indicated previously, they need to acquire not only academic material but also English language necessary to communicate in social and academic settings. It is true that teacher preparation programs include courses that address some of the instruction and assessment of ELs. Nevertheless, given the complexity of the processes of learning English while acquiring academic content, EL-specific courses direct pre-service teachers' attention to issues that are specific only to ELs. As we underscored this point before, teaching ELs is not just good teaching, but teaching is to be done using EL-specific teaching tools.

Finally, we want to emphasize the importance of collaboration among ESL professionals on the one hand and primary, secondary, and special education teachers on the other. The dilemma is that while teacher preparation programs in general do not prepare teachers to be certified ESL teachers, they are expected to prepare them to work with ELs in mainstream classrooms. Therefore, the EL-specific courses should be integrated with the rest of the teacher education curriculum in a seamless way, so that teacher candidates see these courses as an integral part of their preparation. This integration has the potential to foster a strong relationship between EL-specific courses and language arts, content area, or special education classes, which should in turn encourage literacy, content, and special education teachers to seek the support and academic expertise of their ESL-certified colleagues.

CHAPTER 11

A Culturally Responsive Framework for Evaluating EL-Infused Programs

Jeannie Ducher, Martha E. Castañeda, and Amy Fisher Young
Miami University

A s was noted in chapter 1, the One Plus EL infusion model follows established instructional design principles throughout the infusion process. Beginning with an analysis phase, the instructional design cycle includes design, development, implementation, and evaluation, which is both formative and summative.[1] Formative evaluation takes place at each stage of the instructional design cycle, allowing for revision of program elements based on feedback and other data. Occurring at key points during program implementation, evaluation provides the opportunity for improvement from a more complete perspective.

In this chapter, we focus on this fifth component of the instructional design cycle, *evaluation*, and provide a framework for evaluating EL infusion programs and assessing teacher candidates' preparedness to teach EL students. We first depict the EL infusion effort based on the One Plus Model in the form of a logic model, offering an alternative way of considering the individual components that contribute to the project. We then offer suggestions for planning and conducting a culturally responsive evaluation of EL-infused programs and candidate assessment, provide examples from our own past and current development and evaluation work with EL infusion in Ohio and Florida, and discuss how these tasks can be accomplished and aligned with program evaluation standards and key understandings related to the education of ELs.

The EL Infusion Logic Model

The successful evaluation of an EL infusion program begins with the adoption of an established framework, agreed on by stakeholders; aligned with various local, national, and professional requirements; and underscored by a program vision and specific short- and long-term goals.[2] Collecting data without first laying the foundation for assessment may result in laborious efforts compiling information that may not contribute to the decision-making process of program implementation, thus resulting in a loss of resources and momentum. Program evaluation must be seen as a process that informs the development, implementation, and results of the EL infusion project. Evaluation is not a coercive or adversarial process; on the contrary, it is an opportunity for change and improvement, in our case by faculty, administrators, and teacher candidates.[3]

No two infusions are alike. There are numerous contextual factors, ranging from existing needs and resources to desired programmatic change, that make each EL infusion effort unique. Because they link intended outcomes to everything that goes into and occurs during the project, logic models help stakeholders to better understand the "theory and assumptions underlying the project."[4] Frechtling describes logic models as a visual depiction of who does what to reach whom with what resources.[5] In other words, they present the institution's vision of the change planned for its programs by clearly displaying the resources that are allocated to planned activities and how the quantifiable products resulting from the activities lead to the attainment of the desired outcomes. The logic model affords the opportunity to account for contextual factors that impact the way the EL infusion process is undertaken, thus enabling the infusion team to establish the group's theoretical understanding and assumption of change that the infusion is intended to make in faculty, teacher candidates, program(s), and the community. By building the logic model from the earliest planning stage of the EL infusion effort, institutions facilitate the planning for evaluation, which should occur in parallel fashion. The visual display of the components that go into and result in change gives the project team and the evaluation team the opportunity to check along the way whether the components that made up the input were sufficient to implement the activities, whether the activities reached those for whom they were intended, and finally whether these outputs lead to the expected outcomes. In other words, the logic model is helpful in planning for both formative and summative evaluations.

If all goes as planned and the stated components are met at each or most points, the logic model constructed at the beginning of the project explains the changes that occurred in the institution. However, if at any point in the infusion process the project encounters situations that deviate from the established logic model, such as anticipated resources becoming unavailable or when planned activities are either not delivered or don't reach the anticipated level of output, the infusion team can gauge whether the project can still reach the stated outcomes, or whether changes in the process need to be considered. In the scenario where the final outcomes can still be met, the logic model needs to be tweaked to reflect the difference between the planned components and the actual situation. It then presents an accurate visual description of the change that occurred, and the evaluation explains the change that resulted from the infusion. In the scenario where substantive adjustments to the planned process have to be made, the revised logic model becomes the new roadmap for project completion and summative evaluation.

Figure 11.1 illustrates the various categories and elements that comprise the logic model of the One Plus model of EL infusion. In its left-to-right sequence, this logic model illustrates the stakeholders in terms of *input* and the types of activities undertaken and their planned results, or *output*, as well as those entities that are the intended

Figure 11.1 **One Plus logic model**

Inputs	Activities	Outputs	Outcomes
Institutional support: • Teacher preparation faculty • ESL faculty • Clinical faculty • Assessment director • Administration • Teacher candidates PreK–12 school support: • Collaborating teachers • Students State representatives	Selection of programs for infusion Faculty development: • Course modifications • Instructional courses Clinical experiences courses EL-specific course development and approval Assessment model development Program approval Delivery of embedded coursework Delivery of EL-specific courses Collaboration with schools: • Field experiences • Clinical experiences placements	Amount of faculty development delivered # of sustainable faculty development plan # of embedded courses # of infused programs # of ESL-specific courses created # of student credit hours from ESL-specific courses # of clinical experiences placements with ELs # of teacher candidates obtaining content # of teacher candidates obtaining endorsement/certificate	Teacher preparation faculty learning [short term] New collaborations (teacher preparation and ESL faculty) [short term] Candidate learning [short term] Enhanced teacher preparation programs [short term] Improved preK–12 EL student achievement [long term]

beneficiaries of the infusion effort. Specifically, it shows that there are eight potential stakeholder groups involved in and/or affected by the project: (1) teacher preparation faculty, (2) ESL faculty, (3) clinical faculty, (4) administrators, including assessment
director and administration, (5) preK–12 teachers, (6) preK–12 students, (7) teacher
candidates, and (8) state representatives (if state approval of endorsement or certification is needed).

The Activities block of the One Plus logic model presents the actionable items
or individual steps necessary to reach the final outcome. These steps are not sequential; many of them can be undertaken simultaneously. For example, once the programs
slated for EL infusion are selected and faculty development has been initiated, the
content embedding process, EL-specific course design, and approval can begin and the
assessment model can be conceptualized. Other activities obviously require the completion of one step before the next can take place, such as obtaining approval for the
EL-specific course before its first offering. Outputs are always expressed in quantifiable
terms in the logic model, and evaluators typically use this category to determine the
extent to which the project is reaching the declared goal of the activities. In that light,
outputs are used as summative evaluation for activities, but they can also be utilized as
individual points of reference along the way of formative evaluation tasks.

Outcomes differ from outputs in that they aren't represented as quantities produced by the activities, but rather as change in knowledge, skills, behavior, attitude or
condition in the participants that are attributable to the project. The desired short-term
outcomes consist of teacher candidates' and teacher preparation faculty's increased
knowledge and skills in teaching content and language to ELs and in meeting the
needs of ELs. These outcomes reflect today's need for preparing effective teachers of
ELs and may result in scholarly productivity through new or renewed collaborations
among faculty. Determining whether the project accomplished its long-term outcome
of improved academic achievement of ELs along the preK–12 continuum is one part
of the evaluation that can be undertaken only after a substantial number of candidates
have graduated from the EL infused program(s). Although keeping in touch with the
graduates is a challenge for all institutions and attributing student success to individual
teachers presents various philosophical and methodological challenges, we feel strongly
that this outcome must be investigated. After all, it is the underlying reason for undertaking the programmatic change that is EL infusion.

The visual display of input, activities, output, and outcomes in sequential order
helps stakeholders to formulate the evaluation questions that are important to them. We
will touch on the formulation of evaluation questions later in this chapter. As we argue
below, hearing the voices of all stakeholders straight from the beginning ensures that
the findings of the evaluation are valuable because they are focused on those individuals
and groups who are impacted by the project. Therefore, we suggest following a simple,
strategic evaluation and assessment plan based on the logic model that fits the institution's context, combining culturally responsive techniques with a real-world approach
to create a comprehensive plan that is rigorous, yet flexible and responsive to common
obstacles.

Culturally Responsive Evaluation: Taking Context into Consideration

Over the past decade, a clear consensus has emerged that cultural responsiveness should be an integral part of program design, implementation, and evaluation.[6] *Culturally responsive evaluation*—also referred to in the literature as *responsive, collaborative,* or *participatory* evaluation—is a response and challenge to the traditional reductionist and dichotomous evaluation methods that rely heavily on quantitative data; distance the evaluator, researcher, participants, and community; work under the notion that assessment is objective and culture free; and may not honor the cultural context and role the affected community plays in the conception, process, and evaluation of the project. In contrast to traditional evaluation models, a culturally responsive evaluation is descriptive, inductive, participatory, and multidimensional. Frierson et al. describe this type of evaluation as "an examination of impacts through lenses in which the culture of the participants is considered an important factor," an examination that Dobson states resists the "dominant, mainstream thinking that pervades the tradition of scholarship that sees difference as deficit or diversity as deviant."[7]

When a culturally responsive evaluation of an EL infusion project is conducted, we recommend that evaluation teams consult the logic model to see the operational context as well as the participants who are either involved in carrying out the project or are impacted by its activities, outputs, and outcomes. We have already explained how each institution's logic model varies, depending on the operational context in which the infusion efforts take place, and have listed the various stakeholder groups. In EL infusion, the main targeted population coincides to a large extent with the stakeholders actively involved in the project. Teacher preparation faculty engage in faculty development and infuse their courses. ESL faculty provide the faculty development, mentor their partners, and build EL-specific courses. Candidates acquire additional knowledge and skills in the process of going through the infused courses. At the same time, their learning and changed practice are also two of the three short-term outcomes depicted in the logic model. In the process of engaging in the EL infusion process, these individuals may explore issues of inclusion and cultural and linguistic diversity at a deep and sustained level for the first time. They are directly impacted by the change that the teacher preparation programs undergo, at least during the development and implementation of the infusion efforts. Culturally responsive evaluation allows for their voices to be heard.

Preparing to Conduct a Culturally Responsive Evaluation

As stated above, the logic model should be constructed during project planning because it provides the basis of the evaluation plan. The members of the evaluation team need to represent the various stakeholders identified in the logic model. It is equally important that all participants and stakeholders have a shared understanding of and support the development of an evaluation plan that looks at processes and products in an interconnected, mosaic-like manner.

Once agreed upon, the evaluation plan becomes the theoretical roadmap for evaluation activities. Like a roadmap, the plan should provide for flexibility to follow multiple paths to answering the questions the stakeholders desire to investigate. Frierson et al. offer the following critical steps or phases to conduct culturally responsive program evaluations:

- Preparing for the evaluation
- Engaging stakeholders
- Identifying the purpose(s) and intent of the evaluation
- Framing the right questions
- Designing the evaluation
- Selecting and adapting instrumentation
- Collecting the data
- Analyzing the data
- Disseminating and utilizing the results[8]

Preparing for the Evaluation

A critical first step in conducting a culturally responsive evaluation of EL-infused programs involves the selection of an evaluation team that is aware of and responsive to the participants' and stakeholders' cultures. When conducting a culturally responsive evaluation of an EL infusion program, it is advisable to invite educator preparation faculty and staff who have cultural expertise, and ideally language expertise, to the table. Members of participating culturally and linguistically diverse groups might be drawn from teacher educators, teachers from local area schools, or even parents of students representing the predominant languages and cultures of the EL students served.

Through our involvement with EL infusion projects, we have learned that their evaluations are best thought of as a team effort. Depending on institutional resources and staff capabilities, we suggest one of the following three options for assembling dependable evaluation teams:

- An institution that does not have a research and evaluation staff may want to hire an outside evaluator who would serve as an evaluation team leader and who would be supported by program staff. The outside evaluator will provide leadership in determining the focus of the evaluation, developing the evaluation plan, and preparing an evaluation report.
- Institutions that have the resources but need technical evaluation expertise may want to assign an in-house project evaluator who will serve as a team leader but who will draw on the support of the program staff and the outside consultant for assistance in developing an evaluation plan, conducting the evaluation, and disseminating the findings.
- Institutions that have the resources and evaluation/research expertise might simply form an in-house evaluation team. This team would then be responsible for the design, implementation, and oversight of the evaluation plan.

Engaging Stakeholders

In conducting culturally responsive program evaluations, experts advise keeping members of the impacted communities in mind when planning program evaluation.[9] Projects that start the construction of a logic model at the very beginning can draw on key members of the identified stakeholder groups *before* they finalize the design, development, and implementation of the program. Representatives of the various stakeholders can assist in fine-tuning the theory of change of the project. This action increases the probability for long-term engagement in the project. If the state's department of education requires that an EL infusion program be accredited, the accrediting agency and its requirements must be taken into consideration when conducting program evaluation, and a representative should be asked to serve in an advisory role. If accreditation is optional, key purposes guided by indicators and essential questions must be determined and the standards against which program and candidate outcomes will be evaluated should be outlined early in the process for congruity. Representation from the student body should be considered.

What is unique about culturally responsive evaluations is that everyone is given the chance to be heard: those involved in program operations, such as teacher education faculty, ESL faculty, and university administrators, as well as those served or directly affected by the program, namely, teacher candidates, ESL teachers in the community, generalist teachers, school administrators, parents, and EL students themselves. We have found the evaluation process to be valuable and useful when the program evaluation team deliberately engages stakeholders early in the evaluation process. As potential users of the evaluation findings, their input is essential to establishing the focus and direction of the evaluation.

Following the identification of potential stakeholders, we recommend that the lead evaluator invest time and effort in preparing stakeholders for active engagement in the program and its evaluation. This might include providing them with a thorough understanding of the program and the specific components that are being evaluated by explaining when the program started, what resources are allocated to the program, what activities are in place to achieve project goals, and what the expected outcomes are. It might also include building strong relationships with the various individuals and groups representing stakeholders. Learning about their backgrounds and areas of expertise; their diverse viewpoints, experiences, and needs relative to the program and its evaluation; their motivations and interest in participating in the program evaluation; and their preferred mode of communication (e.g., in person or virtually, individual meetings, group meetings or surveys) helps the evaluator determine how to involve each person in helping shape the development and implementation of the evaluation plan.

Identifying the Purpose(s) and Intent of the Evaluation

An essential step in conducting culturally responsive evaluations is to ensure that stakeholders share a common understanding of the purpose(s) or intent of the EL-infused program evaluation so as to prevent hasty decision making regarding how the evaluation should be conducted. Purposes for conducting evaluations in educator preparation often pertain to program effectiveness and teacher candidate preparation. For instance, evaluations focused on program coherence and participant learning might include efforts to: (a) improve the quality, effectiveness, or efficiency of program activities; and (b) examine the relationships between program activities and observed changes in teacher candidates' knowledge, skills, and dispositions to teach EL students. Again, the logic model can be used to explain the relationships between project inputs, activities, and improved quality, efficiency, or teacher candidate learning.

With a clear sense of the purpose(s) and intent of the program evaluation, we have found that one way to ensure the relevance and usefulness of an evaluation is for the evaluation team, working either as a whole or in smaller groups determined by interest, to develop a set of guiding questions that reflect the perspectives, experiences, and insights of as many relevant individuals or stakeholder groups as possible. These questions might include the following: Does the evaluation team have an assessment system in place for monitoring and documenting progress relative to the goals of the EL-infused program? How do members of the evaluation team know that the EL-infused activities or initiatives are working as planned? What specific steps or strategies do members of the evaluation team take when these initiatives in place are not working as envisioned?

Research has shown that while approaches can vary widely with respect to educator preparation, effective preparation programs share three common ingredients that have been associated with improving teacher candidate preparation to teach all students, including EL students: (a) use of assessment data to inform program design and instruction, (b) institutional investment in mentoring as a form of effective professional development, and (c) engaging faculty and staff in collaboration and teamwork.[10]

Framing the Right Questions

Questions establish boundaries for the evaluation by stating which aspects of the program will be addressed. Depending on the purpose(s) or intent of the evaluation, questions can focus on operational aspects of the EL-infused program. For instance, stakeholders might want to study how the EL-infused initiatives operate together as a system of interventions to effect change within the operation of the program. Other questions can focus on the impact of program activities on teacher candidates' preparation to teach EL students. For example, stakeholders might want to examine the relationships between specific EL-infused activities and observed changes in teacher candidates' attitudes, practices, and achievement outcomes. Negotiating and prioritizing questions among stakeholders can further refine the overall focus for the evaluation.

We have emphasized the need for collaboration and teamwork among members of the evaluation team and stakeholders in planning for the project and the evaluation thereof. Collaboration and teamwork are critical when assessing the infusion team's effectiveness in achieving the stated program outcomes. In our work with EL-infused programs, we have focused primarily on key questions pertaining to the program operation and its impact on teacher candidate preparation to teach EL students in mainstream classrooms. Our questions have focused on (a) improving the quality, effectiveness, or efficiency of program activities; and (b) examining the relationships between program activities and observed changes in participant knowledge, skills, and dispositions to teach EL students. For example, in an outcome-oriented evaluation of an EL-infused program, members of the evaluation team and stakeholders worked together to first develop a shared understanding of what teacher candidates should know and be able to do. They then developed a mechanism for (a) determining the degree to which teacher candidates had acquired the knowledge, skills, and dispositions to teach EL students; and (b) responding to instances when they fall short on meeting program expectations.

Designing the Evaluation

Although various types of evaluation designs can be drawn from established scientific research traditions, none is intrinsically better than another, given the diversity of institutional and program structures. However, regardless of the institutional contexts, the evaluation team needs to select methods that directly address the specific questions identified and framed by stakeholders. Decisions regarding which evaluations methods or approaches to use also raise questions about how the evaluation will operate. With respect to evaluating EL-infused programs, discussions among the stakeholders might pertain to the degree to which program participants will be involved in the evaluation process, which and how data sources will be selected, what data collection instruments will be used, who will collect the data, what mechanisms will be needed to manage the data obtained, and what methods will be used to analyze, interpret, and disseminate the results of the evaluation. In general, experts agree that because evaluation methods have their own biases and limitations, evaluations that use a mix of qualitative and quantitative methods are generally more effective.

Selecting and Adapting Instrumentation

EL infusion program team members involved in the evaluation process should strive to collect information that will convey a well-rounded picture of the program and be seen as credible by the program's stakeholders. Although various types of data and data sources have limitations, an evaluation's overall credibility can be improved by identifying, developing, or adapting instruments that can capture the type of data needed to answer the key evaluation questions pertaining to overall program effectiveness and participant achievement outcomes.

To enhance the credibility of the evaluation, we recommend that all data collection instruments and procedures be adapted to the needs of the program and suited to the sources of information, data analysis plans, and strategies for disseminating the findings. Data collection instruments could include surveys of teacher candidates' perceived levels of preparation to teach EL students, tests or exams to gauge their knowledge of key understandings regarding the education of EL students, or rubrics to evaluate their skills in working with EL students; for example, during field experiences. Members of the evaluation team should carefully scrutinize these instruments to help ensure that they are well conceived and developed, and used to address program needs. In our EL infusion work, we identified an established instrument that was designed to determine general education student and faculty efficacy to teach all students, but we adapted it to meet the needs of our program, which was focused on the preparation of faculty and teacher candidates to teach EL students.

Collecting the Data

Conducting an EL infusion project evaluation involves the collection of data related to individuals, and thus requires careful consideration of its human subjects' protection. Members of the evaluation team should check plans for data collection, analysis, and reporting to ensure that the data sources are adequately protected and that the privacy and confidentiality of the information obtained is maintained.

Once the data collection instruments and procedures have been established, members of the evaluation team can devise an overall strategy for collecting the data to document the overall functioning of the EL-infused program activities and their impact on participant preparation to teach EL students. For purposes of evaluating EL-infused programs, we suggest giving special consideration to several key factors, including, but not limited to, (a) the volume of data to be collected, selecting multiple data sources to provide an opportunity to include different perspectives regarding the program and thus enhance the evaluation's credibility; (b) the type of data to be collected, integrating qualitative and quantitative data to increase the chances that the evidence base will be balanced and thereby meet the needs and expectations of diverse users; (c) the timing and frequency for collecting data (e.g., collecting specific types of data before, during, and after the implementation of EL content enables members of the evaluation team to determine program impact on participant learning); (d) the recruitment and training of individuals who will engage in data collection (e.g., experts recommend recruiting data collectors who have a shared lived experience with program participants and/or training them to collect data so as to help them become more attuned to the cultural context in which the program is situated); and (e) the reliability and usability of the data obtained so that it is viewed as useful and usable by its intended audiences.

The assessment data to be collected depend on the EL infusion programs' goals, both short- and long-term, and the evaluation questions identified in the conceptualization phase of the project. With respect to EL-infused program data, such data might include, but should not be limited to, (a) pre- and post faculty surveys, interviews, and focus groups to determine their perceptions of their own efficacy, knowledge, and attitudes relative to EL infusion; (b) document artifacts such as course syllabi, types of EL infusion instruction and assessment activities, and faculty ongoing reflections regarding their own professional learning; and (c) curricular maps to review of the depth and breadth of EL infusion work across educator preparation programs.

With respect to teacher candidate assessment data, data sources might include (a) student portfolios, which comprise various types of artifacts such as teaching philosophies, teaching videos, reflections, sample lessons, or other projects which document the teacher candidates' preparation to teach EL students in mainstream classrooms; (b) pre- and post surveys, interviews, and focus groups to determine the teacher candidates' perceptions of their own efficacy, knowledge, and attitudes relative to their preparation to teach EL students as well as cumulative exams relative to a candidate's knowledge of teaching EL students collected in EL-specific or EL-embedded courses; and (c) program completer certification test scores, documenting teacher candidate knowledge, skills, and dispositions to teach EL students.

Analyzing the Data

Consistent with the basic principles of culturally responsive evaluations, and given the types of data collected, members of the evaluation team need to use a mix of qualitative and quantitative data analysis methods. Doing so increases the chances that evaluation findings are balanced, thereby meeting the needs and expectations of diverse audiences. Because of the biases and limitations inherent in evaluation methods, Frierson and colleagues recommend creating a review panel consisting of representatives from program stakeholder groups to examine evaluation findings gathered by the project evaluator or evaluation team. [11] The creation of such a panel is likely to engage members of the evaluation team in discussions and generate deliberations that are more likely to reflect the complexities of the contexts in which the data were gathered and interpreted.

In our work with EL-infused programs in Ohio and Florida, we assigned different types of data analyses to different members of the evaluation team according to their expertise. For instance, one member of the evaluation team was in charge of analyzing survey data that required quantitative data analyses, while other members analyzed interview and focus group data, which required expertise in qualitative data analysis techniques. Members of the team then discussed the findings in light of the key project purposes and questions. This process helped a great deal in preparing for and writing an evaluation report that was shared with project stakeholders.

Disseminating and Utilizing the Results

The dissemination and use of EL-infused program outcomes represent integral parts of the evaluation process. We suggest that program evaluation findings be communicated to relevant audiences via timely, unbiased, and readable reports. Members of the program evaluation team should tailor the content to the intended audiences, explaining the focus of the evaluation, along with its limitations, strengths, and weaknesses. The information presented will ultimately be used to document the effectiveness of the EL-infused program activities, to determine the resulting benefits of these interventions on faculty practices and teacher candidates' preparation to effectively teach EL students, and to make recommendations for needed program improvements. Our sense is that, by building on the above guidelines for conducting a culturally responsive program evaluation, institutions can design and implement an evaluation system for their EL-infused programs that is developmental, culturally responsive, data-driven, and well-established.

However, we want to conclude this chapter with a cautionary note relative to EL-infused program evaluations. Because not all EL-infused programs are conceived and built alike, we suggest that educator preparation programs use their own insights, along with the guidelines offered in this chapter, to develop EL-infused programs that are responsive to their specific contextual needs. Although our prior and current work with EL infusion projects is derived from a specific model of infusion (including a blend of EL-infused activities, ESL elective courses, extended EL-focused field experiences, and optional completion of specialized ESL-specific coursework, which leads to an EL certificate), our efforts in this chapter focus on general principles that underlie the evaluation of effective EL infusion programs.

The lessons learned from our prior experiences with EL infusion projects indicate that the above key principles, which build on the interrelated benefits of interdisciplinarity, effective instruction and assessment of ELs in preK–12 mainstream classrooms, and instructional design (see chapter 3 for an expanded discussion of these critical components), can be applied to a diverse array of educator preparation settings. While the structure and governance of EL-infused programs can vary as widely as the teacher candidates they seek to serve, the degree to which educator preparation programs apply the principles of high quality EL infusion determine whether the program will lead to enhanced teacher candidate practices and student achievement outcomes.

Notes

Introduction

1. Claude Goldenberg, "Teaching English Language Learners: What the Research Does—and Does Not—Say," *American Educator* 32, no. 2 (Summer 2008): 11–23, 42–43.

2. Ibid.

3. State Title III Directors and 2007/08 State CSPR; National Clearinghouse for English Language Acquisition and Language Instruction Educational Programs (NCELA). *The Growing Numbers of Limited English Proficient Students, 1997/98–2007/08* (Washington, DC: NCELA, The George Washington University, 2010), www.ncela.gwu.edu.

4. Ibid.

5. Wendy Grigg, Patricia Donahue, and Gloria Dion, "The Nation's Report Card: 12thGrade Reading and Mathematics 2005 (NCES 2007-468), U.S. Department of Education, National Center for Education Statistics, (Washington DC: U.S. Government Printing Office, 2007); Jihyun Lee, Wendy Grigg, and Patricia Donahue, *The Nation's Report Card: Reading 2007* (NCES 2007-496), U.S. Department of Education, National Center for Education Statistics (Washington DC: U.S. Government Printing Office, 2007).

6. Jim Cummins, "Language Development and Academic Learning," in *Language, Culture and Cognition: A Collection of Studies in First and Second Language Acquisition*, ed. Lillian Malave and Georges Duquette (Bristol, PA: Multilingual Matters, 1991): 161–175.

7. Cummins's research indicates that it takes five to seven years for ELs to develop the academic language proficiency required for grade-level performance.

8. Committee on the Study of Teacher Preparation Programs in the United States, 2010, *Preparing Teachers: Building evidence for sound policy*, National Research Council. (Washington, DC:, National Academy Press, 2010).

9. Diane August and Timothy Shanahan, *Developing Literacy In Second-Language Learners: Report of the National Literacy Panel on Language-Minority Children and Youth* (Mahwah, NJ: Erlbaum, 2006).

10. Kristin L. McGraner and Laura Saenz, *Preparing Teachers of English Language Learners. (*Washington, DC: National Comprehensive Center for Teacher Quality, 2009).

11. National Center for Education Statistics, "Teacher Quality: A Report on the Preparation and Qualifications of Public School Teachers" (Washington, DC: U. S. Department of Education, 1999).

12. National Center for Educational Statistics, "The Condition of Education 2005—Indicator 5: Language Minority School-Age Children" (Washington, DC: U. S. Department of Education, 2006).

13. Beth Antunez, "The Preparation And Professional Development of Teachers of English Language Learners," ERIC Document ED 477-724 (Washington, DC: ERIC Clearinghouse on Teaching & Teacher Education, 2002).

14. Kate Menken, Beth Antunez, Mary E. Dilworth, and Said Yasin, *An Overview of the Preparation and Certification of Teachers Working with Limited English Proficient (LEP) Students* (Washington, DC: National Clearinghouse for Bilingual Education, 2001).

15. Ibid.

16. Keira Gebbie Ballantyne, Alicia R. Sanderman, and Jack Levy, *Educating English Language Learners: Building Teacher Capacity* (Washington, DC: National Clearinghouse for English Language Acquisition, 2008) http://www.ncela.gwu.edu/practice/mainstream_teachers.htm.

17. Ibid.

18. Susan M. Gass and Alison Mackey, "Input, Interaction, and Output: An Overview," *AILA Review* 19 (2006): 3–17.

19. *Input:* Stephen D. Krashen, *The Input Hypothesis: Issues and Implications,* (New York: Longman, 1985); *output:* Merill Swain, "Communicative Competence: Some Roles Of Comprehensible Input And Comprehensible Output In Its Development." In *Input in Second Language Acquisition*, eds. Susan M. Gass and C. G. Madden, (Rowley, MA: Newbury House, 1985); *interaction:* Michael M. Long, "The Role of Linguistic Environment in Second Language Acquisition," in *The New Handbook Of Second Language Acquisition,* eds. William C. Ritchie and Taj K. Bhatia. San Diego: Academic Press, 1996; and Gass and Mackey, "Input, Interaction, and Output: An Overview."

20. Wayne P. Thomas and Virginia P. Collier, *A National Study of School Effectiveness for Language Minority Students' Long-Term Academic Achievement* (Santa Cruz, CA: Center for Research on Education, Diversity and Excellence, University of California-Santa Cruz, 2002), http://crede.berkeley.edu/research/llaa/1.1_final.html. Although bilingual approaches have been shown to lead to improved outcomes for ELs, our discussion focuses on the traditional ESL model since it is more widely used throughout the nation. This is especially true in areas that have not traditionally served large populations of ELs (see Thomas and Collier).

21. Rod Ellis, *The Study of Second Language Acquisition,* 2nd edition (Oxford: Oxford University Press, 2008).

22. Cummins, "Language Development and Academic Learning."

23. TESOL, *ESL Standards for Pre-K–12 Students*, (Alexandria, VA: Author, 1997), 77.

24. Cummins, "Language Development and Academic Learning." Cummins's research has shown that developing social language can take up to three years, but reaching proficiency in academic language can take seven years or more.

25. Ellis, *Second Language Acquisition.*

26. Anna Uhl Chamot and J. Michael O'Malley, *The CALLA Handbook: Implementing The Cognitive Academic Language Learning Approach (*Reading, MA: Addison-Wesley, 1994); William Grabe and Fredricka L. Stoller, "Content-Based Instruction: Research Foundations," in *The Content-Based Classroom: Perspectives on Integrating Language and Content*, eds. Marguerite Ann Snow and Donna M. Brinton (White Plains, NY: Longman, 1997), 5–21; Jana J. Echevarria, MaryEllen J. Vogt, and Deborah J. Short, *Making Content Comprehensible for English Learners: The SIOP Model (*New York: Allyn & Bacon, 2008).

27. Tamara Lucas, *Teacher Preparation for Linguistically Diverse Classrooms: A Resource for Teacher Educators* (New York: Routledge, 2011), xiv.

28. Minnie Cardona, e-mail message to author, June 21, 2011.

Chapter 1

1. Tamara Lucas and Jaime Grinberg, "Responding to the Linguistic Reality of Mainstream Classrooms: Preparing All Teachers to Teach English Language Learners," in *Handbook of Research on Teacher Education,* 3rd ed. (New York: Routledge, 2008), 606–636.

2. Stephen Fallows and Christine Steven, *Integrating Key Skills in Higher Education* (London: Kogan Page, 2000).

3. University of Central Florida, "The Unifying Theme," http://www.unifyingtheme.ucf.edu/; Faculty Center for Teaching and Learning. "Teaching Sustainability," http://www.fctl.ucf.edu/TeachingAndLearningResources/SelectedPedagogies/TeachingSustainability/.

4. *Vannatta and O'Bannon:* Rachel A. Vannatta and Blanche W. O'Bannon, "Beginning to Put the Pieces Together: A Technology Infusion Model for Teacher Education," *Journal of Computing in Teacher*

Education 18, no. 4 (2002): 112–123; *essential conditions for technology integration:* International Society for Technology in Education, *National Educational Technology Standards for Teachers: Preparing Teachers to Use Technology.* (Eugene, OR: International Society for Technology in Education [ISTE], 2002).

5. Toni R. Van Laarhoven, Dennis D. Munk, Kathleen Lynch, Julie Bosma, and Joanne Rouse, "A Model for Preparing Special and General Education Preservice Teachers for Inclusive Education," *Journal of Teacher Education* 58, no. 5 (2007): 440–455.

6. We refer to those who teach English language learners exclusively as ESL or bilingual specialists and to those who teach ELs together with native speakers as teachers of ELs.

7. Examples of EL-focused topics include characteristics of ELs, stages of SLA, accommodating English learner needs in instruction and assessment, among many others. These will be explained in detail in chapter 3.

8. See www.reading.org; www.tesol.org.

9. P. Gibbons, *Scaffolding Language, Scaffolding Learning: Teaching Second Language Learners in the Mainstream Classroom* (Portsmouth, NH: Heinemann, 2002); C. E. Hite and L. S. Evans, "Mainstream First-Grade Teachers' Understanding of Strategies for Accommodating the Needs of English Language Learners," *Teacher Education Quarterly* 33, no. 2 (2002): 89–110.

10. Jana J. Echevarria, MaryEllen J. Vogt, and Deborah J. Short, *Making Content Comprehensible For English Learners: The SIOP Model* (New York, NY: Allyn & Bacon, 2008).

11. Lucas and Grinberg, "Responding to the Linguistic Reality of Mainstream Classrooms"; Aida Walqui "The Development of Teacher Expertise to Work with Adolescent English Learners: A Model and a Few Priorities," in *Inclusive Pedagogy for English Language Learners*, eds. L. Verplaetse and N. Migliacci (New York: Lawrence Erlbaum Associates, 2007).

12. Jennifer Costa, Gary McPhail, Janet Smith, and María Estela Brisk, "Faculty First: The Challenge of Infusing the Teacher Education Curriculum with Scholarship on English Language Learners," in *Journal of Teacher Education*, 56, no. 2(2005): 104–118; Antoinette Gagné, "Preparing Every Teacher to Be an ESL Teacher: The OISE/UT Experience. *Contact* 28, no. 3 (2002): 34–39; Carla Meskill, "Infusing English Language Learner Issues Throughout Professional Educator Curricula: The Training All Teachers Project," *Teachers College Record* 107, no. 4 (2005): 739-756; Joyce Nutta and Kim Stoddard, "Reducing the Confusion about Infusion: A Collaborative Process of Infusing ESOL into Special Education Teacher Preparation," in *Florida Journal of Teacher Education,* 8(2005): 21–32; see ESOL infusion video @ http://tapestry.usf.edu/video-lectures.html.

13. Gagné, "Preparing Every Teacher to Be an ESL Teacher"; Antoinette Gagné "The Impact of Infusing ESL Issues and Teaching Strategies in Pre-Service Teacher Education Programs" (Research proposal abstract, Social Sciences and Humanities Research Council of Canada (SSHRC), 2002).

14. Nutta and Stoddard, "Reducing the Confusion about Infusion." 2005; Costa et al. "Faculty First."

15. Meskill, "Infusing English Language Learner Issues Throughout Professional Educator Curricula, 2005."

16. "Tapestry," http://tapestry.usf.edu; Nutta and Stoddard, "Reducing the Confusion about Infusion."

17. "Tapestry," http://tapestry.usf.edu.

Chapter 2

1. *League of United Latin American Citizens (LULAC) et al. v. State Board of Education Consent Decree*, United States District Court for the Southern District of Florida (August 14, 1990), "The Florida Consent Decree," http://www.fldoe.org/aala/lulac.asp.

2. In Florida, the term *ESOL* is used instead of *ESL*. This book uses *ESL* when referring to the field in general and ESOL when referring to the Florida ESOL endorsement or the Florida ESOL endorsement standards.

3. Mary Elizabeth Wilson-Patton, "A Legal Study of the Florida ESOL Consent Decree: From Initiation through Fifth Year Implementation" (PhD diss., Florida State University, 2000).

4. Laws of Florida, Ch. 95-306, Section 2, p. 2763; cited in ibid., 839.

5. As detailed in chapters 1 and 3, the One Plus model refers to EL infusion rather than ESOL infusion to indicate that its purpose is to prepare mainstream teachers of ELs rather than ESL specialists. To describe the Florida model discussed in this chapter, the terms *ESOL endorsement through infusion* and ESOL infusion are used.

6. Florida State Board of Education Rule 6A-5.066, F.A.C., Section 240.529, F.S. (March 16, 2006).

7. "Preparing Florida Teachers to Work with Limited English Proficient Students," http://www.fldoe.org/profdev/pdf/final_esol.pdf.

8. Florida Department of Education Bureau of Education Recruitment and Professional Development, "Preparing Florida Teachers to Work with Limited English Proficient Students," http://www.fldoe.org/profdev/pdf/final_esol.pdf.

9. Phillip Smith, "Teaching Inclusivity: Preservice Teachers' Perceptions of their Knowledge, Skills and Attitudes toward Working with English Language Learners in Mainstream Classrooms," *Tapestry Journal* 3, no. 1 (2011), http://www.tapestry.usf.edu/journal/documents/v03n01/Smith percent20FORMATTED.pdf.

10. Ernest L. Boyer, *Scholarship Reconsidered: Priorities of the professoriate* (San Francisco: Jossey-Bass, 1997).

11. Common Core State Standards Initiative, accessed November 1, 2011, http://www.corestandards.org/the-standards/english-language-arts-standards/writing-6-12/grade-11-12/ .

12. "Rate of LEP Growth 1997–98 to 2007–08," http://www.ncela.gwu.edu/t3sis/state/ohio/data.

13. Martha Castañeda, Amy Fisher-Young, and Bruce Perry, "ESOL MIAMI Project: An Overview," *AccELLerate!* 2, no. 3, (Spring 2010).

14. Maria R. Coady, Ester J. de Jong, and Candice Harper, "Preservice to Practice: Mainstream Teacher Beliefs of Preparation and Efficacy with English Language Learners in the State of Florida," *Bilingual Research Journal* 34, no. 2 (2011); Maria R. Coady, Candice Harper, & Ester J. de Jong, "Quality Teacher Preparation for ELLs: Preliminary Findings from Florida," *AccELLerate!* 2 no. 2 (2010): 8-10; Maria R. Coady, Candice Harper, & Ester J. de Jong, (2011). Project DELTA: Preliminary Findings from the State of Florida" (paper presented at Sanibel Leadership Conference, Clearwater, Florida, June 24, 2011).

15. U.S. Department of Education, Institute of Education Sciences, National Center for Education Statistics, 2005, 2007, 2009 Reading Assessments.

16. Joanne Urrutia, Sanibel Leadership Conference, Clearwater, Florida, June 24, 2011.

Chapter 3

1. Joyce Nutta, Nazan U. Bautista, and Malcolm B. Butler, *Teaching Science to English Language Learners* (New York: Routledge, 2011).

2. Joel Colbert, Kimberly Trimble, and Peter Desberg, *The Case for Education: Contemporary Approaches for Using Case Methods* (Boston: Allyn and Bacon, 1996).

3. Julie T. Klein, "Blurring, Cracking, and Crossing: Permeation and the Fracturing of Discipline," in *Interdisciplinarity: Essays From the Literature*, ed. William H. Newell (New York: College Entrance Examination Board, 1998), 273–295.

4. Ernest L. Boyer. *Scholarship Reconsidered* (San Francisco: Jossey-Bass, 1990), 21.

5. William H. Newell, ed. *Interdisciplinarity: Essays from the Literature* (New York: The College Board, 1998), 53.

6. Allen F. Repko, "Interdisciplinary Curriculum Design," *Academic Exchange Quarterly* 11, no. 1 (2007): 130–137.

7. Tony Becher, *Academic Tribes and Territories: Intellectual Enquiry and the Cultures of Disciplines* (Milton Keynes, UK: Society for Research in to Higher Education and Open University Press, 1989).

8. National Center for Education Statistics, "The Nation's Report Card: Mathematics 2009*,*" accessed August 7, 2011, http://nationsreportcard.gov/math_2009/.

9. Teachers of English to Speakers of Other Languages, "TESOL/NCATE Standards for the Recognition of Initial Tesol Programs in P–12 ESL Teacher Education," http://www.tesol.org/s_tesol/bin.asp?CID=219&DID=13040&DOC=FILE.PDF.

10. Keira Gebbie Ballantyne, Alicia R. Sanderman, and Jack Levy, "Educating English Language Learners: Building Teacher Capacity," http://www.ncela.gwu.edu/files/uploads/3/EducatingELLsBuildingTeacherCapacityVol1.pdf.

11. For more information on culturally responsive lessons, see Gloria Ladson-Billings, "Toward a Theory of Culturally Relevant Pedagogy," *American Educational Research Journal* 32, no. 3 (1995): 465–491. For more information on funds of knowledge, see Luis C. Moll, Cathy Amanti, Deborah Neff, and Norma Gonzalez, "Funds of Knowledge for Teaching: Using a Qualitative Approach to Connect Homes and Classrooms," *Theory into Practice* 31, no.2 (2001): 132–141.

12. Florida Department of Education, "Florida Teacher Standards for ESOL Endorsement 2010," Bureau of Student Achievement Through Language Acquisition, http://www.fldoe.org/aala/pdf/ApprovedTeacherStandards.pdf.

13. We use *outcomes* to describe our proposed credentials for teaching English learners (e.g., EL-qualified for teaching language arts). We use *EL curricular competencies* to describe national or state standards or competencies adopted, adapted, or developed by the program as outcome measures of candidates' knowledge, skills, and dispositions for teaching English learners.

14. Walter Dick, Lou Carey, and James O. Carey, *The Systematic Design of Instruction*, 5th ed. (New York: Longman, 2001); Patricia L. Smith and Tillman J. Ragan, *Instructional Design*, 2nd ed. (Columbus, OH: Merrill, Prentice Hall, 1999).

15. The National Council for Accreditation of Teacher Education, *Unit Standards in Effect 2008*, http://www.ncate.org/Standards/NCATEUnitStandards/UnitStandardsinEffect2008/tabid/476/Default.aspx.

Chapter 4

1. Roberta G. Sands, L. Alayne Parson and Josann Duane, "Faculty Mentoring Faculty in a Public University," *The Journal of Higher Education* 6, no. 2 (1991): 174-193.

2. Ann Darwin and Edward Palmer, "Mentoring Circles in Higher Education," *Higher Education Research & Development* 28, no. 2 (2009): 125–136; Sands, Parson, and Duane, "Faculty Mentoring"; Luna Gaye and Deborah L. Cullen, *Empowering the Faculty: Mentoring Redirected and Renewed*, ASHE-ERIC Higher Education Report No. 3. (Washington, DC: The George Washington University, Graduate School of Education and Human Development, 1995).

3. At first, our primary reason for leaning toward conducting faculty development and undertaking the process of embedding EL content simultaneously was the fear that if the latter had to occur after the former is completed, the entire EL infusion project would remain unfinished or be quickly wrapped up in a haphazard fashion when participants lost interest or were distracted by the many obligations in academe. While working with faculty in Florida on "re-infusing" the EL content as a result of the new standards, we also noticed that some teacher preparation faculty who had completed the EL faculty development several years needed a small refresher of EL content that they were going to embed in new and different ways.

4. Carol A. Mullen, "Constructing Co-Mentoring Partnerships: Walkways We Must Travel," *Theory into Practice* 39, no. 1 (2000): 4–11; Frances K. Kochan and Susan B. Trimble, "From Mentoring to Co-Mentoring: Establishing Collaborative Relationships," *Theory into Practice* 39, no. 1 (2000): 21–28.

5. For those interested in reading up on the history of mentoring as well as newer approaches to mentoring in higher education, we recommend the special issue "New Visions of Mentoring" of *Theory into Practice* 39, no. 1 (Winter 2000).

6. Mullen, "Constructing Co-Mentoring Partnerships"; Lois J. Zachary, *The Mentor's Guide: Facilitating Effective Learning Relationships* (San Franscisco: Jossey-Bass, 2000).

7. Technically speaking, faculty development, which is detailed in chapter 5 begins before the mentoring process. Therefore, some readers may want to consult chapter 5 before reading the remainder of this chapter.

8. Kathy E. Kram and Lynn A. Isabella, "Mentoring Alternatives: The Role of Peer Relationships in Career Development," *Academy of Management Journal* 28, no. 1 (1985): 110–132.

9. Sands, Parsons, and Duane, "Faculty Mentoring Faculty in a Public University."

10. Karen W. Verkler and Cynthia Hutchinson, "You Can Lead a Horse to Water but . . . ESOL Faculty Mentors Reflect on Their Experiences," *SRATE Journal* 11, no. 1 (2002): 16–28.

11. Carla Meskill, "Infusing English Language Learner Issues Throughout Professional Educator Curricula: The Training All Teachers Project," *Teachers College Record* 107, no. 4 (2005): 739–756; Sean J. Smith and Blanche O'Bannon, "Faculty Members Infusing Technology Across Teacher Education: A Mentorship Model," *Teacher Education and Special Education* 22, no. 2 (1999): 123–135.

12. Jennifer Costa, Gary McPhail, Janet Smith, and María Estela Brisk, "Faculty First: The Challenge of Infusing the Teacher Education Curriculum with Scholarship on English Language Learners," in *Journal of Teacher Education* 56, no. 2 (2005): 104–118.

13. If graduate students are utilized for this purpose, the institution should make sure that they are individuals with in-field experience teaching English learners, rather than students who are acquiring the exact same knowledge and skills they are presenting to the teacher preparation faculty. In other words, they should be pursuing a doctorate degree in bilingual education or ESL, rather than a master's of arts in ESOL, which often comprises a first introduction to the discipline. Any training sessions conducted by graduate assistants, though, should be guided by the ESL faculty or ESL expert consultant.

14. Walter Dick, Lou Carey, and James O. Carey, *The Systematic Design of Instruction,* 5th ed. (New York: Longman, 2001); Patricia L. Smith and Tillman J. Ragan, *Instructional Design,* 2nd ed. (Columbus, OH: Merrill, Prentice Hall, 1999).

15. The reason for this difference lies partially in the number of hours of suggested faculty development for each course category of the One Plus model. Chapter 5 explains the cumulative nature of faculty development: teacher educators whose courses focus on planning and implementing curriculum, instruction, and assessment require pedagogical competencies in addition to those of 1+ course faculty whose content focuses on the learner and the learning context. Similarly, the more course elements that need to contain an EL focus, the more assistance the mentor will need to provide in terms of designing meaningful connections between the existing course topics and identifying information, material, or media to be used as the basis for the activities and assignments.

16. There are two slightly different versions of the content examination portion in this form. The first is intended for 1+ courses, since these courses do not require candidates to develop and implement curriculum, instruction, or assessment. If graduate assistants with expertise in bilingual education or ESL are part of the faculty development team, they may help the mentor in the pre-infusion review tasks after they have been adequately trained in the expectations for embedding content at each level.

17. The danger of superficial infusion has been noted by the Center for Instructional Development and Research at the University of Washington, where Schmitz invited the faculty who infused diversity issues into courses university-wide to ask themselves how they "can integrate new material so that it is not simply an 'add-on'"; Betty Schmitz, "Transforming a Course," *CIDR Teaching and Learning Bulletin* 2, no. 4 (1999), http://depts.washington.edu/cidrweb/Bulletin/Transforming.pdf.

18. If multiple faculty members typically teach this course and no one faculty member has been designated as the course leader, then all members should be present, as the infused elements will need to be consistent across all sections in order to assure equal coverage for all candidates.

19. Carla Meskill, "Infusing English Language Learner Issues Throughout Professional Educator Curricula."

Chapter 5

1. Thomas H. Levine and Elizabeth Howard, "Developing a Faculty Learning Community to Improve Preservice Teacher's Capacity to Teach ELLs" (paper presented at the American Association of Colleges of Teacher Education annual conference, Atlanta, GA. February, 2010). The candidate instrument is called "Teaching English Language Learners Self-Efficacy Scales (TELLSES)" and the faculty version had been named the "Teacher Educator Self-Assessment of Capacity for Preparing Teachers for English Language Learners (TESCAPTELL)."

2. Woolfolk-Hoy's instrument, the directions for scoring both the long and the short form, and other information related to the *Teacher Sense of Efficacy Scale* are available at http://people.ehe.ohio-state.edu/ahoy/research/instruments/.

3. U.S. Department of Education Office of English Language Acquisition National Professional Development grant, ESOL MIAMI, 2007-2012.

4. These are: ESL Methods, Curriculum, Assessment, Culture, and Applied Linguistics.

5. Carla Meskill, "Infusing English Language Learner Issues Throughout Professional Educator Curricula: The Training All Teachers Project," *Teachers College Record* 107, no. 4 (2005): 739–756; Levine and Howard, "Developing a Faculty Learning Community"; Jennifer Costa, Gary McPhail, Janet Smith, and María Estela Brisk, "Faculty First: The Challenge of Infusing the Teacher Education Curriculum with Scholarship on English Language Learners," in *Journal of Teacher Education*, 56, no. 2 (2005): 104–118.

6. All faculty should be invited to participate in the launch event, but attendance by those faculty who will be embedding the content and who are teaching in that program should be required, if at all possible.

7. As described in chapter 3 and depicted in tables 3.1 and 3.2 and figure 3.1, respectively.

8. We have used this approach with great success in introducing faculty to EL infusion and in providing in-service professional development in preK–12 schools. A similar "shock-therapy" approach is also described in Meskill's article "Infusing English Language Learner Issues Throughout Professional Educator Curricula."

9. As shown in table 5.1, faculty teaching 1+ courses do not require the coverage of 2+ and 3+ course topics, but should be invited to go through all levels. Similarly, 2+ course faculty members should be invited to attend 3+ level sessions, even though the content covered in those sessions exceeds the knowledge and skills their candidates have to master in their course.

10. In states where teacher preparation programs deal with questions of compliance, the faculty may have to provide proof of prior coursework or experience before any component of the faculty development can be reduced.

11. Karen W. Verkler, "Teacher Educators as Students: A University Shares Its Faculty ESOL Professional Development Model," *Foreign Language Annals* 36, no. 2 (2003): 208–222. The faculty involved in Project Jericho, the EL infusion effort in Florida described in this article, signed contracts to infuse their syllabi with EL competencies.

12. Although the series was originally designed for faculty development, the authors use selected video lectures in their own teacher preparation courses and have received feedback that they are also being used within teacher preparation courses and in-service workshops throughout the United States.

13. The first six modules were developed under the original grant work and are still used by the University of South Florida as training materials and modules for faculty who teach EL-embedded courses and need to satisfy the Florida Department of Education's training requirements. The subsequent modules have been produced under the ESOL MIAMI grant funding.

14. In Florida, where the state mandates that each instructor of an EL-embedded course fulfill forty-five hours of EL content training, an institutional professional development plan that stipulates the time frame within which the faculty development must be completed is required.

15. This is because no time is required to select the EL content materials and design the activities, assignments, and/or assessments.

16. Now commonly referred to as the *scholarship of teaching and learning*; see Ernest L. Boyer, *Scholarship Reconsidered: Priorities of the Professoriate* (Princeton, NJ: Carnegie Foundation for the Advancement of Teaching, 1990), 19 and 80.

17. William H. Newell, ed. *Interdisciplinarity: Essays from the Literature* (New York: The College Board, 1998), 53.

18. Boyer, *Scholarship Reconsidered,* 80.

19. Mary Taylor Huber, Pat Hutchings, and Lee S. Shulman, "The Scholarship of Teaching and Learning Today," in *Faculty Priorities Reconsidered*, eds. KerryAnn O'Meara, and R. Eugene Rice (San Francisco: Jossey-Bass, 2005), 34–38.

20. For example, Joyce W. Nutta and Kim Stoddard, "Reducing the Confusion About Infusion: A Collaborative Process of Infusing ESOL into Special Education Teacher Preparation," *Florida Journal of Teacher Education* 8 (2005): 21–32; Verkler, "Teacher Educators as Students"; and Karen W. Verkler and Cynthia Hutchinson, "You Can Lead a Horse to Water but . . . ESOL Faculty Mentors Reflect on Their Experiences," *SRATE Journal* 11, no. 1 (2002): 16–28.

21. John M. Braxton, William Luckey, and Patricia Helland, *Institutionalizing a Broader View of Scholarship Through Boyer's Four Domains* (San Francisco: Jossey-Bass, 2002), 117; Boyer also includes the *scholarship of discovery* and the *scholarship of application* (Boyer, *Scholarship Reconsidered*).

Chapter 6

1. Merton Hill, "A Call for the Americanization of Mexican-American Children [1928]," in *Readings in Sociocultural Studies in Education* (6th ed.), ed. Kathleen Knight Abowitz (Boston: McGraw-Hill Learning Solutions, 2006), chapter 50.

2. "Thinking Box: Theories of Assimilation," in *Readings in Sociocultural Studies in Education* (6th ed.), ed. Kathleen Knight Abowitz (Boston: McGraw-Hill Learning Solutions, 2006), p. 322.

3. Joyce Nutta and Kim Stoddard, "Reducing the Confusion About Infusion: A Collaborative Process of Infusing ESOL into Special Education Teacher Preparation," *Florida Journal of Teacher Education* 8 (2005): 21–32.

Chapter 7

1. Joyce W. Nutta, Nazan U. Bautista, and Malcolm B. Butler, "What We Know from Research," in *Teaching science to English language learners*, eds. Joyce. W. Nutta, Nazan U. Bautista, and Malcom B. Butler (New York, Routledge, 2010), 38–56.

2. Ronald W. Solorzano, "High Stakes Testing: Issues, Implications, and Remedies for English Language Learners," Review of Educational Research 78 no. 2 (2008): 260.

3. Thomas P. Carpenter and Rich Lehrer, "Teaching and Learning Mathematics with Understanding," in Mathematics Classrooms That Promote Understanding, (Mahwah, NJ: Lawrence Erlbaum Associates, 1999); Gina Borgioli, "Equity for English Language Learners in Mathematics Classrooms," Teaching Children Mathematics 15, no. 3 (2008): 185–191.

4. Noah Borrero and Shawn Bird, Closing the Achievement Gap: How to Pinpoint Student Strengths to Differentiate Instruction and Help Your Striving Readers Succeed (New York: Scholastic, 2009).

5. RTI = Response to Intervention; IFSP = Individualized Family Service Plan; IEP = Individualized Education Program; ITP = Individualized Transition Program.

6. Jim Cummins, "Interdependence of First- and Second-Language Proficiency in Bilingual Children," in *Language Processing in Bilingual Children,* ed. Ellen Bialystok (Cambridge, UK: Cambridge University Press, 2000).

Chapter 8

1. National Universal Design for Learning Task Force, "Universal Design for Learning," accessed September 3, 2011, http://www.advocacyinstitute.org/UDL/.

2. Jim Burke, *The English Teacher's Companion*, 3rd ed. (Portsmouth, NH: Heinemann, 2007); Jeff Wilhelm, *"You Gotta BE the Book": Teaching Engaged and Reflective Reading with Adolescents*, 2nd ed. (New York: Teachers College Press, 2007).

3. Ann Jaramillo, *La Línea* (New York: Square Fish, 2008); An Na, *A Step from Heaven* (New York: Penguin, 2002).

4. Gary Paulsen, *The Crossing* (New York: Dell Laurel-Leaf, 1990).

5. Will Hobbs, *Crossing the Wire* (New York: HarperCollins, 2007).

6. Sonia Nazario, *Enrique's Journey* (New York: Random House, 2007).

7. Kris Peterson, e-mail to author, August 16, 2010.

8. *Which Way Home?* directed by Rebecca Cammisa, (New York: HBO, 2009).

9. Sandra Cisneros, *The House on Mango Street* (New York: Random House, 1991).

10. Na, *A Step from Heaven,* 24.

11. Ibid.

12. Ibid., 9.

13. Ibid., 30.

14. Ibid., 31.

15. Ibid.

16. Ibid., 52 and 101.

17. Ibid., 38.

18. Ibid., 39.

19. Ibid., 68.

20. Jamie Gilson, *Hello, My Name Is Scrambled Eggs* (New York: Luthrop, Lee, & Shepard Books, 1985).

21. Linda Crew, *Children of the River* (New York: Delacorte Press, 1989).

22. Pam Muñoz Ryan, *Esperanza Rising* (New York: Scholastic, 2000); Gene Luen Young, *American Born Chinese* (New York: First Second, 2007).

23. Francisco Jiménez, *The Circuit* (Boston: Houghton Mifflin, 1998); Francisco Jimenez, *Breaking Through* (Boston: Houghton Mifflin, 2001).

24. Sonya Sones, *What My Mother Doesn't Know* (New York: Simon Pulse, 2003); Ann E. Burg, *All the Broken Pieces* (New York: Scholastic, 2009); Margarita Engle, *The Surrender Tree: Poems of Cuba's Struggle for Freedom* (New York: Square Fish, 2010); Helen Frost, *Keesha's House* (New York: Farrar, Straus, and Giroux, 2007); Katherine Applegate, *Home of the Brave* (New York: Square Fish, 2008); Carole Boston Weatherford, *Becoming Billie Holiday* (Honesdale, PA: Wordsong, 2008).

25. National Universal Design for Learning Task Force, "National Universal Design for Learning Task Force, "Universal Design for Learning," http://www.udlcenter.org.

Chapter 9

1. Maya Angelou, *I Know Why the Caged Bird Sings* (New York: Bantam, 1983).

2. *Publication Manual of the American Psychological Association,* 6th ed. 2010. Washington, DC: American Psychological Association.

3. American School Counselor Association, *Ethical Standards for School Counselors*, Alexandria, VA, 2010; Zaida McCall-Perez, "The Counselor as Advocate for English Language Learners: An Action Research Approach," *Professional School Counseling* 4, no. 1(2000): 13–23.

4. Alan W. Burkard, Michael J. Martinez, and Casey A. Holtz, "Closing the Achievement Gap: School Counselors' Social Justice Imperative," in *Handbook of Multicultural Counseling,* ed. Joseph G. Ponterotto (Thousand Oaks, CA: Sage, 2009), 547-561.; Jeannie Park-Taylor, Allison B. Ventura, Mary Walsh, "Creating Healthy Acculturation Pathways: Integrating Theory and Research to

Inform Counselors' Work with Immigrant Children," *Professional School Counseling* 11, no. 1, (2007): 25–34; S. Kent Butler, and Franklyn C. Williams, "Concerns of Newly Arrived Immigrant Students: Implications for School Counselors," *Professional School Counseling* 7, no. 1 (2003): 9–14; Michelle L. Spomer, and Emoy L. Cowen, "A Comparison of the School Mental Health Referrals Profile of Young ESL and English Speaking Children," *Journal of Community Psychology* 29, no. 1 (2001): 69–82.

5. Joy J., Burnham, Miguel Mantero, and Lisa M. Hooper, "Experiential Training: Connecting School Counselors-in-Training, English as a Second Language (ESL) Teachers and ESL Students," *Journal of Multicultural Counseling and Development* 37, no.1. (2009): 2–14; Micheline Hagan, "Acculturation and an ESL program: A Service-Learning Project," *Journal of Multicultural Counseling and Development* 32 (2004):, 443–448; Gargi Roysircar, Gregory Gard, Robert Hubbell, and Marilyn Ortega, "Development of Counseling Trainees' Multicultural Awareness Through Mentoring English as a Second Language Students," *Journal of Multicultural Counseling and Development* 33 (2005): 17–36.

6. Rosemarye T. Taylor, *Leading learning: Change Student Achievement Today!* Thousand Oaks, CA: Corwin Press, 2010.

7. Willis Hawley and Rebecca James, "Diversity-Responsive School Leadership," *UCEA Review* 51 (2010): 1–5.

Chapter 10

1. In referring to language arts and literacy teacher candidates we mean candidates whose certification area will include the instruction of language arts and/or literacy. This may be at the early childhood, elementary, middle, or high school levels and may be the only subject taught (i.e., reading coaches, literacy specialists, secondary language arts teachers) or may be one of many subjects taught, as with early childhood and elementary teacher candidates. In some circumstances, exceptional education candidates with responsibility for teaching language arts would also fit in this classification. We contrast language arts and literacy teachers with academic subject teachers in the type of preparation needed to teach and assess ELs in the mainstream classroom. Please see chapter 3 for more details.

2. T. Lucas, A.M. Villegas, and M. Freedson-González, "Linguistically Responsive Teacher Education,"*Journal of Teacher Education*,59, no. 4 (2008): 361–373.

3. Ibid; Lily Wong-Fillmore and Catherine E. Snow, "What Teachers Need to Know About Language," in *What Teachers Need to Know About Language*, ed. Carolyn T. Adger et al. (Washington, DC: Center for Applied Linguistics, 2002), 7–53.

4. A separate course for Exceptional Education teacher candidates, concentrating on the teaching and assessment of ELs with special needs, is also an option. Alternatives could be to include these candidates in any of the three versions of the course, depending on program and candidate needs.

5. A separate course for Exceptional Education teacher candidates, which uses language acquisition principles to distinguish between a language difference and a language disorder and to address language and literacy development for ELs with special needs, is also an option.

6. Keira Gebbie Ballantyne, Alicia R. Sanderman, and Jack Levy, "Educating English Language Learners: Building Teacher Capacity," http://www.ncela.gwu.edu/files/uploads/3/EducatingELLsBuildingTeacherCapacityVol1.pdf.

7. Diane August and Kenji Hakuta, eds., *Educating Language Minority Children* (Washington, DC: National Academy Press, 1998).

8. Josue M. Gonzalez and Linda Darling-Hammond, *New Concepts for New Challenges: Professional Development for Immigrant Youth* (McHenry, IL, and Washington, DC: Delta Systems and Center for Applied Linguistics, 1997); Tamara Lucas, Ana María Villegas, and Margaret Freedson-Gonzalez, "Linguistically Responsive Teacher Education: Preparing Classroom Teachers to Teach English

Language Learners," *Journal of Teacher Education* 59, no. 4 (2008): 361–373; Catherine E. Snow, M. Susan Burns, and Peg Griffin, eds., *Preventing Reading Difficulties in Young Children* (Washington, DC: National Academy Press, 1998).

9. Snow et al., *Preventing Reading Difficulties in Young Children.*
10. Wong-Fillmore and Snow, "What Teachers Need to Know About Language."
11. Kerry L. Purmensky, *Service-Learning For Diverse Communities: Critical Pedagogy and Mentoring English Language Learners* (Charlotte, NC: Information Age Publishing, Inc., 2009).

Chapter 11

1. Walter Dick, Lou Carey, and James O Carey, *The Systemic Design of Instruction,* 5th ed. (New York: Longman, 2001).
2. Joy A. Frechtling, *Logic Modeling Methods in Program Evaluation* (San Francisco: Jossey Bass, 2007).
3. Joy A. Fretchling, "Logic Modeling" in *The 2002 User Friendly Handbook for Project Evaluation*, ed. Joy A. Frechtling (Arlington, VA: National Science Foundation, 2002).
4. W. K. Kellogg Foundation, *Logic Model Development Guide* (Battle Creek, MI: KI.W. Kellogg Foundation, 2000), iii.
5. Joy A. Frechtling, *Logic Modeling.*
6. Henry T. Frierson, Stafford Hood, and Gerunda Hughes, "A Guide to Conducting Culturally Responsive Evaluations," *The 2002 User-Friendly Handbook for Project Evaluation*, 63–73; Rodney K. Hopson, "Reclaiming Knowledge at the Margins: Culturally Responsive Evaluation in the Current Evaluation Movement," in The *SAGE International Handbook of Educational Evaluation,* eds. Katherine E. Ryan and J. Bradley Cousins (Thousand Oaks, CA: Sage Publications, 2009), 429-447.
7. Frierson, Hood, and Hughes, "A Guide to Conducting Culturally Responsive Evaluations," 63; Hopson, "Reclaiming Knowledge at the Margins, 441.
8. Hood, and Hughes, "A Guide to Conducting Culturally Responsive Evaluations."
9. Floraline I. Stevens, "Reflections and Interviews: Information Collected About Training Minority Evaluators of Math and Science Projects," in *The Cultural Context of Educational Evaluation: The Role of Minority Evaluation Professionals*, NSF 01-43 (Arlington, VA: National Science Foundation, 2000).
10. Linda Darling-Hammond, "Assessing Teacher Education: The Usefulness Of Multiple Measures For Assessing Program Outcomes," *Journal of Teacher Education* 15, no. 2 (2006): 120–138; Laura M. Desimone, "Improving Impact Studies Of Teachers' Professional Development: Toward Conceptualizations And Measures," *Educational Researcher* 38, no. 3 (2009): 181–199; Laura Hamilton, Richard Halverson, Sharnell S. Jackson, Ellen Mandinach, and Jonathan A. Supovitz, *Using Student Achievement Data to Support Instructional Decision Making* (Washington, DC: NCEE, 2009).
11. Frierson, Hood, and Hughes, "A Guide to Conducting Culturally Responsive Evaluations."

Acknowledgments

We extend our heartfelt gratitude to Caroline Chauncey, without whom this book would not be possible. We mean this not only for her role as editor-in-chief of Harvard Education Publishing, but more importantly for her willingness to engage in a series of discussions with us about our rather inchoate proposal to assemble the results of over a decade of our work into a book. Caroline's impact on the book cannot be overstated, as she always asked the right questions at the right times, led us thoughtfully from murkiness to clarity, helped us to zoom in and out from detailing our experiences to presenting what would benefit the reader most, and championed this project tirelessly. Her confidence in the value of our work gave us the vision and drive to complete this book.

We are very thankful for the many dedicated and talented professionals at Harvard Education Publishing. Marcy Barnes oversaw the copyediting process and offered perfect big picture as well as key details suggestions. Monica Jainschigg skillfully copyedited our text, showing great sensitivity to our voices while keeping the reader our first priority. Laura Madden creatively and energetically guided the marketing of our book. Sumita Mukherji expertly brought us through the final proofreading phase.

The anonymous reviewers contributed to this book through their constructive recommendations for improvement, and we hope that we have done justice to their helpful comments. We would also like to thank the Florida ESL experts whom we interviewed and consulted on a variety of issues. Jane Govoni and Gloria Pelaez kindly provided the most up-to-date information on state policies and procedures and offered their wealth of experience with infusion with enthusiasm. Mary Elizabeth Wilson-Patton appeared at just the right time to confirm a great deal of lived history in Florida EL infusion with Joyce and Gloria. Her dissertation stands out as a thorough and perceptive record of a major civil rights advancement for English learners. Our colleagues at the University of Florida, Ester deJong, Candace Harper, and Maria Coady have trailblazed research on infusion and have helped us with rich discussions on many fine points that deserved critical analysis.

We greatly appreciate the enthusiasm with which the individual contributors to chapters 6–11 accepted the challenge to share their infusion efforts through course descriptions and reflections of their journeys in "doing" EL infusion. Their insights have given us new understandings into how to better facilitate the process and are bound to inspire others to undertake the effort.

Our deep appreciation goes to Carine Feyten, Dean of the School of Education, Health, and Society at Miami University, for without her foresight and commitment to second language education, we would not have pursued the National Professional Development grant that funded our work in Ohio. Carine has been and continues to be a treasured mentor for Joyce and has made a positive impact on all our careers. We would also like to thank Bruce Perry for his dedicated leadership with the ESOL MIAMI grant and his articulate advocacy for EL infusion. Jan Clegg has been a silent partner in our work on the ESOL MIAMI project and has been invaluable in keeping us organized and in touch.

We are deeply appreciative of the dream team of doctoral candidates and research assistants at the University of Central Florida, Melanie Gonzalez, Alison Youngblood, and Leigh DeLorenzi, who worked magic with preparing the manuscript, carefully checking references and "Chicago-izing" our style. Of the three, we must single out Melanie for her additional contributions in compiling and annotating resources for chapter 5, which we wish we could recognize in a more fitting way than this simple acknowledgment.

Joyce and Carine have been very fortunate to receive support from a great many individuals at the University of Central Florida, all of whom we thank wholeheartedly. Website design expert Wendy Williams took our crudely drawn diagrams and turned them into outstanding graphics. Joyce would like to thank her codirectors, Michael Hynes and Karen Biraimah, for their generous reassignment of her duties to accommodate the expedited production schedule of the book. More importantly, we all thank them for their strong advocacy in preparing teachers to reach English learners. A culture of equity and excellence is best supported from the grassroots level as well as from the top of the organization, and our Dean Sandra Robinson has set the tone for our college's approach to EL infusion. We are very grateful for her example and support and also recognize Executive Associate Dean for Academic Affairs, Jennifer Platt, for being a steady supporter of ESOL infusion at UCF since the early days, for taking the time to provide us with the historical information, and for sharing her perspective as a leader. We would also like to acknowledge Lance Tomei, director of Assessment, Accreditation, and Data Management, for helping us better understand how to design an electronic portfolio system that yields the student learning outcome data we can use for continuous improvement of our EL-embedded courses.

Librarian Terrie Sypolt has stood by on call for any requests of database searches and offered insightful ideas on reviewing teacher education curricula throughout the nation. We thank our colleagues in ESOL Education, also known as the ESOListas, Silvia Diaz, Donna Frazee, Donita Grissom, Donna Lawless, and Irina McLaughlin for their commitment to giving our candidates a solid basis in becoming effective teachers of culturally and linguistically diverse students and for all their assistance in countless projects throughout the years.

Joyce is deeply grateful to her family for their boundless love, support, and tolerance of her work demands. Her husband Giorgio is always represented in her writing, explicitly or not. Every measured word of Giorgio's counsel is priceless, and his own experiences as an English learner have made him not only a spouse but also a muse. Son Marco Nutta offers inspiration in abundant doses, delighting in each of Joyce's professional accomplishments. Daughter Francesca Scrimgeour has given both practical and emotional support, offering help however and whenever needed. Francesca's husband, Troy Scrimgeour, proofread the manuscript meticulously and cheerfully. Joyce thanks her mother Betty Watson and aunt Gloria Cann for their understanding of her writing responsibilities and for their encouragement and love.

A special thanks is due to Jessica Santos for her considerate care and aesthetic sensibility.

Kouider thanks wife Carla Reichard and children Adam and Ben Mokhtari for their patience and support throughout the planning and writing of the book. He also expresses his gratitude to many of his students and colleagues whose help and support have come in remarkable and unpredictable ways. Oftentimes their insights, reactions, and stories altered his perceptions, clarified his thinking, and gave shape to his ideas regarding the education of all students, including English learners.

Carine is immensely thankful for her husband Ray's infinite love and patience throughout the writing of this book, her friends Deborah Horzen, Ali Korosy, Lisa Nalbone, and Anne Prucha for knowing exactly when words of encouragement were needed, and her parents Max and Sonja Strebel back home in Switzerland, who sparked in her the love for language learning by being role models.

About the Editors

Joyce W. Nutta, PhD, is an associate professor and the ESOL/Foreign Language Education and TESOL PhD Track Coordinator of the College of Education at the University of Central Florida. She ventured into preparing pre-service teachers from all subject areas to reach ELs in 1997, since when she has applied pleasant persistence to engaging colleagues from a wide range of disciplines in the process of infusing EL content into their teacher preparation curricula. Extending these interpersonal collaborations to broader outreach, she founded and maintains the ESOL TAPESTRY (Training for All Pre-Service Educators Stressing Technology-based Resources) website and coedits *The Tapestry Journal: An International Multidisciplinary Journal on English Learner Education*, which is dedicated to the advancement of research and instruction for ELs. Her research focuses on the use of technology to teach second language learners and the integration of EL issues into teacher education curricula, which has been published in *Foreign Language Annals*, *TESOL Journal*, and *CALICO Journal*, among others. Prior to becoming a teacher educator, Joyce taught ESL and coordinated the adult ESL program of Pinellas County Schools, working closely with governmental and community-based agencies to support resettlement of refugee families.

Kouider Mokhtari, PhD, serves as the Anderson-Vukelja-Wright Endowed Professor of Education within the School of Education at UT-Tyler University, where he engages in research, teaching, and service initiatives aimed at enhancing teacher practice and student achievement. Kouider's research focuses on the acquisition of language and literacy by first and second language learners, with particular emphasis on children, adolescents, and adults who can read but have difficulties understanding what they read. His research has been published in books and journals such as the *Journal of Educational Psychology*, the *Canadian Modern Language Review, Journal of Research in Reading,* and *System: an International Journal of Educational Technology and Applied Linguistics*. Kouider currently serves as a member of the Language and Diversity Committee of the International Reading Association, whose work is focused on enhancing the education of English learners in all classrooms. He also serves as coeditor of *Tapestry*.

Carine Strebel, PhD, is an accreditation and program approval specialist in the College of Education at the University of Central Florida, where she also teaches graduate and undergraduate TESOL courses. She has conducted ESOL-focused professional development for teacher educators at several institutions, facilitates the infusion of EL content into initial certification courses, and is a regular guest speaker in educational leadership courses. Having previously taught French and German and provided online mentoring for practicing teachers around the world on the implementation of language learning technology, Carine's research focuses on second language literacy, in particular the development of strategic competence, content-based language instruction aided by computer mediated communication and interactive whiteboard applications, and the preparation of all teachers to work with English learners. She is a founding member of *The Tapestry Journal*'s editorial board and continues to serve as assistant editor.

About the Contributors

Nazan U. Bautista, PhD, is an assistant professor of science education at Miami University. She has received grants to support her research and published in the areas of teaching science to English language learners, teaching and learning of nature of science, and science teacher education.

Martha E. Castañeda, PhD, is an assistant professor of foreign language education at Miami University, Oxford, OH. She has published numerous articles and book chapters, and co-authored books in language learning and teaching, examining the use of technology in language classrooms, the impact of study abroad in developing language and cultural competencies, and the infusion of ESOL competencies into general education.

Edwidge Crevecoeur-Bryant, PhD, is an assistant professor of ESOL Education at the University of Central Florida. She has conducted research in the area of low level literacy among Haitian adults in the U.S., has co-authored five bilingual (Haitian Kreyòl and English) picture dictionaries, and has designed on-line English as a Foreign Language courses for students in Haiti.

Darrel R. Davis, PhD, is an assistant professor of Educational Psychology and Instructional Design and Technology at Miami University. His current interests include teaching and learning in the online environment and the use of technology in diverse educational settings.

Leigh DeLorenzi is a doctoral candidate in the Counselor Education program at the University of Central Florida who teaches graduate counseling students how be multiculturally competent practitioners for clients and families. She has taught courses in group counseling, techniques, and theories of family therapy, and is a supervisor for counseling students in practicum. Her dissertation is in the area of trauma, child sexual abuse, and treatment attrition.

Jeannie Ducher, EdS, is clinical faculty of ESOL education at Miami University, Oxford, Ohio. She has extensive experience teaching ESOL and foreign language methods courses, and has conducted numerous workshops for practitioners and administrators for ESOL compliance. She is interested in helping prepare and support effective, culturally competent teachers to excel in our increasingly diverse schools.

Jennifer Flory Edwards, MS, teaches early grades English Language Learners at Kramer Elementary School in Oxford, Ohio, and adult English learners at the Oxford Family Resource Center through a partnership with the Middletown City School District. Her interests include the teaching of writing and reading with technology at all grade levels.

Michael Todd Edwards, PhD, is an associate professor in the Department of Teacher Education at Miami University. He is the co-director of the GeoGebra Institute of Ohio and co-editor of the Ohio Journal of School Mathematics and the Midwest GeoGebra Journal.

Keith Folse, PhD, is professor of TESOL in the Department of Modern Languages and Literature at the University of Central Florida. The author of over 55 books on teaching ESL/EFL (University of Michigan Press, Cengage National Geographic Press, Oxford University Press), he has also published research articles on language teaching and his second language research in *TESOL Quarterly and Modern English Teacher*, among others. He is a frequent conference presenter in the U.S. and abroad on best teaching practices.

Suzanne R. Harper, PhD, is an associate professor in the Department of Mathematics at Miami University. Her primary research interest is studying the development of technology, pedagogy and content knowledge of mathematics teachers.

Cynthia J. Hutchinson, EdD, is an associate professor in the School of Teaching, Learning, and Leadership in the College of Education at the University of Central Florida. Her areas of research include best practices in teaching and learning with a recent emphasis on classroom management and bullying prevention in K–12 classrooms.

Lauren B. Isaac is a doctoral candidate in Curriculum and Cultural Studies in the Department of Educational Leadership at Miami University. She is formerly a K-6 grade Spanish teacher and High school/Adult School ESOL specialist. Her dissertation research focuses on the politics of language and race in multilingual educational settings.

Glenn W. Lambie, PhD, is an associate professor and school counseling program director in the College of Education at the University of Central Florida. He has worked in the fields of education and counseling for 17 years as a counselor educator, professional school counselor, and family and individual therapist. He has published in the areas of professional school counseling, counselor development and supervision, and counseling children and adolescent "at-risk" populations.

Judith N. Levin, EdD, is the undergraduate program coordinator in the Early Childhood Development and Education Program at the University of Central Florida, where she teaches undergraduate and graduate students. Her interests include young children's social development and studying the impact on families and young children living in poverty. She recently spent a semester teaching emergent bilinguals at Head Start sites in New York.

Florin M. Mihai, PhD, is an assistant professor in the TESOL program at the University of Central Florida. His research interests and publications include language and content-area assessment for English learners, pre- and in-service teacher education, implications of form-focused instruction, and the influence of globalization on curriculum development. His most recent book is *Assessing English Language Learners in the Content Areas: A Research-into-Practice Guide for Educators* (University of Michigan Press, 2010).

Donna Niday, PhD, is an associate professor in the department of English at Iowa State University where she teaches future secondary English teachers and supervises student teachers. Her research interests include mentoring of beginning teachers.

N. Eleni Pappamihiel, PhD, is an associate professor at the University of North Carolina Wilmington. Her research focuses on improving academic outcomes for English learners in the mainstream classroom.

Richard A. Quantz, PhD, is a professor of social foundations of education in the Department of Educational Leadership at Miami University, Oxford, OH. His area of teaching and scholarly interest is sociocultural theory and education. He recently published *Rituals and Student Identity in Education: Ritual Critique for a New Pedagogy* (Palgrave Press, 2011).

William B. Russell III, PhD, is associate professor of Social Science Education at the University of Central Florida. He has authored numerous books and articles related to social studies education. Dr. Russell is the Editor of *The Journal of Social Studies Research* and the Director of The International Society for the Social Studies.

Melissa M. Schulz, PhD, is an associate professor of education at Miami University. Her research and publications focus on literacy acquisition of students who are English learners. Her most recent book is *Literacy for Diverse Learners: Finding a Common Ground in Today's Classrooms* (Christopher-Gordon Press, 2007).

Nicholas Shay, MS is professor of mathematics at Central Ohio Technical College. He graduated from Miami University with a Masters of Arts in Teaching and is currently researching effective teaching methods in developmental mathematics.

Kim Stoddard, PhD, is an associate professor at the University of South Florida St. Petersburg. Her research interests include effective practices for developing inclusive environments for students with disabilities. Her most recent publication regarding this issue can be found in *Preventing School Failure* (2011).

Rosemarye T. Taylor, PhD, is associate professor of educational leadership at the University of Central Florida. She has published widely on leadership to improve learning, particularly in literacy. Her latest book is *Leading Learning: Change Student Achievement Today!* (Corwin Press, 2010).

Michael F. Woodin, PhD, is an assistant professor in Educational Psychology and director of the School Psychology Program at Miami University. He is a licensed school psychologist as well as a pediatric neuropsychologist who has published in the areas of behavioral genetics, response to intervention, learning disabilities, and working memory. He is currently conducting research in the areas of evidence-based interventions, response to intervention, and supplemental reading instruction with English learners.

Amy Fisher Young is a doctoral candidate in the educational leadership department at Miami University. Her research interests include the development of literacy and language in the high school English classroom, as well as teacher resistance in public education. Her work was most recently published in *10 Great Curricula: Lived Conversations of Progressive, Democratic Curricula in School and Society* (Information Age Publishing, 2011).

Vassiliki ("Vicky") I. Zygouris-Coe, PhD, is associate professor of education at the University of Central Florida. She has published extensively on reading in the content areas, teacher professional development, and teacher knowledge and instruction. Her development of the Florida Online Reading Professional Development (FOR-PD) project has had a major impact in over 43,000 K–12 teachers and their students in Florida.

Index